The fragile tropics of Latin America

Note to the reader from the UNU

The United Nations University research and training programme area entitled "Sustaining Global Life-Support Systems" responds to the priorities identified in the UN system-wide Agenda 21 emanating from the United Nations Conference on Environment and Development (UNCED). The University's work has been organized according to five complementary programmes: (i) Eco-restructuring for Sustainable Development; (ii) Integrated Studies of Ecosystems; (iii) Information Systems for Environmental Management; (iv) Natural Resources in Africa; and (v) Environmental Law and Governance. UNU research is multidisciplinary, encompassing both natural and social science approaches.

The present book falls within the second programme, Integrated Studies of Ecosystems. This programme aggregates issues of environmentally sustainable development from the entry point of ecosystems and their ability to support, resist, or recuperate from the long-term impacts of major transformations. The programme has two main thrusts, one focusing on integrated studies of fragile ecosystems and vulnerable places in given geographical zones; the other focusing on critical resources and their management.

The research carried out for this volume was initiated under an earlier UNU programme on Sustainable Development in the Humid Tropics. The first step for the research, the outcome of which is the present book, was the symposium on the Fragile Tropics of Latin America: Changing Environments and Their Sustainable Management, organized in Tsukuba, Japan, 1990. The work forms a part of a larger UNU effort to understand the man–environment relationships in the humid tropical areas of Asia, Africa, and Latin America.

The fragile tropics of Latin America: Sustainable management of changing environments

Edited by Toshie Nishizawa and Juha I. Uitto

United Nations University Press

TOKYO · NEW YORK · PARIS

United Nations University Press
The United Nations University, 53-70, Jingumae 5-chome, Shibuya-ku, Tokyo 150, Japan
Tel: (03) 3499-2811   Fax: (03) 3406-7345
Telex: J25442   Cable: UNATUNIV TOKYO

Typeset by Asco Trade Typesetting Limited, Hong Kong
Printed by Permanent Typesetting and Printing Co., Ltd., Hong Kong
Cover design by Jonathan Gullery/Abel Graphics, Thornwood, New York, USA

UNUP-877
ISBN 92-808-0877-X
03500P

Contents

Contents

Acknowledgements

The editors wish to acknowledge with gratitude a large number of individuals and institutions who have contributed towards the finalization of this book.

The preparations for the volume began with the symposium on The Fragile Tropics of Latin America: Changing Environments and Their Sustainable Management, organized by the Centro de Estudios Latinoamericanos, University of Tsukuba, 29–31 May 1990. The symposium was sponsored by the University of Tsukuba, Japan, the United Nations University, and the Associação Central Nipo-Brasileira.

The co-editor, Prof. Nishizawa, who served as Chairman of the Organizing Committee, would like to acknowledge the help of the members, including Vice-Chairmen Prof. Takashi Maeyama of Shizuoka University and Prof. Em. Shozo Yamamoto of the University of Tsukuba; the late Mr Shunjo Matsuda; Prof. Tomio Fujita of Kanagawa University; Prof. Mario Hiraoka of Millersville University of Pennsylvania; Prof. Em. Hilgard O'Reilly Sternberg of the University of California, Berkeley; Amb. Keiichi Tatsuke; Mr Masahiro Maeda of the Sociedad Latino-Americana; Mr Katsuhiro Kotari of the Japan International Development Agency (JICA); Dr Eiji Matsumoto of the University of Tsukuba; Mr Hajime Mizuno of Sophia University; Dr Ichiroku Hayashi of the University of Tsukuba, Mr Masao Kosaka, then with the Institute of Developing Economies in Tokyo; Mrs Iyo

Kunimoto of Chuo University; Dr Takao Ueda of the University of Tsukuba; Dr Noritaka Yagasaki of Yokohama National University; Dr Fujio Masuda of the University of Osaka; Mr Yoichi Koike of the Institute of Development Economies; Dr Chiyoko Mita of Sophia University; Dr Toshihiko Naito of Tohoko University; Dr Isao Saito of the University of Tsukuba; Dr Hiroaki Maruyama of Kanazawa University; Dr Shuji Yamashita of Tokyo Gakugei University; Dr Noboru Hida of Akita University; Mr Motoko Iwami of the Long-Term Credit Bank of Japan; and Mr Kentaro Nagata of the Associa-ção Central Nipo-Brasileira.

The symposium was supported financially by the Inoue Foundation for Science; the Japan Automobile Manufacturers' Association, Inc.; the Japan–Brazil Economic Committee; the Japan Electrical Manu-factures' Association; the Japan Iron and Steel Federation; Mitsui & Co., Ltd.; SYNNYO-EN; the Federation of Electric Power Compa-nies; the Japan Shipbuilding Industry Foundation; the SOKA GAK-KAI; and the Tokyo Bankers' Association.

We would particularly like to thank Prof. Em. Hilgard O'Reilly Sternberg again for his important input to the symposium, as well as his constructive review and criticism of the manuscript. We are also indebted to the following individuals for their critical review and con-structive comments on various chapters in the manuscript: Prof. Rior-dan Roett, Johns Hopkins University, USA; Dr David W. Goodall, CSIRO, Australia; Prof. Jeremiah F. Epstein, the University of Texas at Austin, USA; Prof. John Saunders, Missisippi State Univer-sity, USA; Prof. Cyrus B. Dawsey, Auburn University, USA; Prof. Stefan Hastenrath, the University of Wisconsin, USA; Prof. Geo-ffrey Scott, the University of Winnipeg, Canada; Prof. Carl F. Jor-dan, the University of Georgia, USA; Dr Vernon E. Kousky, the National Meteorological Center, USA; Prof. Michael Eden, the Uni-versity of London, UK; Prof. Brian J. Godfrey, Vassar College, USA; and Prof. Takeshi Matsui, Nihon University, Japan.

At the United Nations University, we would like to acknowledge the role of the Academic Officer, Mr Dieter Koenig (now with the United Nations Conference on Trade and Development, Geneva) for his support.

The constructive comments of all the above have been very helpful in completing the book. Nevertheless, any remaining mistakes or mis-interpretations are the responsibility of the editors.

Toshie Nishizawa
Juha I. Uitto

1

Introduction

Toshie Nishizawa and Juha I. Uitto

Since its discovery, the Amazon region has been a source of fascination for humanity. In years past, adventurers flocked to the unknown and uncharted expanses seeking fame and fortune. Today, Amazonia is recognized as an important part of the global ecology and many concerned with environmental issues, often outsiders, are now trying to impede the overexploitation and destruction of this region.

The first European explorers of Amazonia were the sixteenth-century *conquistadores* who came in search of *El Dorado*. At that time, the rain forest was only an obstacle with its great size, density, and lushness. Some three centuries later the explorer scientists began to investigate the Amazon rain forests. Among these scientists were Alexander von Humboldt, Alfred Russel Wallace, and Henry Walter Bates, who viewed the rain forest as a subject of intense scientific curiosity.

The rain forest at that time was often evaluated to have high potential, based on the knowledge gained in the temperate latitude forests, where larger trees indicated greater soil potential. However, the size of trees in the tropical regions generally does not indicate soil potential because the nutrient cycle of the region is quite different from that of the temperate regions.

Amazonia is hot, humid, and rainy, drained by a dense network of large, year-round rivers mostly debouching into the Amazon River, which alone accounts for about one-fifth of all the fresh water discharged into the world's oceans. Although there are many different ecosystems in Amazonia, most of them fall into two major groups: those of the *várzea* (floodplains) and those of the *terra firme* or *tierras firmes* (uplands). About one-third of the world's tropical rain forests is located in Amazonia, mostly within Brazilian territory. Those on the highly leached soils of the terra firme exhibit a number of adaptations to their oligotrophic milieu. The fertile soils of the várzea, where traditional agriculture is carried out, are rejuvenated by yearly flooding and occasionally subjected to catastrophic inundations.

North-East Brazil or the *Nordeste* comprises nine states and includes 18 per cent of the area and 30 per cent of the population of the country. Its development began with the arrival of the Portuguese in the sixteenth century, but it still remains one of the poorest regions in Latin America. The Nordeste is divided into three longitudinal zones, starting from the seashore: the humid *zona da mata*, an intermediate *agreste*, and the interior *sertão*. The latter, characterized by deficient and erratic rainfall falling on largely impervious rocks, experiences severe and frequent droughts. The scorching backlands are devoid of perennial streams, except for one exotic river, the São Francisco. The vegetation is typically drought-resistant xerophytic forest (*caatinga*).

The coastal humid region was originally covered by seasonal tropical rain forest. Gradual deforestation in the area has caused serious environmental problems. Development of the coastal humid region started with forest cutting of Brazil-wood for red dye. The Portuguese and other Europeans also found the climate and the fertile alluvial coastal lowlands ideal for sugar cane production. The forest on the nearby uplands was cleared for use as firewood at the sugar cane mills. Recent expansion of sugar cane production for gasohol has resulted in environmental as well as socio-economic distress.

Frontier settlements advanced into the semi-arid interior during the seventeenth century. Due to the limited natural resources, this region was not initially attractive to the settlers, but it gradually developed when cattle grazing became widespread. Despite striking contrasts, the Brazilian portion of Amazonia and the Nordeste, especially the sertão, have been intimately linked historically, demographically, and culturally.

2

After the middle of the nineteenth century, penetration and settlement of Brazilian Amazonia was to reflect the spatial distribution of the *seringueira*, or rubber tree (*Hevea brasiliensia*). Following the discovery of vulcanization, and at a time when the demand for rubber was increasing, the disastrous droughts of 1855 and 1866 uprooted a considerable part of the rural population of the sertão, intensifying an incipient migration to the Amazon.

When the drought struck again in 1877 and 1888, the government directed to Amazonia a good part of those *flagelados* (lit. "lashed"; victims of drought) who managed to reach the coast. The tattered refugees were to form the backbone of Brazil's rubber extractive industry, and put the stamp of their culture on Amazonia, a region whose Amerindian stock had been dramatically depleted following contact with Europeans, and where the Portuguese and their African slaves had never represented more than a modest, mostly urban, demographic contingent.

During the Second World War, when the Allies were cut off from the Asian sources, Brazil, pursuant to what became known as the Washington Agreements, undertook to supply them with rubber. The federal government in Rio de Janeiro turned to the Nordeste and, with appropriate propaganda, mobilized its people for a second assault into the rubber forests. During the so-called *Batalha da Borracha*, the ill-fated Rubber Battle, malaria and other diseases took a heavy toll on the north-easterners.

Amazonia and the Nordeste, each in its own way, have long been the cause of serious apprehension on the part of successive Brazilian governments. The former, a sparsely settled economic backwater isolated from the seat of government, has been perceived as an easy prey to foreign covetousness. The latter, a victim of endemic poverty, is a traditional exporter of people. When the backlands are smitten by catastrophic droughts, farm families are uprooted and transformed into refugees, who make their way to the humid coast. Here, a teeming, landless population, born of the plantation system, embittered and dehumanized, has been seen by nervous officials and landowners as a potential hotbed of social and political unrest.

Significantly, when the 1946 Brazilian Federal Constitution was drafted, two consecutive articles addressed the twin problems of Amazonia and the Nordeste. Article 198 mandated that "in implementing the plan to provide for protection from the effects of the so-called *sêca* [drought] of the Nordeste, the [federal government] shall expend annually ... an amount never inferior to three percent of its

3

tax revenue." The same article also called for "the States included in the drought area to expend three percent of their tax revenue in the construction of dams,... and in ... assistance to their populations." According to Article 199, the federal government was enjoined to "appropriate, during at least twenty consecutive years, an amount not inferior to three percent of its tax revenues" to be applied in executing the plan for economic development of Amazonia. The same directive applied to the "States and Territories within that region, as well as to their respective *Municípios*."

When the Programme of National Integration (PIN) was launched in 1970, construction of the Trans-Amazon and Cuiabá–Santarém highways was linked to the plight of the semi-arid backlands, afflicted by yet another drought. While the PIN stressed effective occupation of the vastness of Amazonia, it also addressed itself to the source region of the settlers, and was perceived as a means, in the words of President Medici, "to absorb the population of areas considered totally unfit for human life." Amazonia is frequently thought of, by those who eschew a deep-cutting agrarian reform, as a convenient substitute, a safety valve to absorb surplus populations, especially from the Nordeste.

With water as its most limiting resource, an option long considered for the Nordeste is the importation of this most basic resource. One possibility, examined in the early 1980s, was the transposition of water from the Tocantins River into the sertão. While not properly an affluent of the Amazon River, the Tocantins, a tributary of the Pará River, is part of Amazonia. Although the idea is not being pursued at present, it serves as a final example to underline the linkages between Amazonia and the Nordeste.

With international attention focused especially on Brazilian Amazonia, a dilemma exists between development and preservation, or conservation, of Amazonian resources. What should scientists do to resolve this dilemma? Are the traditional forest management and agriculture methods effective today?

The origin of this volume stems from an international symposium entitled The Fragile Tropics of Latin America: Changing Environments and Their Sustainable Management, organized by the Centro de Estudos Latinoamericanos of the University of Tsukuba, Japan, in May 1990. The symposium was sponsored by the University of Tsukuba, the United Nations University (UNU), and the Associação Central Nipo-Brasileira.

The symposium had as its background the recognition of the severity, multiplicity, and global nature of the environmental problems facing humanity on the threshold of the twenty-first century. A central theme underlying several contributions was, therefore, the dilemma confronting the countries of Latin America: on the one hand, the desire to utilize the resources of their tropical regions to improve the living standard of their citizens; on the other, a growing concern with the ecological fragility of such regions, and the realization of the urgent need to find sustainable alternatives to the prevalent models of destructive so-called economic development, which is only too often at the service of special interests. Because some aspects of environmental degradation have the potential to affect remote corners of the earth, and because the explosive growth of global, satellite-based TV coverage has stimulated worldwide interest in a "green" Earth, such preoccupations now transcend political boundaries.

Issues highlighted by the agenda of the symposium included the following: (1) the fragility of tropical ecosystems, both humid and arid or semi-arid; (2) changes wrought in the natural environment of the neotropics by human activities; (3) multiple interactions and complementarity between tropical and other regions; and (4) technological, cultural, and land tenure strategies in greater harmony with nature than those promoted by prevalent models and hence more favourable to the sustained development of tropical regions.

Some questions that surfaced during the meeting, such as the palaeoclimatic history of Amazonia, or the size and antiquity of pre-contact Amerindian populations, remain controversial, and it was not the editors' purpose to generate a unified point of view on any issue. The authors alone are responsible for the opinions set forth in their contributions. That said, it must be pointed out that during the period between the symposium and the publication of this volume, the papers selected for publication have gone through extensive review and revisions.

The chapters are classified into four groups. Environmental problems are discussed for Peruvian and Brazilian Amazonia, North-East Brazil, and the entire tropical Latin American region. From an ecological point of view, these regions span an enormous variety. Similarly, the myriad of subjects makes generalized conclusions difficult. The disciplines represented include meteorology, physical and human geography, plant ecology, anthropology, archaeology, and economics. Such a variety of viewpoints may help facilitate solutions to local, regional, and global environmental problems. Each chapter discusses problems unique to the tropics of Latin America.

Gilberto C. Gallopín and Manuel Winograd outline the results of a modelling exercise containing two basic scenarios for the ecological prospects of Latin America, one based on the continuation of present trends, and another for achievement of ecological sustainability. They conclude that, based on the application of present technological and management options, it would be possible to reach sustainability for the entire region in the coming fifty years, assuming major changes in development and land use policies. However, the actual recent trends in the region give less reason for optimism.

Emilio F. Moran, emphasizing the diversity of Amazonian ecosystems, recognizes and describes the extreme environments in the region, differentiating between the oligotrophic black-water river basins and the anthropogenic forests with nutrient-rich soils. The goal is not simply to describe them, but also to move from characterization to understanding how such areas might be managed to balance the conservation and production concerns. He suggests that agricultural development should largely be confined to the latter in order to maximize benefits and to minimize harm to the environment and biological diversity.

Betty J. Meggers issues a warning on the delicacy and vulnerability of the tropical rain forest, based on archaeological evidence utilizing specialized methods of ceramic analysis. Her analysis suggests that surviving unacculturated groups preserve a way of life already established by the beginning of the Christian era, that this represents a sustainable adaptation under normal conditions, that ethnohistorical accounts exaggerate pre-Columbian population densities, and that several episodes of climatic fluctuation during the past two millennia seriously disrupted populations in many parts of the lowlands.

Minoru Tanaka, Akio Tsuchiya, and Toshie Nishizawa clarify the cause of low rainfall from the standpoint of tropospheric circulation. The variability of rainfall is also correlated with the sea surface temperature of the tropical Atlantic Ocean. Moreover, the differences of interannual fluctuation of rainfall between southern and northern North-East Brazil are discussed. The details of regional characteristics of rainfall are important to an understanding of the recurrent droughts and floods that contribute to the poverty cycle of the semiarid interior.

Hilgard O'Reilly Sternberg, after reviewing aspects of the aquatic and wetlands ecosystems of Amazonia, examines changes in the Amazon Basin discharge due to deforestation and the consequential influences on floodplain land use and wetland fauna. He suggests that it is reasonable to believe that the opening of Amazonia will affect the regimen of the trunk stream, but that, given the great number of variables involved, it is impossible to predict when human-induced changes will become manifest. The future remains elusive as the range of uncertainties, influenced, for instance by political and economic decisions, increases. In addition, Amazonian floodplains will be affected by a number of other factors, such as global warming and associated sealevel rise, contributing to the uncertainties.

Roberto M.C. Motta discusses the rationale for the establishment in 1967 of the Free Trade Zone of Manaus as a growth pole, and focuses on the problems of origin and recruitment of entrepreneurs and the role of state bureaucracies. The zone epitomizes some of the characteristics of Latin American economic development, including the alliance of an entrepreneurial élite, often of foreign extraction, supported by tax incentives and protective trade barriers, and a large state bureaucracy able to share in the profits of economic growth and to assert their social and political supremacy. Yet, according to Motta, the ecological and demographic peculiarities of the Amazon region seem to preclude a self-sustained process of development independent of state-supported incentives.

Mario Hiraoka studies the floodland management practices of riverine inhabitants of the Peruvian Amazon, known collectively as *ribereños*. The biological productivity of the floodlands is undeniable, but his findings suggest that the key to understanding the dense and permanent occupation of these areas should be sought in aboriginal resource management techniques. The ribereño production and management practices are based largely on the aboriginal patterns.

Christine Padoch and Wil de Jong describe five agroforestry systems found in the vicinity of Iquitos in north-eastern Peru. Although all begin as shifting cultivation fields, they differ greatly in species composition and richness, in intensity and length of management, in economic orientation, and in adaptation to particular ecological conditions. Their information shows that the basic traditional swidden-fallow agroforestry practices are adaptable to varying environmental and economic situations, including market access.

Miguel Pinedo-Vasquez, Daniel Zarin, and Peter Jipp outline the diverse and complex indigenous systems of forest management in a ribereño community in the lowland Peruvian Amazon. In the detailed case study, they examine the conditions for sustainable use of the forest resources in the communal *monte alto* areas.

Moving the focus to north-eastern Brazil, Eiji Matsumoto shows

7

that the white sand soils are also associated with podzolic and lato-zoic red-yellow soils in the coastal region. Sandy soil is one of the most infertile tropical soils and is distributed throughout the humid coastal North-East and Amazonia. Thus, it is very important to know the characteristics, formation, and geographical distribution of this white sand soil type. Matsumoto concludes that the soil on the *tabuleiros*, the low uplands of the North-East, have suffered severe modifications, especially in the development of white sand soil formations through a long, continuous deforestation process.

Ichiroku Hayashi contrasts the nitrogen content from tree leaves of the North-East with those found in Amazonian *caatinga*, finding those of the North-East to contain three times as much nitrogen as those in Amazonia. Caatinga is a unique vegetation that has adapted to the poor soil and cycles of drought and floods. Hayashi shows that caatinga soils contain 0.01–0.14 per cent nitrogen and 0.39–1.65 per cent carbon. The nitrogen content is very low compared with well-developed soils in the temperate forests. Finally, Hayashi stresses the importance of soil preservation for sustainable production of caatinga trees.

Toshie Nishizawa, Akio Tsuchiya, and Maria Magdalena Vieira Pinto estimate the response rates to water storage and water deficits, and the magnitude of tolerance of water deficits, for seventeen different caatinga tree species. As a consequence of the transformation of agricultural land-use patterns, the original caatinga has been deforested and a secondary growth of vegetation has resulted. The need for a holistic development approach benefiting both the North-East and Amazonia is demonstrated by the case of charcoal production in North-East Brazil.

Finally, Isao Saito and Noritaka Yagasaki present results from detailed field data on the changes in agriculture due to reservoir and river irrigation projects. Major problems related to irrigation are plant diseases and soil salinization. Solutions to these problems point to the necessity of an effective crop rotation system and processes to remove accumulated salt. Although their observations clearly suggest that irrigation farming has largely modified the traditional landscape and land use, they emphasize the need for continued observation of the process of change in the semi-arid interior.

The problems related to Amazonia and North-East Brazil should be approached individually as well as in a complementary fashion in order to benefit both regions. The complementary relationships of geographical characteristics of the regions are important to the resolution of environmental problems. Moreover, perceptions and assessments of the future trends in global and/or continental scale environments are required.

The need for scientific research that strikes a balance between nature, socio-economic and political factors, and technology is demonstrated by the variety of issues raised in the present volume. Emphasis must be placed on the necessity of fieldwork for primary data gathering. Harmony between nature and human activities must be achieved in order to develop sustainable management for the fragile tropics.

Part I
The ecological outlook

2

Ecological prospective for tropical Latin America

Gilberto C. Gallopín and Manuel Winograd

1 Introduction

The Latin American tropics and subtropics contain many unique ecosystems of high biological diversity, many endemic species, and a great potential in terms of renewable natural resources. The ecosystems have evolved under climatic regimes of relatively low variability, characterized by high temperatures and precipitation, resulting in very complex and intricate ecological interrelationships. On the other hand, the ecosystems exhibit a high degree of fragility in face of human perturbations, particularly those associated with the indiscriminate application of modern technologies originating in the industrialized countries and generated under quite different climates and social settings.

However, indigenous pre-Hispanic cultures and civilizations had reached a rather sophisticated level of technology in the management of complex ecosystems, which proved to be sustainable over long spans of time. Different civilizations, such as the Maya, the Inca, and the hydraulic cultures of Brazil, Bolivia, Colombia, Ecuador, and Mexico, maintained sustainable agricultural production for centuries, developing original and efficient solutions for managing the environmental resources without destroying the ecological base of production, at relatively high population densities and often including metropolises of considerable size (Gallopín, 1985; Gligo and Morello, 1980; Vitale, 1983).

The fragility of the Latin American tropical ecosystems, therefore, must be considered in relation to the technology utilized, and not necessarily as an intrinsic attribute precluding any kind of human intervention.

It is clear, however, as will be discussed later, that the current trends in the region are characterized by very high and accelerated rates of ecological deterioration, expressed as deforestation, desertification, soil erosion and depletion, agricultural, industrial, and domestic pollution, accumulation of wastes, and increased vulnerability to catastrophic landslides, droughts, and floods (CEPAL/PNUMA, 1983a; Damascos et al., 1989; Doureojeanni, 1982; Sancholuz et al., 1989; Sunkel and Gligo, 1980). A large proportion of those changes occur in the tropical and subtropical areas of the region, where the advance of the agricultural frontier is most dynamic.

The problem lies not in the transformation or alteration of the natural ecosystems (transformations that in principle could be positive), but in the actual modality and results of these transformations, implying an accelerated degradation of the ecological basis of production, a veritable impoverishment and destruction of the region's renewable natural resources and vital ecological processes. It should be emphasized that many alterations, such as desertification and soil erosion, are irreversible in practical terms.

The destruction of the Latin American tropical ecosystems, and particularly of the tropical forests, is cause for serious concern. From the regional and local viewpoints, the destruction of forests, besides representing a waste of resources for development, has serious ecological impacts, generating micro- and mesoclimatic changes, through variations in the albedo and residence time of rainwater, increases in surface runoff, reductions in evapotranspiration, increases in maximum temperatures and daily thermal amplitudes, and reductions in precipitation (Salati et al., 1989), as well as soil erosion, floods, and other effects. From the global viewpoint, tropical deforestation is a significant contributor to the greenhouse effect, and might possibly affect the regulation of the planetary atmospheric circulation; tropical deforestation is also considered one of the major current causes of species extinction.

In the face of this situation, it is worth investigating the potential for a sustainable management of the major tropical ecosystems in

Latin America. While a number of studies are available around the world, addressing the issue of sustainability at the micro-level and examining alternative technical solutions for the sustainable use of natural resources by a particular human community, or for a given specific ecosystem, studies at the macro-level (regional or global) are very scarce. This paper presents the results of an investigation of sustainability for the whole of tropical Latin America, centred on an ecologically and technically feasible prospective scenario. This scenario is defined as an alternative to the ecologically degrading trajectory being followed in the region.

2 The current condition of the tropical Latin American ecosystems

Latin America is a region where tropical (including subtropical) ecosystems predominate. They cover about 85 per cent of the total surface area of the region, including dense forests (55 per cent), open forests and savannas (33 per cent), and deserts and semi-deserts (12 per cent).

By 1980, 23.5 per cent of the surface of the tropical ecosystems was exploited for ranching and 7 per cent for crop agriculture; 0.6 per cent was under urban uses and 0.3 per cent under plantations. The original (virgin or semi-virgin) ecosystems represented 46 per cent of the total tropical area; the altered ecosystems accounted for 20.5 per cent, and the wastelands (irreversibly desertified or degraded lands) amounted to 2 per cent (see table 2.1).

The tropical portion of Latin America is relatively well endowed with natural resources. It includes 46 per cent of the tropical forests of the world, containing an estimated minimum of 40 per cent of the tropical plant and animal species. It has important reserves of fresh water and minerals, and the highest untapped hydroelectric potential in the world. About 10 per cent of its lands are suited for intensive agriculture and ranching, and another 32 per cent are suitable for agroforestry, agro-silvo-pastoralism and ranching.

However, owing to the advance of the agricultural frontier, as well as the inappropriate management of pastures and agricultural lands associated with high rates of soil erosion and desertification, the degradation of productive lands, deforestation, and land reconversion are advancing at accelerating rates.

The contribution of Latin America to the emissions of carbon dioxide by 1988 has been estimated (Gallopín et al., 1991) as roughly

Table 2.1 **Surface area (10^3 km^3) under each category for the major life-zones of tropical Latin America in 1980 (percentages of total life-zone area appear in parentheses)**

	Natural	Agricultural	Grazing	Altered	Plantations	Urbanized	Wasteland	Total
T & ST moist forests	5,795 (71.3)	583 (7.2)	683 (8.5)	1,023 (12.5)	20 (0.2)	17 (0.2)	3 (0.1)	8,124
T & ST montane moist forests	158 (12.6)	178 (14.2)	473 (37.8)	390 (31.2)	6 (0.5)	41 (3.2)	5 (0.5)	1,251
T & ST dry forests	1,068 (22.5)	377 (7.9)	1,612 (33.9)	1,557 (32.8)	21 (0.5)	20 (0.5)	92 (1.9)	4,747
Tropical savannas	423 (39.7)	32 (3.0)	485 (45.5)	125 (11.7)	0 (0)	1 (0.1)	0 (0)	1,066
T & ST mangrove forests and deltas	52 (28.0)	8 (4.3)	42 (22.6)	82 (44.0)	0 (0)	2 (1.1)	0 (0)	186
Paramo and puna	173 (18.8)	23 (2.5)	422 (45.8)	253 (27.4)	0 (0)	6 (0.5)	45 (5.0)	922
T & ST deserts and dry scrub	354 (30.5)	79 (6.8)	392 (33.7)	146 (12.6)	0 (0)	26 (2.2)	165 (14.2)	1,162
Tropical Latin America	8,023 (46.0)	1,280 (7.3)	4,109 (23.5)	3,576 (20.5)	47 (0.3)	113 (0.6)	310 (1.8)	17,458
Latin America	8,287 (40.5)	1,562 (7.6)	5,476 (26.8)	4,505 (22.1)	58 (0.3)	136 (0.7)	393 (2.0)	20,417

Source: Winograd, 1989a.

Key: T & ST = tropical and subtropical.

14 per cent of the world total, of which about 2.9 per cent is due to the burning of fossil fuels and the rest is mainly from biomass burning associated with tropical deforestation. By contrast, the developed countries contribute more than 70 per cent of the total carbon emissions (Holdgate et al., 1989).

Deforestation is certainly the most pressing ecological problem of the region in terms of land use and the loss of renewable natural resources. In the 1980s,[1] the destruction of tropical dense forests (including both natural and already altered forests) amounted to 4.34 million hectares per year, or 0.59 per cent per year, and the elimination of tropical open forests added another 1.37 million hectares per year.[2] If only natural (virgin and semi-virgin) forests are considered, dense forests are being depleted at a rate of 0.63 per cent per year, and open forests at a rate of 1 per cent per year. Mangrove forests, deltas, and savannas are also diminishing fast. On the other hand, only 0.5 million hectares per year were reforested during the same period, implying an average reforestation to deforestation ratio of 1:11, ranging from 1:7 in the mountain and dry forests to 1:15 in the lowland moist forests (tables 2.2 and 2.3).

Deforestation in tropical Latin America is mainly caused by commercial and subsistence ranching, shifting agriculture, and land speculation. Shifting agriculture accounts for 35 per cent of the deforestation in tropical and subtropical moist forests, and 15 per cent in the tropical dry forests (FAO, 1981; Lanly, 1985; Winograd, 1989a). Peasant and shifting agriculture together generate more than 50 per cent of the agricultural products for final consumption. On the other hand, the expansion of pastures and commercial ranching exhibited sharp increases in the 1960s in Central America and in the 1980s in South America. In the Brazilian Amazon, for instance, this activity is responsible for about 80 per cent of the deforestation in its tropical moist forests. Despite the allocation of important subsidies to this activity, commercial ranching accounted for less than 0.1 per cent of the Brazilian gross internal product in 1981 and employed only 1 per cent of the labour force in the Amazonian agricultural sector (Browder, 1989).

Besides the waste of valuable natural resources, tropical deforestation is a major engine of species extinction. Recent calculations (Lugo, 1988), although lower than other previous figures, suggest that from 30,000 to 100,000 species could disappear irreversibly by the year 2000 in tropical Latin America.

In the dry forests and woodlands, deforestation is also affecting a

17

Table 2.2 **Deforestation by life-zone in tropical Latin America in the 1980s**

	Natural (10^3 km²)	Altered (10^3 km²)	Deforestation On natural (km²/yr)	On altered (km²/yr)	Total (km²/yr)	Annual rate (%/year)
TF	5,588	752	30,350	4,000	34,350	0.54
STF	207	271	3,300	1,200	4,500	0.94
T&ST F	5,795	1,023	33,650	5,200	38,850	0.57
TSTMF	128	283	3,000	450	3,450	0.84
TLMF	30	108	850	290	1,140	0.83
T&ST MF	158	391	3,850	740	4,590	0.84
TDF	393	632	6,800	1,700	8,500	0.83
TVDF	496	311	2,380	535	2,915	0.36
STDF	179	614	1,885	450	2,335	0.29
T&ST DF	1,068	1,557	11,065	2,685	13,750	0.52
TS	423	125	1,280	200	1,480	0.27
D&M	52	82	450	150	600	0.45
Total	7,496	3,178	50,295	8,975	59,270	0.56

Source: Winograd, 1989a.

Key: TF = tropical moist forests
STF = subtropical moist forest
T&ST F = tropical and subtropical moist forests
TSTMF = tropical amd subtropical montane forests
TLMF = tropical lower montane moist forests
T&ST MF = tropical and subtropical montane moist forests
TDF = tropical dry forests
TVDF = tropical very dry forests and thorn woodlands
STDF = subtropical dry forests
T&ST DF = tropical and subtropical dry forest
TS = tropical savannas
D&M = tropical and subtropical deltas and mangrove forests

growing number of people. It is estimated that in 1980 about 26 million persons were suffering from acute fuelwood deficits (Lanly, 1985; Lugo, 1987).

Soil erosion and desertification are also a problem in tropical Latin America. In 1980, about 226 million hectares of tropical and semi-arid lands were suffering from desertification, affecting primarily productive lands (pastures and rainfed and irrigated croplands), and 50 to 75 per cent of the productive lands in the mountain areas were exposed to soil erosion (Doureojeanni, 1982; Masson, 1987; Winograd, 1989a).

18

Table 2.3 **Forest losses and gains in tropical Latin America in the 1980s**

	Forest area[1] (10^3 km^2)	Annual deforesta- tion rate (%/year)	Annual deforesta- tion (km^2)	Annual reforesta- tion (km^2)	Reforesta- tion/defor- estation ratio
T&ST F	6,818	0.57	38,850	2,600	1:15
T&ST MF	549	0.84	4,590	700	1:7
Total dense forests	7,367	0.59	43,440	3,300	1:13
T&ST DF	2,625	0.52	13,750	2,050	1:7
Total dense and open forests	9,992	0.57	57,190	5,350	1:11
TS	548	0.23	1,480	0	—
D&M	134	0.45	600	0	—
Tropical Latin America	10,674	0.56	59,270	5,350	1:11

Source: Winograd, 1989a

Key: (1) Natural + altered
    T&ST F = tropical and subtropical moist forests
    T&ST MF = tropical and subtropical montane moist forests
    T&ST DF = tropical and subtropical dry forests
    TS = tropical savannas
    D&M = tropical and subtropical deltas and mangrove forests

The human population in the tropical and subtropical areas reached about 280 million (80 per cent of the total for Latin America) in 1980. Per capita agricultural land in 1980 amounted to 0.46 hectares per person. However, this average hides large disparities in the availability of agricultural land, as well as in the destiny of agricultural products. For instance, in the same year, agricultural land amounted to 1.17 ha/person in the tropical and subtropical moist forests, where a large part of the production is directed towards export. On the other hand, in densely populated zones such as the tropical and subtropical mountain moist forests, and the paramo and puna, per capita agricultural land reaches only an average of 0.19 and 0.14 ha/person, respectively. There, subsistence crops (corn, beans, potatoes, etc.) dominate (table 2.4).

In general terms, inappropriate modalities of land use in tropical Latin America translate into low grain production, insufficient har-

19

Table 2.4 **Current (1980) and anticipated (simulated for 2030) per capita availability of agricultural land in the Latin American tropics**

| | 1980 | | 2030 | | | |
| | | | Reference | | Sustainable | |
	ha/person	PIL	ha/person	PIL	ha/person	PIL
T&ST F	1.17	L	0.73	L–I	0.96	I
T&ST MF	0.19	L–I	0.13	I	0.084	H
T&ST DF	0.88	L–I	0.46	I	1.1	I–H
TS	1.6	L	0.79	L–I	1.5	I
D&M	0.17	L	0.08	L–I	0.09	I
P&P	0.14	L	0.11	L–I	0.11	I
T&ST DDS	0.11	L	0.06	L–I	0.08	I–H
Total	0.46	L–I	0.27	I	0.32	I–H

Source: Winograd, 1989a.

Key: PIL = predominant input level: L = low; I = intermediate; H = high
T&ST F = tropical and subtropical moist forests
T&ST MF = tropical and subtropical montane moist forest
T&ST DF = tropical and subtropical dry forests
TS = tropical savannas
D&M = tropical and subtropical deltas and mangrove forests
P&P = paramo and puna
T&ST DDS = tropical and subtropical deserts and dry scrub

vests of roots and tubers, and the decline and even disappearance of traditional food crops; alternatively, the latter are produced to satisfy external demand (Winograd, 1989a).

In 1980, livestock amounted to 270 million animal units (AU) in tropical Latin America; that represents an average of 0.96 AU/person. However, the efficiency of ranching is very low, average meat production being about 45 kg/ha/year. Ranching is essentially extensive, with low animal loads: in ten-year-old pastures they may diminish to 0.2 AU/ha (Hecht et al., 1988).

3 Modelling ecological changes

For the purpose of exploring alternative ecological futures for tropical Latin America it was necessary to choose a land classification system capable of including the ecological characteristics of the region and its potential and limitations, and adaptable to the type and quality of the available information. The life-zone approach (Holdridge,

1967) was considered appropriate, subdivided into specific categories (e.g. savannas, mangrove forests) according to the criterion of actual vegetation.

The spatial extent of the tropical zone was adjusted by taking into account the ecological and productive characteristics of the different areas (Brown and Lugo, 1980; Winograd, 1989b); as a consequence, some ecological units exceed the geographical limits (23°27′ South to 23°27′ North) of the strict definition of the tropics. A total of twelve tropical and subtropical life-zones were identified for the region, aggregated into seven major zones for the purposes of the present paper (figs. 2.1 and 2.2).

Simulation models were implemented (Gallopín and Gross, 1989; Winograd, 1989a) for each of the twelve zones. Each zone is modelled as a set of compartments representing different ecological categories or conditions and with different structural, functional, and productive characteristics. The following seven categories were defined:

(1) "Natural": virgin areas, and areas with past alteration but currently similar to the original ecosystems; (2) "Altered": denotes a mosaic of patches of land under production coexisting with patches of original and secondary vegetation, and areas with slight to moderate soil erosion; (3) "Agricultural": annual, permanent, and non-traditional (i.e. coca, marijuana) crop areas, including fallow from permanent agriculture;[3] (4) "Grazing": ranching areas in natural or artificial pastures; (5) "Plantations": reforested areas used for forestry and watershed protection; (6) "Wastelands": unproductive lands irreversibly transformed by extreme soil erosion and desertification (natural deserts are not included here); and (7) "Urban": urbanized areas (mainly cities).

Every year, land shifts from one category to others according to the intensity and nature of the human activities (defined by an assumed scenario) and of the natural processes occurring on it (fig. 2.3). Simulations span the period 1980–2030. A simple compartment model was used. Each compartment represents the surface of a land category, for each life-zone, and it changes according to the following equation:

$$S_{t+1}^i = S_t^i + \sum_{j \in J} Inflows_{t,t+1}^{ij} - \sum_{k \in K} Outflows_{t,t+1}^{i,t}$$

$$J \subseteq I, K \subseteq I \qquad 0 \leq S_t^i \leq S_{max}^i$$

where S = surface of a given land category (km^2); *Inflows* = surface of land of other categories converted into the considered category in

21

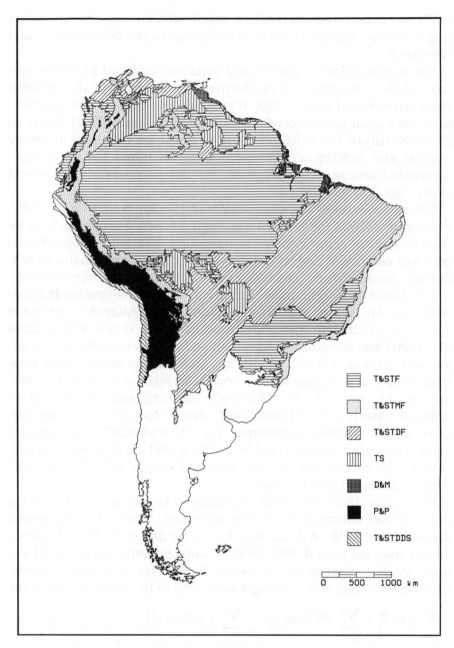

	T&STF
	T&STMF
	T&STDF
	TS
	D&M
	P&P
	T&STDDS

0   500   1000 km

Figure 2.1 **The major tropical and subtropical life-zones of South America. T&ST F = tropical and subtropical moist forests; T&ST MF = tropical and subtropical montane moist forests; T&ST DF = tropical and subtropical dry forests; TS = tropical savannas; D&M = tropical and subtropical deltas and mangrove forests; P&P = paramo and puna; T&ST DDS = tropical and subtropical deserts and dry scrub.**

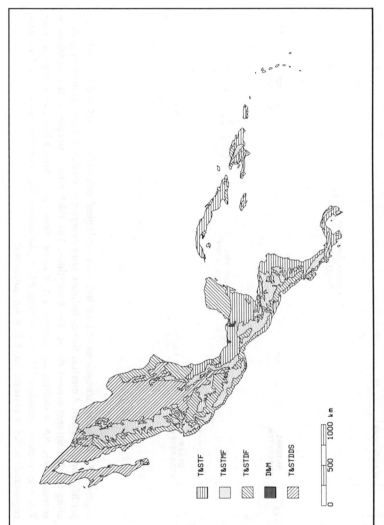

Figure 2.2 **The major tropical and subtropical life-zones of Central America and Mexico. T&ST F = tropical and subtropical moist forests; T&ST MF = tropical and subtropical montane moist forests; T&ST DF = tropical and subtropical dry forests; D&M = tropical and subtropical deltas and mangrove forests; T&ST DDS = tropical and subtropical deserts and dry scrub.**

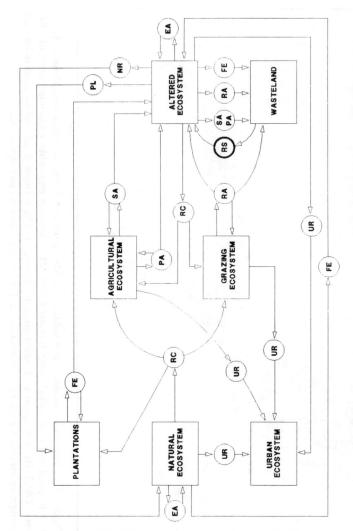

Figure 2.3 **Potential transitions of land between ecological categories, simulated for each major life-zone of Latin America. Boxes indicate land categories; circles indicate processes generating the transitions; arrows denote the transitions. The thick circle operates in the sustainable scenario only. SA = shifting agriculture; PA = permanent agriculture; RA = ranching; PL = plantation; EA = extraction activities; RA = ranching; PL = plantation; RC = reconversion; NR = natural regeneration; RS = restoration; UR = urbanization.**

a given year (km²/year); *Outflows* = surface of land of the considered category converted into other categories (including itself) in a given year (km²/year); S_{max} = maximum potential surface of the category (km²); I = set of all land categories. The scenario yearly defines the process generating the transformations (human activities or natural regeneration; see fig. 2.3) for each category and life-zone, specifying the portion of the category affected by the activity and the rates of conversion to other categories. The scenario is exogenously defined, taking into account the current situation, the assumed rate of growth of the activity, and the availability of land. Models were run under both a reference and a sustainable development scenario (see next section).

While the simulation models, in their present state, do not calculate production, but only the surfaces of land under different categories and production systems, the estimates of production are based upon the expected improvements in agricultural yields (compatible with the historic changes within the region and probably underestimating the future increases).

4 The reference scenario

Based on the current situation and the trends already visible, the expected reference scenario of changes in the region in the next forty years has been specified (Furtado, 1984; Gallopín, 1986, 1989a; Winograd, 1989a). The scenario implies a partial continuation of the current stagnation followed by a moderate increase in economic growth, but at a level lower than before the current crisis. The pattern of development would be fundamentally unchanged, with an expanding influence of transnational corporations. The regulating role of the state will diminish and market forces will become increasingly dominating. The current social disparities and income concentration would be maintained or increased. Environmental policies will continue to be weak and little enforced, and additional pressures on the ecological base will arise. These will originate in the increasing emphasis on exports for the servicing of external debt, for compensating for the deteriorating terms of trade, and for occupying a niche in the changing world economy. The major dynamic factor in the economy will continue to be industrial production oriented towards the internal market of consumer goods, but with an increasing preponderance of the export sector (raw materials and industrial goods). The new and emerging technologies will enter essentially exogenously, with the region maintaining its current passive attitude, and generating a number of ecological (as well as social) impacts (Gallopín, 1988). At the international level, closer cooperation between the industrialized countries is expected, leading to a higher coordination of their economic policies. The external debt of the third world would be reformulated, eventually reversing the current net capital flow from the South to the North.

A number of general hypotheses regarding variables directly related to land use have been specified for each scenario, and adjusted for each of the life-zones, by taking into account the current pattern of use, the potential availability of land, the ecological limitations, and the expected pressures for exploitation. The basic reference scenario has been subdivided into a pessimistic and an optimistic sub-scenario (table 2.5).[4] Besides the hypotheses, a gradual decrease in the rate of advance of the agricultural frontier in tropical zones, and a general increase in the intensity of land and inputs use, is assumed for the reference scenario.

The aggregated results from the simulation runs under the reference scenario appear in table 2.6, and the results for each life-zone in table 2.7.

For the whole region, the figures imply the transformation of 4.7 million hectares per year (as an average for the fifty years) of virgin and semi-virgin ecosystems. As much as 80 per cent of the surface will come from the tropical areas, and 20 per cent from the subtropical areas. As much as 45 per cent of this transformed area will become agricultural (30 per cent under shifting agriculture, 15 per cent under permanent agriculture); 30 per cent will be used for grazing and 22 per cent for forest exploitation (timber, charcoal, and fuelwood).

Two major driving forces account for a large part of the dynamics: (1) the advance of the agricultural frontier, translating into a decrease of the natural ecosystems and the growth of the agricultural, grazing, and altered areas; and (2) the intensification of land use, which in the dry zones increases the wastelands at the expense of the altered ecosystems, and in the humid zones increases the area of altered ecosystems, within which subsistence agricultural activities intensify.

The loss of natural forests will reach from 3.7 to 6.8 million hectares per year, in the optimistic and pessimistic scenarios respectively (table 2.8).

Soil erosion problems originating from deforestation, inappropriate agricultural techniques, overgrazing, and overexploitation will

Table 2.5 **General hypothesis of the simulation scenarios for tropical Latin America**

Variable	Pessimistic reference subscenario	Optimistic reference subscenario	Sustainable scenario
Population growth	From 2.2%/yr in 1980 to 1.2% in 2030	From 2.2%/yr in 1980 to 1.2% in 2030	From 2.2%/yr in 1980 to 1.2% in 2030
Average growth of per capita agricultural production	Within the range 0 to 0.5%/yr	0.5%/yr	Within the range 0.5 to 1%/yr
Average growth of crop yields	0.5%/yr	1%/yr	Within the range 1.5 to 2%/yr.
Animal carrying capacity (animal units)	From 0.6AU/ha in 1980 to 0.9AU/ha in 2030	From 0.6AU/ha in 1980 to 1.2AU/ha in 2030	From 0.6AU/ha in 1980 to 1.5AU/ha in 2030
Annual harvested area	65% of the agricultural land	65% of the agricultural land in 1980; 75% in 2030	65% of the agricultural land in 1980; 85% in 2030
Land allocation	Emphasis on export crops	Emphasis on export crops; secondarily, on crop diversification for internal consumption and export	Emphasis on crop diversification for internal consumption and export; secondarily, on export crops

Source: Gallopín, 1989a; Winograd, 1989a.

Table 2.6 **Simulated total changes in land categories for tropical Latin America 1980–2030, under the reference scenario**

	1980	2030	Total change (%)
Natural	46.0	33.5	−27.1
Altered	20.5	19.2	−5.6
Agricultural	7.3	11.2	+52.4
Grazing	23.5	30.2	+28.2
Plantations	0.3	1.5	+459.6
Urban	0.6	1.3	+96.5
Wastelands	1.8	3.1	+72.9
Total	100.0	100.0	

Table 2.7   **Evolution of land use under the reference scenario (10^3 km²)**

	Natural			Agricultural			Grazing		
	1980	2000	2030	1980	2000	2030	1980	2000	2030
T&ST F (8,124)	5,795	5,193	4,436	583	744	849	683	745	1,040
T&ST MF (1,251)	158	98	48	178	273	319	473	472	550
T&ST DF (4,747)	1,068	884	678	377	486	576	1,612	1,861	2,183
TS (1,066)	423	367	286	32	46	51	485	543	627
D&M (186)	52	43	34	8	8	8	42	50	53
P&P (922)	173	145	112	23	43	49	422	437	487
T&ST DDS (1,162)	354	309	252	79	92	99	392	366	328
Tropical L. America (17,458)	8,023	7,042	5,845	1,280	1,692	1,951	4,109	4,474	5,268
Latin America (20,417)	8,287	7,286	6,071	1,562	1,995	2,284	5,476	5,806	6,597

Source: Winograd, 1989a.

Key: T&ST F = tropical and subtropical moist forests
T&ST MF = tropical and subtropical montane moist forests
T&ST DF = tropical and subtropical dry forests
TS = tropical savannas
D&M = tropical and subtropical deltas and mangrove forests
P&P = paramo and puna
T&St DDS = tropical and subtropical deserts and dry scrub

particularly affect the tropical and subtropical mountain rain forests and the subtropical rain forest of Central America, the Andean countries, and Brazil.

Watershed degradation due to deforestation and damming will affect mainly the tropical and subtropical mountain and lowland rain forests in Central America, the Andean countries, parts of South America, Brazil, and Mexico.

Floods due to watershed degradation, deforestation, and natural processes will mainly affect the tropical and subtropical mountain and lowland rain forests in Central America, the Andean countries, and Brazil, and some of the savannas and subtropical forests of the Andean countries and Brazil.

Plantations			Urban			Altered			Wastelands		
1980	2000	2030	1980	2000	2030	1980	2000	2030	1980	2000	2030
20	62	122	17	26	39	1,023	1,350	1,634	3	4	4
6	16	31	41	45	53	390	338	235	5	9	15
21	58	110	20	31	47	1,577	1,310	1,001	92	117	152
0	0	0	1	2	3	125	109	99	0	0	0
0	0	0	2	3	4	82	81	84	0	1	3
0	0	0	6	9	12	253	238	202	45	50	60
0	0	0	26	42	64	146	132	119	165	223	302
47	136	263	113	158	222	3,576	3,558	3,374	310	404	536
58	165	316	136	187	264	4,505	4,467	4,217	393	511	688

Desertification associated with overgrazing, excessive extraction of fuelwood, and cyclic droughts will advance mainly in the puna, the dry tropical forests, and the tropical and subtropical desert shrublands in the Andean countries, Brazil, Peru, Mexico, and Central America.

Agricultural pollution will continue in many parts of the cultivated lands in the whole region, and agricultural, industrial, and urban pollution will increase in the deltas and mangrove forests of Central America, the Caribbean, and parts of South America.

The fuelwood deficit will continue to increase in most of the ecosystems. It is anticipated that, by the year 2030, not less than 50 million people will suffer from an acute fuelwood deficit in the western dry areas, the Andean plateau, and in densely populated zones.

The results from the models suggest that agricultural land will become critically scarce by the year 2030 in tropical Latin America, being reduced from 0.46 to 0.27 hectares per person on average. A total of 710 million people (90 per cent of the projected total population of Latin America) will be living in the tropical areas. In order to produce enough food for the population, agricultural inputs will have

Table 2.8 **Anticipated losses of natural forests in tropical Latin America according to two reference sub-scenarios (figures in parentheses indicate percentages of total surface of the corresponding life-zone)**

	1980	2000		2030	
		O	P	O	P
T&ST F					
Natural condition (10^3 km^2)	5,795 (71)	5,193 (64)	5,035 (62)	4,436 (55)	3,512 (43)
Annual deforesation (km^2/year)	33,650	30,100	38,000	25,550	50,750
Deforestation rate (%/year)	0.58	0.58	0.75	0.58	1.40
T&ST MF					
Natural condition (10^3 km^2)	158 (13)	98 (8)	80 (6)	48 (4)	0 (0)
Annual deforestation (km^3/year)	3,850	3,000	3,900	1,700	0
Deforestation rate (%/year)	2.4	3.0	4.8	3.5	0
T&ST DF					
Natural condition (10^3 km^2)	1,068 (22)	884 (19)	793 (17)	678 (14)	274 (6)
Annual deforestation (km^3/year)	12,950	9,200	13,750	7,000	17,300
Deforestation rate (%/year)	1.2	1.0	1.7	1	6.3

Key: O = optimistic reference sub-scenario.
P = pessimistic reference sub-scenario.
T&ST F = tropical and subtropical moist forests
T&ST MF = tropical and subtropical montane moist forests
T&ST DF = tropical and subtropical dry forests

to increase from the current low to an intermediate level, or to an intermediate to high level (the latter is comparable to the level applied today in the industrialized countries) (Gómez and Gallopín, 1989a, and table 2.4, above). The situation will be worst in the mountainous areas; the results indicate that agricultural land availability will be reduced to 0.13 hectares per person in the tropical and subtropical mountain forests, and to 0.11 ha/person in the paramo and puna.

Species extinctions could range from 100,000 to 350,000 species in the next forty to fifty years, considering only those existing in dense tropical forests (Lugo, 1988; Winograd, 1989a).

Table 2.9   **Carbon contents of forest biomass in Latin America (tons C/ha)**

		Altered	
Life-zone	Natural	fallow	exploited
T&ST F	164	63	119
T&ST DF	40	19	—
T&ST MF	133	51	97

Sources: Brown and Lugo, 1982, 1984; Fearnside, 1987; Detwiler et al., 1985.

Key: T&ST F = tropical and subtropical moist forests
   T&ST MF = tropical and subtropical montane moist forests
   T&ST DF = tropical and subtropical dry forests

Table 2.10   **Calculated carbon emissions (10^6 tons of C) due to deforestation in Latin American tropical forests under three alternative scenarios**

	1980	2000			2030		
		P	O	S	P	O	S
T&ST F	599.3	676.5	536.4	354.0	903.4	455.4	46.0
T&ST MF	31.1	31.5	24.3	9.4	0.0	13.7	5.5
T&ST DF[1]	35.2	43.0	30.3	19.2	52.5	24.0	3.6
Total	665.6	751.0	591.0	382.6	955.9	492.7	55.1

Key: P = pessimistic reference scenario; O = optimistic reference scenario; S = sustainable
   scenario
   T&ST F = tropical and subtropical moist forests
   T&ST MF = tropical and subtropical montane moist forests
   T&ST DF = tropical and subtropical dry forests

[1] Including tropical savannas.
Note: it is assumed that all the carbon in the biomass is converted into CO_2 during forest
   burning.

By using the estimated contents of carbon in forest biomass presented in table 2.9 and the detailed simulated changes in land use, it
is possible to anticipate that carbon emissions associated with deforestation could change from 665.6×10^6 tons of carbon (1980) to between 493×10^6 tons and 956×10^6 tons in the year 2030 (table 2.10).

5 The sustainable scenario

A possible and desirable scenario for the sustainable development
of the region was identified (Furtado, 1984; Gallopín, 1986, 1989b;
Winograd, 1989a). This scenario emphasizes the satisfaction of the
needs of the population, a better distribution of wealth, and a partici-

patory and decentralized approach. It assumes the implementation of national and regional environmental policies and an active strategy for research and development (R&D) focused upon regional problems and opportunities; the implementation of social and economic reforms; land use zoning and regulation of the agricultural frontier; policies for the reinforcement of the industrial sectors associated with renewable and non-renewable natural resources and agriculture; the development of local energy sources (mainly hydroelectricity and biomass); promotion of technological innovations in relation to the revalorization of the renewable natural resources and to the development of new sustainable productive uses and internal and international market "windows of opportunity," particularly in relation to tropical forests and agricultural production.

In terms of environmental sustainability, the issues of **technological pluralism** (complementary use of traditional, modern, and high technology) and of **technological blending** (constructive integration of new and emerging technologies into traditional or modern technologies) will assume paramount importance, requiring new forms of social organization and an integrated strategy for technological development and diffusion. The re-evaluation and upgrading of traditional technology and of the empirical knowledge existing in the region will be specially important for the medium and small-scale sectors of the rural areas. While many of the traditional technologies are extensive rather than intensive, they are often well adapted to the local ecological and social characteristics. They represent a good basis for building new, efficient, high-yielding, and ecologically sound production systems. A number of already tested systems of forestry, agroforestry, and agro-silvo-pastoralism support this point (Hecht, 1981).

Special emphasis will be given to the development of new systems of production based on the utilization of the ecosystems already altered, including the "neo-ecosystems" generated by past human activities on virgin and abandoned lands, and to modernization and yield improvements in the high-quality lands that are already being exploited.

Strategies will be developed concerning the allocation of ecological areas for protection (and in some cases management) of large-scale ecological functions and processes (i.e. watershed regulation, bio-geo-chemical cycles, etc.), often requiring cooperation among different countries.

Regarding the major rural productive activities, integrated production systems will be favoured when appropriate. Particular emphasis will be placed upon the development of productive activities according to ecological suitability zoning (see table 2.11). A general criterion is the maintenance (at least during a transition period) of **productive pluralism**, with the coexistence of different types of agriculture, integrated through subnational, national, and regional policies (Gallopín, 1988). Structural reforms and technological innovations directed towards the transformation of the present subsistence agricultural sector into an efficient and sustainable peasant agriculture will be required. New forms of high-technology diversified agriculture will be developed, directed towards the selective exploitation of the local genetic resources for food, medicine, industry, and so on. It will imply the development of technologies for a new efficient agriculture in diversified ecosystems, as well as new ranching and wildlife management systems, viewing ecological diversity, heterogeneity, variability, and singularities as resources rather than as hindrances or constraints. Forestry will emphasize the re-evaluation of the forests as multi-purpose producers (wood, energy, wildlife, special products, ecological functions).

The scenario was derived using the following conclusions from the EPLA project:

1. There are no important **ecological constraints** (at the regional level) to the satisfaction of human needs and to sustainable development, including food production. It is not necessary to sacrifice conservation areas needed to maintain essential ecological functions and services (Coutou, 1988; Gómez and Gallopín, 1989a, 1989b; Higgins et al., 1982; Morello et al., 1989).
2. There is no **lack of available technologies** impeding the sustainable management of Latin American ecosystems. Even where more research is needed and knowledge of the management of some ecosystems is seriously incomplete, there exist many socially, economically, and ecologically sustainable management techniques for a wide variety of ecosystems (Fuentes Godo, 1989; Gligo, 1989; Winograd, 1989a, 1989b).
3. Regarding **new and emerging technologies**, the following broad regional priorities for R&D will be emphasized (Gallopín, 1987): (i) the fertility limitations of tropical red soils (covering 50 per cent of South America) for traditional agriculture; (ii) sustainable use of deserts and semi-deserts (covering 15–20 per cent of South America and 35–40 per cent of Central America and Mexico) and of superficial and underground freshwater; (iii) sustainable management of tropical forests and their ecological functions; (iv)

Table 2.11 **Land use suitability for the tropical life-zones of Latin America (surface area in 10^3 km²; percentages in parentheses)**

	T&ST F	T&ST MF	T&ST DF	TS	D&M	P&P	T&ST DS	Total
Protection	4,358.5	312.5	1,542.0	374.0	74.0	323.0	930.0	7,914.0
	(54)	(25)	(33)	(35)	(40)	(35)	(80)	(45)
Ranching	480.0	148.5	1,019.5	533.0	0.0	184.5	116.0	2,481.5
	(5)	(12)	(21)	(50)	(0)	(20)	(10)	(14)
Agro-silvo-pastoralism	147.5	227.5	1,162.5	53.0	0.0	184.5	58.0	1,833.0
	(2)	(18)	(24)	(5)	(0)	(20)	(5)	(10)
Agroforestry	886.0	187.5	94.5	53.0	19.0	92.0	0.0	1,332.0
	(11)	(15)	(2)	(5)	(10)	(10)	(0)	(8)
Forestry	1,551.0	187.5	335.0	0.0	84.0	46.0	0.0	2,203.5
	(19)	(15)	(7)	(0)	(45)	(5)	(0)	(13)
Intensive agriculture and ranching	701.0	187.5	593.5	53.0	9.0	92.0	58.0	1,694.0
	(9)	(15)	(13)	(5)	(5)	(10)	(5)	(10)
Total	8,124.0	1,251.0	4,747.0	1,066.0	186.0	922.0	1,162.0	17,458.0
	(47)	(7)	(27)	(6)	(1)	(5)	(7)	(100)

Source: Winograd, 1989a.

Key: T&ST F = tropical and subtropical moist forests
T&ST MF = tropical and subtropical montane moist forests
T&ST DF = tropical and subtropical dry forests
TS = tropical savannas
D&M = tropical and subtropical deltas and mangrove forests
P&P = paramo and puna
T&ST DS = tropical and subtropical deserts and dry scrub

management and protection of regional germplasm and wildlife; (v) sustainable increment of agricultural yields and sustainable livestock management; (vi) evaluation and use of the regional empirical cultural experiences in agro-ecological management; (vii) management and conservation of fragile ecosystems; (viii) management, rehabilitation, and restoration of degraded or over-charged regional environments;[5] (ix) management of the stabilized "neo-ecosystems" generated by human actions; (x) treatment of regional and sub-regional bio-geo-chemical cycles and intercountry coordination of human activities affecting them. (The general hypothesis for variables directly affecting land use appears in table 2.5, above.)

Under the sustainable scenario, the simulations indicate that the region is capable of satisfying the agricultural, livestock, fishing, and forestry internal requirements in a sustainable manner within the considered time-horizon of the next forty years, with a substantial surplus for exports.

Three major processes account for a large part of the dynamics in this scenario: (1) implementing science and technology and economic policies emphasizing the productive rehabilitation of deteriorated and altered ecosystems, which cover 20 per cent of the total land area; (2) implementing policies favouring integrated rural production systems (agriculture–animal husbandry–forestry–aquaculture) whenever appropriate; and (3) actively implementing policies directed to integrating the new technologies into traditional and modern technologies.

The results from the simulation runs under the sustainable scenario appear in aggregated form in table 2.12, and for each life-zone in table 2.13.

Table 2.12 **Simulated total changes in land categories for tropical Latin America 1980–2030, under the sustainable scenario**

	1980	2030	Total change (%)
Natural	46.0	40.9	−11.0
Altered	20.5	19.3	−31.8
Agricultural	7.3	13.1	+78.8
Grazing	23.6	20.2	−14.4
Plantations	0.3	3.6	+1,253.2
Urban	0.6	1.2	+85.8
Wastelands	1.8	1.7	−31.6
Total	100.0	100.0	

Table 2.13 **Evolution of land use under the sustainable scenario (10^3 km^2)**

	Natural			Agricultural			Grazing		
	1980	2000	2030	1980	2000	2030	1980	2000	2030
T&ST F (8,124)	5,795	5,325	5,100	583	852	1,118	683	667	568
T&ST MF (1,251)	158	126	165	178	255	206	473	432	316
T&ST DF (4,747)	1,068	949	999	377	623	686	1,612	1,742	1,396
TS (1,066)	423	372	356	32	69	95	485	515	486
D&M (186)	52	47	54	8	10	9	42	35	44
P&P (922)	173	153	157	23	64	50	422	430	416
T&ST DDS (1,162)	354	319	312	79	97	125	392	336	292
Tropical L. America (17,458)	8,023	7,291	7,143	1,280	1,970	2,289	4,109	4,157	3,518
Latin America (20,417)	8,287	7,548	7,424	1,562	2,288	2,662	5,476	5,490	4,780

Source: Winograd, 1989a.

Key: T&ST F = tropical and subtropical moist forests
　　 T&ST MF = tropical and subtropical montane moist forests
　　 T&ST DF = tropical and subtropical dry forests
　　 TS = tropical savannas
　　 D&M = tropical and subtropical deltas and mangrove forests
　　 P&P = paramo and puna
　　 T&St DDS = tropical and subtropical deserts and dry scrub

In addition to the quantitative differences with the pattern derived from the current trends, the qualitative changes in the modality of rural production imply a drastic reduction of the ecologically degrading processes exhibited by the reference scenario. For the whole region those figures imply the transformation of 2.2 million hectares per year of virgin and semi-virgin ecosystems. Protected areas represent 45 per cent of the remaining natural ecosystems. Altered ecosystems will cover 19 per cent of the area, the same figure as in the reference scenario. However, in this case most of the altered lands become productive lands (13 per cent under sustainable forestry and 6 per cent in rehabilitation). Cultivated lands increase to 13 per cent (10 per cent under intensive agriculture and 3 per cent under shifting cultivation). Rangelands decrease because of increments in carrying

Plantations			Urban			Altered			Wastelands		
1980	2000	2030	1980	2000	2030	1980	2000	2030	1980	2000	2030
20	88	214	17	25	34	1,023	1,163	1,088	3	3	1
6	24	130	41	44	50	390	361	378	5	8	6
21	83	254	20	31	44	1,557	1,217	1,285	92	102	83
0	2	10	1	2	3	125	105	116	0	0	0
0	2	12	2	3	4	82	89	63	0	1	1
0	2	16	6	9	13	253	219	234	45	45	35
0	0	0	26	41	62	146	169	202	165	200	169
47	201	636	113	155	210	3,576	3,323	3,366	310	359	295
58	249	818	136	184	249	4,505	4,206	4,113	393	452	371

capacity (14 per cent is under intensive and semi-intensive grazing systems and 10 per cent is integrated with forestry). Eight per cent of the land will be under agroforestry. As a consequence of the rehabilitation and restoration activities, wastelands are reduced.

The ecological and technical feasibility of the sustainable scenario is supported by a number of additional considerations. By conservative estimates, not less than 15 per cent of the territory of tropical Latin America is suitable for crop agriculture (7.5 per cent for intensive agriculture and 7.5 per cent for agroforestry, agro-silvo-pastoralism, and shifting agriculture) (Winograd, 1989a). The requirement of agricultural lands in order to nourish the total projected population of Latin America by the year 2030 is estimated as 4 per cent of the total land surface under a high level of agricultural inputs, 7 per cent if an intermediate level is used, and 19 per cent with a low input level agriculture (Gómez and Gallopín, 1989a). The major constraint to food production (at the regional level) is thus not the absolute scarcity of agricultural land, but the low effectiveness of its utilization. Only 65 per cent of the tropical agricultural lands are harvested annually (FAO, 1986); however, this figure can be increased to at least

85 per cent. This implies a large potential increase in agricultural production by the improvement of this single factor.

On the other hand, the agroclimatological conditions in 75 per cent of the tropical areas of the region permit up to 2.5 annual harvests of short-cycled crops. The yields of those crops can be duplicated just by applying currently known technological systems (FAO, 1981, 1988).

Taking all those factors into account, it can be estimated that average food production could be multiplied by four within a relatively short period, merely by introducing known technical improvements in the allocation and utilization of agricultural land.

Agricultural land availability will reach 0.32 hectares per person in the year 2030 (table 2.7, above).

Important improvements are also feasible regarding tropical ranching, which currently exhibits a very low efficiency. By using existing techniques (Hecht et al., 1988), production can be increased from the present 45 kg/ha/year to 90–120 kg/ha/year and animal loads from 0.6 AU/ha to 1.5 AU/ha. This would allow increased production while reducing by 30 per cent or more the extent of pasture lands, land that could be allocated to more sustainable uses (Winograd, 1989a).

Other major opportunities for sustainable development are associated with the richness and diversity of the flora and fauna of the Latin American tropics, a potential much underutilized so far. It is estimated that 36 per cent of the 250,000 known species of flowering plants live in the region. About 1,000 plant species have a clear economic potential (Myers, 1984; Tosi, 1980). About 250 plant species and 45 animal species of the Andean mountain areas are appropriate for cultivation or domestication (Patiño, 1982). The tropics of the region possess areas with the capacity to provide unique products: in the puna, for instance, more than 30 potato varieties are grown, and a large economic potential exists for the production of fine wool from camelids such as alpaca, vicuña, and llama (CEPAL/PNUMA, 1983b). These alternative production systems can be not only ecologically but also economically better suited than the prevailing ones (see table 2.14 for some illustrative examples).

In the sustainable scenario, it is anticipated that carbon dioxide emissions from biotic sources would be reduced by 90 per cent from the 1980 level, to about 55×10^6 tons of carbon per year (table 10, above) by the year 2030. This is associated with the strong reforestation emphasis embodied in the scenario, aiming at a reforestation rate of 1.3 million hectares per year. This would result in 64 million

Table 2.14 **Some examples of alternatives systems of production for tropical areas of Latin America**

	Prevailing			Alternative			References
	Activity	yield of main product	Other products	Activity	yield of main product	Other products	
T&ST moist forests	Cattle ranching	0.1 ton/ha/yr of meat	Leather	Iguana breeding	1.2 ton/ha/yr of meat	Skins	Cohn, 1989; Hecht et al., 1988
T&ST moist forests	Selective forest exploitation	100 to 120 m³ of timber	—	Natural forest management	150–200 m³ of timber	Fruits, wildlife	Harshorn et al., 1987
T&ST montane moist forests, puna	Monoculture	1 to 2 ton/ha of wheat	—	Agriculture in terraces	40 ton/ha of potatoes	Vegetables	Masson, 1987
T&ST montane moist forests	Sunny coffee cultivation	0.65 to 2 ton/ha	—	Shade coffee cultivation	0.5 to 0.65 ton/ha	Fruits, wood	Carrizosa, 1987
Tropical savannas and tropical dry forests	Cattle ranching	15 kg/ha/yr of meat	Leather	Capybara breeding	64 kg/ha/yr of meat	Leather	González-Jiménez, 1979
Tropical deltas and mangrove forests	Monoculture	2 tons/ha of rice	—	Chinampa agriculture	3 to 4 tons/ha of corn	Vegetables, fishes, manure, wood, livestock	Jiménez Osornio et al., 1987
Puna	Sheep ranching	0.5 kg/yr of wool	Leather	Camelid ranching	1.5 to 5 kg/yr of wool	Leather	CEPAL–PNUMA, 1983

hectares reforested by the year 2030. This represents 14 per cent of the new reforested area that could compensate the excess atmospheric carbon due to human activities (Sedjo, 1989). This value should be compared with the present estimated regional biotic emission of between 8.5 and 10.4 per cent of the world total.

6 Conclusions

The elements presented in this paper suggest the technical and ecological feasibility of an environmentally sustainable scenario for the region. While its economic feasibility has not been investigated in depth, our preliminary estimates of the costs specifically associated with the necessary changes in land use range between US$ 2,300 and 3,500 million per annum for the whole region (Winograd, 1989a) – not an exorbitant figure.

As a general conclusion, it can be stated that the ecological future of Latin America, and the possibilities of benefiting from the ecological opportunities while minimizing the constraints, are much more directly tied to the great social options adopted in the region than to the search for new knowledge and new ecosystem management techniques. Unfortunately, the more recent trends in the region are going in the direction of the reference scenario, with a disordered abandonment of the regulating role of states (rather than true modernization) and increasing pressures to produce for export, neglecting internal social needs.

The prospects of a sustainable scenario for Latin America will depend also to a large degree upon the attitudes adopted by the industrialized countries, and their willingness to assume their full share of the responsibility for the reversal of the worldwide ecological degradation and social impoverishment.

Acknowledgements

A large part of the results presented here has been generated by the project "Ecological Prospective for Latin America" (EPLA) supported by the United Nations University, the International Development Research Centre of Canada, and the National Council for Science and Technology of Argentina (Gallopín, Gómez, and Winograd, 1989). This project is a component of the wider international project "Technological Prospective for Latin America." We wish to acknowledge the collaboration of Miguel Gross, who developed the digitizing, processing, and printing software for the production of the maps, the valuable suggestions and criticisms generously provided by Isabel Gómez and Anahí Pérez, and the collaboration of Alejandro Dezzotti in the digitizing of part of the cartographic information.

Notes

1. Based on data for the period 1980–85, which, after examining partial data available for later years, are considered approximately valid for the whole decade.
2. Estimates of deforestation in tropical Latin America are polemic, although all imply very significant rates. For instance, estimates for the "Pan-American" Amazon (covering about 7 million km^2) range from not less than 20,000 km^2 per year (Salati, 1989) to 23,000 km^2 year (Freitas, 1989). For the Brazilian Legal Amazon (an area of 4.9 million km^2), Fearnside (1982) estimated that 44% of the Legal Amazon would be deforested by the end of the 1980s. However, the same author (Fearnside, 1989) corrected his calculations, estimating a deforestation rate of 35,000 km^2 year for 1989, with a cumulative deforestation of 352,000 km^2 (7.2% of the Legal Amazon) for the decade. Those figures yield an average rate of some 25,000 km^2 per year for the period 1975–1989. Recent studies, based on the analysis of satellite images (Landsat-TM) made by INPE (Brazil), indicate an average rate of 15,649 km^2 per year for the period 1975–78, and of 17,678 km^2 per year for the period 1978–1988. Those figures yield a cumulative figure of 251,500 km^2 per year for the period (Pereira da Cunha, 1989). It should be noted that the Legal Amazon includes tropical moist forests (84%), tropical dry forests or *cerrado* (11.5%), and tropical moist savannas or *campos* (4.5%). Later estimates (Fearnside, 1990) indicate that, in the period 1960–1988, 6.4% of the tropical moist forests and 9.6% of the dry tropical forests were eliminated. Deforestation rates for 1988 reached 20,000 km^2 per year in the Amazon moist forests and 18,000 km^2 per year in the dry forests. This implies a total deforestation rate of 38,000 km^2 per year and a total cumulative figure of 459,734 km^2 (9.2% of the Legal Amazon) in 1988. The range of figures discussed here is compatible with our estimates (not limited to the Amazon forests) presented in table 2.1 and table 2.2. The often-cited figures of the World Bank (Mahar, 1989), giving a cumulative deforestation of 600,000 km^2 or 12% of the Legal Amazon by the year 1989, should be discarded. They do not represent estimates, but are mere extrapolations assuming exponential growth based on data from 1975, 1978, and 1980. Other extreme estimates (Setzer and Pereira, 1991) suggesting a deforestation rate of 1.6% per year for 1987 are probably unreliable (Cunha, 1989; Goldemberg, 1989).
3. Note that, contrary to other authors' definitions, fallow from shifting and peasant agriculture within forest areas in included in "Altered."
4. The run of the models for the initial period 1980–1990, for which independent estimates are available, show that the optimistic reference sub-scenario results in a better reproduction of the real trends for that period than the pessimistic sub-scenario. Unless otherwise stated, simulation results presented for the reference scenario refer to the optimistic sub-scenario.
5. E.g. Andean zone, coastal and island areas, deforested, desertified, and overgrazed areas.

References

Browder, J. 1989. "Development alternatives for tropical rain forests." In J.W. Leonard et al. (eds.), *Environment and the poor: Development strategies for a common agenda* (US World Policy Perspectives no. 11, Overseas Development Council; Transaction Books, New Brunswick), 111–33.

Brown, S., and A.E. Lugo. 1980. *Models of carbon flux in tropical ecosystems with emphasis on the role in the global carbon cycle.* US Department of Energy; CONF-800350. Río Piedras.

———. 1982. "The storage and production of organic matter in tropical forests and their role in the global carbon cycle." *Biotropica* 14 (3): 161–87.

———. 1984. "Biomass of tropical forests: A new estimate based on forest volumes." *Science* 223: 1290–93.

CEPAL/PNUMA. 1983a. *Expansión de la frontera agropecuaria y medio ambiente en América Latina*. CIFCA, Madrid.

———. 1983b. *Sobrevivencia campesina en ecosistemas de altura*,vols. I and III. Santiago de Chile.

Coutou, A.J. 1988. "Latin America." In Board for International Food and Agriculture Development, *Development partnership in world agriculture for the 1990s: A symposium* (Occasional Paper no. 13; Agency for International Development, Washington, DC), 151–62.

Damascos, M.A., N.M. Gazia, and G.C. Gallopín. 1989. "Consecuencias de la transformación de los ecosistemas latinoamericanos. Estudios de caso." In Gallopín et al., 1989 (Chapter 9).

Davies de Freitas, M.L. 1989. "Desmatamento na Amazonia: Causas, efeitos y soluçoes." *Interciencia* 14 (6): 298–303.

Detwiler, R.P., and C.A.S. Hall. 1988. "Tropical forests and the global carbon cycle." *Science* 239: 42–7.

Detwiler, R.P., C.A.S. Hall, and P. Bogdonoff. 1985. "Land use change and carbon exchange in the tropics: II. Estimates for the entire region." *Environmental Management* 9 (4): 335–44.

Doureojeanni, M.J. 1982. *Renewable natural resources of Latin America and the Caribbean: Situation and trends*. World Wildlife Fund, Washington, DC.

FAO. 1981. *Los recursos forestales de América tropical*. Food and Agriculture Organization, Rome.

———. 1986. *Production yearbook 1986*. FAO, Rome.

———. 1988. *Potentials for agricultural and rural development in Latin America and the Caribbean*. Annex IV, Natural resources and the environment. FAO, Rome.

Fearnside, P.M. 1982. "Deforestation in the Brazilian Amazon: How fast is it occurring?" *Interciencia* 7: 82–8.

———. 1987. "Summary of progress in quantifying the potential contribution of Amazonian deforestation to the global carbon problem." In D. Athie, T.E. Lovejoy, and P. de M. Oyens (eds.), *Proceedings of the Workshop on Biogeochemistry of Tropical Rain Forests; Problems for Research* (University of São Paulo, Centro de Energia Nuclear na Agricultura (CENA), Piracicaba, São Paulo), pp. 75–82.

———. 1989. "A prescription for slowing deforestation in Amazonia." *Environment* 31 (4): 17–40.

———. 1990. "Greenhouse gas contribution from deforestation in Brazilian Amazonia." *Chapman Conference on Biomass Burning*, Williamsburg, VA, 19–23 March.

Fuentes Godo, P. 1989. "Rescate de tecnologías productivas y conservacionistas." In Gallopín et al., 1989 (Chapter 14).

Furtado, A.T. 1984. *Cenarios socio-economicos para América Latina* (Primeira versão). Proyecto Prospectiva Tecnológica para América Latina. Centro Brasileiro de Análisis e Planejamento (CEBRAP), Rio de Janeiro.

Gallopín, G.C. 1985. "Opciones sociales y el futuro ambiental de América Latina." In: L. Pinguelli Rosa and M. D'Olne Campos (organizers), *A crise presente e o futuro da América Latina* (Anais, CESP, São Paulo), 58–66.

———. 1986. "Problemas del futuro ecológico de América Latina." *Boletín de Medio Ambiente y Urbanización* 4 (15): 3–10.

———. 1987. "Prospectiva ecológica de América Latina." *Realidad Económica* no. 78: 55–83.

————. 1988. "Ecologia e mudança tecnológica na América Latina: Uma visão prospectiva." In P. Leitão & S. Albagli (organizers), *Prospectiva, avaliação de impactos, e participação social no desenvolvimento científico e tecnológico* (CNPq, Rio de Janeiro), 169–183.

————. 1989a. "Medio ambiente, desarrollo y cambio tecnológico en América Latina." In Gallopín et al., 1989 (Chapter 19).

————. 1989b. "Sustainable development in Latin America: Constraints and challenges." *Development* 1989: 2/3: 95–99.

Gallopín, G.C., I. Gómez, and M. Winograd (eds.). 1989. *El futuro ecológico de un continente. Un análisis prospectivo para América Latina*. Final Report. United Nations University, Tokyo.

Gallopín, G.C., and M. Gross. 1989. "Modelos de simulación: Estructura conceptual y funcionamiento." In: Gallopín et al., 1989 (Chapter 17).

Gallopín, G.C., M. Winograd, and I.A. Gómez. 1991. *Ambiente y desarrollo en América Latina y el Caribe: Problemas, oportunidades, y prioridades*. Grupo de Análisis de Sistemas Ecológicos, S.C. Bariloche.

Gligo, N. 1989. "En torno a la sustentabilidad ambiental del desarrollo agrícola latinoamericano." In Gallopín et al., 1989 (Chapter 15).

Gligo, N., and J. Morello. 1980. "Notas sobre la historia ecológica de la América Latina." In O. Sunkel and N. Gligo (eds.), *Estilos de desarrollo y medio ambiente en la América Latina* (Fondo de Culture Económica, Mexico, DF), 129–57.

Goldemberg, J. 1989. "Help Brazil preserve the Amazon." *New York Times*, September.

Gómez, I., and G.C. Gallopín. 1989a. "Potencial agrícola de América Latina." In Gallopín et al., 1989 (Chapter 7).

————. 1989b. "Oferta ecológica en América Latina: Productividad y producción de los grandes ecosistemas terrestres." In Gallopín et al., 1989 (Chapter 6).

Hecht, S. 1981. *Amazonia: Investigación sobre agricultura y uso de tierras*. CIAT (Centro International de Agricultura Tropical), Calí.

Hecht, S., et al. 1988. "The economics of cattle ranching in Eastern Amazonia." *Interciencia* 13 (5): 233–40.

Higgins, G.M., H.H. Kassam, L. Naiken, G. Fisher, and M.M. Shah. 1982. *Potential population supporting capacities of lands in the developing world*. Technical Report, project "Land Resources for Population of the Future." FAO/United Nations Fund for Population Activities/International Institute for Applied Systems Analysis, Rome.

Holdgate, M.W., J. Bruce, R.F. Camacho, N. Desai, O. Mascarenhas, W.J. Maunder, H. Shibab, and S. Tewunga. 1989. *Climate change: Meeting the challenge*. Commonwealth Secretariat, London.

Holdridge, L.R. 1967. *Life zone ecology*. Revised edition. Tropical Science Center, San José, Costa Rica.

Lanly, J.P. 1985. "Les ressources forestières de l'Amérique du Sud tropical." Doctorat d'état, Université Paul Sabatier, Toulouse.

Lugo, A.E. 1987. *Uso de las zonas boscosas de América Latina tropical*. Reunión "Nuevas Tecnologías y el Futuro Ecológico de América Latina," Grupo de Análisis de Sistemas Ecológicos (FB)/United Nations University. S.C. Bariloche, Argentina, 9–12 November 1987.

————. 1988. "Estimating reductions in the diversity of tropical species." In F.M. Peter and E.O. Wilson (eds.), *Biodiversity* (National Academy Press, Washington, DC), 58–76.

Mahar, D.J. 1989. *Government policies and deforestation in Brazil's Amazon region.* World Bank, Washington, DC.

Masson, L. 1987. "La ocupación de andenes de Perú." *Pensamiento Iberoamericano* 12: 179–200.

Morello, J., R. Burkart, and B. Marchetti. 1989. "Las áreas protegidas en el tercer milenio." In Gallopín et al., 1989 (Chapter 16).

Myers, N. (ed.). 1984. *Gaia. An atlas of planet management.* Gaia Books, London.

Patiño, U.M. 1982. "Biotic resources for potential development." *Mountain Research and Development*, vol. 2, no. 3: 333–6.

Pereira da Cunha, R. 1989. *Deforestation estimates through remote sensing: The state of the art in the Legal Amazonia.* International Symposium of the Amazon, University of São Paulo, 31 July–2 August 1989.

Salati, E. 1989. "Problemas ambientais decorrentes da ocupação de espaço Amazonico." Unpublished report to UNDP/RBLAC.

Salati, E., R.L. Victoria, L.A. Martinelli, and J.E. Richey. 1989. "Deforestation and its role in possible changes in the Brazilian Amazon." In R.S. De Fries and T.H. Malone, (eds.), *Global change and our common future* (National Academy Press, Washington, DC), 159–171.

Sancholuz, L.A., M.A. Damascos, G.C. Gallopín, and N.M. Gazia. 1989. "Aprovechamiento de ecosistemas y recursos naturales renovables en América Latina: Un análisis comparativo." In Gallopín et al., 1989.

Sedjo, R.A. 1989. "Forests: A tool to moderate global warming?" *Environment* 31 (1): 14–20.

Setzer, A.W., and M.C. Pereira. 1991. "Amazonian biomass burnings in 1987 and estimate of their tropospheric emissions." *Ambio* 20 (1): 19–22.

Sunkel, O., and N. Gligo (eds.) 1980. *Estilos de desarrollo y medio ambiente en la América Latina.* Fondo de Cultura Económica, Mexico, DF.

Tapia, M. 1982. *Los cultivos andinos, su papel en las economías campesinas.* Proyecto G/R 35, CEPAL, Santiago de Chile.

Tosi, J. 1980. *Desarrollo forestal del trópico americano frente a otras actividades económicas.* Curso "Uso y manejo de suelos forestales tropicales." CATIE (Centro Agronómico Tropical de Investigación y Enseñanza), Costa Rica.

Vitale, L. 1983. *Hacia una historia del ambiente en América Latina.* Nueva Imagen,Mexico, DF.

Winograd, M. 1989a. "Simulación del uso de tierras: Escenarios tendencial y sostenible." In Gallopín et al., 1989.

————. 1989b. "Clasificación de los grandes ecosistemas de Sudamérica, México y América Central por zonas de vida." In Gallopín et al., 1989.

3

Rich and poor ecosystems of Amazonia: An approach to management

Emilio F. Moran

1 Introduction

The Amazon always brings out the grandiose vision in us. It is by any measure an enormously vast area. The drainage basin encompasses about 4 million km², an area the size of the continental United States. Contrary to the popular opinion, the Amazon Basin is not mostly tropical rainforest. It is made up of a patchwork of different vegetations, reflecting environmental conditions as well as past use and abuse. In it we find deciduous forests, seasonal forests, vine forests, palm forests, flooded forests, moist forests, well-drained and poorly-drained savannas, and xeromorphic scrub forests or *caatingas amazônicas*.

In this paper I will focus on two extremes of the environmental gradient in Amazonia. This gradient is based not only on the criteria of nutrient availability in soils and their pH, but relies also on assessment of other environmental and social processes (such as above-ground biomass and vegetation transformations by prehistoric populations) relevant to the future use and management of these areas. The two extremes chosen are the oligotrophic black-water river basins – of which the Rio Negro Basin is the best known – and the anthropogenic forests found associated with nutrient-rich soils in the lower Xingú, lower Tapajós, and lower Tocantins basins and in portions of the state of Rondônia like the Guaporé valley.

This contrast departs from the traditional one commonly made between the *terra firme* (uplands) and *várzeas* (floodplains) of Amazonia. I do not dispute the validity and usefulness of the contrast between the floodplain and the uplands – a contrast that has served to highlight the differences between those areas enriched by Andean alluvial deposition and areas lacking these favourable conditions. However, this contrast has also hidden the heterogeneity present within the terra firme, an area that accounts for 98 per cent of the entire basin. As this paper hopes to show, the terra firme is very diverse in environmental conditions. The two extreme points of the gradient which I will discuss serve simply to suggest a more extensive exploration that makes more detailed discriminations within the terra firme (Moran, 1990, 1993). This heterogeneity has implications to the management of the region.

Within the terra firme, to which I will confine myself in this paper, annual precipitation varies from a low of 1,500 mm to a high exceeding 3,600 mm (Salati, 1985: 33), with considerable micro-ecological variation. The number of meteorological stations is still very small and the variability is probably even greater than figure 3.1 suggests.

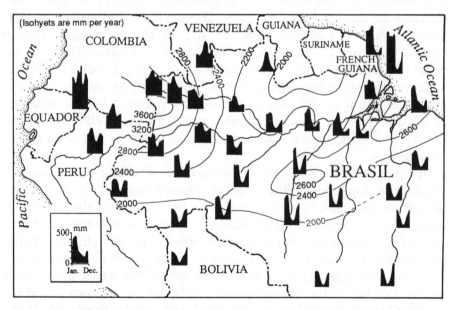

Figure 3.1   **Rainfall distribution patterns in Amazonia. (Source: Salati, 1985: 36.)**

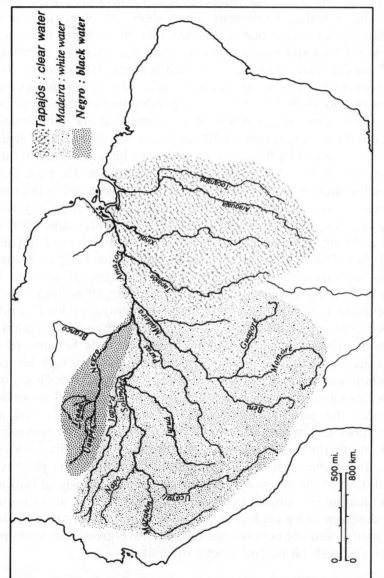

Figure 3.2 **River "types" of Amazonia.**

Average monthly temperatures do not fluctuate annually by more than 3°C, but the daily variation can be greater than 15°C.

An important ecological distinction was made long ago between the rivers of the Amazon (Sioli, 1951). Three types were distinguished: black-water, white-water, and clear- or blue-water rivers. See figure 3.2 for illustration of the areal extent of these three types of rivers. White-water rivers drain the Andean area and commonly, but not always, carry sediments of high fertility. Black-water rivers drain areas with white sand, podzolic soils, and are extremely acid and of poor optical quality owing to suspended undecomposed organic matter. Clear-water rivers drain areas of the Guiana and Brazilian plateaux and are of medium quality in terms of nutrients and acidity.

The areas drained by black-water rivers can be considered to fall at the poorest extreme of the ecosystems of Amazonia. They are dominated by the most nutrient-deficient and acid soils found in the basin. The forests have such a tight nutrient-cycling that hardly any nutrients escape the forested areas, and the river water has been described as being of near-distilled-water quality in terms of nutrients (Sioli, 1951). The productivity of black-water lakes is 15 to 19 times less than in várzea lakes and the fish show signs of nutrient deficiency in their vertebrae (Geisler and Schneider, 1976; Smith, 1979).

The extremely low levels of nutrients or oligotrophy lead to other responses that create additional difficulties for organisms exploiting such areas: organic matter decomposes more slowly because of the extreme acidity of the soils; native plants have evolved high levels of polyphenols and other toxic substances that appear to reduce nutrient loss through herbivory but which require specialized processing to detoxify the plant material. The extreme cycles of flood and drought have led to the selection of plants with highly specialized adaptations to these conditions, in the form of unusually high root biomass and leaves that are either leathery or spiny. The poor optical resolution of the rivers makes techniques like the use of bow and arrow in fishing less productive than elsewhere. These areas require careful description by ecologists and ethnographers because of their patchy nature and the coexistence of low above-ground biomass productivity and high biotic and abiotic diversity.

2 Characterization of the oligotrophic environment

Unlike other areas of terra firme, the characteristic vegetation of this habitat is *campina* or *caatinga amazônica* rather than tropical moist or rain forest. Caatinga is a dwarfed scrub-forest vegetation of about 6 to 20 metres above ground level growing on hydromorphic quartzy sands (Klinge, 1978; Takeuchi, 1961). It is found chiefly in the Guianas and portions of the Rio Negro basin and its affluents (chiefly the Vaupés and the Içana). This type of vegetation develops in areas with a humid tropical climate where there is no dry season and which is dominated by podzolic soils or spodosols. The vegetation varies along a gradient from high caatinga to low caatinga or *bana*, which is the poorest of all. With increased oligotrophy, the herbaceous cover increases in dominance and the proportion of roots in total biomass increases. Figure 3.3 illustrates the interrelation between hydrology, soils, and vegetation in an area of the upper Rio Negro.

Leaves of caatinga vegetation are hard and leathery (sclerophyllous). Leaf area index is smaller in this type of vegetation (5.2) as compared with the mean of 8.0 in tropical forests, probably to reduce the effects of the drought stress period. Wood volume is less and the canopy is smaller than in areas less limited (Jordan, 1982: 395). Vines are uncommon, in contrast to epiphytes. In oligotrophic areas, there is a tendency for species dominance, in contrast to the pattern, more common in Amazonia, where dominance is rare in native forests. In a region near San Carlos de Río Negro in Venezuela, *Micrandra spruceana* and *Eperua leucantha* constituted 50.3 per cent of the biomass (Klinge, 1978: 260).

Caatingas are not restricted to the Amazon. In Sarawak this vegetation is known as *kerangas*, growing on poor soils where rice cultivation is not possible (Jacobs, 1988: 188). In other areas of Asia they are known as *padangs*. Areas with xeromorphic vegetation in the humid tropics have also been noted in Borneo, Sumatra, and Malacca. Richards (1952) compared the padangs of Malaysia to *wallaba* vegetation in the Guianas. In all these cases, these vegetations are associated with extremely leached white sandy soils. When cleared of their native vegetation, the areas take an uncommonly long time to return to their original state (perhaps as much as one hundred years), confirming the poverty of the environment (Jacobs, 1988: 189; Uhl, 1983; Uhl et al., 1982).

Low bana reaches a height of 3–7 metres, with dwarfed trees and bushes occurring mixed with grassy vegetation. In high caatinga the height may reach 20 metres, approximating the structure of upland tropical forest. High bana can be seen as a transitional zone between low bana and caatinga amazônica (Klinge, n.d.: 20). Biomass in caatinga is twice that of bana (i.e. 28 kg/m^2 *vis-à-vis* 10–17 kg/m^2).

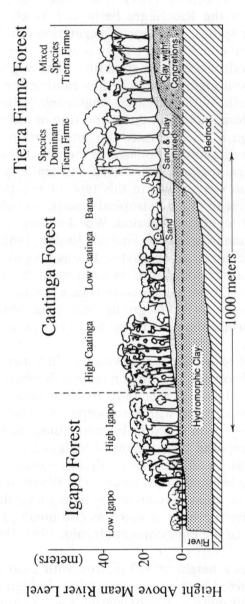

Figure 3.3 Hydrology, geology, soils, forests in the Rio Negro. (Source: Clark and Uhl, 1987: 5; Jordan, 1985.)

Table 3.1   **Ecological characteristics of types of forest**

	Bana & caatinga	Rio Negro upland forest	Other moist and rain forests
No. of tree spp. with 10 cm dbh/ha	18–69	80–100	80–100
No. of individual trees with 10 cm dbh/ha	39–173	650–800	600
Canopy height in metres	6–20	25–30	30–50
Basal area in m²/ha 10 cm dbh	0.15–22	25–30	40–50
Above-ground biomass in metric tons/ha	170–335	320–340	400–700
Percentage of total biomass in roots	34–87	20–38	20

Source: Modified from Klinge, 1982 and Uhl and Murphy, 1981: table 3.

Other indices of the differences between bana/caatinga and upland tropical forests elsewhere in Amazonia clearly indicate the substantial differences between them (see table 3.1). Of particular note is the substantial increase in species diversity when moving from bana/caatinga to upland forests in the Rio Negro. The species diversity is comparable in upland forests of the Rio Negro to tropical moist and rain forests elsewhere in Amazonia. However, it is important to observe that the upland forests in the Rio Negro have a shorter canopy, a considerably smaller basal area, lower above-ground biomass, and a higher proportion of total biomass in the root layer than tropical moist and rain forests elsewhere in Amazonia. Thus, not all terra firme tropical forests are the same. The Rio Negro terra firme forests, because they are at the extreme end of the gradient of poverty, are more geared to nutrient conservation and recycling than they are to producing net yield available to herbivores or humans.

Also implicated in the presence of this type of vegetation are the hydrologic patterns. Medina et al. (1978) demonstrated that even with 3,600 mm of annual rainfall and rains of more than 200 mm each month, seasonal drought is common in these areas. By the time rainfall declines to the range of 200 to 300 mm in a month there is a high probability of wilting due to the high evapotranspiration (5.4–11.5 mm/day), high albedo, and the excellent drainage of the sandy soils. The water table is near the surface, due to an impermeable B horizon, characteristic of podzolic soils (Herrera, 1979). With every rain the water can flood an area immediately, and draining will occur only slowly over the next few days.

The soils are sandy and composed of near-pure quartz. They have

51

a high erosion potential. These soils are known variously as spodo-sols, podzolic soils, and hydromorphic podzols. They have a super-ficial layer with a great deal of undecomposed organic matter, pH below 4.0, and a diagnostic B horizon (i.e. a spodic horizon) of greyish colour of impermeable clays.

Further evidence for the oligotrophy of this environment is evident in the heavy investment in root biomass. Above-ground biomass is lower in this ecosystem but total biomass is comparable to other parts of terra firme. Roots constitute between 34 and 87 per cent of total biomass, as compared with 20 per cent in most areas of forested terra firme. Eighty-six per cent of the roots are found in the A hori-zon of the soils, and 70 per cent are considered extremely fine (Klinge and Herrera, 1978). In an experiment, 99.9 per cent of calcium and potassium was absorbed by the fine roots (Stark and Jordan, 1978). This is due to the mutualistic relation between mycorrhizae and the vegetation. In other areas of Amazonia the nutrient capture mecha-nisms are more porous and more nutrients escape from the immedi-ate area of leaf-fall near a tree. The micro-organisms in the root layer incorporate the available nitrogen, the nutrient which seems most limiting in this ecosystem. Denitrifying bacteria are almost non-exis-tent in this system, as compared to other areas of Amazonia. The poorer the ecosystem, the greater the development of the fine root layer, and the greater the presence of toxic substances which inhibit predation of leaves. Herbivore populations are very low in these areas, owing to the lack of palatable biomass. Research in Africa and in Venezuela confirms the presence of bacteriostatic and fungi-static substances like alkaloids and polyphenols in oligotrophic areas (McKey et al., 1978). These chemical defences are of considerable importance for research in both medicine and agriculture.

3 Characterization of eutrophic forests

One of the general characteristics of the upland forests found in Amazonian terra firme is their biotic diversity and environmental patchiness. Figure 3.4 illustrates just one type of patchiness present, in this case vegetational patchiness, in an eutrophic area of the lower Tapajós valley. One way in which human populations cope with ex-treme diversity is by simplifying the initial heterogeneity present, giv-ing preference to resources to which they give particularly high value. Indeed, human beings do not simply adapt to the environment but also modify it so that its limitations are replaced with opportunities

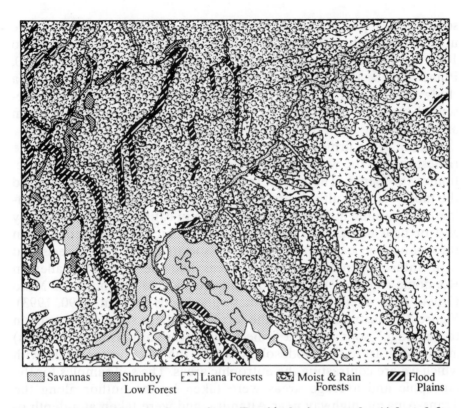

Savannas   Shrubby   Liana Forests   Moist & Rain   Flood
              Low Forest   Forests   Plains

Figure 3.4 **Patchiness in Amazonia, a Tapajós basin example. (Adapted from Prance, 1978: 210.)**

for future use. As we will see in this section of the paper, prehistoric populations of terra firme brought about major transformations in the vegetation formations in the more productive areas of terra firme. These anthropogenic vegetations serve as indicators of areas of high potential for human occupation and agriculture. Indeed, there is much we can learn from indigenous peoples of Amazonia about how to manage the ecosystems.

The more favourable conditions of these eutrophic areas are reflected in the lower proportion of total biomass in the root component, with only about 20 per cent of the total, in contrast to 34–87 per cent of the total in the black-water basins (see table 3.1, p. 51). Thus, the above-ground biomass is nearly twice that of the black-water regions.

These forests' natural diversity has been simplified by management to the point where some of them have overwhelming dominance of

53

some species, particularly of some valuable palms. In areas that have not been notably modified by human management, one finds 80 to 100 tree species per hectare with 10 cm dbh (Black et al., 1950; Prance et al., 1976; Takeuchi, 1961; Uhl and Murphy, 1981). In a study by Uhl and Murphy, 67 per cent of the species were represented by fewer than four individuals. This diversity is reduced in areas that have been modified by prehistoric populations.

Soils in terra firme include some of the poorest and some of the richest soils in the world. The poorest we examined in the earlier section of this paper. The richest soils of terra firme are the alfisols and the mollisols. The alfisols are soils of medium to high fertility, resulting from basaltic intrusions, and are high in cation exchange capacity and of near-neutral pH. They occur in a highly dispersed pattern throughout the basin but are often associated with vine forests and with anthropogenic black soils. Areas like the Guaporé valley in Rondônia, the lower Tocantins and Xingú, and the north of Mato Grosso have sizeable areas of these good soils (Moran, 1990, 1993). Figure 3.5 illustrates visually the fertility of these soils in comparison to "average" soils of terra firme (the proverbial oxisols or latosols) and in contrast to the spodosols typical of the black-water basins with which we are contrasting the eutrophic areas. The soil samples for the eutrophic and average areas were taken by the author along the Trans-Amazon highway near Altamira, and were taken at a depth of 0–20 cm (i.e. fertility cores). The oligotrophic soil samples were taken by Rafael Herrera (1979).

At least 11.8 per cent of the terra firme forests are now thought to be anthropogenic in nature, resulting from prolonged management by prehistoric populations (Balée, 1989). The population did not eliminate diversity entirely in this process, as this would have been foolhardy and ineffective, but promoted, instead, islands of concentrated resources within a sea of diversity. They did this by creating favourable conditions for the dominance of species that they valued highly and with characteristics that facilitated their competitiveness over time in an environment where succession is remarkably vigorous. Among the vegetations that are likely to be anthropogenic in contemporary Amazonia one may cite palm forests, bamboo forests, Brazil nut forests, and vine forests.

Palms are excellent indicator species of archaeological sites. Pupunha (*Bactris gassipaes*), inajá (*Maximiliana maripa*), and burití (*Mauritia flexuosa*) have been used as indicative of prolonged human occupation sites (Balick, 1984; Boer, 1965; Heinen and Ruddle, 1974;

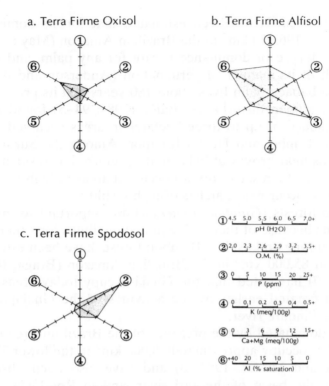

a. Terra Firme Oxisol

b. Terra Firme Alfisol

c. Terra Firme Spodosol

① 4,5 5,0 5,5 6,0 6,5 7,0+
pH (H2O)

② 2,0 2,3 2,6 2,9 3,2 3,5+
O.M. (%)

③ 0 5 10 15 20 25+
P (ppm)

④ 0 0,1 0,2 0,3 0,4 0,5+
K (meq/100g)

⑤ 0 3 6 9 12 15+
Ca+Mg (meq/100g)

⑥ +40 20 15 10 5 0
Al (% saturation)

Figure 3.5   **Comparison of terra firme soils.**

Pesce, 1985). Burití is found most often in areas of flooded forest and várzea, in contrast to the other two. Tucumã (*Astrocarium vulgare*), caiaui (*Elaeis oleifera*), and babaçú (*Orbignya phalerata*) are important, favoured species in the terra firme forests.

Boer (1965: 132) views *Astrocarium vulgare*, or tucumã, as a species that "never is found in virgin" areas, but only in areas that have been extensively disturbed by human managers. The Urubú Ka'apor of the state of Maranhão value it as a tree that attracts tapir and cutias, making hunting easier and more productive. It is also valued for its fibres, which are used to make hammocks, child-carrying slings, and other articles of daily use (Balée, 1989).

Andrade (1983: 23) found an association between the presence of *Elaeis oleifera* and anthropogenic black soils in areas of the Madeira river and south of the city of Manaus. Its uses are similar to those of the African palm and it seems to have come originally from Central America.

Perhaps the best-known palm of the palm forests is *Orbignya pha-*

lerata or babaçú. It has been estimated that forests dominated by babaçú cover 196,370 km² in the Brazilian Amazon (May et al., 1985: 115). This degree of dominance is rare for any palm, and seems to be a result of its manner of germination (Anderson and Anderson, 1985). The babaçú palm lives about 180 years and its presence is indicative of human disturbance. Balée (1984: 94–5) found forest islands of babaçú of up to three hectares in areas occupied today by the Guajá, Tembé, and Urubú Ka'apor. Among the Suruí of Rondônia, areas near groves of babaçú are preferred as residential sites. Babaçú forests themselves do not occur on areas of high fertility, but they seem to occur near patches of high fertility.

Bamboo forests (*Guadua glomerata*) are important to indigenous populations because of their value in making flutes for rituals and arrows for hunting and fishing. Bamboo forests have been estimated to cover about 85,000 km² in the Brazilian Amazon (Braga, 1979: 55). Balée (1989) has noted that the Guajá occupy today areas of bamboo forest created earlier by the activities of the Guajajara in the area of the Pindaré river.

Forests dominated by the presence of the Brazil nut tree (*Bertholletia excelsa*) occupy approximately 8,000 km² in the lower Tocantins (Kitamura and Muller, 1984: 8) and have also been observed in Amapá, in the basin of the Jarí river, and in Rondônia, although their areal extent has not been mapped. Some observers have noted that these forests seemed to be associated with archaeological sites and with areas of anthropogenic black soils (Araújo-Costa, 1983; Simões and Araújo-Costa, 1987; Simões et al., 1973). The Kayapó at Gorotire plant Brazil nut trees because of their importance as food (Anderson and Posey, 1985; Posey, 1985). Besides its local food value, this free is also an important economic resource for export (Laraia and da Mata, 1968). Brazil nut trees live even longer than babaçú, and are important indicator species of anthropogenic forests.

Perhaps most extensive of all, after the babaçú palm forests, are the vine or liana forests (*matas de cipó*), estimated to occupy 100,000 km² in the Brazilian Amazon (Pires, 1973: 152). They occur in particular concentration in the lower Tocantins, Xingú, and Tapajós river basins (see the area of vine forests in figure 3.4). Vine forests have a lower basal area than presumably "virgin" forests of terra firme (18–24 *vis-à-vis* 40 m² per hectare, respectively), an unusually high density of woody vines, and a tendency towards dominance by a few species (Pires and Prance, 1985: 120–2).

In these vine forests one finds a concentration of resources that is suggestive of complex, long-term management: food items, fruits that attract game, construction materials, medicinal plants, insect repellents, and firewood. The number of useful species is larger than in other types of upland forest. Observers have long noted the preference of farmers for vine forests (Moran, 1977, 1981; Sombroek, 1966: 195). Although no simple correlation between these forests and a particular soil order has been made, they seem to be more frequently associated with anthropogenic black soils (Heindsdijk, 1957; Smith, 1980) and with alfisols (Falesi, 1972; Moran, 1981). Balée (1989) found anthropogenic black soils in vine forests of Maranhão, of 39 cm depth, and with 31.8 meq/100 g of phosphorus – levels much higher than in adjacent soils. He also noted the higher pH (5.8) and the high concentration of calcium.

In contrast to the black-water regions of Amazonia, in these anthropogenic forests one finds an unusually high frequency of corn cultivation, in some cases leading to the near-total loss of bitter manioc cultivars and to the abandonment of manioc flour production. By contrast, in the black-water regions, one sees a predominance of extremely bitter varieties of manioc and a near-total absence of corn cultivation. One should note that in the white-water basins of the western Amazon, one also finds a low incidence of bitter manioc varieties and more corn cultivation. Corn is much more demanding of nutrients than can be sustained in many parts of Amazonia, particularly in the black-water regions.

4 Management of oligotrophic areas

There is much we can learn about the proper management of Amazonian ecosystems from the region's indigenous population, which coped with its limitations and in some cases rose above them by changing the composition of forest and soil. What we conclude from our examination of these two ecosystems is that native populations used both areas, but that they restricted their manipulations of the ecosystem to the "islands" of terra firme forest in the oligotrophic regions and focused on the eutrophic "islands" within the vaster nutrient-poor areas of terra firme.

Human populations have inhabited the upper Rio Negro for at least 6,000 years. Ceramics and anthropogenic soils have been identified in the Rio Negro, dated at 3750 BP (Clark and Uhl, 1987: 7; Saldarriaga and West, 1986; Sanford et al., 1985). The anthropogenic soils are found not in the caatinga areas but in upland tropical forests growing on oxisols, suggesting a very ancient preference for the patches of tropical forest, rather than caatinga, for occupation and agriculture.

Populations of the upper Rio Negro practise slash-and-burn agriculture, clearing areas of between 0.5 and 2.0 hectares between September and November each year. It has been observed that contemporary native populations generally avoid locating their swiddens in areas of caatinga, which through ethno-ecological taxonomies are identified as inappropriate for agriculture (Hill and Moran, 1983). Clark and Uhl (1987) estimated that in the region near San Carlos de Río Negro, in Venezuela, only about 20 per cent of the soils were not spodosols. This extremely restricted availability of soils capable of supporting crops for even a couple of years runs counter to very old assumptions about the ease with which native populations could relocate in Amazonia and the lack of "environmental circumscription" in the basin (Carneiro, 1970). There have been no reports of nutrient-rich alfisols (*terra roxa estruturada eutrófica*) in the Rio Negro Basin. Galvão (1959: 24) noted another factor limiting the agricultural potential of the upper Rio Negro: the apparent avoidance of areas which required penetration into the forest and a preference for areas along river banks by horticultural populations. Chernela (1983) observed a similar preference among the Uanano, a Tukanoan population in the Vaupés, as have those who have studied the Bara Makú (Silverwood-Cope, 1972) and the Hupdu Makú (Reid, 1979). This tendency to limit territorial occupation to the river-banks may represent a compromise response to the poverty of the terrestrial ecosystem, the availability of restricted areas of fertile levees, and the importance of fisheries based on ancient territorial claims.

Similarly, flooded forests (*igapós*) are avoided for agriculture, given their importance for fisheries (Chernela, 1983; Clark and Uhl, 1987; Dufour, 1983). Many of the fish in Amazonian river channels enter the flooded forest during the rainy season to gain weight and to spawn (Goulding, 1980, 1981). When fishing gives poor results, the Wakuenai in Venezuela say that the fish are spawning and locate their swiddens distant from the flooded forests. Chernela (1982, 1986a) noted the same explicit avoidance of flooded forest for agriculture among the Uanano in Brazil.

The length of the cultivation period and the size of clearings is of special significance in these oligotrophic habitats. The smaller the area cleared, the easier it will be for seeds from the native vegetation to recolonize the area. The length of the cultivation period affects the levels of nutrients available to the incoming seeds and the growth rate of secondary vegetation. In black-water ecosystems, the return of the original vegetation may take over a hundred years (Uhl, 1983; Uhl et al., 1982). Uhl et al. (1982: 319) found 271 seeds per m^2 in an area studied at the end of the cultivation cycle, 90 per cent of them secondary successional species. It is quite likely that secondary successional species are better adapted to low levels of nutrients and can thrive where domesticated plants cannot. Succession is much slower in black-water ecosystems: above-ground biomass after three years was only 870 g/m^2 compared to 2,000 g/m^2 in areas of oxisols on upland forest. It appears that oligotrophy, as well as the flooding, are responsible for this lower level of above-ground biomass production (Uhl et al., 1982: 320). After sixty years, the above-ground biomass is only 40 per cent of that of the original vegetation (Clark and Uhl, 1987: 12; Jordan and Uhl, 1978), compared to 90 per cent of above-ground biomass in eight years on ultisols in the Peruvian Amazon (Sanchez, 1976: 351).

One of the ways in which native peoples help accelerate the recolonization of cleared areas is by planting fruit trees in the swiddens. Not only does this increase the utility of the land, but it serves to attract birds and bats, which are the principal agents of primary forest seed dispersal in the humid tropics. In a controlled experiment, areas planted in this manner had nine times the number of seeds of native trees than an area which was not planted with fruit trees at the end of the cultivation cycle. The shade of the fruit trees serves to provide the needed shade to primary tree species of slow growth, and reduces leaching of nutrients.

The lack of a marked dry season in this region would lead us to expect that burns would be of poor quality. Generally, it is the quality of the burn that determines the yield of slash-and-burn cultivation in non-volcanic areas of the humid tropics (Moran, 1981). That is clearly the case in areas with high above-ground biomass. But in areas with lower biomass, high insolation, and high albedo resulting from reflection from the white sands, the biomass dries sufficiently to burn so well that, in fact, areas of xeromorphic vegetation tend to experience burns beyond the areas cleared. Clark and Uhl (1987) documented the problem of natural burns in this habitat, where hundreds of hectares can catch fire when twenty rainless days occur. The destructive impact of fire is a real threat in this ecosystem, in contrast to other areas of the humid tropics, where fire rarely extends beyond the area cleared (or in areas scarred by logging activities). Planting follows, and is dominated by bitter manioc.

Dufour (1988) found more than a hundred varieties of bitter manioc among a Tukanoan population in the Colombian Vaupés. Very few varieties of sweet manioc were known and cultivated. Chernela (1986b) found that repeated efforts by Uanano peoples in the Vaupés of Brazil to introduce sweet cultivars of manioc failed and only bitter cultivars persisted, when she did a study of their manioc varieties. Bitter manioc resembles the native vegetation of black-water regions by its toxic quality, which serves to conserve nutrients for the plant through reduction of herbivory. Montagnini and Jordan (1983) found that insects consumed less than 3 per cent of the tissue of bitter manioc plants due to the cyanogenetic glucosides present.

Bitter manioc cultivation solves one of the great problems of Amazonian populations: how to cultivate soils that are extremely poor in nutrients, extremely acid, and have toxic levels of aluminium. Manioc, a plant that appears to have evolved in just such areas of South America, can produce impressive yields in areas where nothing else will grow (Moran, 1973). One of the few limitations to its cultivation is its inability to withstand water-logging, which explains why it is cultivated on higher ground. Manioc is even adapted to drought, during which it loses its leaves and goes into dormancy, gaining its leaves again with the return of soil moisture. Beans and corn, by contrast, are unable to produce a predictable crop in these nutrient-poor areas, and unable to cope with even short-term droughts. Galvão (1959: 24) noted that corn had been abandoned by the populations of the Içana and that it probably never had much importance in the Rio Negro Basin.

Bitter manioc produces the bulk of the calories for black-water basin populations. Dufour (1983) showed that among the Tukanoans she studied in Colombia, 70 per cent of the energy came in the form of manioc flour and manioc bread (*casabe* or *beijú*), tapioca, manioc beer, and other forms of prepared manioc. The energy efficiency of manioc is impressive: it yielded 15.2 calories for every calorie spent on its production. Seventy percent of the production costs occur during processing. Nevertheless, the oligotrophy of the black-water regions depresses the total yields. Yields vary between 3 and 8 tons per hectare, with a mean of 4.7 (Clark and Uhl, 1987). By comparison, the world mean is 8.4 tons per hectare, and reaches 12.7 tons in

Brazil. The relatively low mean harvests confirm the nutrient-poor conditions of the environment.

Clark and Uhl (1987: 19) estimated the fish productivity of the Rio Negro–Casiquiare–Guainía rivers to be between 6.6 and 13.2 kg/ha/year – one of the lowest values for any tropical basin. In Africa and Asia the mean values are 40–60 kg/ha/year and Goulding (1979) estimated the productivity of the Madeira River in Brazil at 52 kg/ha/year.

The lower mean productivity results, in large part, from the absence of some particularly large species like pirarucú or paiche (*Arapaima gigas*), aruanã (*Osteoglossum bicirrhosum*), several large species of the genus *Colossoma*, and several large catfishes or pimeloids (Goulding, 1979: 15). The absence of aquatic grasses in black-water rivers, an important food source for many of the larger fishes, influences the species composition of these rivers and favours smaller species. This is not to say that black-water rivers are species-poor. Goulding et al. (1988) have shown that the lower Rio Negro is among the most species-rich rivers in the world, with approximately seven hundred species. Fish species in the Rio Negro, however, are dominated by smaller species with a mean length of only 40 mm – with over one hundred species of less than 30 mm length (Goulding et al., 1988: 109).

Success in fishing in black-water ecosystems depends mostly on territorial control over cataracts and flooded forest, where the fish volume is greatest. The most successful method of fishing is through the use of large fixed traps which require considerable investment in their construction and maintenance. The importance of control over the best fishing spots is evident in such a situation, and reaches a considerable level of sophistication in the Rio Negro (Chernela, 1986a; Moran, 1990). Fish was found to be a part of meals in 78–88 per cent of cases sampled by Dufour (1987: 389).

5 Management of eutrophic areas

By contrast, management of the eutrophic areas of terra firme offers the challenge of diversity. This was handled by native populations by creation of "islands of resources." They concentrated species of economic interest within close proximity to soils favourable for horticulture and favourable in locational factors, such as ease of river transportation, well-drained areas for habitational sites, and cool breezes to provide comfort and freedom from insects.

The creation of anthropogenic forests and soils solves two of the commonly mentioned problems posed by Amazonia: poor soils and species dispersal. This process need not have been conscious. The behaviour of ancestors could very well have been certified in myths and descendants continued traditions found to be favourable to their lifestyle.

For agriculture, the preferred areas were the vine forests, because of their association to alfisols. Near the villages, the population concentrated further resources by creating palm forests, bamboo forests, food/fruit-rich forests – and the garbage from their settlements built up over time anthropogenic soils which would serve in the future as usable soils in previously inferior areas from an agronomic viewpoint. This is equivalent to the population creating ecotones, or transitional areas, to favour high productivity.

In eutrophic areas, cultivation of grains and other nutrient-demanding plants is possible, although this will shorten the time before fertilization will be required. On the other hand, it makes no sense to build cities on top of these superb soils (as has been done in recent years, for example, at Tucumã, Pará) or to put them into the production of export and tree crops (as was the case in Rondônia with cacao). Agricultural zoning of these areas will need to achieve particularly high levels of sophistication, matching the quality of the soils to the products developed. Unfortunately, much of this will have more to do with market forces than with the micro-ecological characteristics of the areas.

The eutrophic areas of terra firme can be put to intensive use. Doing so should begin with attention to the processes of environmental modification undertaken by indigenous populations, and build on these efforts. The better soils can withstand cultivation for prolonged periods of time because of their fine structure and high initial cation exchange capacity. However, fertilization will be required for any form of continuous and intensive cultivation. The viability of continuous cultivation in these areas of terra firme is not an environmental issue *per se* but, rather, a political and economic one, of the government providing the conditions for access to fertilizers at competitive prices and of matching market demand to the products supplied by the areas put under cultivation. So far, for most of Amazonia, this has been poorly done. One of the few success stories has been the Japanese colony at the favourably located Tome-Açú, in which the inhabitants identified a low-weight/high-value crop early on, and which invested in technical and human resources from the outset.

6 Conclusions

Black-water ecosystems such as those found in the Rio Negro, Vaupés, and Içana represent the poorest and most limited areas of Amazonia. Above-ground biomass is lower, litterfall is poor in nutrients, decomposition is slow due to the acidity of the soils and the water, and the drainage limitations resulting from the podzolic soils contribute to making these areas a true challenge to human populations.

Selection of particularly toxic varieties of bitter manioc and hierarchical control over fishing spots further adjusted native peoples to these poor areas of Amazonia. The areas are rich in endemic species and in toxic plants with secondary compounds with great promise for advances in medicine and pharmacology. More than any others they should be protected from large-scale development activities. These are important ethnic refuge areas, with low potential for intensification but high potential for specialized and more selective exploitation for genetic, pharmacological, and medical research. While the total biomass is less than elsewhere in Amazonia, the species diversity is as high, if not higher, than other phytogeographic areas of the Amazon Basin. The native populations of this region are particularly attuned to the limitations of this ecosystem and their expertise should guide land use and research in the years ahead. Their potential for medicine and pharmacology, in particular, should have highest priority, especially the caatinga and bana areas, which are too poor for most other economic uses. On the "islands" of terra firme forests, extensive forms of resource use and extraction may continue, but intensive use is out of the question except in very restricted areas.

By contrast, intensive agriculture in Amazonia is possible and should largely be restricted to the eutrophic areas, especially where there are anthropogenic forests and soils. These have demonstrated productivity and, under the right market conditions, are likely to be economical. In contrast to more virgin areas, use of these areas will have minimal significance in terms of species extinction and biodiversity, since these areas are already simplified versions of the original ecosystems, with a predominance of species of economic value. This strategy would, in turn, recommend that for the foreseeable future large areas of the Amazon be protected from further clearing until such time as, through research and conservation, their potential can be better known.

Acknowledgements

The author wishes to thank the John Simon Guggenheim Memorial Foundation for a Fellowship during 1989–1990, which permitted him to take the time to reflect upon some of the matters discussed in this paper. He also wishes to thank the Institute for Advanced Study at Indiana University for the space in which to work during the Fellowship year; and Prof. Toshie Nishizawa for the invitation to participate in the stimulating meeting at Tsukuba.

References

Anderson, A., and E. Anderson. 1985. "A 'tree of life' grows in Brazil." *Natural History* 94: 41–6.

Anderson, A., and D. Posey. 1985. "Manejo de cerrado pelos Indios Kayapó." *Boletim do Museu Paraense Emílio Goeldi*, Botánica 2 (1): 77–98.

Andrade, E.B. 1983. *Relatório da expedição para coleta de germoplasma de "caiaui," Eleais oleifera, na Amazônia Brasileira*. Biblioteca da EMBRAPA/CPATU (Empresa Brasileira de Pesquisa Agropecuaria/Centro de Pesquisa Agropecuaria do Trópico Umido), Belém.

Araújo-Costa, F. 1983. "Projeto Baixo Tocantins: Salvamento arqueológico na região de Tucuruí." Dissertação de Mestrado, USP.

Balée, William. 1984. "The ecology of ancient Tupi warfare." In R.B. Ferguson (ed.), *Warfare, culture and environment* (Academic Press, New York), 241–65.

———. 1989. "The culture of Amazonian forests." *Advances in Economic Botany* 7: 1–21.

Balick, M.J. 1984. "Ethnobotany of palms in the neotropics." *Advances in Economic Botany* 1: 9–23.

Black, G.A., T. Dobzhansky, and C. Pavan. 1950. "Some attempts to estimate species diversity and population density of trees in Amazonian forests." *Botanical Gazette* 111: 413–25.

Boer, J.G. 1965. "Palmae." In J. Lanjouw (ed.), *Flora of Suriname*, vol. 5, part 1. Brill, Leiden.

Braga, P. 1979. "Subdivisão fitogeográfica, tipos de vegetação, conservação, e inventário florístico da floresta Amazônica." Supplement to *Acta Amazônica* 9 (4): 53–80.

Carneiro, Robert. 1970. *The transition from hunting to horticulture in the Amazon basin*. Eighth Congress of Anthropological and Ethnological Sciences 3: 243–51.

Chernela, Janet. 1982. "Indigenous forest and fish management in the Vaupés basin of Brazil." *Cultural Survival Quarterly* 6 (2): 17–18.

———. 1983. "Hierarchy and economy of the Uanano speaking peoples of the middle Vaupés basin." Ph.D. dissertation, Columbia University.

————. 1986a. "Pesca e hierarquização tribal no alto Uaupés." In B. Ribeiro (ed.), *Suma Etnológica Brasileira*, vol. 1 (Editôra Vozes, Petrópolis), 235–50.

————. 1986b. "Os cultivares de mandioca na área do Vaupés. In B. Ribeiro (ed.), *Suma Etnológica Brasileira*, vol. 1 (Editôra Vozes, Petrópolis), 151–8.

Clark, K., and C. Uhl. 1987. "Farming, fishing, and fire in the history of the upper Río Negro region of Venezuela." *Human Ecology* 15: 1–26.

Dufour, Darna. 1983. "Nutrition in the northwest Amazon." In R. Hames and W. Vickers (eds.), *Adaptive responses of native Amazonians* (Academic Press, New York), 329–55.

————. 1987. "Insects as food: A case study from the northwest Amazon." *American Anthropologist* 89: 383–97.

————. 1988. "Cyanide content of cassava cultivars used by Tukanoan Indians of Northwest Amazonia." *Economic Botany* 42: 255–66.

Falesi, I.C. 1972. *Os solos da Rodovia Transamazônica*. IPEAN (Instituto de Pesquisa Agronomica do Norte), Belém.

Galvão, Eduardo. 1959. "Aculturação indígena no Rio Negro." *Boletim do Museu Paraense Emílio Goeldi*, n.s. Antropología 7: 1–60.

Geisler, R., and J. Schneider. 1976. "The element matrix of Amazon waters and its relationship with the mineral content of fishes." *Amazoniana* 6 (1): 47–65.

Goulding, Michael. 1979. *Ecologia da pesca do Rio Madeira*. INPA (Instituto Nacional de Pesquisas da Amazônia), Manaus.

————. 1980. *The fishes and the forest*. University of California Press, Berkeley.

————. 1981. *Man and fisheries on an Amazon frontier*. W. Junk, The Hague.

Goulding, M., M.L. Carvalho, and E.G. Ferreira. 1988. *Rio Negro: Rich life in poor water*. SPB Academic Publishing, The Hague.

Heindsdijk, D. 1957. *Forest inventory in the Amazon valley*. FAO, Rome.

Heinen, H.D., and K. Ruddle. 1974. "Ecology, ritual and economic organization in the distribution of palm starch among the Warao." *Journal of Anthropological Research* 30 (2): 116–38.

Herrera, Rafael. 1979. "Nutrient distribution and cycling in an Amazonian caatinga forest on spodosols in S. Venezuela." Ph.D. dissertation, University of Reading.

Hill, J., and E. Moran. 1983. "Adaptive strategies of Wakuenai people of the Rio Negro basin." In R. Hames and W. Vickers (eds.), *Adaptive responses of native Amazonians* (Academic Press, New York), 113–35.

Jacobs, Maurius. 1988. *The tropical rain forest: A first encounter*. Springer-Verlag, New York.

Jordan, C.F. 1982. "Amazon rain forests." *American Scientist* 70: 394–401.

————. 1985. *Nutrient cycling in tropical forest ecosystems*. Wiley, New York.

Jordan, C.F., and C. Uhl. 1978. "Biomass of a tierra firme forest of the Amazon basin." *Oecologia Plantarum* 13: 387–400.

Kitamura, P.C., and C.C. Muller. 1984. *Castanhais nativos de Marabá: Fatores de depredaçãoãe bases para sua preservação*. Documentos no. 30. EMBRAPA/CPATU, Belém.

Klinge, Hans. 1978. "Studies of the ecology of Amazon caatinga forest in S. Venezuela." *Acta Científica Venezolana* 29: 258–62.

————. n.d. "Low Amazon caatinga or bana." Mimeo.

Klinge, H., and R. Herrera. 1978. "Biomass studies in Amazon caatinga forest in S. Venezuela." *Tropical Ecology* 19 (1): 93–110.

Laraia, R., and R. da Mata. 1968. *Indios e castanheiros*. Zahar, São Paulo.

May, P.H., A. Anderson, J. Frazão, and M. Balick. 1985. "Subsistence benefits from the babassu palm." *Economic Botany* 39 (2): 113–29.

McKey, D., P. Waterman, C. Mbi, J. Gartlan, and T. Struhsaker. 1978. "Phenolic content of vegetation in two African rain forests: Ecological implications." *Science* 202: 61–3.

Medina, Ernesto, M. Sobrado, and R. Herrera. 1978. "Significance of leaf orientation for leaf temperature in an Amazonian sclerophyll vegetation." *Radiation and Environmental Biophysics* 15: 131–40.

Montagnini, F., and C.F. Jordan. 1983. "The role of insects in productivity decline of cassava on a slash and burn site in the Amazon territory of Venezuela." *Agriculture, Ecosystems, and Environment* 9 (3): 293–301.

Moran, Emilio F. 1973. "Energy flow analysis and Manihot esculenta crantz." *Acta Amazônica* 3 (3): 28–39.

———. 1977. "Estrategias de sobrevivencia: o uso de recurses ao Longo da Rodovía Transamazônica." *Acta Amazônica* 7 (3): 363–79.

———. 1981. *Developing the Amazon*. Indiana University Press, Bloomington.

———. 1990. *A ecologia humana das populacões da Amazônia*. Editôra Vozes, Petrópolis.

———. 1993. *Through Amazonian eyes: The human ecology of Amazonian populations* (revised English edition). University of Iowa Press, Iowa City.

Pesce, C. 1985. "Oil palms and other oilseeds of the Amazon." Cited in Balée, 1989.

Pires, J.M. 1973. *Tipos de vegetação da Amazônia*. Publicacões Avulsas do Museu Paraense Emílio Goeldi, Belém.

Pires, J.M., and G. Prance. 1985. "The vegetation types of the Brazilian Amazon. In G. Prance and T. Lovejoy (eds.), *Key environments: Amazonia* (Pergamon Press, Oxford), 109–45.

Posey, Darrell. 1985. "Indigenous management of tropical forest ecosystems: The case of the Kayapó Indians of the Brazilian Amazon." *Agroforestry Systems* 3: 139–58.

Prance, G.T. 1978. "The origin and evolution of the Amazon Flora." *Interciencia* 3(4): 207–22.

Prance, G.T., W. Rodrigues, and M.F. da Silva. 1976. "Inventário florestal de um hectare de mata de terra firme km 30 da estrada Manaus-Itacoatiara." *Acta Amazônica* 6: 9–35.

Reid, Howard. 1979. "Some aspects of movement, growth, and change among the Hupdu Makú Indians of Brazil." Ph.D. dissertation, University of Cambridge.

Richards, Paul. 1952. *The tropical rain forest*. Cambridge University Press, Cambridge.

Salati, Eneas (1985). The climatology and hydrology of Amazonia. In G. Prance and T. Lovejoy (eds.), *Key environments: Amazonia* (Pergamon Press, Oxford), 18–48.

Saldarriaga, J., and D. West. 1986. "Holocene fires in the Northern Amazon basin." *Quaternary Research* 26: 358–66.

Sanchez, Pedro. 1976. *Properties and management of soils in the tropics*. Wiley–Interscience, New York.

Sanford, R.L., J. Saldarriaga, K. Clark, C. Uhl, and R. Herrera. 1985. "Amazon rainforest fires." *Science* 227: 53–5.

Silverwood-Cope, P. 1972. "A contribution to the ethnography of the Colombian Makú." Ph.D. dissertation, University of Cambridge.

Simões, M., and F. Araújo-Costa. 1987. "Pesquisa arqueológicas no baixo Rio Tocantins." *Revista de Arqueología* 4 (1): 11–28.

Simões , M., C. Correa, and A. Machado. 1973. "Achados arqueológicos no baixo Rio Fresco." *O Museu Goeldi no Sesquicentenario*. Publicações Avulsas do Museu Paraense Emílio Goeldi, Belém.

Sioli, Harald. 1951. "Zum Alterungsprozess von Flussen und Flusstypen in Amazonas Gebiet." *Archiv für Hydrobiologie* 45 (3): 267–84.

Smith, Nigel. 1979. *A pesca no Rio Amazonas*. INPA, Manaus.

————. 1980. "Anthrosols and human carrying capacity in Amazonia." *Annals of the Association of American Geographers* 70: 553–66.

Sombroek, W. 1966. *Amazon soils*. Centre for Agriculture Publications and Documents, Wageningen.

Stark, N., and C.F. Jordan. 1978. "Nutrient retention by the root mat of an Amazonian rain forest." *Ecology* 59 (3): 434–7.

Takeuchi, M. 1961. "The structure of the Amazonian vegetation, II: Tropical rain forest." *Journal of the Faculty of Science* (University of Tokyo), 8: 1–26.

Uhl, Christopher. 1983. "You can keep a good forest down." *Natural History* 92: 69–79.

Uhl, Christopher, C. Jordan, K. Clark, H. Clark, and R. Herrera. 1982. "Ecosystem recovery in Amazon caatinga forest after cutting, cutting and burning and bulldozer treatments." *Oikos* 38: 313–20.

Uhl, Christopher, and P. Murphy. 1981. "Composition, structure and regeneration of a tierra firme forest in the Amazon basin of Venezuela." *Tropical Ecology* 22 (2): 219–37.

4

Archaeological perspectives on the potential of Amazonia for intensive exploitation

Betty J. Meggers

1 Introduction

The first European visitors were astonished by Amazonia. The lush vegetation, immense rivers, healthy climate, strange animals, and attractive people were truly a "new world," unlike anything known at home. Five hundred years later, the region continues to elicit wonder. Its biological diversity has raised the estimated number of species on the planet from three million to 30 million, and even that may be conservative. Interactions among species are intricate, life cycles are peculiar, and morphology is often exotic, especially among insects. These traits reflect the remarkably complex interaction among biota, soil, and climate, achieved during tens of millennia of biological evolution.

This successful natural configuration is now in conflict with the most successful product of cultural evolution, namely, modern industrial civilization. We desire to replace it with the kind of landscapes we understand, to make it produce the foods we prefer and support the social and economic institutions we consider most suitable. To this end, we are converting forest to pasture, constructing roads, damming rivers, and encouraging immigration on a larger scale. But things are not working out as expected. Urban sprawl is affecting local weather. Cleared land rapidly declines in productivity and costs often exceed gains. Malaria has become a serious health hazard. The biologists warn of global disaster; the politicians say there is nothing to worry about. Who is right? How fragile are the tropics of Latin America?

We cannot answer these questions unless we recognize and rid ourselves of biases inculcated by our immersion in temperate eco-systems. We continue to judge the carrying capacity of tropical envir-onments using temperate-zone criteria and to design projects for maximizing productivity using temperate-zone models, although sci-entific evidence and practical experience make it increasingly evi-dent that temperate and tropical ecosystems behave very differently. We assess the complexity of tropical forest cultures on the scale of hierarchical organization and urbanism evolved in the riverine cra-dles of Old World civilization, although archaeological and ethno-graphic evidence attests to alternative forms of social integration and population distribution. In this context, the numerous and often extensive archaeological habitation sites on the terra firme as well as along the várzea are equated with large sedentary populations orga-nized into stratified political entities. Similarly, the low density and high mobility of surviving indigenous groups are attributed to deci-mation and deculturation since European contact (Roosevelt, 1989: 31, 45; Smith, 1980: 553, 564, 566).

The temperate-zone perspective also pervades assessments of the disappointing results of development programmes. Poor planning, in-sufficient credit, corrupt administration, inadequate transportation, shortage of labour, defective infrastructure, and other sociopolitical and economic factors implicated in the failure of temperate-based projects are judged responsible, with the consequence that attention is focused away from potentially significant environmental and eco-logical factors (e.g. Collins, 1986; Schumann and Partridge, 1989).

I shall attempt to demonstrate that surviving unacculturated groups accurately depict pre-Columbian settlement behaviour and that their way of life reflects an ancient and remarkable accommodation to complex and variable conditions. In so doing, I will make two assump-tions: (1) the fundamental physical–chemical processes and evolu-tionary principles that have guided the transformation of life during the past five billion years remain unchanged and immune to our con-trol; and (2) our survival depends on exploiting necessary resources in sustainable ways. All organisms affect and are affected by their environments; humans differ mainly in the range of resources they use and in the elaboration of cultural mechanisms for obtaining them. Our global dominance is testimony to the superiority of cultural behaviour over non-symbolic forms of learning, but does not justify assuming that the evolutionary processes responsible for this situation have been neutralized. By shedding another of our biases – namely, that culture is exempt from evolutionary constraints – we can take advantage of a large body of theory to discover clues for reconstructing prehistoric cultural adaptation in Amazonia, where the predominant physical remains are small undecorated fragments of pottery.

2 Evolutionary principles

Although natural selection is the best known evolutionary process, drift is also a significant mechanism of change. Characters relevant to survival and reproduction are subject to selection, whereas those that are adaptively neutral change directionally by drift. As long as the members of a population interact socially and reproductively, behavioural and genetic variations among individuals are homogenized. If interaction is impeded, however, the resulting segments begin to diverge, in part because of different adaptive constraints and in part because of drift. The best-known cultural manifestation occurs in language, where drift accounts for gradual alterations in pronunciation, meaning, and grammar, but it also operates in other aspects of culture.

The recent history of the Panare in south-eastern Venezuela provides an excellent illustration of the process. Less than a century ago, they began expanding from their traditional territory in the Guyana highlands toward the north-west, into land vacated by the previous occupants (fig. 4.1). Dispersal along several tributaries segregated the original community into three semi-isolated populations, which have begun to diverge in dialect, kinship terminology, dress, and ornament, as well as in ceremonies associated with male initiation, female puberty, and funerals (Henley, 1982: 11–14). Similar incipient linguistic and cultural differentiation has been observed among other recently separated Amazonian groups (e.g. Yanomami: Spielman, Migliazza and Neel, 1974; Campa and Machiguenga: D'Ans, 1982: 252; northern Ge: Seeger, 1981: 229–30).

Temper and firing are among the characteristics of pottery susceptible to unconscious directional change. Classifying unselected sam-

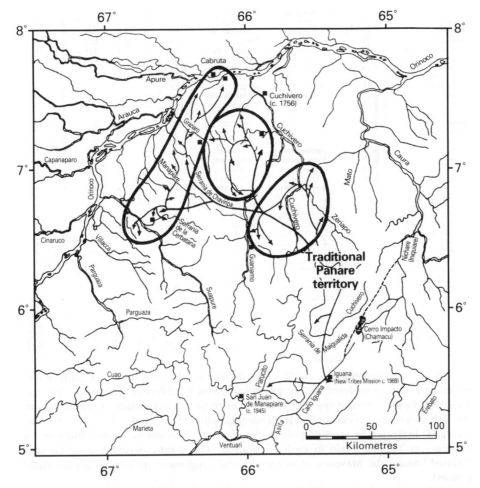

Figure 4.1 **Panare expansion during the past hundred years from their traditional territory south-east of the Orinoco into lands vacated by the previous indigenous population. Groups occupying different rivers have begun to drift apart linguistically and culturally as a consequence of reduced interaction (After Henley, 1982.)**

ples of fragments using uniform criteria permits recognizing distinct trends in the relative frequencies of undecorated types. All samples that can be interdigitated into a single sequence represent the same prehistoric community, termed a phase (fig. 4.2). Phases that share a specific set of decorative characteristics are assigned to the same tradition. After these communities have been identified, their settlement behaviours can be reconstructed and their population densities can be inferred. Comparing the resulting patterns with those of surviving

71

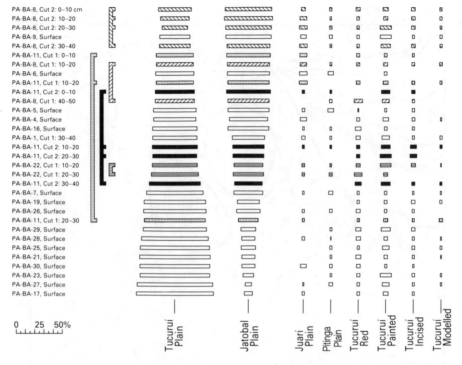

Figure 4.2 **Seriated sequence of the Tucuruí Phase, Rio Tocantins. The pottery was classified into four undecorated types distinguished by differences in tempering material and four decorated types defined by technique of decoration. Vertical bars at the left connect successive levels of stratigraphic excavations. The direction of change is indicated by stratigraphic evidence for an increase in Jatobal Plain and a decrease in Tucuruí Plain in each excavation. The erratic occurrence of Turucuí Painted implies the presence of two matrilocal exogamous residential groups (subphases).**

indigenous groups makes it possible to assess whether or not the latter are representative of the pre-Columbian demographic situation.

3 Past and present settlement behaviour

Survey along the principal tributaries of the Amazon during the past fifteen years by participants in the Programa Nacional de Pesquisas Arqueológicas na Bacia Amazônica (PRONAPABA) has located and sampled hundreds of archaeological sites (fig. 4.3). The resulting data permit dozens of phases to be distinguished and their settlement behaviour to be described.

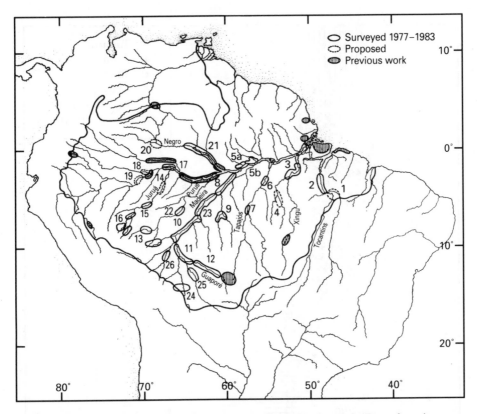

Figure 4.3 **Regions surveyed during the Programa Nacional de Pesquisas Arqueo-lógicas na Bacia Amazônica between 1977 and 1983. Areas 2, 5a, 5b, 8, and 21 by Mário Simões; Areas 3, 6, 7, and 22 by Celso Perota; Areas 9–12 and 23 by Eurico Th. Miller; Areas 13–17 by Ondemar Dias, and Areas 24–26 by Bernardo Dougherty.**

Territorial configurations

The spatial distributions of habitation sites belonging to contemporary phases generally suggest contiguous territories along rivers. Along the lower Tocantins, for example, the sharp boundaries between the phases coincide with changes in the character of the river. Each zone provides different aquatic resources and requires different methods of exploitation (fig. 4.4). Similar contiguous territories have been reported among surviving indigenous communities in various parts of the lowlands, among them Akawaio River groups in west-central Guyana (fig. 4.5).

73

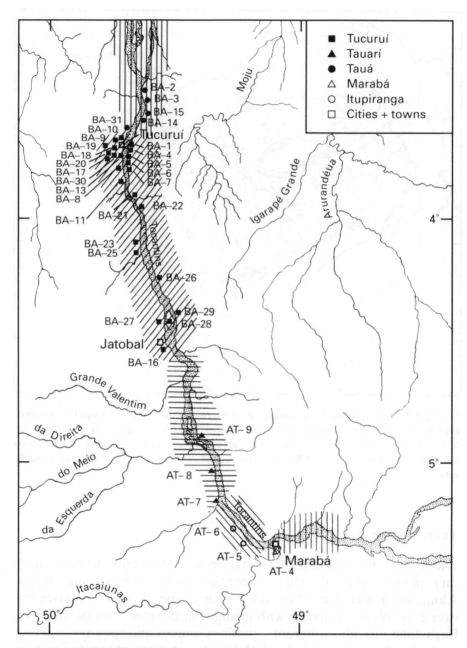

Figure 4.4 **Territorial distributions of four contemporary phases (prehistoric communities) on the lower Tocantins, inferred from the locations of habitation sites. The boundaries correlate with physical changes in the character of the river and associated differences in subsistence resources.**

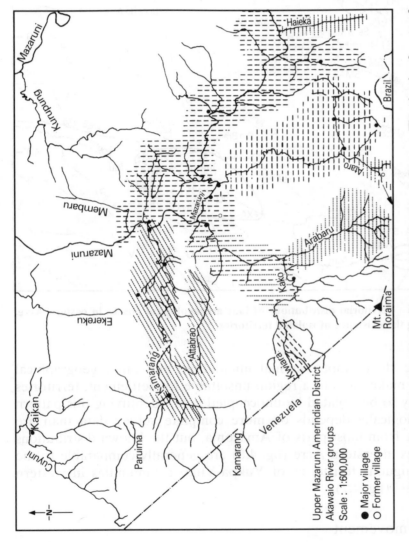

Figure 4.5 **Territories of Akawaio River groups in west-central Guyana. The riverine focus and contiguous boundaries along the river are shared with the prehistoric territories reconstructed in figure 4.4, suggesting that the archaeological phases represent similar endogamous communities. (After Colson, 1983/4, map 2.)**

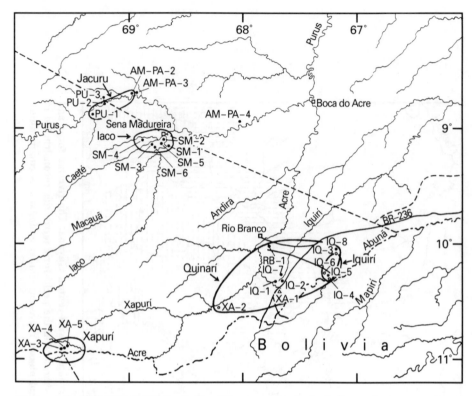

Figure 4.6 **Territorial distributions of four archaeological phases in eastern Acre, suggesting the existence of isolated territories.**

Where steep slopes, annual inundation, and other geographical features make parts of a region unsuitable for settlement, territories are likely to be isolated by unoccupied land. Identifying this pattern archaeologically depends on more complete survey data than are available from most parts of Amazonia, but the known distributions of phases in eastern Acre (fig. 4.6) are generally comparable to the non-contiguous territories of Yukpa-Yuko communities in western Venezuela (fig. 4.7).

Village movement

Since a seriated sequence is a relative chronology, comparing the locations of sites with their chronological positions permits tracing village movement. The schematic settlement history of the Tucuruí

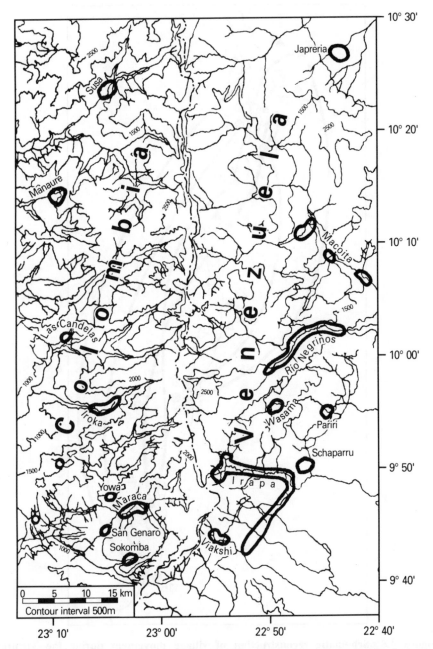

Figure 4.7 **Isolated territories of Yukpa-Yuko communities on the border between Colombia and Venezuela, resembling the disjunct pattern reconstructed for the archaeological phases in figure 4.6. (After Ruddle, 1971, map 1.)**

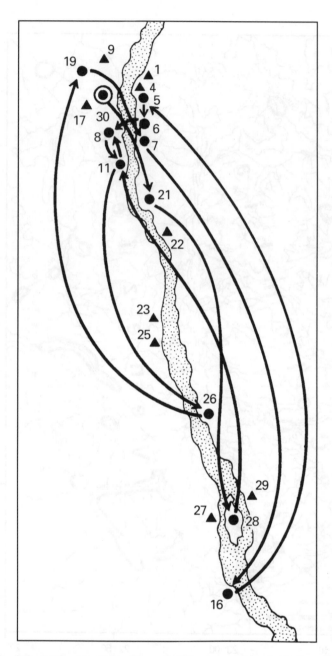

Figure 4.8 **Schematic reconstruction of village movement during the Tucuruí Phase, by subphase B derived from sequential positions of sites represented in the seriated sequence (fig. 4.2). Although more intensive investigation would undoubtedly identify additional episodes of occupation at many of the sites, the general pattern would not be affected.**

Phase on the lower Tocantins is typical. Differences in the relative frequencies of painted decoration suggest the community was divided among two matrilocal villages, each of which moved independently and occasionally fissioned and refused. Although the sites are seldom shared, both patterns are centripetal within the territory and combine short and long moves, some to pristine and some to previously occupied locations (fig. 4.8).

The actual history of village movement during the past seventy-five years by the Mekragnoti of the upper Xingu, reconstructed from interviews with informants, also incorporates long and short movements, reoccupation of several locations, and episodes of fission and fusion (fig. 4.9).

Reoccupation

Changes in the relative frequencies of the undecorated pottery types in successive levels of a stratigraphic excavation provide the basis for estimating continuity and discontinuity of occupation of a site by the same phase and for recognizing reoccupation by a different phase or phases of the same or different traditions. The procedure is exemplified by the seriated sequences of the Kiusiu and Ibare phases on the Llanos de Moxos (fig. 4.10).

Two kinds of discontinuities are evident in both seriations. First, successive levels of each excavation (connected by vertical bars at the left) are separated by one or more levels from the other excavation. This interdigitation implies that the portion of the site represented by the excavation was abandoned and subsequently reoccupied. Second, the seriated positions of some levels are contiguous, but the magnitude of the differences in relative frequencies of the principal undecorated type is equal to or greater than that between levels with disjunct positions (e.g. BE-MO-8, Levels 60–80 and 80–100 cm). This situation also implies discontinuous occupation of the location sampled.

This seriation provides evidence not only for discontinuous occupation at both sites during the Kiusiu Phase, but also for reoccupation of both by the Ibare Phase. The boundary is marked by reversal of the trend in the principal undecorated pottery type and by abrupt changes in occurrence of most of the decorated types. Carbon-14 dates confirm the stratigraphic evidence for priority of the Kiusiu Phase. This pattern of reoccupation of sites by the same phase and

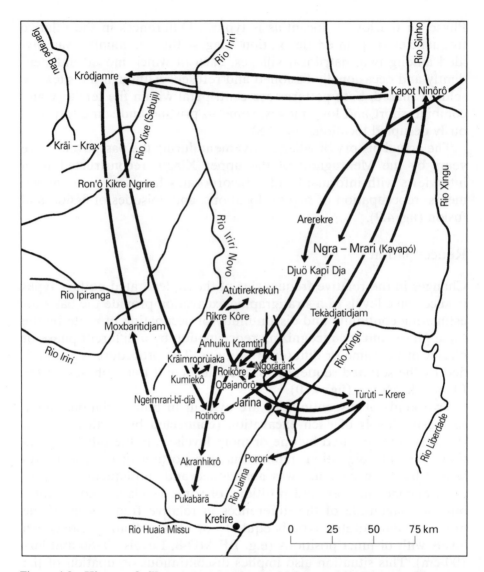

Figure 4.9 **History of village movement by the Mekragnoti in the upper Xingu region during 75 years, reconstructed from interviews with informants. The centripetal pattern, long and short moves, fissioning and fusing, and reoccupation of several locations are characteristics shared with the Tucuruí Phase reconstruction in figure 4.8. (After Verswijver, 1978.)**

by successive phases of the same or different traditions is characteristic throughout the lowlands.

Multiple reoccupation of the same locations is relatively common

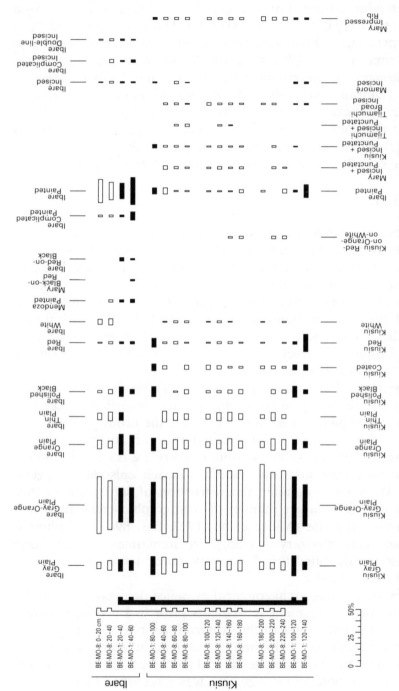

Figure 4.10 Seriated sequences derived by interdigitation of levels of stratigraphic excavations at two sites on the central Llanos de Moxos, identified by the vertical bars at the left. Replacement of the Kiusiu Tradition by the Ibare Tradition, marked by discontinuities in the trends of the undecorated pottery types and in the techniques of decoration, coincides with a brief, intense episode of aridity c. 700 BP (fig. 4.12).

81

among surviving groups. For example, the Mekragnoti have moved their village thirty-six times since AD 1900. Ten of the sites had been occupied previously. Five were reoccupied once, several twice, and one three times (Gross, 1983: 439). Reoccupation of former locations is also characteristic among the Siona-Secoya and Tatuyo of eastern Colombia (Dufour, 1983: 330; Vickers, 1983: 471) and the Yanomami of southern Venezuela (Hames, 1983: 412–14). Archaeological evidence that the same location was reoccupied by phases belonging to different traditions has a modern counterpart in the reoccupation of prehistoric sites by contemporary groups (e.g. Balée, 1987).

Village area

Sites of several phases in Acre vary from 3 m diameter to 8 × 15 m, comparable to the ranges of house dimensions among the Mojo, Panare, Camayurá, Kayapó, and Witoto. Along the Xingu and Tapajós, by contrast, the minimum dimensions of sites are close to the upper limit of dwellings reported ethnographically (65 × 30 m and 50 m diameter). Differences in house size are associated today with differences in the size of the domestic group, rules of marriage and residence, and other social behaviour, implying the existence of similar variation prior to European contact.

The maximum dimensions of contemporary single-house villages suggest that archaeological sites with surface extensions exceeding about 50 m in diameter or 65 m in length are the product of multiple occupation. When a site is represented by more than one stratigraphic excavation, it is often possible to correlate the levels and estimate the maximum area attributable to each episode (Meggers, 1992, fig. 5). A more detailed reconstruction of settlement history can be made from a larger number of stratigraphic excavations distributed across the site (Miller et al., 1993, figs. 69–71). Although two or more contemporary dwellings are sometimes implied, none of the episodes identified thus far covers more than a small fraction of the surface of the site.

In summary, existing archaeological evidence does not confirm the existence of large permanent settlements prior to European contact along any of the tributaries of the Amazon. Rather, it indicates that the settlement behaviour exhibited by surviving unacculturated indigenous communities, including territorial configuration, village movement, village duration, and village size, was established by the beginning of the Christian era.

4 Relations between várzea and terra firme groups

Two scenarios have been proposed for interaction between the groups exploiting the várzea of white-water rivers and those occupying the terra firme drained by black- and clear-water rivers. One envisions the várzea as a region of constant population increase, creating demographic pressure that was relieved by expansion up the principal tributaries (Lathrap, 1970: 74–7). The other views the várzea as prime agricultural land coveted by occupants of the terra firme.

Examining the affiliations of the phases identified thus far along the Madeira, Tocantins, and Xingu reveals a sharp boundary coincident with the first rapid on each river. Phases below this point are affiliated with the Polychrome Tradition and those above it belong to traditions restricted to the terra firme. This segregation is particularly clear on the Tocantins (fig. 4.4) and on the lower Xingu, where sites above and below the barrier are in close proximity. Expansions of the Polychrome Tradition up the Negro and the Solimões are late and seem attributable to the advent of the Incised and Punctate Tradition rather than to local population increase.

These distributions are compatible with environmental evidence that the várzea and terra firme habitats are distinct and require different specialized knowledge and procedures for effective utilization, such that groups adapted to either are ill equipped to exploit the other. A case can be made that the terra firme was a more stable environment than the várzea, which was subject to drastic fluctuations in subsistence productivity because of unpredictable variations in the rate, timing, and extent of annual inundation (Irion, 1984; Meggers, 1971: 146).

5 The impact of climatic fluctuation

It is generally accepted that Amazonia experienced episodes of climatic fluctuation during and since the Pleistocene, but until recently evidence for their impacts on humans was restricted to the disjunct distributions of languages and cultural traits (Meggers, 1987). The existence of detailed relative chronologies and numerous carbon-14 dates throughout the lowlands now makes it possible to correlate local cultural discontinuities with environmental oscillations.

When humans entered South America toward the end of the Pleistocene, some 12,000–14,000 years ago, the lowlands were less densely forested than at present. Although details are unclear, it seems likely that the savannas of Roraima and northern Pará are relics of a corridor of relatively open vegetation that extended from Venezuela to eastern Brazil (Barbosa, 1992). The availability of similar kinds of resources across the basin would have facilitated movement by hunter-gatherers and carbon-14 dates indicate they had reached the south-eastern margin of the lowlands by 11,000 BP (Schmitz, 1987, table II). The only evidence thus far for their presence in the central Amazon takes the form of rare stone projectile points (Simões, 1976) and early carbon-14 dates from the lower levels of ceramic sites, which may represent campfires of pre-ceramic occupants of the same locations. The oldest result is 7320 ± 100 BP (SI-4277) from a tributary of the middle Madeira.

The vegetation assumed its current composition and extent during subsequent millennia, but the process was disrupted by several widespread episodes of climatic fluctuation. Pollen records from marginal locations indicate that prior to the Christian era savanna replaced forest during several centuries and briefer episodes occurred about 1,500, 1,200, 700, and 400 years ago (Absy, 1982; Van der Hammen, 1982). These episodes coincide with cultural replacements in well-dated archaeological sequences throughout the lowlands.

Oscillations reflected in a pollen profile from Lago Ararí on eastern Marajó correlate with successive archaeological phases in the surrounding region (fig. 4.11). The Ananatuba Phase, the earliest pottery-making group on the island, arrived when forest vegetation was dominant. By 2590 ± 100 BP (Beta-2289), forest pollen had declined from 65 per cent to 30 per cent, implying significant alteration in the climate and biota (Absy, 1985, fig. 4.9). The terminal date for the Mangueiras Phase probably marks the point during the transition at which declining subsistence resources could no longer sustain sedentary communities. The inception of the Formiga Phase coincides with re-expansion of the forest about 2000 BP. The arrival of the Marajoara Phase follows the shorter period of aridity about 1500 BP and its termination coincides with the 700 BP episode.

Similar cultural discontinuities are evident in all the regions where local sequences are sufficiently complete and well dated to minimize the probability of sampling error. With rare exceptions, the initial ceramic complexes throughout the lowlands postdate 2000 BP (fig. 4.12). On the Llanos de Moxos in north-eastern Bolivia, most phases begin or end about 1500, 1000, and 700 BP. In the Silves–Uatumã region on the left bank of the middle Amazon, replacements take place about 1,500, 1,100, 800, and 400 BP. On the lower Xingu, transitions

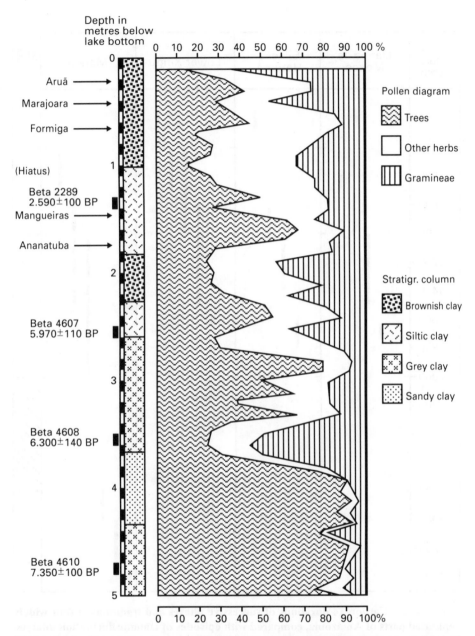

Figure 4.11 **Correlation between the inceptions of archaeological phases on Marajó and local fluctuations in arboreal vegetation. A carbon-14 date of 2590 ± 100 BP for a decline in tree pollen falls within the hiatus between the end of the Mangueiras Phase _c._ 2800 BP and the inception of the Formiga Phase _c._ 2000 BP. (After Meggers and Danon, 1988.)**

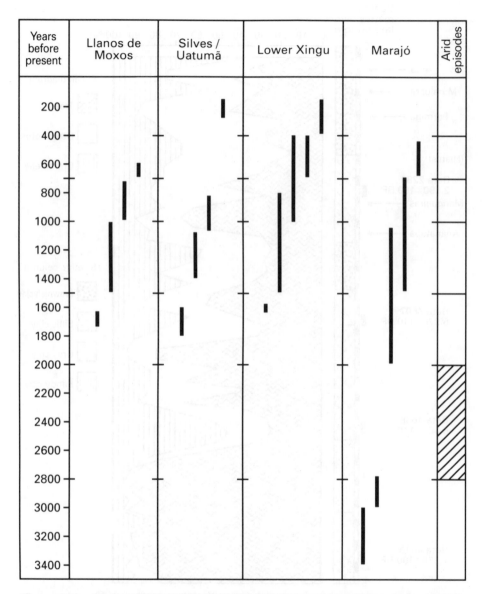

Figure 4.12 **Carbon-14 durations of successive phases and traditions in four widely separated parts of Amazonia, compared with episodes of climatic fluctuation inferred from pollen cores. Cultural discontinuities in all four regions coincide with the 1500 BP episode and also tend to be associated with the episodes *c.* 700 and 400 BP. Disagreement between the concentration of cultural discontinuities *c.* 1000 BP and vegetational changes *c.* 1200 B.P. probably reflects the greater number of dates for this episode from archaeological sites.**

occur about 1,500, 1,100, 800, and 400 BP. The only significant disagreement between the timing of climatic changes inferred from pollen profiles and the cultural replacements is the clustering of the latter about 1000 BP rather than 1200 BP. This may reflect more precise dating for the archaeological sequences. Droughts too brief to leave a pollen record are more frequent (Meggers, 1994; Sternberg, 1987: 206; Stockton, 1990) and failure to incorporate their effects places unwise schemes for "development" in greater jeopardy.

The contemporaneity of climatic fluctuations and cultural discontinuities implies a cause and effect relationship. Evidence that many plants respond to variations in rainfall by failing to flower and fruit indicates that the cause was deterioration of local subsistence resources below the requirements of small semi-sedentary communities (Leigh et al., 1982). The effect may have been emigration, decimation, adoption of a wandering way of life, or a combination of solutions. Although emigration cannot yet be traced archaeologically, it is implied by the disjunct distributions of the principal Amazonian languages as well as by the different ceramic affiliations of successive phases in the archaeological sequences.

6 Overcoming environmental constraints

From the perspective of temperate-zone observers, the failure of indigenous inhabitants of Amazonia to equal the population density and sociopolitical complexity achieved in the adjacent Andean region signifies cultural stagnation. From the perspective of the tropical environment, however, their way of life represents highly successful exploitation of unpromising and unpredictable resources. Wild plants and animals are solitary and dispersed, agricultural intensification is precluded, and food cannot be stored for future consumption (Bergman, 1980: 109–10; Good, 1989: 78). The number, variety, and ingenuity of the cultural practices that have developed for manipulating environmental constraints, inhibiting overexploitation, and optimizing the productivity of this complex ecosystem are no less remarkable than the intricate interactions among the climate, soils, and biota.

Comprehensive knowledge of the flora provides alternatives when primary resources fail (Berlin, 1984: 32; Boom, 1989: 82–3; Carneiro, 1978; Cavalcante and Frikel, 1973: 5). The Yanomami are reported to experiment continuously with new plants they encounter (Fuentes, 1980: 23). The abundance of useful species is enhanced by selective cutting and weeding and by transplanting (Irvine, 1989). Multiple varieties of the principal cultigens with differing tolerances for disease, moisture, soil, and other variables are usually planted to minimize loss (Boster, 1987: 41–2; Johnson, 1983: 44–5). Knowledge of the fauna is equally detailed and includes many species not ordinarily consumed (Berlin and Berlin, 1983: 320–2).

Prenatal and postnatal practices offsetting population increase are numerous and varied (Meggers, 1971: 103–10), and include prolonged lactation, contraception, abortion, infanticide, abstinence from intercourse, blood revenge, and warfare. Their effectiveness is implicit in calculations of the consequences of uncontrolled reproduction. A four per cent rate of increase would have created a population of 4–5 trillion in 5,570 years, half of the time since human colonization of the lowlands (Cowgill, 1975: 510; cf. Frank, 1987: 114). Both ecological studies (Clark and Uhl, 1987; Fearnside, 1990) and ethnographic evidence for environmental degradation following forced sedentarism (Gross, 1983: 438) also indicate that the densities of surviving unacculturated groups represent sustainable carrying capacity.

Although formal and informal trade for commodities not locally available has been characteristic of human groups since the Upper Palaeolithic, the extensive networks of the neo-tropical lowlands are peculiar in several respects. Items exchanged are often necessities that could be manufactured locally, trading partners must accept what is offered whether they desire it or not, and hostile relations among the groups involved make participation perilous (Chagnon, 1968; Coppens, 1971; Jackson, 1983: 99; Mansutti R., 1986: 13–15; Meggers, 1971: 65; Oberg, 1953). Several ethnographers have pointed out the role of these networks in creating and perpetuating regional and ethnic interdependence (Bodley, 1973: 595; Colson, 1985: 104; Coppens, 1971: 40). They also serve as channels for transmitting all kinds of potentially useful information among groups with different linguistic and tribal affiliations and occupying different environments.

The similarities between prehistoric and recent settlement behaviour (territoriality, impermanent residence, centripetal village movement, site reoccupation, small homesteads) imply that associated practices maximizing sustainable exploitation of essential resources had evolved by the beginning of the Christian era (when the adoption of pottery permits their recognition) and probably earlier. The archaeological data provide no support for the existence during pre-Columbian times of urban centres, highly stratified sociopolitical organization, or expansive states. Rather, they suggest a dispersed pattern of settlement by small communities that were politically autonomous but socially and economically interdependent.

7 Conclusion

During tens of thousands of years, the changing courses of rivers and the fluctuations of climate divided and redivided the landscape, segregating and reuniting populations of plants and animals. Drift and natural selection enhanced divergence and guided interactions, creating increasingly intricate configurations that not only conserved the limited nutrients but also moderated the range of variation in heat and humidity. Arriving at the end of the Pleistocene, humans were the last of a series of mammalian immigrants that entered via the Central American passage and melted into the ecosystem. Like the rest of the fauna, they returned in services as much as they took in sustenance, sometimes knowingly, sometimes unaware.

Contemporary humans in the northern temperate zone came to terms with a different set of edaphic, climatic, topographic, and biotic conditions. Initially, their cultural development followed a similar course. They too conserved resources and enhanced their productivity. The motivation was the same: degradation meant extinction. Slowly at first and then with increasing success, some groups expanded their sustaining areas and their capacities to transport commodities. By neutralizing the immediate impact of overexploitation, they were able to increase consumption while degrading resources both locally (since deficits were compensated by imports) and at a distance (since decimation in one location could be compensated by moving to another).

During the past decade, the human sustaining area has become synonymous with the surface of the planet. The scale of our activities is now sufficient to alter the global climate, an achievement equalled only once before in the history of the earth. The blue-green algae that added oxygen to the atmosphere eons ago and established the conditions for terrestrial life did so unaware. Although we are conscious of our impact and its potential consequences, we appear as helpless as the algae to alter our behaviour. They survive inconspicuously today. Whether humans will be so resilient is questionable.

Amazonia will play a critical role in the future of the biosphere because of its influence on global climate. During the past several millennia, the vegetation has suffered the vicissitudes of repeated climatic fluctuations and recovered. Whether it will survive the impacts of accelerating human-induced deforestation, erosion, and pollution seems less likely. The pursuit of inappropriate policies will persist as long as incentives and perceptions of alien origin remain dominant (Ledec and Goodland, 1989: 448–51). Their continuing strength in spite of negative economic, social, and environmental results bodes ill for the future of the tropical forest and, if the climatologists are correct, for the future of the biosphere as well.

Acknowledgements

The archaeological investigations undertaken under the Programa Nacional de Pesquisas Arqueológicas na Bacia Amazônica have been funded principally by the Neotropical Lowland Research Program of the National Museum of Natural History, Smithsonian Institution. I am grateful to the following colleagues for use of their data: Bernardo Dougherty, Museo de La Plata, Argentina; Ondemar F. Dias, Instituto de Arqueologia Brasileira, Rio de Janeiro; Eurico Th. Miller, Eletronorte, Brasília, and Celso Perota, Universidade Federal do Espírito Santo, Vitória. The sequences on the lower Negro and Tocantins are based on the work of Mário F. Simões, Museu Paraense Emílio Goeldi, Belém.

References

Absy, Maria Lucia. 1982. "Quaternary palynological studies in the Amazon basin." In G.T. Prance (ed.). *Biological diversification in the tropics* (Columbia University Press, New York), 67–73.

———. 1985. "Palynology of Amazonia: The history of the forests as revealed by the palynological record." In G.T. Prance and T.E. Lovejoy (eds.), *Amazonia* (Pergamon Press, Oxford), 72–82.

Balée, William. 1987. "A etnobotânica quantitativa dos índios Tembé (Rio Gurupí, Pará)." *Boletim do Museu Paraense Emílio Goeldi* 3: 29–50.

Barbosa, Altair Sales. 1992. "A tradição Itaparica: Uma compreensão ecológica e cultural do povoamento inicial do planalto central brasileiro." In B.J. Meggers (ed.), *Prehistoria sudamericana: Nuevas perspectivas* (Taraxacum, Washington, DC), 145–60.

Bergman, Roland. 1980. *Amazonian economics: The simplicity of Shipibo Indian wealth*. Dellplain Latin American Studies no. 6. Syracuse, NY.

Berlin, Brent. 1984. "Contributions of native American collectors to the ethnobotany of the neotropics." *Advances in Economic Botany* 1: 24–33. New York Botanical Garden, New York.

Berlin, Brent, and Elois A. Berlin. 1983. "Adaptation and ethnozoological classification: Theoretical implications of animal resources and diet of Aguaruna and Huambisa." In Hames and Vickers, 1983), 301–25.

Bodley, J.H. 1973. "Deferred exchange among the Campa Indians." *Anthropos* 68: 589–96.

Boom, Brian M. 1989. "Use of plant resources by the Chácobo." *Advances in Economic Botany* 7: 78–96. New York Botanical Garden.

Boster, James S. 1987. "Classification, cultivation, and selection of Aguaruna cultivars of *Manihot esculenta* (Euphorbiaceae)." *Advances in Economic Botany* 1: 34–47. New York Botanical Garden, New York.

Carneiro, Robert (1978). "The knowledge and use of rain forest trees by the Kuikuru Indians of central Brazil." In *The nature and status of ethnobotany* (University of Michigan Anthropological Papers 67), 201–16. Ann Arbor.

Cavalcante, Paulo B., and Protasio Frikel. 1973. "A farmacopeia Tiriyó." *Museu Paraense Emílio Goeldi, Pubs. Avulsas* 2. Belém.

Chagnon, Napoleon A. 1968. *Yanomamo: The fierce people*. Holt, Rinehart and Winston, New York.

Clark, Kathleen, and Christopher Uhl. 1987. "Farming, fishing, and fire in the history of the upper Rio Negro region of Venezuela." *Human Ecology* 15: 1–26.

Collins, Jane L. 1986. "Smallholder settlement of tropical South America: The social causes of ecological destruction." *Human Organization* 45: 1–10.

Colson, Audrey Butt 1983/4. "The spatial component in the political structure of the Carib speakers of the Guiana highlands: Kapon and Pemon." *Antropológica* 59–62: 73–124.

———. 1985. "Routes of knowledge: An aspect of regional integration in the circum-Roraima area of the Guiana Highlands." *Antropológica* 63–4: 103–149.

Coppens, Walter. 1971. "Las relaciones comerciales de los Yekuana del Caura-Paragua." *Antropológica* 30: 28–59.

Cowgill, George L. 1975. "On the causes and consequences of ancient and modern population changes." *American Anthropologist* 77: 505–25.

D'Ans, André-Marcel. 1982. *L'amazonie péruvienne indigène*. Payot, Paris.

Dufour, Darna. 1983. "Nutrition in the Northwest Amazon." In Hames and Vickers, 1983, 329–55.

Fearnside, Philip M. 1990. "Estimation of human carrying capacity in rainforest areas." *Trends in Ecology and Evolution* 5: 192–6.

Frank, Erwin. 1987. "Delimitaciones al aumento poblacional y desarrollo cultural en las culturas indígenas de la Amazonía antes de 1942." In G. Kohlhepp and A. Schrader (eds.), *Hombre y naturaleza en la Amazonía* (Tübinger Geographische Studien 95, Tübingen), 109–23.

Fuentes, Emilio. 1980. "Los Yanomami y las plantas silvestres." *Antropológica* 54: 3–138.

Good, Kenneth. 1989. "Yanomami hunting patterns: Trekking and garden relocation as an adaptation to game availability in Amazonas, Venezuela." Ph.D dissertation, University of Florida.

Gross, Daniel R. 1983. "Village movement in relation to resources in Amazonia." In Hames and Vickers, 1983), 429–49.

Hames, Raymond B. 1983. "The settlement pattern of a Yanomamo population block: A behavioral ecological interpretation." In Hames and Vickers, 1983, 393–427.

Hames, R.B., and W.T. Vickers (eds.). 1983. *Adaptive responses of native Amazonians*. Academic Press, New York.

Henley, Paul. 1982. *The Panare: Tradition and change on the Amazonian frontier*. Yale University Press, New Haven, CT.

Irion, G. 1984. "Sedimentation and sediments of Amazonian rivers and evolution of the Amazonian landscape since Pliocene times." In Harald Sioli (ed.), *The Amazon* (Dr W. Junk, Dordrecht), 201–14.

Irvine, Dominique (1989). "Succession management and resource distribution in an Amazonian rain forest." *Advances in Economic Botany* 7: 223–37. New York Botanical Garden, New York.

Jackson, Jean E. 1983. *The fish people*. Cambridge University Press, Cambridge.

Johnson, Allen. 1983. "Machiguenga gardens." In Hames and Vickers, 1983, 29–63.

Lathrap, Donald W. 1970. *The upper Amazon*. Praeger, New York.

Ledec, George, and Robert Goodland. 1989. "Epilogue: An environmental perspective on tropical land settlement." In D.A. Schumann and W.L. Partridge (eds.), *The human ecology of tropical land settlement in Latin America* (Westview, Boulder.), 435–67.

Leigh Jr., Egbert G., A. Stanley Rand, and Donald M. Windsor (eds.). 1982. *The ecology of a tropical forest*. Smithsonian Institution Press, Washington, DC.

Mansutti Rodríguez, Alexander. 1986. "Hierro, barro cocido, curare y cerbatanas: El comercio intra e interétnico entre los Uwotjuja." *Antropológica* 65: 3–75.

Meggers, Betty J. 1971. *Amazonia: Man and culture in a counterfeit paradise*. Harlan Davidson, Arlington Heights.

———. 1987. "The early history of man in Amazonia." In T.C. Whitmore and G.T. Prance (eds.), *Biogeography and quaternary history of South America* (Clarendon Press, Oxford), 151–74.

———. 1992. "Prehistoric population density in the Amazonian Basin." In J.W. Verano and D.H. Ubelaker (eds.), *Disease and demography in the Americas* (Smithsonian Institution Press, Washington, DC), 197–205.

———. 1994. "Archeological evidence for the impact of mega-Niño events on Amazonia during the past two millennia." *Climatic Change* 28: 1–18.

Meggers, Betty J., and Jacques Danon. 1988. "Identification and implications of a hiatus in the archeological sequence on Marajó Island, Brazil." *Journal of the Washington Academy of Sciences* 78: 245–53.

Miller, Eurico Th., et al. 1992. *Arqueologia nos empreendimentos hidrelétricos da Eletronorte; Resultados preliminares*. Centrais Elétricas do Norte do Brasil S.A., Brasília.

Oberg, Kalervo. 1953. *Indian tribes of Mato Grosso, Brazil*. Institute of Social Anthropology Publ. 15. Washington, DC.

Roosevelt, Anna C. 1989. "Resource management in Amazonia before the conquest: Beyond ethnographic projection." *Advances in Economic Botany* 7: 30–62. New York Botanical Garden, New York.

Ruddle, Kenneth. 1971. "Notes on the nomenclature and the distribution of the Yukpa-Yuko tribe." *Antropológica* 30: 18–27.

Schmitz, Pedro Ignacio. 1987. "Prehistoric hunters and gatherers of Brazil." *Journal of World Prehistory* 1: 53–126.

Schumann, Debra A., and William L. Partridge, eds. 1989. *The human ecology of tropical land settlement in Latin America*. Westview, Boulder.

Seeger, Anthony. 1981. *Nature and society in central Brazil: The Suyá Indians of Mato Grosso*. Harvard University Press, Cambridge, MA.

Simões, Mário F. 1976. "Nota sobre duas pontas-de-projetil da Bacia do Tapajós (Pará)." *Boletim do Museu Paraense Emílio Goeldi*, Antropológia 62.

Smith, Nigel J.H. 1980. "Anthrosols and human carrying capacity in Amazonia." *Annals of the Association of American Geographers* 70: 553–66.

Spielman, R.S., E.C. Migliazza, and J.V. Neel. 1974. "Regional linguistic and genetic differences among Yanomama Indians." *Science* 184: 637–44.

Sternberg, Hilgard O'Reilly. 1987. "Aggravation of floods in the Amazon River as a consequence of deforestation?" *Geografiska Annaler*, Series A, 69A: 201–19.

Stockton, Charles E. 1990. "Climatic variability on the scale of decades to centuries." *Climatic Change* 16: 173–83.

Van der Hammen, Thomas. 1982. "Paleoecology of tropical South America." In G.T. Prance (ed.), *Biological diversification in the tropics* (Columbia University Press, New York), 60–6.

Verswijver, Gustaaf. 1978. "Separations et migrations des Mekragnoti: Groupe Kayapó du Brésil central." *Boletin, Société Suisse des Américanistes* 42: 47–59.

Vickers, William T. 1983. "The territorial dimensions of Siona-Secoya and Encabello adaptation." In Hames and Vickers, 1983, 451–78.

5

Distribution and interannual variability of rainfall in Brazil

Minoru Tanaka, Akio Tsuchiya, and Toshie Nishizawa

1 Introduction

Climatological studies on annual change in rainfall regimes in South America were conducted by Ratisbona (1976) and Caviedes (1981). Similar studies on the atmospheric circulation patterns were conducted by Virji (1981). The rainfall regime of the Brazilian Nordeste is divided into northern (north of 10°S) and southern Nordeste by Hastenrath and Heller (1977). Markham and McLain (1977), Moura and Shukla (1981), and Hastenrath (1984) suggest a link between rainfall in the northern Nordeste and sea surface temperature (hereafter called SST) anomalies in the Atlantic Ocean. Walker (1928), Ramos (1976), Kousky and Chu (1978), and Kousky (1979, 1985) studied the rainfall in the Nordeste and atmospheric circulation over Brazil and the Atlantic Ocean. The influence of the northern hemisphere circulation on the rainfall in the Nordeste was investigated by Namias (1972). Yamazaki and Rao (1977) studied the tropical cloudiness over the South Atlantic Ocean.

A pilot study on annual change in tropospheric circulation and its relationship to the monthly mean rainfall in South America was conducted by Nishizawa and Tanaka (1983), as was a similar survey on interannual change also by Tanaka and Nishizawa (1985). Collectively, these studies show a trough at the 150mb level over the Nordeste which can be linked to regional subsidence and to the relatively low amount of the rainfall in the Nordeste in the drought year of 1983.

Empirical orthogonal function (EOF) analyses of rainfall in Brazil on monthly, seasonal, and interannual time scales were carried out by Tsuchiya et al. (1988) and Tanaka et al. (1988). In addition, Aceituno (1988, 1989) analysed the rainfall and atmospheric circulation associated with the Southern Oscillation. These studies show that the inverse relationship between the northern Nordeste and southern Brazil (hereafter called the NS pattern), which appears in the First EOF, is best developed for an interannual time scale of more than one year. The rainfall difference between northern and southern Nordeste appears for all time scales in the Second EOF. For the present study, the relationship between the NS pattern and the Southern Oscillation Index (SOI) is based on the normalized sea level pressure difference between Tahiti and Darwin in the tropical Pacific Ocean and the SST in the tropical Atlantic Ocean.

2 Data source and distribution of rainfall in South America

The source of the data for rainfall distribution and 850mb height are from the *Monthly Climatic Data for the World* published by the US National Oceanic and Atmospheric Administration (NOAA) for the 10-year period from 1969 to 1978. The data for EOF analysis (36 stations, 1968 to 1985) come from the Superintendência do Desenvolvimento do Nordeste (SUDENE) for the Nordeste region and from *Boletim Agroclimatológico* published by the Agricultural Ministry of Brazil for the rest of Brazil. Because locations of the rainfall data for the EOF analysis are unevenly distributed, six of the locations shown are the average of closely spaced stations. This averaging was conducted because the EOF components can shift toward the area of high concentration of the stations. Annual cycles in rainfall are removed by subtracting the long-term mean (1968–85 average) for each month of the year. The interannual component of rainfall variability was extracted by filtering rainfall data by the 24-month triangular weighted running means (see Burroughs, 1978 for details). The triangular running means reduce short period oscillations much more efficiently, compared to the simple unweighted running means. However, about twice as many terms are required compared to the simple running means. Hence, filtering frequency below 12 months requires about 24-month triangular means. This filter was used because the regional variations in the rainy season in Brazil are large. This means that the rainy season is observed in certain regions in Brazil during any months of the year. Hence it is difficult to define a cutoff month for obtaining the annual totals. The EOF analysis of the anomaly rainfall time series employed filtered data. Similar smoothing was applied to the 850mb height and SST over the Atlantic Ocean. Distribution of rainfall in South America and its relationship to the tropospheric circulation are shown in detail by Nishizawa and Tanaka (1983), as shown only by the examples for December (fig. 5.1) and April (fig. 5.2). In December, rainfall is especially heavy in the Amazon Basin and the interior of Brazil. Because the Intertropical Convergence Zone (ITCZ) over the Atlantic Ocean is located north of the equator, dry areas are observed in the Nordeste. In April, rainfall in the interior of Brazil begins to decrease, while a southward dis-

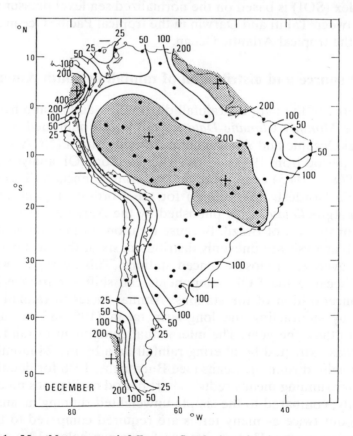

Figure 5.1 **Monthly mean rainfall over South America in December (1969–78) (mm). Stations are shown by dots.**

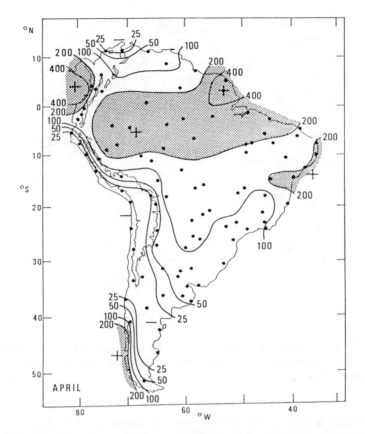

Figure 5.2 **Monthly mean rainfall over South America in April (1969–78) (mm).**

placement of the ITCZ over the Atlantic Ocean produces a brief rainy season in the Nordeste.

3 Interannual variability of rainfall in Brazil

The interannual variability of rainfall in Brazil is analysed by empirical EOF analysis for an 18-year period from 1968 to 1985 by using filtered data, as discussed previously.

The primary reasons for conducting EOF analysis are its capability to reduce the dimensionality and to describe coherent variability in the rainfall data. Since 27 locations are shown in figure 5.3, there are 27 dimensions in the rainfall data. The EOF analysis reduces the dimensions to few major components while retaining the information contained in the original data. These components are calculated to maximize the variance explained in the original data. Hence, coherent variability in the original data can be described by the first few

97

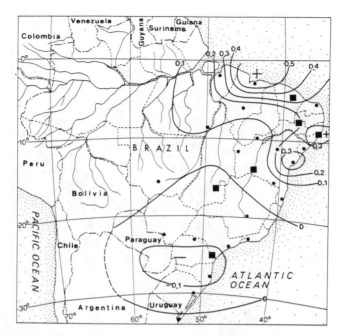

Figure 5.3 **Distribution of eigenvector of First EOF (24 M1) of rainfall EOF explaining 46.7% of variance, for 27 locations as shown by dots and squares for averages of closely spaced stations.**

components which contain most of the variance. For these reasons, we believe that EOF analysis depicts large-scale variability of the rainfall much more clearly than the simple correlations between the 27 locations.

Figure 5.3 shows the distribution of the eigenvector of the First EOF (24 M1) explaining 46.7 per cent of variance. The pattern shows an inverse relationship in rainfall between northern and southern Brazil (NS pattern). This pattern is analysed by Aceituno (1988, 1989). The highest values are concentrated near São Luiz and Fortaleza, where rainfall variability is strongly influenced by the interannual variation in intensity and location of ITCZ located near the equator. Figure 5.4 shows the time coefficients for the First EOF. Positive values in 1974 and 1985 show wet years in the northern Nordeste. Negative values in 1972, 1976, and 1983 coincide with dry years in northern Brazil and severe flooding in 1983 in southern Brazil (see Tanaka and Nishizawa, 1985 for a detailed case study).

Figure 5.5 shows the correlation of the 850mb height over South America to the First EOF (24 M1). A region of high negative correla-

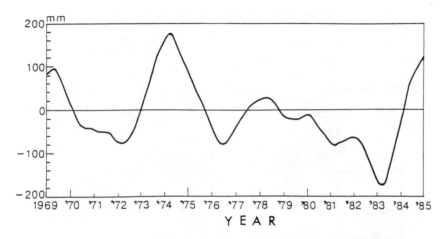

Figure 5.4   **Time coefficients for First EOF (24 M1) of rainfall EOF.**

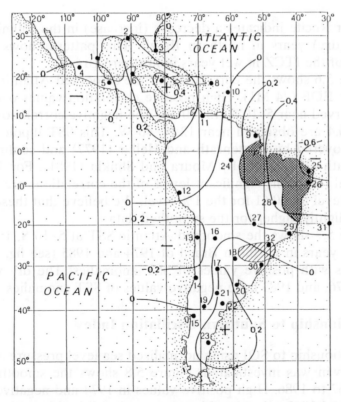

Figure 5.5   **Correlation of smoothed 850mb height to First EOF (24 M1) of rainfall EOF.**

99

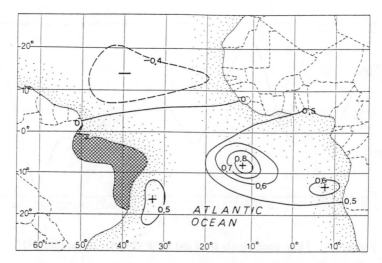

Figure 5.6 **Correlation of smoothed SST (C) to First EOF (24 M1) of rainfall EOF.**

tion near Recife indicates a decrease (increase) in the 850mb height in wet (dry) years in northern Brazil. This pattern shows intensification of the ITCZ in wet years in northern Brazil.

Figure 5.6 shows the correlation of the smoothed Atlantic SST to the First EOF (24 M1). High positive correlation values over +0.8 are observed near 5–10°S, 15–10°W. The negative correlation values over −0.4 are observed near 12°N, 40°W. This SST dipole pattern was discovered by Hastenrath and Heller (1977) and confirmed by Hastenrath (1978), and by Moura and Shukla (1981). For 17 years of annual totals, the significant levels of the correlations are 0.49 for the 5% level and 0.61 for the 1% level. We believe that these values will be slightly higher for the smoothed data.

Figure 5.7 shows the smoothed Atlantic SST at 5–10°S, 15–10°W. The wet years in northern Brazil of 1974 and 1985 (see fig. 5.4) are the years with positive values of SST anomalies. The dry years of 1972, 1976, and 1983 have negative values of SST anomalies.

4 Relationship to Southern Oscillation Index

The relationship to SOI using normalized sea level pressure at Tahiti and Darwin was investigated. Figure 5.8 shows the smoothed SOI from 1967 to 1986. High positive values in 1974 and negative values in 1972 and 1983 coincide with extreme rainfall in the northern Nordeste (see fig. 5.4). This relationship is reversed for the periods from

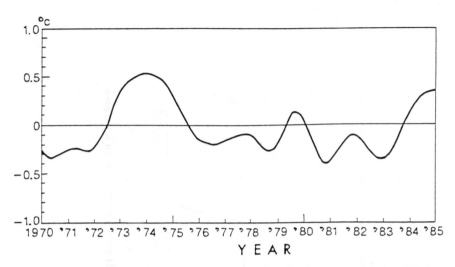

Figure 5.7   **Time change of smoothed Atlantic SST (C) at 5–10°S, 15–10°W.**

1969 to 1971 and from 1976 to 1978. Figure 5.9 shows the correlation of smoothed rainfall values (not EOF) for 27 locations in Brazil compared to the smoothed SOI. The correlation pattern is similar to the First EOF (24 M1) (see fig. 5.3). However, the regions with moderately high correlation over 0.4 are restricted to northern Brazil and to central and southern Brazil. Figure 5.10 shows the correlation of the smoothed 850mb height to the smoothed SOI. This pattern is very similar to Hastenrath (1984). When this pattern is compared to the Atlantic SST (fig. 5.5), it shows a high correlation to the subtropical high near 20°S.

5 Seasonal variability of rainfall in Brazil

EOF analyses of monthly and seasonal (defined here as a consecutive 4-month period) variability of rainfall in Brazil show the shorter time-scale interaction between SST and rainfall. The monthly EOF analysis of rainfall (Tanaka et al., 1988) reveals rainfall distribution patterns of three distinct seasons.

Table 5.1 shows the variance explained by the first three components of the seasonal and smoothed interannual rainfall (24 M). The First EOF in the December to March season is centred on interior Brazil and has a component which shows a low month-to-month persistence pattern. (Persistence is defined here as the persistence from

101

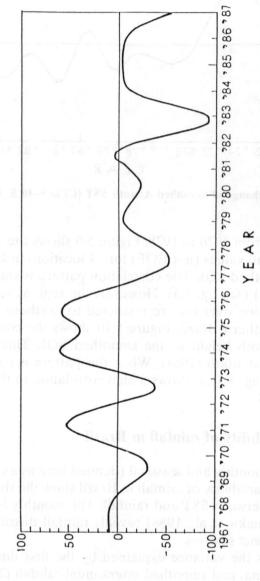

Figure 5.8   Time change of smoothed Southern Oscillation Index (SOI) using normalized sea level pressure at Tahiti and Darwin (Tn-Dn).

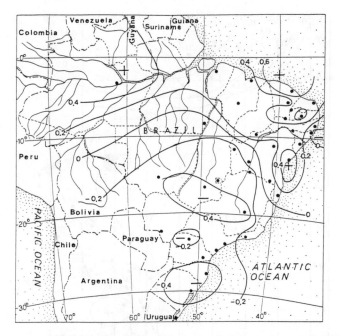

Figure 5.9   **Correlation of smoothed rainfall values to smoothed SOI.**

one month to the next month.) The low persistence indicates that the monthly EOF pattern does not persist in the next month. The First EOF (fig. 5.11) in the April to July season is very similar to the First EOF (24 M1) of the interannual time scale, which has a high month-to-month persistence. The First EOF in August to November season is centred on southern Brazil and has a low month-to-month persistence.

Since the First EOF in April to July (4–7 M1) seasonal rainfall has high month-to-month persistence and is very similar to the NS pattern (24 M1) in interannual time-scale, correlation to Atlantic SST was computed (see fig. 5.12). This pattern is similar to the interannual time-scale (see fig. 5.6). An area of negative correlation is located near 5–10°N, 45–40°W. This resultant pattern is very similar to that of Moura and Shukla (1981), who employed data from Fortaleza and Quixeramobim. Our study shows that rainfall in northern Brazil is related to this SST pattern.

Figure 5.13 shows the time change of the SST at 0–5°S, 15–10°W and the First EOF (4–7 M1) of seasonal rainfall. The time changes of both parameters are very similar.

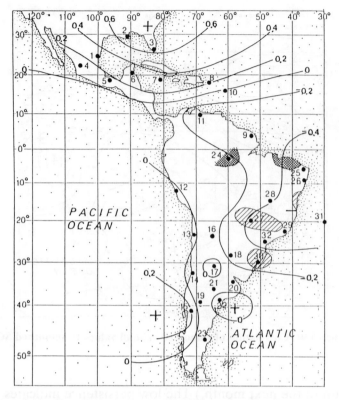

Figure 5.10   **Correlation of smoothed 850mb height to smoothed SOI.**

Table 5.1   **Variance explained by first three EOFs of seasonal and smoothed inter-annual rainfall (24 M)**

	Variance explained %		
Months	M1	M2	M3
12–3	30.44	18.66	14.93
4–7	50.52	13.85	8.54
8–11	27.93	16.91	10.18
24M	46.66	12.46	10.28

6 Comparison of the rainfall in northern Brazil to other tropical regions

The rainfall in the semi-arid region has high interannual variability. However, Nishizawa et al. (1986) have shown that part of the sub-

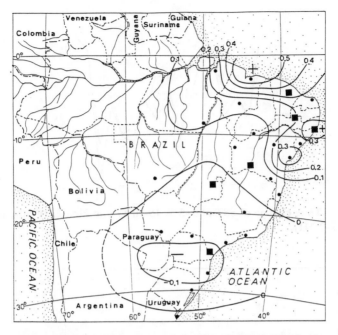

Figure 5.11 **Distribution of eigenvector of the First EOF (4–7 M1) of seasonal rainfall EOF explaining 50.5% of variance.**

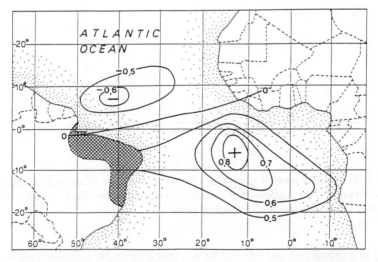

Figure 5.12 **Correlation of March to May SST (C) to First EOF of seasonal rainfall EOF (4–7 M1). 5% level = 0.49; 1% level = 0.61.**

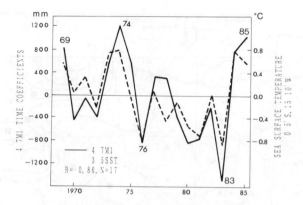

Figure 5.13 **Time change of SST at 0–5°S, 15–10°W and First EOF of seasonal rainfall EOF (4–7 M1).**

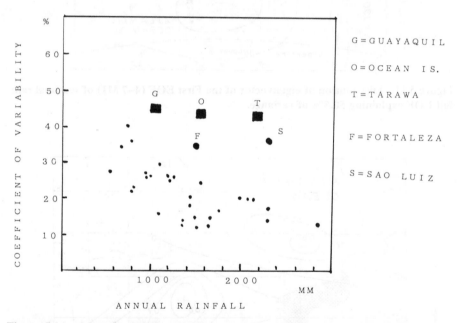

Figure 5.14 **Annual rainfall variability shown as function of annual rainfall in mm (horizontal scale) and coefficient of variability (vertical scale) for 27 locations in Brazil and three selected stations in tropical area.**

humid northern coastal region in north-eastern Brazil, with more than 1,000 mm of annual rainfall, has a high (30–50 per cent) coefficient of variability in rainfall. Figure 5.14 shows annual rainfall variability in Brazil based on the 27 locations used in this study. As shown in the lower part of this figure, most locations in Brazil show a decrease in rainfall variability as the total rainfall increases. However, Fortaleza and São Luiz show both greater variability and annual rainfall, which indicates the unstable nature of the climate at these locations. An inspection of other regions of tropical climate shows that unstable rainfall of similar magnitude (approximately over 1,000 mm per year) in relatively humid locations is restricted to the regions directly influenced by El Niño–Southern Oscillation (ENSO) in the equatorial Pacific (e.g., Ocean Island and Tarawa) and coastal Ecuador (Guayaquil).

An interesting study on this topic was published recently by Nicholls and Wang (1990), which showed that the annual rainfall variability is typically higher for a specific mean rainfall in areas affected by ENSO. In these areas of unstable climatic regimes, any human development must consider careful water and forest resource management in order to reduce the possible impact of drought or floods caused by unusually wide fluctuations in rainfall.

7 Conclusion

EOF analysis of interannual variability of rainfall in Brazil confirmed an inverse relationship in the rainfall in the First EOF between northern and southern Brazil (NS pattern), analysed by Aceituno (1988, 1989). This pattern is best developed in interannual and seasonal (April to July total) time-scales. The relationship between the NS pattern and the atmospheric circulation pattern shows an intensification of the ITCZ in wet years in northern Brazil. The correlation analysis of SOI and the tropical Atlantic SST confirmed the earlier findings by Hastenrath and Heller (1977) and Moura and Shukla (1981), that the NS pattern is highly correlated ($+0.80$ to 0.86) to the SST near 0–10°S, 15–10°W on the interannual and seasonal time-scales. Although detailed atmospheric circulation data over the South Atlantic ocean are not available, weakening of the trade winds in the South Atlantic is the probable cause of the rise in SST in the equatorial South Atlantic. The negative correlation in the SST near 5–10°N, 45–40°E suggests that southward migration in South America of the ITCZ coincides with the increase in rainfall in northern Brazil. The influence of the Southern Oscillation is found to be less than Atlantic SST. However, the extreme cold event in 1974 (wet year in northern Brazil) and the warm event in 1983 (dry year) coincided with rainfall extremes of the NS pattern.

The EOF analysis of the seasonal variability of rainfall in Brazil have shown that the First EOF in the December to March season is centred on interior Brazil and has a low month-to-month persistence pattern. The First EOF in August to November season is centred on southern Brazil and has a low month-to-month persistence.

Acknowledgement

The writers wish to express their sincere gratitude to the SUDENE office in Recife, Pernambuco, for providing part of rainfall data in this study.

References

Aceituno, P. 1988. "On the functioning of the southern oscillation in the South American sector. Part I: Surface climate." *Monthly Weather Review* 116: 505–24.

———. 1989. "On the functioning of the southern oscillation in the South American sector. Part II: Upper air circulation." *Journal of Climate* 2: 341–55.

Burroughs, W.J. 1978. "On running means and meteorological cycles." *Weather* 33: 101–9.

Caviedes, C. 1981. "Rain in South America, seasonal and spatial correlations." *Erdkunde* 35: 107–18.

Hastenrath, S. 1978. "On modes of tropical circulation and climate anomalies." *Journal of Atmospheric Sciences* 35: 2222–31.

———. 1984. "Interannual variability and annual cycle: Mechanisms of circulation and climate in the tropical Atlantic sector." *Monthly Weather Review* 112: 1097–1107.

Hastenrath, S., and L. Heller. 1977. "Dynamics of climate hazards in Northeast Brazil." *Quarterly Journal of Royal Meteorological Society* 103: 77–92.

Kousky, V.E. 1979. "Frontal influences on Northeast Brazil." *Monthly Weather Review* 107: 1140–53.

———. 1985. "Atmospheric circulation changes associated with rainfall anomalies over tropical Brazil." *Monthly Weather Review* 113: 1951–7.

Kousky, V.E., and P.S. Chu. 1978. "Fluctuations in annual rainfall for Northeast Brazil." *Journal of Meteorological Society of Japan* 57: 457–65.

Markham, C.G., and D.R. McLain. 1977. "Sea surface temperatures related to rain in Ceará, Northeastern Brazil." *Nature*, 265: 320–3.

Moura, A.D., and J. Shukla. 1981. "On the dynamics of drought in Northeast Brazil: Observations, theory and numerical experiments with a general circulation model." *Journal of Atmospheric Science* 38: 2653–75.

Namias, J. 1972. "Influence of northern hemisphere general circulation on drought in Northeast Brazil." *Tellus*, 24: 336–42.

Nicholls, N., and K.K. Wang. 1990. "Dependence of rainfall variability on mean rainfall, latitude, and the Southern Oscillation." *Journal of Climate* 3: 163–70.

Nishizawa, T., and M. Tanaka. 1983. "The annual change in the tropospheric circulation and the rainfall in South America." *Archiv für Meteorologie, Geophysik, und Bioklimatologie*, Series B, 33: 107–16.

Nishizawa, T., M. Tanaka, T. Iwakuma, and T. Kushima. 1986. "Fluctuations of spatial distribution of rainfall in Northeast Brazil and their relationship to the tropospheric circulation." *Latin American Studies* 8: 11–30.

Ramos, R.P.L. 1976. "Precipitation characteristics in the Northeast Brazil dry region." *Journal of Geophysical Research* 80: 1665–78.

Ratisbona, C.R. 1976. "The climate of Brazil." *Climate of Central and South America, World Survey of Climatology*, vol. 12 (Elsevier), 219–93.

Tanaka, M., and T. Nishizawa. 1985. "The atmospheric circulation and the major drought and flood of 1983 in Brazil." *Geographical Review of Japan* 58 (Ser. B): 165–71.

Tanaka, M., A. Tsuchiya, and T. Nishizawa. 1988. "The empirical orthogonal function analysis of the seasonal and interannual rainfall in Brazil." *Latin American Studies* 10: 27–45.

Tsuchiya, A., M. Tanaka, and T. Nishizawa. 1988. "Empirical orthogonal function analysis of the monthly rainfall in Brazil." *Latin American Studies* 10: 13–26.

Virji, H. 1981. "A preliminary study of summertime tropospheric circulation patterns over South America estimated from cloud winds." *Monthly Weather Review* 109: 599–610.

Walker, G.T. 1928. "Ceará (Brazil) famines and the general air movement." *Beitr. Phys. D. Freien Atmosphere* 14: 88–93.

Yamazaki, Y., and V.B. Rao. 1977. "Tropical cloudiness over the South Atlantic Ocean." *Journal of Meteorological Society of Japan* 55: 205–7.

Part II
The Brazilian Amazon

6

Waters and wetlands of Brazilian Amazonia: An uncertain future

Hilgard O'Reilly Sternberg

Sweet sea

Sailing along the coast of South America in 1500, and reckoning their position to be forty leagues offshore, a party under Vicente Yañez Pinzón came upon a body of "fresh water of unsurpassable quality." To learn whether it extended all the way to the bottom, the seafarers adapted a barber's chafing bowl (*escalfador de barbero*), "so that it would open only upon reaching the seabed," which was at six fathoms. They ascertained that the fresh water at the surface was present to a depth of $2\frac{1}{2}$ fathoms, overlying salt water identical to that of the sea. The mariners "discarded the water they brought with them, and took on the supply needed to continue their voyage" (Ferrando, [1515]). The "great river," source of the fresh water, named by Pinzón Santa María de la Mar-Dulce (Saint Mary of the Sweet Sea), is generally believed to have been the Amazon.[1]

The existence of surface lenses of fresh water bounded by a sharp halocline, discovered five centuries ago with the aid of an improvised device, has now been substantiated by state-of-the-art techniques. These have also confirmed the fact that the Amazon River plume, overriding denser sea water, can extend more than 100 km from the mouth, across the continental shelf (Curtin, 1986a, 1986b; Curtin and

113

Legeckis, 1986; Nittrouer and DeMaster, 1986; Gibbs and Konwar, 1986).

The Amazon discharge, estimated to average some 200,000 m³/sec (Nordin and Meade, 1986),[2] affects a large region in the tropical Atlantic (Gibbs, 1970; Johns et al., 1990; Nittrouer and DeMaster, 1986; Ryther, Menzel, and Norwin, 1967). Satellite images, obtained by coastal zone colour scanners, show the distribution of near-surface pigments (e.g. chlorophyll), revealing, in an impressive way, the trajectory of the effluent. During the first part of the year, it is carried into the Caribbean Sea by the North Brazil Coastal Current and the Guiana Current. From June to January, however, an offshore retroflection occurs in the flow, and an appreciable fraction of Amazon water is transported eastward, being detectable near Africa (Muller-Karger, McClain, and Richardson, 1988; Muller-Karger and Varela, 1989/1990).

The advection of Amazon sediments by the north-west-setting coastal current explains, at least in part, the sharp contrast between the coast to the north-west and that to the east of the embouchure. The former is a relatively straight, prograding littoral; the latter, a convoluted shoreline of ria-like inlets, giving the impression that submergence affected a zone previously dissected by subaerial erosion.

The Amazon River system

The watershed

The source of the Amazon's huge discharge, which affects the chemistry of ocean water over thousands of square kilometres and transports sediments that build up distant shorelines and overspread remote seabeds, is a catchment area of almost six million square kilometres, two-thirds of which are in Brazil. Not all of the world's largest hydrographic basin shares the "Amazon look" (Spruce, 1908) one associates with the tropical rain forest. It includes snow-capped Andean peaks and *cerrado*-covered plateaus in West-Central Brazil.[3] Conversely, some adjacent areas, while Amazonian in character, do not drain into the Amazon River. Such is the case of the 800,000 km² Tocantins basin, tributary to the Rio Pará, a cul-de-sac connected to the Amazon proper by a maze of deep narrow channels. It is also the case of about 100,000 km² of watersheds in Amapá state that discharge directly into the Atlantic.

Whereas in the Cordilleras the pattern of the Amazon drainage is determined by the alignment of the Andean orogenic belt, the low-land west–east course of the main stem corresponds to the axis of a deep sedimentary basin. This is filled to depths of more than 5,000 metres with Palaeozoic sediments and associated magmatic intrusions. It is underlain by a very old portion of the earth's crust, a complex of Precambrian metamorphic and plutonic rocks that surfaces north and south of the trough. The areas of relatively modest elevation where the ancient core is exposed are the tectonically stable, so-called "shields." There is, thus, a Guiana Shield and a Central-Brazilian (sometimes named Guaporé) Shield. The downflexed beds of the intervening structural basin are covered by extensive subhorizontal sedimentary strata, which, attributed to the Mesozoic and Cenozoic (Caputo, 1984), constitute the extensive Amazonian Plain (fig. 6.1).

As the seas retreated during the last glacial stage, coming to a stand more than 100 m lower than that of today, the Amazon adjusted to the change by deepening its bed. With this, erosion advanced up tributaries, frequently exploiting a lattice of rectilinear and right-angled fractures (Bemerguy and Costa, 1991; Bremer, 1971, 1973; Projeto RADAMBRASIL, 1978; Sternberg, 1950, 1955; Sternberg and Russell, 1952). This incision left standing above the valley bottoms all but a fraction of the central sedimentary plain, a vast area of relatively flat or gently undulating landscapes known as the *terras firmes*.

When sea level rose again, it caused the flow of the Amazon to back up. Thus, was created a freshwater gulf thousands of kilometres long, with ramifications into the lower reaches of tributary valleys. This drowned river system is the theatre of the ongoing alluviation that has shaped the present-day riverine wetlands, or *várzeas* (fig. 6.2).

Volcanic renewal of nutrients, through convection in the upper mantle and the creation of new rock, occurs near active plate margins. Brazilian Amazonia, however, lies in an essentially stable province that experiences only modest epeirogenic activity (Sternberg, 1950, 1975; Sternberg and Russell, 1952). With the exception of those developed on rare, and generally small, basaltic outcrops, terra firme soils are derived from nutrient-deficient parent rocks, further impoverished by intense biochemical weathering. Overall stability and low energy relief have favoured the accumulation *in situ*, over a time span estimated to reach some ten million years, of the depleted regolith (Fyfe et al., 1983), reported to extend down to a depth of 10 to 60 metres (Costa, 1993). Locally, it has been identified at more

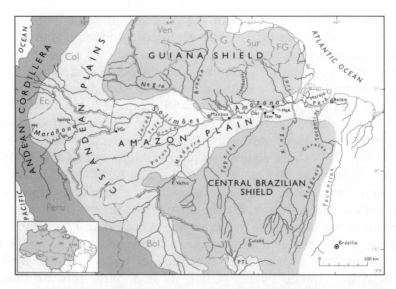

Figure 6.1 **The Amazon Basin (features mentioned in text). The youngest strata of the Amazonian Plain, including non-flooded *terras firmes* and (not differentiated here) recent alluvial wetlands, overlie a deep, sediment-filled trough. Dipping toward the axis of the structural basin, older beds are largely buried under the superficial accumulations. The whole is underlain by a complex of very ancient metamorphic and igneous rocks. Exposed north and south of the axial plain, this worn-down platform constitutes the Guiana and Brazilian "shields." The Cis-Andean Plains, essentially a mantle of debris from the cordilleras and front ranges, decline eastward, merging with the Amazon Plain or lapping over the Guiana and Brazilian oldlands.**

Inset: **"Amazônia Legal," an operational region, originally defined in 1953 for the purpose of implementing the development activities provided for by the 1946 Constitution.**

Abbreviations: **Ita, Itacoatiara; MtA, Monte Alegre; Óbi, Óbidos; P.Velho, Porto Velho; Stm, Santarém; Tap, Taperinha; VGr, Vargem Grande. PM, Pongo de Manseriche; PTL, Pantanal. Bol, Bolivia; Col, Colombia; Ec, Ecuador; FG, French Guiana; G, Guyana; P, Peru; Sur, Surinam; Ven, Venezuela. *Abbreviations in inset*: AC, Acre; AM, Amazonas; MA, Maranhão; MT, Mato Grosso; PA, Pará; RO, Rondônia; RR, Roraima; TO, Tocantins.**

than 300 m below the surface, as in the Serra dos Carajás (Coelho, 1986), which may have been uplifted after the weathered mantle had been formed. Nutrients released at deep-seated weathering fronts are, of course, unavailable to plant roots. If Amazonian soils developed on rocks of the basement, or oldlands, are poor, those generated on the clastics of the central plain are even more so. Yet, in spite of inherent geological and climatic constraints to the formation and maintenance of fertile soils, lush rain forests clothe not only shield areas but also much of the sedimentary axial plain.

Figure 6.2   **Sealevel, rising after the last glacial, backed up the Amazon River, drowning the main stem and the terminal sections of its lowland tributaries. Sediment-poor affluents have been unable to alluviate the resulting lake-mouths; such is the case of the Tapajós River, partially closed off by an alluvial deposit of the trunk stream. Despite its huge sediment load, even the Amazon has left extensive areas of its giant freshwater embayment to be filled. This is evidenced by the intricate pattern of channels and natural levees that enclose thousands of shallow bottomland lakes. Some lacustrine basins are partly bounded by upland bluffs, as is the case of Lake Maicuru, also known as Lago Grande de Monte Alegre or, simply, Lago Grande (upper right). (Projeto RADAMBRASIL, 1972, Semi-controlled mosaic of radar images executed in 1971–1972, Sheet SA-21-Z-B. Original scale 1:250,000. Departamento Nacional da Produção Mineral, Rio de Janeiro.)**

Inset: **An attempt, made "in the face of every kind of protest," to create new land by silting up Lago Grande and the surrounding marshes, began in 1950, when the Piapó, a 4-km-long natural channel through the levee of the Amazon (Sioli, 1951), was cleared and straightened with the use of manual labour. Following up with mechanical excavators, several artificial channels were cut, and were named after public figures. Novais Filho, the first to be excavated, was completed in 1953, reaching a high-water inflow into Lake Maicuru of 275 m^3/sec in 1954, when the aggregate discharge of all six cuts came to 670 m^3/sec (Camargo, 1958). According to a recent denunciation, the so-called "siltation canals," instead of accomplishing their purpose, are allegedly bringing about the expansion of Lago Grande, which, it is claimed, is swallowing up neighbouring lakes and threatening the levee that separates it from the Amazon (*O Liberal*, 1989). (Excerpted and re-drawn from Camargo, approximate scale added, width of canals exaggerated. Differences in the size and shape of the lake as represented on a sequence of maps, air photos, and satellite images cannot be used to follow its evolution. This is because of the diffuse boundary between lakes and marshes, as well as the fact that surveys made at different, and mostly unspecified, river stages reflect seasonal contraction and expansion.)**

117

This fact indicates an efficient adaptation to oligotrophic conditions, as in the case of "direct nutrient cycling" through the agency of mycorrhizal fungi, described a quarter-century ago by Went and Stark (1968). Recent research suggests, further, that exogenous nutrients are being imported in the form of aerosols. Chemical "fingerprinting" of the allochthonous particulates and satellite observation of dust plumes over the Atlantic point to material originating mainly on the African continent, nearly 5,000 km away (Swap, Garstang, and Greco, 1992; Talbot et al., 1990). A nutrient cycling pathway, recently reported from the Rio Negro headwaters in Venezuela, would appear particularly well adapted to utilize such wind-borne particulates: plants with upward-growing roots intercept stem flow and absorb the precipitated nutrients before they enter the soil solution, where they might be lost to competitors or become generally unavailable (Sanford, 1987).

Provenance and characteristics of Amazonian waters

The source for most of Amazonia's waters is evaporation from the Atlantic Ocean. The moisture precipitated over the basin is wafted upvalley by an easterly flow of air, driven by the convergence of trade winds from the Azores and South Atlantic highs (Salati and Vose, 1984). Average precipitation over Brazilian Amazonia amounts to 2,200 mm per annum;[4] accentuated relief introduces marked spatial variations in the Andean portion of the drainage. Thus, the upper Madeira basin exhibits extremes of less than 500 and more than 7,000 mm (Roche et al., 1990). Westward advection of oceanic moisture does not occur in a continuous flux. Preliminary observations suggest that a considerable proportion of the precipitation that falls on the basin is "recycled" water, returned to the atmosphere by evapotranspiration from the rain forest (Lettau, Lettau, and Molion, 1979; Salati and Vose, 1984).

Reflecting the paucity of nutrients in the sedimentary areas whence they flow, the relatively short streams that drain the central plain are among "the most electrolyte-poor natural waters on earth" (Fittkau et al., 1975), and carry almost no solid load. Those that rise in the flanking, lithologically complex, shield areas are somewhat more favoured geochemically. But it is the youthful Andean belt, estimated to represent a mere 12 per cent of the total area of the basin (Gibbs, 1967), that is believed to supply more than 90 per cent of the sediments and nutrients carried by the Amazon River (Meade et al.,

1985). This load is diluted downstream by the influx of large volumes of sediment-poor waters from the deeply weathered oldlands or from the central plain. The Rio Negro, for instance, has been calculated to contribute 20 per cent of the Amazon's outflow, but less than one per cent of its sedimentary discharge (Meade, Nordin and Curtis, 1979).

Related to the particulate and dissolved load of Amazonian waters are their optical properties,[5] which Native Brazilians incorporated in their fluvial nomenclature. Those appearing black are especially striking, and several Amazonian streams bear the Tupi designation Ipixuna ("black water") or include the diagnostic suffix *-una*. Early Europeans were equally impressed by the seeming inkiness of the water, "*negra como tinta*" (Carvajal 1942) of one major affluent, since known as the Rio Negro (fig. 6.3).

Alfred Russel Wallace (1853) perceived a simple threefold division of Amazonian streams into "white-water rivers, blue-water rivers, and black-water rivers," and recognized the association between optical properties and source areas. Issuing most characteristically from the Andean Cordillera and its foreland, so-called "white"-water rivers, such as the Madeira or the Amazon itself, are actually muddy-yellow to light reddish-brown because of the inorganic particulates they transport in suspension. Their pH values tend to lie close to neutral. Streams carrying minimal amounts of suspended sediments may be either clear-water or, if tinged by organic matter, "black"-water rivers, such as the Negro. Clear-water streams, of which the Tapajós is an example, may appear blue or green. Typically, they rise in the worn-down Guiano-Brazilian oldlands, and carry little dissolved salts and suspended solids. Their pH values vary widely. The earliest reference to the provenance of tropical black-water streams from areas of bleached sands or podzols may have been that of Lochead (1798). Imbued with fulvic and humic acids derived from the breakdown of plant tissue, the tea-colored water, which appears jet black in a stream or lake, may have pH values below four (Sioli, 1975).

Variation in water level and its ecological significance

The fact that summer rainfall maxima in the southern and northern hemispheres are out of phase offsets, to some extent, the peak discharges of major right- and left-bank tributaries of the lowland Amazon.[6] Storage provided by a vast floodplain also contributes to damp the seasonal variation of main stem discharge. The estimated high-flow/low-flow ratio of, at most, 3:1, is significantly less than that of

Figure 6.3 **Confluence of Negro and Solimões rivers, the "black," sediment-poor waters of the former flowing side by side with the "white," silt-laden waters of the latter. The fact that optical differences can no longer be discerned several tens of kilometres downstream does not signify that complete mixing has been achieved. Thus, some 100 km below the confluence, electrical conductivity still shows significant contrasts, increasing from the left to the right bank (Sternberg, 1975). Upstream end of alluvial Careiro Island at right. Terras firmes at top left. Photographed on or about 25 February 1952, with water level roughly 1 m above mean-stage. (Serviços Aerofotogramétricos Cruzeiro do Sul S.A. Original scale approximately 1:25,000.)**

other large rivers of the world (Nordin and Meade, 1986). Even so, the average yearly amplitude reaches 10 m at Manaus, which, situated 20 km up the Rio Negro, provides a reasonable approximation of the stage level in the trunk stream at the confluence.

The rise and fall of the waters, the great "drama of nature," in the words of Martius (Spix and Martius, 1831), is of supreme ecological consequence. The invasion of the várzea by floodwaters provides an opportunity for seed or fruit to bob away, leaving behind pests concentrated near the parent tree. Many floodplain plants are successfully adapted to dissemination by water. Ducke (1949) compared strategies for dispersal in species of the same genera belonging, respectively, to upland and bottomland habitats. In addition to mechanisms that involve the aquatic fauna (referred to below), he noted, among features that are adaptive in areas subject to inundation, indehiscence of fruit, favouring flotation, as contrasted with dehiscence in corresponding upland species.

Variation in river level is no less important for hydrophytes. In the case of white waters – or even black or clear waters, when seasonally invaded by silt-bearing floods – penetration of light is blocked by the very turbidity that denotes the presence of mineral nutrients. Here, buoyant plants are optimally adapted: regardless of water-level oscillations, they can use the radiant energy available at the surface. Vast areas are covered by "floating meadows" (Gessner, 1959; Junk, 1970, 1973) made up mainly of grasses, but sometimes bearing full-sized trees. The *matupás*, preferred habitat of the manatee (*Trichecus inunguis*) and home to a complex aquatic fauna, may also shelter amphibious and terrestrial animals, e.g. pacas (*Agouti paca*), capybaras (*Hydrochoerus hydrochaeris*), peccaries (*Tayassu pecari*), and tapirs (*Tapirus terrestris*).

Both free-floating plants and those that, rooted in the floodplain, are capable of pacing the rising waters play a key role in the nutrient and energy budget of the várzea, by capturing throughflowing nutrients. In one study that exemplifies the capacity of such macrophytes to concentrate critical elements, levels of potassium and phosphorus in the plants were, respectively, eight and four times higher than in the supporting soils and waters (Howard-Williams and Junk, 1977). With falling stage, the plant tissue deposited on the emerging land substantially enriches the soil.

The periodic appropriation of the várzea by floodwaters also has profound implications for Amazonian aquatic wildlife. During high water, many kinds of fish and other components of the riverine fauna, such as turtles, pass freely into flooded forests, which serve as breeding grounds and provide an appreciable part of the annual food intake. This is the time when a number of species develop the fat stores that carry them through the "physiological winter" of low water (Lowe-McConnell, 1967; Marlier, 1967), acquiring the energy necessary for gonad development and spawning migrations (Junk, 1985a).

Huber (1909) recognized the role of phytophagous fish in the dissemination of várzea plants. Ducke (1949) took the matter one step

121

further, suggesting that the frequent tartness of floodplain fruit, in contrast with the insipidness or sweetness of upland counterpart species, may have been selected for by the aquatic fauna, which, by passing viable seed, contributes to plant dispersal. The correlation acquired an additional mutualistic dimension in the light of evidence that, in the course of evolution, at least some fishes have lost the capacity to synthesize ascorbic acid (Chatterjee, 1973). It has been suggested (e.g. by Gottsberger, 1978) that the relative homogeneity of the wetland vegetation may be due to the alimentary regime of Amazonian fishes.

Riverine, estuarine, and coastal wetlands

The chemistry and fluctuations in stage of Amazon waters exert a decisive influence on the riparian and aquatic vegetation, as well as on the faunistic components of the ecosystems involved. Their sediment burden governs the evolution of the várzeas. Thus, the small load of rivers like the Tapajós and Xingu accords with the fact that they have yet to silt up their drowned lower courses. Other tributaries, rich in sediments, like the Juruá and Purus, describe meandering courses on the alluvium they themselves deposited.

This is not the pattern of the main stem. The incomplete filling of its drowned valley has produced an intricate mosaic of open water and wetlands. Lenticular alluvial islands split the stream-bed into a master channel and one or more laterals, or *paranás* (fig. 6.4). As the Amazon and major paranás shift back and forth, they leave behind gently curving strands of higher ground, *restingas*. Owing, among other reasons, to compaction of sediments, areas from which active channels have pulled away are lower then the youthful riverside levees. Major inundations submerge the entire alluvial plain; even during lesser floods, water flows into the bottoms through low sections in the natural levees. With their capricious windings and ramifications, the depositional strips laid down by distributary channels partition the floodplain into inumerable sub-basins, occupied by seasonal or permanent lakes (figs. 6.2 and 6.5) (Sternberg, 1956).

A widely-used estimate, giving the Amazonian várzeas a total of 64,400 km^2 (Camargo, 1958), has recently been revised upward, on the basis of airborne radar images. According to the new computation (Sippel, Hamilton, and Melack, 1992), wetlands along the main stem add up to 92,400 km^2 (11 per cent of which is covered by lakes), and, along major tributaries, to another 62,000 km^2, making

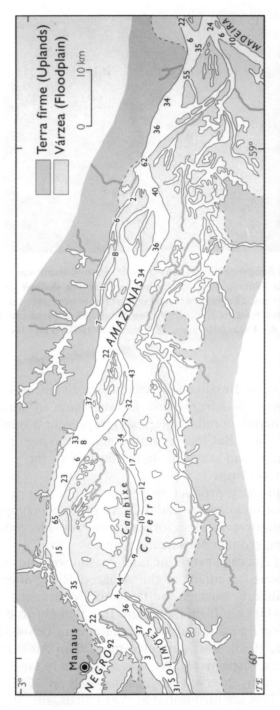

Figure 6.4 Stretch of the Amazon River, showing lenticular islands dividing the stream-bed into a master channel and one or more side channels, or *paranás*. Selected soundings (in metres) from the 1967 hydrographic survey by the Brazilian Navy; datum is mean lower low-water stage. (Taken, together with most water surface lines, from Brasil, *Rio Amazonas, Cartas de Praticagem da Flotilha do Amazonas*, Marinha do Brasil, Sheets P 4 106 A and B, 2nd ed., 1970. Original scale 1:100,000. Approximate outline of terra firme lakes, and boundary between uplands and floodplains, from aerial photographs.)

123

Figure 6.5   **Fed by silty floodwaters from the Amazon, sinuous distributary channels flow into and, with their flanking deposits, further partition the shallow basins created by major natural levees. The pattern is best seen at low water, since the expanding and contracting lakes tend to coalesce during floods. Floodplain southeast of Manaus, in the Paraná do Autaz Miri area, 28 November 1963. Water level almost 7 m below mean stage.**

a total of 154,400 km^2 in Brazilian Amazônia.[7] The várzeas, covered by grasslands (*campos de várzea*) and forests, some of which are more or less permanently inundated (*igapós*), represent a small fraction of the Amazon Plain. But they contain some of the region's most productive ecosystems, and stand in sharp contrast to the generally poor, non-flooded, terra firme.

In terms of net primary production per unit area (e.g. g/m^2/yr), Amazonia's estuarine and coastal wetlands are probably comparable to the várzeas. Mangrove forests, for example, provide privileged nurseries and feeding grounds for aquatic fauna.

The continuum of riverine, estuarine, and coastal wetlands reflects the remarkably subdued gradient of the Amazon River after it escapes from the Cordilleras through the Pongo de Manseriche, at 200 metres a.s.l., some 4,000 km from its mouth. It is thought to descend about 2–3 cm/km near Iquitos, and less than 1 cm/km below Óbidos (Nordin and Meade, 1986), towns situated more than 3,000 km and 1,000 km from the sea, respectively. As a consequence, a far-reaching tidal influence has been observed, at least as early as 1743, by La Condamine (1745). This scientist noted at Fort Pauxis, site of today's

Óbidos, where the river is constricted to a channel about 2,400 m wide, that "the flux & reflux of the Sea reaches as far as these narrows ... From Pauxis to the sea, ... over two hundred and some leagues ..., the River must not descend more than $10\frac{1}{2}$ feet."

Human use of Amazonian aquatic and wetland ecosystems

Native Amazonians

Millennia before a band of Europeans was swept downstream by eastward-flowing Andean waters (Carvajal, 1942) and others had paddled west against the current to remote Cordilleran headwaters (Acuña, 1942), Amerindians had introduced a human dimension to the Amazonian landscape. Indeed, early reports by soldiers and missionaries suggest very large numbers of indigenes at the time of conquest. Yet high estimates for the pre-contact population generally have been viewed with some reserve. Perhaps the reason lies in the failure to allow for the precipitous demographic decline during the early years of contact, whether from deliberate extermination, lack of immunity to Old World diseases, or the general disruption of indigenous ways of life.

Several scholars admit the possibility that Indian nations in Amazonia might have reached several million individuals before this collapse. In considering such estimates, it should be remembered that the pre-Conquest inhabitants might not have had to face some of the hardships presently seen as inherent to the region. Thus, areas now malarial, and shunned as such, may have been free of the disease. Several parasitologists suggest that the aetiological agents of malaria were introduced into the New World by Europeans and their African slaves (Dunn, 1965, 1993; Coatney et al., 1971; Wood, 1975).[8] The proposition has not gone unchallenged (e.g. Noble et al., 1989), and much research remains to be done with respect to the initial manifestation in the Americas of malaria and other diseases.

The fact is that substantial archaeological evidence exists for large pre-contact populations in Amazonia: e.g. pictographs, petroglyphs, and the widespread occurrence of charcoal and kitchen middens in the soil of what might appear to be virgin forests. Salvage work carried out in connection with large-scale hydropower projects has revealed a number of prehistoric sites. In the case of the Balbina reservoir, for example, a map of the lower Uatumã and tributaries shows no less than 121 such sites (SAUHEB, n.d). Similarly, a survey in the

125

area of the projected Porteira hydroelectric station, on the Trombetas River, Pará, identified 43 prehistoric localities (Costa et al., 1986).

The archaeological significance of *terra preta* (black earth) was recognized more than a century ago. This anthrosol is derived from middens, and contains abundant potsherds and ceramics, some of considerable sophistication, such as the striking Santarém pottery (Palmatary, 1960). The terras pretas are found both on floodplains (Sternberg, 1960) and uplands, where they have long been "highly prized as agricultural grounds" (Brown and Lidstone, 1878).[9] Indeed, indigenous settlements were so large and persistent that soil scientists have come to recognize the black earth as a "taxonomic unit" (Falesi, 1967).

In sum, there are grounds to believe that, when Europeans arrived upon the scene, Indians numbered in the millions, and that the Amazon had been, in the words of Palmatary (1939), "a busy ... part of the New World."

As to the time depth involved, indications are that it is greater than formerly thought. Thus, caves and rock shelters under the plinthite that caps the vast reserves of iron ore in the Serra dos Carajás of southern Pará have begun yielding artifacts whose oldest radiocarbon ages are reported to be $8,140 \pm 130$ years (Lopes and Silveira, 1990), or $8,065 \pm 360$ (Magalhães, 1993). They are interpreted as evidence of the presence of pre-ceramic hunter-gatherers and, later, of potters. Among other indications of human antiquity in Amazonia is the eighth-millennium pottery from a prehistoric shell midden at Taperinha, near Santarém, taken to be the earliest yet found in the western hemisphere (Roosevelt et al., 1991). One may expect that continued research will further push back the record of human presence in the region.[10] Obviously, this presence relates to the more general and highly controversial issue of timing the entry of Amerindians into the New World. And here, some students (e.g. Torroni et al., 1993; Torroni et al., 1994; Wallace and Torroni, 1992), having applied a new high-tech tool, the analysis of mitochondrial DNA, to the problem, are interpreting the results as consistent with an "early" arrival, possibly some 30,000 years before present or even earlier.

Thanks to the mobility provided by an extensive fluvial network, comprising tens of thousands of kilometres of navigable channels, the water-oriented tribes ranged far and wide. Alexandre Rodrigues Ferreira (1972), whose *Viagem Philosophica* from 1783 to 1792 has been seen as the forerunner of nineteenth-century scientific reports on Brazil, remarks on the intimate knowledge of Native Brazilians concerning Amazonia's hydrography. He recounts how a Macuxi, questioned about the Rio Branco, took a cord to represent this affluent of the Rio Negro, and attached to it, left and right, as many strands as are the sub-affluents, spacing them correctly and endowing them with appropriate windings. Additionally, knots indicated the number and position of Indian villages.

True, not all Indian groups were riparian peoples, a fact evidenced by numerous archaeological sites on the upland interfluves (Smith, 1980). But the "personality" of Amazonia, to a considerable degree, rests on, and is defined by, its waters and wetlands. To them are attached some of the region's most fascinating myths, such as that of the *iara* or *mãe d'agua*, siren of rivers and lakes, that of the lecherous *bôto*, or Amazon River dolphin (*Inia geoffrensis*), seducer of streamside maidens, or yet that of the supernatural *cobra grande*, big snake.

Even the cosmologies of contemporary Amazonian fishermen occasionally translate an ethos that, at least theoretically, favours sustained use of aquatic resources (Furtado, 1992; Smith 1981). One belief, for instance, enjoins fishermen to abstain from overfishing and to diversify their catch, in order to avoid angering the "mother-of-fish." Also to be shunned is the wrath of another spirit that punishes those who disturb spawning female turtles.

The Amerindians' economy did not demand the stockpiling of vast food resources. An abundant storehouse was at hand, and they knew how to preserve the product of their fishing, hunting, and gathering, for instance by smoke-drying, *moquém*, or potting meat in its own rendered grease, *mixira*. Some carry-over of seasonally abundant fare was thus assured, and they had little incentive to overexploit the waters and wetlands.

Referring to the numerous alluvial islands on which the natives laid out their crops, Acuña observed in 1639 :

The river washes [over] these islands every year, fertilizing them with its muds, so they [are ... never] sterile, even though, year in and year out, one demands of them ... maize [*Zea mays*] and yuca or manioc [*Manihot utilissima*].

In addition to the staples mentioned by Acuña (1942), Amerindians assembled in their floodplain gardens a variety of food plants. Some of these are believed to have been domesticated thousands of years ago, such as a number of cucurbits (*Cucurbita* spp.), beans (*Phaseolus vulgaris*), peanuts (*Arachis hypogaea*), papaya (*Carica papaya*), and several species of *Capsicum* (Ducke, 1946; Kerr, Campos, and Barros, 1986).

127

Things would change with the arrival of Europeans and Neo-Brazilians. Instead of a moderate, diversified use, mainly for consumption, of aquatic and wetland bioresources, a mercantilist world pushed many species to the brink of extinction.

Conquest and colonization: The waters

Incorporation of Amazonia into the Portuguese empire occurred in the seventeenth and eighteenth centuries. As the Amazon Basin was conquered, river after tributary river, it yielded up all sorts of drugs and spices – aromatic and valuable cargo for Europe-bound ships. Plants and animals enriched merchants, and suffered great havoc in the process. The aquatic fauna early became the object of veritable carnages, as in the case of the Amazon turtle (*Podocnemis expansa*) and the previously mentioned manatee.

Coutinho (1868), writing about turtles, once present in vast numbers, decried their capture before oviposition, and recalled guidelines no longer observed:

Nobody was allowed to approach before the eggs had been laid. Only when this was completed, did one proceed to the *viração* [the "turnover," by which the chelonians were immobilized], each person receiving half a turtle, the remainder being given back to the river.

While two-thirds of the clutch of eggs had been used in the manufacture of *manteiga* (literally, "butter," an oily substance derived from the yolks), one-third had been reserved for reproduction. With commercialization, the destruction of eggs reached mind-boggling proportions. Fat obtained from the eggs was used in the preparation of food and as lamp oil, as was that extracted from turtle meat (fig. 6.6).

Manteiga was also melted down from fatty tissues of the manatee and put to the same use. The massive slaughter of the sirenian got under way in the seventeenth century (Vieira, 1659; Heriarte, *c.* 1662). Part of the resultant products, notably rendered fat, was shipped to Europe. Much of the flesh apparently was consumed in the Guianas and the Caribbean, where English and French colonies were supplied by Dutch traders.[11]

The preceding illustrates how overexploitation directly endangers bioresources.[12] These may also be threatened indirectly by habitat modification. A wide range exists of potential anthropic impacts of this kind on the waters of Amazonia, which hold sway over the alluvial wetlands and are complex ecosystems in themselves.

Figure 6.6 **Exploitation of the Amazon turtle. Alexandre Rodrigues Ferreira's Amazonian expedition (1783–1792) included two artist-illustrators, and resulted in a valuable iconography, including the above composition (Ferreira, 1971). It shows the production of** *manteiga* **(literally, "butter"), a fatty oil from the yolk of turtle eggs. The sand is probed for nests (left), from which the eggs are taken – 100, 150, sometimes 200 to a clutch (left and centre). They may be allowed to ferment, or placed in a canoe (centre), to be trampled "as grapes are trodden in Portugal" (Ferreira, 1972). Water is stirred in and the supernatant oil is skimmed off, boiled in cauldrons, and, eventually, put in earthenware jars (right), to be marketed regionally and abroad. Manteiga was used in cooking, as lamp oil, and, mixed with pitch, in caulking boats. Turtle meat was an important commodity, dried as well as preserved in its own manteiga or in manatee fat. The practice of keeping live turtles in a stockade (left background), was noted in 1542 (Carvajal, 1942).**

Human activities may subvert hydrologic characteristics, such as volume and seasonal variations of runoff. They may also affect the particulate and dissolved load of river waters, altering their chemical and other properties, and modifying their interaction with soils, plants, and animals. Further, they may trigger obscure biological chain reactions by eliminating keystone species or, conversely, by introducing disruptive exotic organisms.

Any of these, and a number of other anthropogenic changes, would probably have a noticeable impact on the human population. The life of floodplain dwellers (*varzeanos, varzeiros, ribeirinhos*) is closely linked to the yearly rise and fall of water levels, which conduct the cadence of current economic activities on, and in the proximity of, the várzea. One example is the gathering of aquatic macrophytes as fodder for cattle huddled on platforms or rafts during high water. Another is the felling and removal of timber in várzea forests, the former at low, the latter at high, stage. To the degree in which waters saturate, submerge, or leave the land dry, they influence not only the extent of the area available for cropping but the span of time during which it can be used, and even the manner of its use.

Conjectured human-induced trends in river stage

An upswing in the severity and frequency of major floods in the Amazon lowlands was predicated at least as early as 1903 by Paul Le Cointe, who returned to the subject several times (Le Cointe, 1922, 1935, 1948). Leaving aside the possibility of water slope adjustment to neotectonic events (Sternberg, 1950, 1955, 1987a), shown to be significant in westernmost Amazonia (e.g. Dumont, 1993; Räsänen, 1991, 1993),[13] elevation of flood levels such as suggested by Le Cointe could result from increased highwater flow, siltation of channels and bottomlands, or a combination of both processes. Although these might be induced or exacerbated by societal behavior, Le Cointe did not invoke the possible role of human activities.

However, given the contemporary rate of deforestation, it is now reasonable to anticipate that, in time, and starting with small or medium-sized, intensely ravaged, tributary watersheds, streamflow will be affected. Reduced transpiration, as moisture extraction by plant roots decreases, compounded with curtailment of water storage, due to soil degradation and erosion, may be expected to raise flood levels. An increased delivery of debris may contribute to the silting up of waterways and thus to a general elevation of gauge readings. In the case of low-water discharge, impairment and removal of soil should lead eventually to a diminished carry-over into dry periods.

Prominent among activities that contribute to deforestation and thus might affect the flow patterns of Amazonian waters is the construction of new roads opening the interfluves to "economic development." In Brazil, this was translated essentially in terms of giant cattle ranches, established at the expense of pristine selva. In addition, following the new roads came wave upon wave of farm folk, either landless or desiring to exchange minuscule, worn-out plots in the south or north-east of Brazil for larger tracts carved out of the forest.

New inducements for the destruction of Amazonia's rain forest have arisen. Mining is one of them. Take, for instance, the Grande Carajás region,[14] named after the massif noted for its immense mineral reserves, especially high-grade iron ore. Far more extensive than the forest areas directly affected by opencut mining in the district are those where wood is extracted for the charcoal used in smelting (Penna, 1989). Charcoal kilns that use forest trees are found in a wide radius around the blast furnaces. One estimate is that an area of 26,000 km² for tree plantations eventually will be needed to satisfy the demand (Kohlhepp, 1987).[15]

Other incitements to forest clearing, less readily discernible at this time, are certain to lie ahead. One might be the commercial production of lowland coca (*Erythroxylum coca*, var. *ipadu*), a close relative of the Andean *E. coca*, var. *coca* (Plowman, 1981). Grown initially by Indians, the powdered leaf had been observed in use in 1774 by a Portuguese administrator (Sampaio, 1825). Later, planted under conditions of shifting cultivation, it was noted by Martius (Spix and Martius, 1822–1831) on "a hill, cleared of forest south of the village of Ega," now Tefé. In the Andean realm, for example in the Huallaga Valley of Peru, coca has become the single most important cause of deforestation and a significant factor in water pollution by fertilizer, herbicide, and industrial wastes (Dourojeanni, 1992). To the degree that eradication programmes are effective in the mountains, production may shift to the Amazon lowlands.[16]

Given actual and potential motivations to divest cordilleran and lowland watersheds of their cover, it is defensible to argue that hydrologically disruptive effects of clearing will eventually spread to the main stem. It is another thing to posit present-day changes in the lowland Amazon induced by deforestation in the Andes. Yet it has been suggested that higher and more persistent flood crests, as well as decreased low-water stages, were perceived as far downstream as Iquitos (Gentry and López-Parodi, 1980, 1982). Consistent with this suggestion is the claim by varzeanos in the Itacoatiara area that floods had become increasingly severe. Confirmation of this observation was sought in the stage levels at Manaus (Smith, 1981), but the suspected tendency of the maxima at this station, after a spike in 1976, did not hold. Indeed, trend analyses relative to heights, duration, and timing of yearly floods, applied to data for the period 1902–1985, showed no statistical significance, and did not support the above propositions (Sternberg, 1987a). When the series was extended to 1992 (fig. 6.7), both annual maxima and mean daily water levels continued to reveal no significant tendency. However, the slope

131

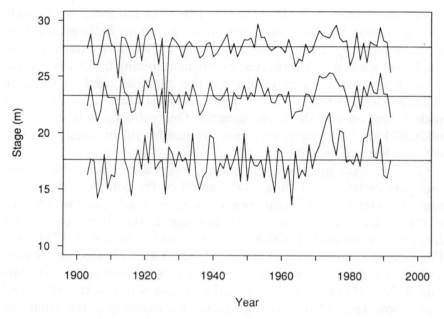

Figure 6.7 **Annual maximum, mean, and minimum stages of the Rio Negro at Manaus. Series for the period 1 January 1903 to 31 December 1992. Given the negligible gradient of the water surface, the Manaus gauge, about 20 km up the Negro estuary, provides a reasonable surrogate for the stage of the Amazon River at the confluence. Upper graph: annual maximum for each year; middle graph: mean of all daily values for each year; lower graph: annual minimum for each year. The horizontal lines give the mean level of the respective series for the entire 90-year period. In the search for a possible change in the level of the water surface, trend analyses were carried out for the three series in the manner of Brillinger (1988). The results were as follows. For the maximum: slope, 0.0068440m/yr; SE, 0.0055143; ratio (t-statistic, with 17 degrees of freedom), 1.241); two-sided p-value, 23.14%. For the mean: slope, 0.011471m/yr; SE, 0.0062402; ratio, 1.834; two sided p-value, 8.36%. For the minimum: slope, 0.019263m/yr; SE, 0.0081425; ratio, 2.366; two-sided p-value, 3.01%. Whereas the trends for the annual maximum and for the mean of daily values lack significance at the commonly employed 5% level, the upward trend of the annual minimum is significant at this level. (*Source of data*: Manaos Harbour Ltd. and Portobrás).**

of the linear trend relative to the *low*-water stage exhibited a slight, but distinct, *upward* bent, and requires further investigation.

Deterioration of aquatic ecosystems
The hydrograph can be significantly altered by manipulation of the natural conduit through which the river flows (e.g. by impoundment

or construction of embankments). When, in the 1960s, the Hudson Institute of New York proposed the building of a gigantic earth dam across the Amazon at the Óbidos narrows (Panero, 1967, 1969), the scheme met with strong opposition – largely on emotional issues of sovereignty, rather than because of its inherent silliness – and was abandoned. By contrast, a programme to harness affluents of the trunk stream or of the Rio Pará has been actively pursued. As a result, the Tucuruí hydroelectric power plant, one of the world's largest, was inaugurated in 1984 on the Tocantins River, which has been envisaged as an unbroken chain of huge reservoirs (Sternberg, 1981). Plans for similar development on other tributaries were drawn up in rapid succession, and some were implemented before the country's financial difficulties interrupted the programme.

Engineers argue that the area of forest drowned by even the largest hydroplant is but a small fraction of what goes up in smoke every year. They are probably right. However, it is not the *area* lost to reservoirs that is so important, but the effects of the impoundment on entire aquatic ecosystems. Recall that the life cycles of many species of freshwater fauna are, in great measure, adjusted to yearly inundations of the forest and to an open communication between river channels and floodplain lakes (Goulding, 1980; Marlier, 1967; Smith, 1981; Sternberg, 1975). It seems quite possible, therefore, that an important supply of protein, of special value to underprivileged rural populations, will be much reduced by impounding Amazonian rivers. Dams do not merely affect characteristics of flow; they can also alter physical and chemical properties of the water.

Noteworthy among other activities that constitute a direct menace to the quality of Amazonia's waters are the extraction, processing, and transportation of mineral resources. In some tributary catchments, the purity of water has already been seriously vitiated by mining and metal refining. Illustrations are found typically in Andean headwaters, but, increasingly, in the lowlands. An example comes from the Madeira River basin, in the state of Rondônia. The region has been the scene of a gold rush that mobilized an adventitious labour force, estimated, at times, to exceed half a million *garimpeiros* (folkminers, prospectors) in Brazil's Amazonia.[17] On the Madeira, gold is extracted from the channel bed by means of locally-built suction-dredges (fig. 6.8). In 1989, the Rondônia Cooperative of Garimpeiros (COPEGRO, 1989) denounced the frenzied increase in the use of heavy equipment on the river, alerting against an exhaustion of the placer. That COPEGRO suggested a minimum distance of

Figure 6.8 **The frenzied scramble to build suction dredges (*dragas*) for operation on the Madeira River, whose alluvial channel deposits have been counted among the world's richest sources of riverine placer gold. The dragas incorporate a platform supported by two iron cylinders some 14 m in length, and a structure that houses the machinery and includes the operators' living quarters (a smaller and more rudimentary version are the *balsas*). The river gravels are worked by a powerful cutterhead at the extremity of a lance, while a diesel-driven pump draws in the slurry. After the gold particles are trapped and concentrated in a sluice, liquid mercury is used in amalgamation. Although every dredge now is theoretically required to employ a retort to recover the mercury for reuse, the amalgam is often heated over an open flame (Veiga, 1993). In this case, the vaporized mercury is eventually precipitated, polluting soils and waters. A paper accepted for publication in 1986 refers to some 100 dragas in operation along a 180-km stretch of the Madeira River upstream of Porto Velho (Bastos, 1988). Their number was reported to have reached 5,000 in 1989 (Hilde, 1989) and 10,000 in 1990 (Dias, 1993); however, a possible source of uncertainty in the count is the inclusion of balsas in some reports. After this peak, the number of dragas fell off sharply, and many, having been built at a cost of several kilograms of gold each, were abandoned on the riverbanks. The drop is attributed by some to a partial exhaustion of recoverable gold (Veiga, 1993) – at least in terms of the low efficiency of the dragas. (Photographed 6 June 1989.)**

50 m between dredges, in order to reduce congestion and the frequent collision of outboards, gives some idea of the crowded conditions at the time on bountiful sections of the river. Prospecting for gold along the 180-km stretch known as the *reserva garimpeira* fell off considerably since COPEGRO's pronouncement, after a high

point of some five to ten thousand dredges was reached – a fact that appears to reflect the depletion of the deposit (Veiga, 1993).[18]

Reworking of the channel bed, roiling of the waters, redeposition of sediments downstream, and dumping of spent diesel oil in the rivers are not the most serious impacts of gold mining in Amazonia. Metallic mercury is used on the dredges, as it is in land-based operations, to amalgamate fine gold particles. When the precious metal is recovered by ustulation, the vaporized quicksilver eventually falls back to earth, contaminating soils and waters. No form of pollution can be more insidious. It is hard to believe, for instance, that the limpid, apparently pure, waters of the Tapajós River, downstream from Itaituba, an important gold-mining centre, can pose serious health risks. Yet, there is evidence that this, precisely, is the case. Mercury (particularly the organic compound, methylmercury) identified in Amazonian river sediments, plants, and fish (see, for instance, Castro, Albert, and Pfeiffer, 1991; Malm et al., 1993; Pfeiffer et al., 1991; and the review by Pfeiffer et al., 1993), has a profound and generally irreversible impact on the human central nervous system. The levels of this metal in several fish samples collected in Amazonia have exceeded the World Health Organization's safety limit for human consumption; high values found in species widely consumed by humans, such as the omnivorous tambaqui (*Colossoma macropomum*), are of the greatest concern. Some plants, such as the water hyacinth (*Eichornia crassipes*), used to feed domestic animals, seem to concentrate mercury (Martinelli et al., 1988).

In contrast to pollution by mercury, which is not perceptible to the senses, the presence of even a thin film of petroleum, another threat to Amazonian aquatic and wetland environments, is betrayed by iridescence. However, Brazil, an unequally developed country, aspires for "first world" status. It is committed to an urban-industrial model of development, having chosen to rely on highways and airways for its long-distance transportation – notably in its attempts to end the isolation of Amazonia. Oil spills, while potentially catastrophic to waters and wetlands, are not immediately life-threatening to human communities. The national society is likely to see economic benefits and pay little, if any, attention to the possible environmental costs of a petroleum-driven development of Amazonia.

What appear to be important oil and gas reserves were found in 1986 more than 600 km west of Manaus (fig. 6.9), in the Urucu river drainage (Pimentel, 1986). The prospect of drilling for, pumping, transporting, and refining oil in Amazonia is disquieting, given the

135

Figure 6.9 **Oil well in the Urucu River drainage, where petroleum was found in the late 1980s. What seems to have been a limited oil spill occurred in 1988, when, pending construction of a pipeline to the year-round navigable Tefé River, the barge *Celetra I*, loaded with crude, struck a floating log in the Urucu – more a narrow and shallow *igarapé* than a river. The Urucu debouches into the Solimões some 660 km upstream from the mouth of the Rio Negro. (Photograph by Jônio Machado, courtesy Petróleo Brasileiro S.A.—PETROBRÁS).**

effects that a major spill could have on waters and wetlands. A relatively minor mishap occurred in 1988 but received little or no attention outside the region. An estimated 20,000 litres of crude befouled the narrow Urucu River (*A Crítica*, 1988a, 1988b, 1988c, 1988d, 1988e), whose waters eventually reach the Solimões, about 450 km upstream from this river's confluence with the Rio Negro.

Despite the billions of dollars spent on cleanup efforts in the Gulf of Alaska following the 1989 *Exxon Valdez* spill of more than 40 million litres of oil, the results have been judged unsatisfactory. Destructive as were the environmental effects of the Alaskan disaster,[19] they pale in comparison with what could happen if a large discharge of oil were to take place in Amazonian waters. In the Prince William Sound, the land area directly affected, mainly rocky headlands and pebbled beaches, was limited to the intertidal zone. In the mosaic of levees, backswamps, ridge-and-swale features, and shallow lakes of the Amazon wetlands (see figs. 6.2 and 6.5), the very concept of shoreline has little meaning. At floodtime, waters spread over an area that may comprise as much as 90 to 95 per cent of the várzea (Junk, 1985b). In a low-energy environment lacking the wave action that

136

helps break up oil spills at sea, the slick, depending on the river stage, could be carried dozens of kilometres through open water, flooded forest, and floating meadows. One can imagine the immediate effects of oil settling on, and penetrating, the fine sands, clays, and silts of the floodplain, impacting on soil organisms, plant life, and aquatic as well as terrestrial fauna. In the long term, however, the intense microbial activity of the tropical milieu may expedite the weathering of the pollutant. As to the chances of a significant oil discharge into waters and wetlands of Brazil's Amazonia, the question is not whether, but when and how much.

One final instance of the kinds of human activities that have the potential for causing grievous harm to the region's aquatic ecosystems: consider the plan for a waterway from the Caribbean to the Rio de la Plata, to be achieved by linking the Orinoco with the Amazon system, and this with the Plata basin. Given Brazil's current lack of interest, there is no immediate prospect of its implementation.[20] Nevertheless, the point needs to be made that interbasin linkages, involving the Amazon drainage – an idea which has been under consideration for at least two centuries (*Anal*, 1773; Humboldt and Bonpland, 1820–1822) – could produce environmental changes of unforeseeable ramifications. A major concern among many students stems from the role of waterways in the diffusion of organisms. Although not all exchanges need prove harmful, the gamut of possible biological consequences from the intermingling of biotas pertaining to previously discrete ecosystems is considerable. Hazards include competition for resources, direct predation, perhaps even the spread of parasitic diseases among geographic isolates. An estimation of this risk must be based on an understanding of the degree of biological separateness of the catchments involved, and the specific co-evolutionary history of hosts and pathogens, in the case of both endemic fauna and potential invaders.

Conquest and colonization: The fertile interface

Because waters create, refashion, and exert a dominant influence on the wetland ecosystem, human actions that denature the former can injure the latter. Thus, given the importance of ichthyocory, modification of the waters qua habitat for dispersal agents may indirectly affect the makeup of the wetlands vegetation. Naturally, the most demonstrable anthropic pressures on an ecosystem are those applied to it directly – and the Native Amazonian farmers stepped lightly on these lands. Numerous tracts of terra preta testify to sustained use of the floodplains. The same is true, downvalley, for the estuarine and tidal lands, whose mudflats and mangrove forests, in the words of the historian Varnhagen (1927), "offered ... inexhaustible *mines* of crabs." They also offered an abundant harvest of molluscs, easily harvested from the roots of mangroves (*Rhizophora mangle, Avicennia, nitida,* and *Laguncularia racemosa*). That the utilization of such resources by humans goes far back in time is evidenced by the number and size of coastal shell mounds, long quarried by colonists as a source of lime (Le Cointe, 1945).

Among the earliest Europeans to cultivate the Amazonian wetlands were the religious orders: first, in the manner of subsistence farming, to feed the missions; then in the production of cash crops, such as bananas, sugar cane, cacao, cotton, rice, maize, and manioc, with which to finance their evangelization activities. Plantations and cattle ranches were established in the estuarine section of the river, where ruins of sugar mills and vestiges of drainage and irrigation canals have been identified (Lima, 1956). One mid-eighteenth-century inventory of Jesuit holdings on Marajó Island (fig. 6.10) lists seven ranches, running more than a hundred thousand head of cattle.

The Portuguese and neo-Brazilian upriver settlements were essentially punctate, dispersed, allowing ample room for new arrivals to settle out interstitially, along the riverine avenues of penetration. Gradually, farming developed alongside the basic gathering activity. Although some plants were introduced, indigenous crops took pride of place. Native manioc, or cassava, was then – as it is now – the staple food crop, and the transformation of the tuber into *farinha*, or meal, was among the first rustic industries.

After the middle of the nineteenth century, penetration and settlement of Amazonia followed a pattern that mirrored the geographical distribution of the *seringueira*, or rubber tree (*Hevea brasiliensis*). At a time when the demand for rubber was increasing, disastrous droughts uprooted a considerable part of the rural population in Brazil's semi-arid north-east, the Nordeste. Arriving in Amazonia, they formed the workforce of the new extractive economy. Other *nordestinos*, eschewing the dream of making a fortune in the distant rubber-rich headwaters (*"altos rios"*), settled on the floodplain with their families, to be joined later by those who beat a retreat from the *seringais* when the boom collapsed. To the fertile river-banks that emerge during falling stages they applied the traditional *lavoura de vasante* ("ebb farming") they had used in the seasonally dry river-

Figure 6.10 **Marajó Island, at the mouth of the Amazon, with the palafitte-like village of Genipapo. Rain forests cover the western half of the island's almost 50,000 km², while low-lying grasslands, including some park landscapes and gallery forests, predominate in the eastern part. Cattle ranching has a long tradition on Marajó, reaching back to Jesuit ranches in colonial times, when it was known as the Island of Joannes. (Photographed 12 July 1970.)**

beds of their homeland. Well-drained natural levees were cultivated with a diversity of native and exotic crops: annuals, replanted after each flood, and, starting with endemics, arboreal perennials capable of surviving the yearly inundation. Home gardens contained native fruit trees, such as cupuaçu (*Theobroma grandiflorum*), graviola (*Annona muricata*), papaya (*Carica papaya*), açaí (*Euterpe oleracea*), and cacao (*Theobroma cacao*) – for a time an important cash crop. Much later came jute (*Corchorus capsularis*), introduced in the early 1930s by Japanese settlers and once a significant element of the *varzeano*'s economy (Pinto, 1966).

The end result is a landscape incorporating a rich repertory of native and introduced crops, distributed in conformity with the topography of the várzea. Crops intolerant of humidity or requiring more time for maturation, such as banana, cacao, manioc, or beans, are located on the levee crests, and those more tolerant to humidity, notably jute, make use of the bottoms (fig. 6.11), In addition to current agricultural pursuits and animal husbandry, there has been some

139

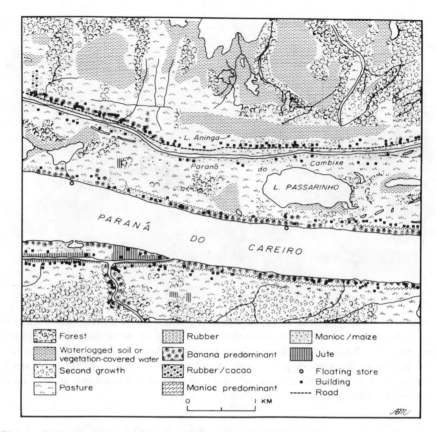

Figure 6.11 **Land use along the white-water Paraná do Careiro and its ancillary Paraná do Cambixe, near the confluence of the Rio Solimões and the Rio Negro. The distribution of various crop combinations (in 1956), adjusted to the subdued relief of the floodplain, is indicated in a generalized manner by segments of streambank, not by individual establishments. The depiction of some crops, such as beans, sweet potato, rice, and vegetables, which are significant on certain farms, is not compatible with the degree of generalization of the map. Fruit trees are disseminated throughout most properties, and some stretches of the paranás are lined with mangoes. (Source: Sternberg, 1975.)**

small-scale rubber tapping, logging, and extraction of non-wood products of the selva. With the river and the forests supplying a rich bounty of animal protein, this land-use system has been treated as an example of what now goes by the designation "agroforestry" (Bahri, 1992).

Nowhere is it better represented than on the floodplain island of Careiro,[21] especially on the levees of the Paraná do Careiro, which

Figure 6.12   **Upstream section of the Paraná do Careiro, near its diversion from the Solimões River. Where natural levees are wide, long-lot holdings, roughly perpendicular to the river, predominate. Each farmer thus has access to the privileged higher and better-drained ground immediately contiguous to the river. This is where houses are built and crops less tolerant to flooding are planted. Waterlogged backswamps may be left with forest; where it is cleared, the objective is to create supplementary pastures.**

bounds it on the south, and the subsidiary Paraná do Cambixe (figs. 6.4, 6.11 and 6.12). Here, refugees from the 1888 drought in the Nordeste received small long-lot tracts of a size proportionate to the number of active family members. The stable, close-knit community that resulted favoured the retention, alongside truck gardening, of the north-east's time-honoured livestock farming tradition. The landscape came to be increasingly influenced by dairying, with the island becoming a key component of the Manaus milkshed (Sternberg, 1956, 1966). The spatial organization of the Careiro wetlands permits the periodic utilization, as supplementary pastures, of low-lying areas, where native fodder plants become available as the waters recede.

During severe floods, however, forage must be cut and transported by boat to cows bunched on patches of unsubmerged levee crest, or

Figure 6.13 During severe inundations, cattle raised on the floodplains of Amazonia are likely to be sheltered on *marombas*, stable-like structures built either on land or on large rafts, such as this one, which afforded sanctuary to 50 cows in the Careiro region, part of the Manaus milkshed. Marombas on piles can accommodate as many as 150 head; those on raised earthen platforms, 400. The cows placed on marombas subsist on canarana (*Echinochloa polystachya*) and other aquatic and semiaquatic gramineae, tossed from a boat. During the flood of 1953, the highest on record, 4,029 head of cattle had been given refuge on marombas along the Paraná do Careiro and the ancillary Cambixe channel. (Photographed 1 July 1953, river level at Manaus 6.31 m above average.)

confined to barns upraised on piles or waterborne on rafts (fig. 6.13). The main native forage, canarana (*Echinochloa polystachya*), which thrives in white water, is indispensable for getting through critical inundations. When not consumed by cattle, it and other grasses are set on fire after the flood subsides, nutrients carried in the turbid water then being incorporated as ash into the soil.

Although the humanized landscape of the Careiro represents an alteration of the wetlands, it is far from the radical make-over some might find desirable. Swamps, marshes, and forest-covered tropical floodplains in their natural state tend to have few champions. The most extreme transformation of the aquatic-terrestrial ecosystems is, of course, to take the "wet" out of "wetlands." The word *saneamento* (from L. *sanare*, to restore to health), as used in Brazil, is most aptly translated by the English "reclamation." In Western thinking, improvement and proper use of wetlands often is equated with exsiccation. Perhaps this mindset derives, in part, from the widely acclaimed achievements of Dutch hydraulic engineers. Generations of dykemasters from the Netherlands have been called to work all over the world (Veen, 1962) and it is not surprising that, early in this century, a Dutch engineer was hired to study the manner in which Marajó Island might be drained.

The optic of certain ancient civilizations, such as those that flourished on the east coast of Mexico, appears to have been very different. The density and achievements of these pre-Columbian populations do not seem compatible with what, to modern eyes, appears as an inhospitable, waterlogged region. But, instead of removing water, the natives chose to discipline it and use it to supply protein in the form of aquatic fauna, while raising ridges, upon which they presumably produced the necessary complements of carbohydrates (e.g. Flannery, 1982; Harrison and Turner, 1978; Turner and Denevan, 1985). Water, properly organized, represented a resource, not an obstacle.[22]

A major hydrogeomorphic transformation of wetland and lacustrine environments along the Amazonas was attempted by the federal Agronomic Institute of the North in 1949, when it set out to effect, on a gigantic scale, what várzea farmers sometimes accomplish on their property: the diversion of silt-laden floodwaters into low-lying tracts. The target was Lake Maicuru, also known as Lago Grande de Monte Alegre, or, simply, Lago Grande (see fig. 6.2), between Santarém and Monte Alegre, Pará State (Camargo, 1958; Sioli, 1951). Eventually, the lacustrine depression was to have been

143

brought under cultivation, but it was thought that, even during the initial stages of siltation, water buffalo could be raised there. A number of canals from the Amazonas were cut. The largest, completed in 1953, was 30 m across and 6 m deep at bank full stage, and in 1954 was discharging 275 m³/sec. (Camargo, 1958). Recently, the President of the Society for the Preservation of Amazonia's Natural Resources issued a warning, based on his perception that, as water pours in, Lake Maicuru is expanding, swallowing up small neighbouring lakes and streams, and threatening the natural levees that separate it from the Amazon (*O Liberal*, 1989).

The most ambitious operation hitherto attempted to remake Amazonian wetlands was begun in the mid-1970s by São Raimundo Agro-industrial Ltda. (SRAL). This was a division of the empire established by US billionaire Daniel K. Ludwig on the banks of the Amazon and its left-bank tributary, the Jari. With Amazonia envisaged as Brazil's most promising rice bowl, the project to cultivate the grain on 12,700 hectares of wetlands used powerful earthmoving equipment to build 460 km of dikes and 250 km of canals. Agricultural operations were mechanized, employing heavy farm machinery; seeding, and the application of fertilizer, herbicides, and pesticides were carried out by aeroplanes (SRAL, n.d.). However, weed control is very difficult in the Amazonian wetlands. An exploratory survey had signalled the presence of several potentially dangerous weeds in floodplain rice fields and the difficulty of targeting them selectively (Barrett, 1975). Also, elevated temperatures, coupled with high humidity, favour pests and diseases. Indeed, biocides did prove to be a significant part of production costs on the 3,500 ha eventually brought under cultivation (SRAL, 1984).

In 1982, a Brazilian consortium incorporated the Companhia do Jari, with the objective of taking over Ludwig's tree farm, pulp plant, and mineral deposits. Two years later, it also acquired the rice operations. The buyers have stated that, although aware of the serious problems faced by SRAL, they were motivated by the social merit of an enterprise dedicated to the production of a food staple, and by the desire to complete the "nationalization of 'Projeto Jari'." Four years and US$ 13 million later, officers of the Companhia became convinced that "the degree of technological sophistication" built into the gigantic project was just "not compatible with rice farming in Amazonia," stating that this should be undertaken "with simple and inexpensive processes that rely more on people, less on machines" (Companhia do Jari, 1988).

The future, a cascade of uncertainties

The foregoing pages have touched upon some of the complex phys-ico-biotic phenomena inherent to Amazonian waters and wetlands, and have briefly exemplified the many human activities that impact on such ecosystems. The future of these remains obscure, deter-mined as it is by the interplay of a myriad factors – some not even identified.

Incertitudes regarding the destiny of Amazonian aquatic and wet-land ecosystems increase in an exponential-like manner as forecasts extend deeper into the future. An appropriate metaphor for this pro-gression might be that of a cascade of cause and effect (Roberts et al., 1980), a succession involving natural processes, human disruptions of them, and attempts to mitigate, prevent, or reverse the resulting environmental dysfunctions.

The uncertainties may be grouped into three, frequently inter-twined, categories. First, those properly addressed by the natural sci-ences. Second, those of a cognitive and behavioural nature, involving human perception of, and conduct toward, the environment. Finally, those that stem most directly from the dynamic of political life.

The scientific context

There is much uncertainty even in the establishment of a natural, un-disturbed base line from which to assess anthropic influences on Amazonia.[23] Not enough is known, for instance, regarding the circu-lation of the atmosphere, including the El Niño (ENSO), as it affects the region's climate; or regarding the dissimilar proportions of rain which, falling on different plant covers (e.g. rain forest, savanna), are returned to the atmosphere by evapotranspiration.

The possible role of humans in deflecting the evolution of ecosys-tems of which they are part should never be overlooked. One exam-ple of a chain of events in which people are believed to play an initia-tory role relates to the issue of sealevel rise, with its sequence of incertitudes *vis-à-vis* the future of Amazonian waters and wetlands. The hypothetical sequence starts with an anthropogenic buildup of atmospheric carbon dioxide and other so-called greenhouse gases, or GHGs, which increase mean surface air temperature, leading, in turn, to an eustatic rise of sealevel.

The upturn in atmospheric CO_2 is well established by measurements such as those taken at Mauna Loa. It is ascribed mainly to the use of fossil fuels, but also to deforestation, especially in the tropics. The extent to which removal of the selva contributes to a gain in CO_2 is a question fraught with incertitudes. Yet the answer is essential to determine whether potential damage to Amazonia by rising sealevel can be exacerbated by activities within the region.

In the second stage of the progression, although GHGs are widely believed to elevate the global temperature, there is disagreement as to the extent of the warming. Note, further, that some scholars even question whether the observed increase is not, in part at least, due to the location of weather stations in "urban heat islands," or simply to increased solar activity.

Although the first two stages in the postulated enchainment of cause and effect might impact on Amazonian ecosystems, e.g. through disruption of weather patterns, or plant responses to CO_2 enrichment,[24] it is the third stage that relates with greatest specificity to Amazonia's most productive ecosystems. Global warming, leading to the melting of ice sheets and glaciers, combined with the thermal expansion of oceanic waters, is generally predicted to bring about a perceptible rise in mean sealevel. Again, however, there is no consensus as to the amount and timing of the postulated change. Various scenarios recently proposed for the rise that might be expected by the end of next century are generally lower than those advanced in the mid-1980s. Changes then considered within the realm of possibility ranged, for example, from a conservative 56.2 cm to a very high 345.0 cm, as in Hoffman (1984). By contrast, most projections now under discussion suggest a rise of less than one metre by the year 2100. Although the forecasts are more subdued, projected rates of sealevel rise are "still very large," being, in fact roughly four times that estimated for the past century (Wigley and Raper, 1992). Moreover, it has been pointed out that, in the light of the many incertitudes woven into the projections, one may not exclude the possibility of a substantially greater rise. Given the minimal slope of the Amazon River valley, even a relatively modest sealevel rise would impact some low-lying wetlands, in terms of exacerbated flooding, while several coastal areas might experience saltwater intrusion.

A number of secondary effects may be anticipated. Waterlogging of soils, for instance, would favour anaerobic decay and thus contribute to an increase in atmospheric methane, the Amazon Basin already being responsible, it is said, for one-tenth of the world output of this gas (Devol et al., 1988; Mayer et al., 1982). Since methane is thought to be even more effective than CO_2 in producing the green-house effect, there is the possibility here of a positive feedback.

The postulated chain that starts with CO_2 emissions illustrates, sim-ultaneously, scientific uncertainties and the importance of appropri-ate programmatic decisions (e.g. clean air legislation), combined with the political resolve to have these implemented.

The programmatic context

The yardstick by which the "success" of a given undertaking is meas-ured reflects community understanding of, and values relative to, the environment. A giant hydroplant, possibly an outstanding civil engi-neering feat, may be a failure when assessed from the perspective of this paper, if it compromises the health of waters and wetlands. Or, take the promise seen in the application of biotechnology to crop plants as a means to increase the world's food supplies. Janzen (1988) has some sobering thoughts on this score. He conjectures whether genetic engineering, by producing crops capable of coping with environmental handicaps (such as are found on oligotrophic soils of Amazonian watersheds), might not provide the incentive to clear lands today "protected," as it were, by their very poverty. "Agroecosystem inviability," he submits, is "the most powerful conservation force in the tropics."

And so, misgivings and uncertainties are generated, not only by the stated goals of a programme, but also by the often unintentional effects of its implementation – assuming it is implemented. Certainly, there exists in Amazonia a conspicuous legacy of failed programmes that either came to naught or have produced results bearing no re-semblance to announced objectives. A few examples may be men-tioned.

The most tragic failure in Amazonia has been that of the govern-ment's "Indianist" policy. In the wake of a centuries-long history of ethnocide, the Indian Protection Service, set up in 1910, left a record of corruption and mismanagement that made a mockery of the agen-cy's name. It was replaced in 1968 by the National Indian Foundation (FUNAI), whose annals are hardly more inspiring. To give a current example, consider the delay in demarcating Brazil's portion of the tribal lands belonging to the Yanomami, which straddle the Brazil-ian–Venezuelan frontier. FUNAI has been incapable of protecting this nation against invading miners, guaranteeing the Indians their territory, their culture, their livelihood, indeed, their very lives. Only recently, Brazilian garimpeiros murdered a number of Yanomami tribespeople,[25] a crime that brought forth a powerful international outcry. As a consequence, President Itamar Franco was driven to institute an extraordinary ministry for the coordination of action in Amazonia, the Ministry of the Environment and Amazônia Legal.

In addition to being an outrageous violation of moral principles, the elimination or demoralization of Indian peoples has been accompanied by the replacement of sustainable land use with destructive exploitation. The forfeiture of know-how acquired in the course of millennia is a loss of no small consequence in the management of Amazonian watersheds.

Another unsuccessful government policy was mandated by the 1946 Constitution. This instrument ordained that, for at least 20 consecutive years, three per cent of tributary revenues be allocated to the implementation of a plan for economic *"valorização"* (increase in value) of Amazonia. However, it was only in 1953 that the operational area, *Amazônia Legal,* was defined, a blueprint for development adopted, and the Superintendency for the Plan for Economic Valorization of Amazonia (SPVEA) created. A balance-sheet of this agency's activities, drawn up more than a decade later by the then Superintendent, describes a "chaotic" situation that had prevailed since its institution, a "vast field of illicit deals and irresponsibilities under the most varied forms that resulted in the complete discredit of the organism" (Cavalcanti, 1967).

Extinguished in 1966, SPVEA was replaced by the Superintendency for the Development of Amazonia (SUDAM). This entity became identified with the use of fiscal incentives to promote cattle ranching in Amazonia, with a view to the export of beef. The ease with which big business, mostly based in São Paulo, was able to reduce federal tax liabilities by investing the corresponding savings in projects approved by SUDAM resulted in deforestation at an unprecedented scale. The tax incentive programme (see, for instance, Mahar, 1989) has been the single most important cause of watershed degradation. Forests were felled, burned, put into pasture, and, only too often, abandoned, leaving millions of hectares of debased and unproductive soils.

During the 1970s, the government mounted an all-out effort to integrate Amazonia into the Brazilian body politic. This was the Programme for National Integration, of which the Transamazônica and Cuiabá–Santarém highways were to be the cornerstone. Construction of a transportation network intensified deforestation of watersheds by land-seekers, notably large-scale ranchers or would-be ranchers (Fearnside, 1993; Smith, 1982), and directly affected the streams intersected by the roads.

A further instance of failed strategy is the so-called "Polamazônia programme," established in 1974 to promote "Poles of growth," for instance *polos agropecuários, polos agrominerais* (MINTER, 1976) – a concept already applied to Brazil in the 1950s (see, e.g., Boudeville, 1957, 1973). No more than lip service was paid to the cultivation of land connoted by the first part (*agro*) of each paired modifier. Meanwhile, the region's alleged vocation for *pecuária*, i.e. to be a major producer of beef cattle, has been disproved.[26] As to the *polos agrominerais*, impressive ore bodies were viewed less as levers for long-term, sustainable development of neighbouring areas than as assets to confront a massive foreign debt.

A final example of nugatory government plans is one created in 1988 and aimed specifically at environmental issues: the *Nossa Natureza* ("Our Nature") programme. The title is reminiscent of the nationalist slogan, "The petroleum is ours." Indeed, the agenda was hurriedly crafted to silence foreign denunciations of Brazil's handling of the environment, particularly in Amazonia, by demonstrating the country's determination to confront the issue on its own terms. But, when the National Environmental Council reviewed the Nossa Natureza package, it pointed out several flaws, such as "technical and juridical inappropriatenesses," "hurried elaboration," "conceptual confusion," and the "inadmissibly centralized cast of some of the projects" (*Folha de São Paulo*, 1989).

The political context

Domestic programmes that affect the quality of Amazonian waters and wetlands have, of course, been decided rather less often in the arena of scientific ideas than in the political market place.[27] Despite the volatility of politics, certain lines of force have persisted in Brazil. One is a pervasive sensitivity in relation to sovereignty over an isolated and sparsely settled backwater. As a consequence, policy has often been reactive to real or perceived moves by international players (Sternberg, 1987b). Even after independence in 1822, substantial portions of Brazilian Amazonia were unsuccessfully claimed by France and England. Among other nineteenth-century territorial

149

ambitions focused on the region[28] was one that obsessed Matthew Fontaine Maury, Superintendent of the US Observatory and Hydrographic Office (Sternberg, 1987b). Such foreign designs upon Amazonia, a legitimate concern of Brazilians in the past, are used to justify today's unceasingly invoked apprehensions – whether genuine or feigned.

With the Amazon problematic seen through the prism of national security, the role of the military looms large. Thus, the 1985 "North Trough Project" proposed additional military outposts in the 150-km wide frontier zone or belt, *Faixa de Fronteiras*, that hugs the international boundary from the point where the Amazon River enters Brazil to the Atlantic, a distance of some 6,500 km (Sternberg, 1987b). The rhetoric can be fevered: José Sarney, when president, was quoted as exhorting the armed forces to defend Amazonia, so as to prevent it from being transformed by long-existing covetousness "into an internationalized Persian Gulf" (Teixeira, 1989). And General Antenor de Santa Cruz Abreu, one-time military commandant of Amazonia, reportedly declared that, in the event of the region's internationalization, the army would transform it into a new Viet Nam. At this, Governor Gilberto Mestrinho of Amazonas state is quoted as announcing that he would be the first to take up arms and enlist in the general's forces (*O Liberal*, 1991).

One of the more intemperate voices among officials in the region has been that of Mestrinho, who would like to roll back all legislation protecting the environment and indigenous populations. His proposed "Amazonian Code," after expressing respect for the environment "in which we all live," was designed to repeal the entire federal legislation involving parks, ecological stations, and Indian reservations.

Nothing illustrates better the unpredictability of Amazonia's future, given its dependence on domestic politics, than the mercurial administration of President Fernando Collor de Mello. Perhaps wishing to demonstrate to external critics that Brazil's handling of the environment would be different in his administration, he appointed as secretary for the environment José Lutzenberger, "one of Brazil's ... most vociferous environmentalists" (Bonalume, 1990). Collor did take several praiseworthy measures, but the news that he had invited Mestrinho to be his personal advisor in environmental matters was commented on with irony by the latter's political opponents in Manaus (*Jornal do Comércio*, 1991). Then, less than three months prior to the 1992 United Nations Conference on Environment and Development in Rio de Janeiro, Collor dismissed both Lutzenberger and the head of the environmental agency. Within months, Collor himself was indicted on the charges of corruption that led to his impeachment.

Uncertainties of political origin regarding Amazonian ecology do not stem from domestic vagaries alone. They also may be related to the internal politics of other countries, when these impact on global ecosystems individually, or when, as members of the world community, they support or oppose international environmental agreements. Furthermore, the outcome of domestic politics in nations who are major contributors to multilateral funding agencies can influence the priorities set by such bodies.

Observe, for instance, the result of the 1992 elections in the United States. As an aftermath, the White House, in an action that could conceivably affect Amazonian ecosystems, reversed the position of the preceding chief executive and gave its full support to two recently-drawn-up international treaties. One was to reduce carbon dioxide emissions worldwide (the United States being the largest emitter); the other, to protect biological diversity. It would be consistent with the positions embraced by the current administration *vis-à-vis* the environment if it were to urge the World Bank and other multilateral lending agencies to finance only ecologically sound projects. Although the performance of such institutions in respect to environment and native rights has improved, past policies bear considerable blame for the breakdown of ecosystems and human communities in Amazonia. A notable example is the Polonoroeste programme, financed by the World Bank. Had it been preceded by, or combined with, an agrarian reform capable of anchoring Brazil's destitute and drifting rural population (see, e.g., CEM, 1986) the outcome might have been different. But in the absence of such an undertaking, this "pole of growth" was an arrant failure. The reconstruction and paving of the Cuiabá–Porto Velho road merely opened up the state of Rondônia and adjacent areas in Mato Grosso to an unprecedented and devastating land rush (Coy, 1988).[29]

Extraregional linkages

The issue of agrarian reform is an example of the many ties between Amazonian concerns and those of Brazil as a whole. A more equitable access to land, nationwide,[30] would tend to relieve the pressure on the area's ecosystems.

151

Another type of extraregional articulation is created by pro-grammes intended to recruit Amazonian ecosystems as suppliers to outside markets, both domestic and foreign. Given the possibility of changes in demand, they introduce further uncertainties into the environmental equation.

An example is the drive for energy. Part of the hydroelectric power produced in Amazonia, at considerable social and environmental cost to local inhabitants, is destined for densely populated areas such as Brazil's north-east and south-east (Sternberg, 1986b, 1988b). A na-tional energy-conserving policy would favour the environment of Amazonia by decreasing the call for energy of whatever kind (e.g. hydroelectric, petroleum, biofuels) generated there.

Moreover, several regions envisaged as recipients of Amazonian power are capable of producing substantial amounts themselves, in ways that would reduce their need to import. To illustrate: prelimi-nary studies show that the highest potential windpower in the coun-try exists along the east–west section of the Nordeste coast (Funda-ção Padre Leonel Franca, 1988; Picanço, 1993). Primitive windmills made from carnauba palm stems have long been employed in pump-ing sea water in the area's salterns. Now, it is believed that wind plants using the new variable-speed, computerized turbines may prove cost-effective in the near future. Furthermore, favoured by a relatively modest cloud cover and a high number of hours of sun-shine, the Nordeste receives abundant solar radiant energy and is also a candidate for solar-thermal and photovoltaic technologies (Eletrobrás, 1992).

Since conversion to pasture, designed to promote beef production for extra-regional consumers, has been the major cause of deforesta-tion, shifting dietary patterns in putative markets may be of direct significance to the future of Amazonian ecosystems. Generated by medical concerns, there has been a trend in the developed countries away from red meat,[31] accompanied by a sharp rise in the consump-tion of poultry products (Brown, 1993). Greater use of native animal species that provided the Amerinds with a bountiful source of protein and probably are more efficient converters of the natural vegetation may represent an additional disincentive to deforestation. A form of rational cropping of wildlife, or game ranching – perhaps as a supple-ment to the raising of water buffalo, fish, and turtle – would seem par-ticularly promising in floodplain environments. The drive for artifi-cially established grasslands also would be weakened by a partial turning away from animal protein itself, on the part of prospective consumers of Amazonian beef. Along these lines, McDonald's, with its world-wide franchises, is testing a vegetable hamburger that is a mix of potato, peas, carrots, corn, onion, and spices.

Among the extraregional linkages that stem from Amazonia's actual or potential role as supplier to the outside, one commodity is central to this paper, and deserves some additional comments.

The primordial element

Water has been treated here as the habitat for aquatic lifeforms and as an essential component of wetland ecosystems. However, it must also be considered as a substance detached from its ecosystemic relationships – a separate resource in its own right, vital for human consumption, for irrigated agriculture, and as industrial raw material. Water is an increasingly scarce and disputed commodity, and not only in arid and semi-arid regions.[32] For some time it has been reasonably assumed that "water will become an item in foreign trade" (L'vovich, 1979). In fact, one geographer wondered if the "capacity [of Brazil's Amazonia] to sell great quantities of fresh water" should not be listed among the region's resources (Gourou, 1982). In conjectures such as these, even contiguity of donor and recipient no longer appears as a necessary condition for the transfer. Thus, according to a hydrologist who spoke off the record, one oil company has inquired about the chemical quality of the Amazon River water near Santarém, with the idea of transporting it by tanker to Aruba (Anon., 1984).[33]

Actually, there are areas adjacent to the Amazon Basin where water is already at a premium, for example the Peruvian coast and the Nordeste of Brazil. For such regions, derivation of Amazonian waters has, in fact, been effected (Peru), or is being contemplated (Nordeste). A plan to import water into the latter drought-prone region has surfaced at intervals since the early nineteenth century (Sternberg, 1967). Traditionally, the proposed donor has been the São Francisco River, draining an area of 650,000 km^2 in eastern Brazil. With the implementation of major hydroelectric and irrigation projects, and a growing urban, rural, and industrial demand for water within this basin, the idea seemed increasingly unrealistic (Pessoa, 1989).[34] In fact, some recent proposals envisaged a transfusion from eastern Amazonia (fig. 6.14), specifically from the basin of the Tocantins (Budweg, 1981; DNAEE/DCRH, 1983) – despite the fact that the energy establishment has slated this river to become a stairway of reservoirs and hydroelectric plants (Sternberg, 1981).

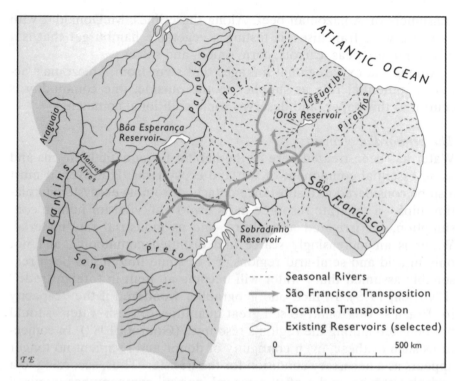

Figure 6.14 **Suggested diversion of waters from the Tocantins basin into Brazil's
semi-arid Nordeste. The idea of transporting water from the São Francisco River,
which rises in the humid eastern highlands of Brazil, into the dry north-east was put
forward in the early nineteenth century. However, with the implementation of major
hydroelectric and irrigation projects and the general growth of water demand in the
valley of the proposed donor, some planners have been turning further afield for a
source, namely to the Tocantins – although it too is slated for extensive hydropower
development (Sternberg, 1981). Several schemes have been advanced that involve a
combination of impoundments, pumping, and gravity flow through canals, tunnels,
and river beds. One plan would carry water from the Tocantins drainage through a
reversed Sono River to the Preto, an affluent of the São Francisco, and into the Sobradinho Reservoir (34 billion m³), thus boosting the volume that could be diverted
from the São Francisco. Water derived from this river would be distributed through
so-called peripheral canals to the headwaters of streams in the droughty backlands,
such as the Poti, the Jaguaribe, or the Piranhas. Another plan would tap the Tocantins drainage by reversing the direction of the Manoel Alves and leading the diverted
flow into the catchment area of the Boa Esperança Reservoir (5 billion m³) on the
Parnaíba River. Part of the Tocantins water thus diverted might also be relayed to
the Sobradinho Reservoir (Budweg, 1981; DNAEE/DCRH, 1983).**

The intercourse of ideas

To conclude these examples of uncertainties resulting from extraregional influences, one might speculate whether adoption of, or

154

changes in, environmental management practices elsewhere could inspire emulation in Amazonia. Take the recent case of a remarkable turnabout in the Netherlands, the country most closely identified with the drainage of wetlands. Concerns raised by a decline in plant and animal species led to a 1990 government plan aimed at increasing nature areas by 250,000 hectares in 30 years, when they are to exceed 20 per cent of the national territory. Where people have been dyking and draining for centuries, substantial areas of impoverished farm-land will be converted to wetlands (Netherlands, 1990, 1993a, 1993b). Will such a remarkable reversal prompt second thoughts relative to schemes for Amazonia's wetlands?

The health of Amazonian waters and wetlands might also be favoured by borrowing from an idea now being tested in Costa Rica (Janzen, 1991). In what has been called a "dollars-for-diversity" transaction, Merck & Co. Inc. pays the Central American country for the opportunity to search out promising natural compounds in its forests. Should a marketable product result, the host country will benefit from royalties and the transfer of pertinent technology (Joyce, 1991; Roberts, 1992). This procedure is in line with the Biodiversity Convention that resulted from the 1992 Earth Summit, recognizing the rights of a country to its genetic resources (Simpson and Sedjo, 1992), and thus supporting such types of arrangements.

A broader picture: Environmental perspectives in Brazil

Some uncertainties specific to the future of Amazonian waters and wetlands embody, to a degree, uncertainties regarding Brazil's over-all approach to the environment and indigenous people. Actually, there are no monolithic views on these issues, only a number of unresolved contradictions.

Integrity of ecosystems: Economic and ecological evaluations

For their health, waters and wetlands require, in addition to the soundness of related ecosystems, workable societal institutions, since dysfunctions along the human/environment interface (e.g. inequitable land tenure) often lead to a breakdown of natural systems.

The benefits offered by a forested catchment area in Amazonia derive from its substance and from its function. The former may be exemplified by a supply of lumber; the latter, by the damping of run-off. It is through its functioning that the selva, in its wholeness and diversity, contributes to the quality of waters and wetlands. Commonly, however, the forest is appraised on the basis of a narrowly defined economic use – and this is often synonymous with its demise. An evaluation that considers the system's more comprehensive worth – for example as repository of germplasm or as producer of marketable non-timber products – argues more forcefully in favour of appropriate safeguards. Sampling a species-rich forest near Iquitos, Peters, Gentry, and Mendelsohn (1989) are among students who maintain that the financial benefits from the continued harvest of non-wood resources exceed by far those that would accrue from logging the tract, converting it to pasture, or planting it to *Gmelina arborea* for the production of pulp, as was done in the Jari project.

In order to publicize the existence of non-wood products from the Amazon forest and simultaneously provide income for forest dwellers, some effort has been made to promote the use abroad of such resources (e.g. Pará nuts, in confectionery; and Pará nut oil, in cosmetics).[35] A recent bid was also made to showcase the assets of Amazonia's aquatic domain. Fish such as the already mentioned tambaqui, the tucunaré (*Cichla* spp.), and the pescada (*Plagioscion* spp.), were flown frozen to the United States. Here, they were prepared by renowned chefs for a benefit in favour of an organization dedicated to the conservation of tropical rain forests. The rationale behind the exercise was that a larger market would lead to the development of fish farms in Amazonia (Fabricant, 1993). Laudable intentions, but caution is called for: when new roads linked Amazonian rivers to several major cities in Brazil, thus opening a domestic market for the region's piscifauna, gross overfishing resulted.

Environmental quality and economic growth: Opposition or opportunity?

Does this inauspicious outcome of making riverine resources accessible to markets demonstrate, one more time, an irreconcilable conflict? From the Greek word *oikos*, house, have come, on the one hand, ecology, and on the other, economics. It is ironic that knowledge and management of the habitat should have become almost antithetical. However, where some see opposition, others see opportunity. The idea is beginning to sink in that environmental activities can, in themselves, bring financial benefits and create jobs. Carneiro (1993), writing in Brazil's most prestigious economic monthly, hails the "perfect marriage" between ecology and economy, and envisions the opening up, to joint-venture companies, of promising new markets in other developing countries. He concludes that economic development not only is compatible with strict environmental standards but could actually benefit from them, while the resultant business opportunities may even reveal an unexplored source of foreign exchange. Simultaneously, one of Brazil's ten largest conglomerates, with world-girdling engineering operations, has launched a subsidiary entirely devoted to environmental technology, targeting an international market (*Odebrecht Informa*, 1993). Such fresh viewpoints should be placed in the context of often contradictory – and evolving – mindsets in Brazil regarding the environment.

Evolution of environmental awareness in Brazil

The last decades have witnessed mounting concern among many Brazilians regarding the deterioration of the environment.[36] At first, attention focused on those insults to the habitat that offended the senses. In the eighties, concepts such as "biodiversity" and "ozone layer" came into their own. Belching smokestacks, formerly featured as a metaphor for progress, inviting investment in industry, became in due course a symbol for degradation of the milieu.

The United Nations Conference on the Human Environment, held in Stockholm, June 1972, and the UN Conference on Environment and Development, convened in Rio de Janeiro twenty years later, provide two points of reference to gauge the unfolding of Brazil's official position on the environment.

During the first session of the Preparatory Committee for the 1972 Conference, the Permanent Representative of Brazil to the United Nations claimed that his government had always followed policies "consistent with ... a safe and ecologically balanced human environment for present and future generations" (Brasil, 1972).

A Brazilian geographer, invited to represent his country on the Preparatory Committee, in a report to the Minister of External Relations, stressed the need "to leave aside [such] frivolous and ... complacent pronouncements." He argued that they "do not resist the evidence of the facts [and] must give way to a realistic diagnosis and to a serene account of what has been done and what is left to do ... for the environment" (Sternberg, 1970). The tenor of government statements remained unchanged, however, before, during, and after the 1972 Conference. One of many made by the aforementioned Permanent Representative was typical. Addressing the United Nations, he

157

cautioned against using "the environment ... to enforce economic stagnation, and 'hands-off' measures designed [*sic*] to perpetuate a situation of economic and social injustice, to the detriment of the developing countries" (Brasil, 1972).

At the opening of the Conference, Brazil's Minister of the Interior, speaking as Head of Delegation, made light of environmental hazards: "solutions will arrive in time to avoid dangers in some remote future. A sensible and objective attitude will prevent us from seriously believing in threats to humanity presented in an exaggerated and emotional manner." Then, a warning against restrictions to unimpeded sovereignty over natural resources: "international cooperation ... should not ... be hampered by ... mechanisms that ... limit and dilute the ... sovereignty and independence of States" (Cavalcanti, 1972).

During the Stockholm Conference and related meetings, few if any specifics regarding Brazil's numerous ecological problems were discussed. The accent was on denial and sovereignty.

The different attitude with which the government prepared for the 1992 Earth Summit in Rio de Janeiro evidences progress in the willingness of at least certain sectors of government to face up to ecological deterioration. This time, 45,000 copies of a 172-page publication containing draft reports were circulated a year in advance for comments (Brasil, 1991). Although of unequal quality, it contains several candid assessments of environmental problems.

A career foreign service officer, then Secretary General for Foreign Policy (Ministry of External Relations), went on record regarding Brazil's position on environment and development:

the international community has a right to be concerned by the violation of human rights and by the damage done to the environment, wherever such may occur. In dealing with these and other issues, Brazil no longer resorts to allegations of sovereignty to deflect criticism. Instead, it shoulders its responsibilities, conscious that its actions have repercussions for the whole planet. (Azambuja, 1990)

Significantly, in the period between the two international conferences, elected representatives of the Brazilian people in 1988 enacted what may be the world's "greenest" constitution. This affirmed that "all persons have the right to an ecologically-balanced environment, it being the duty of the public power and the community to defend it and preserve it for present and future generations." According to article 5, "any citizen is a legitimate party in bringing ...

suit to annul ... actions detrimental ... to the environment." Such litigation was facilitated by the stipulation that, "except in case of proven bad faith, the plaintiff shall be exempt from court costs and other burdens of a losing litigant" (Brasil, 1993b).

Given the assumption that, by and large, traditional forms of land management practised by Indians in the areas they occupy are generally conducive to environmental integrity,[37] it is relevant to note that the 1988 constitution guaranteed, to an unprecedented extent, the protection of Amerindian tribal lands.

However, with the new constitution, new and troubling uncertainties. Would there be the political will to stand up to the powerful interests that opposed its precepts regarding the environment and the indigenes?

It is axiomatic that legislation lacking grass-roots support is doomed to failure. The 1988 constitution's provision for citizen involvement in the protection of the environment could only remain a dead letter without informed, committed – and assertive – members of the public. Recent years did see a groundswell of green militancy develop across the country. In fact, impatient with accomplishments that remained on paper, ordinary people have shown anger at what they see as foot-dragging by the political establishment in terms of practical action. The denunciation displayed on the T-shirt of a young woman encountered in 1991 on a street in Itacoatiara, a small Amazon riverfront town, is an illustration (fig. 6.15).

The unpredictability of circumstances having the potential to affect Amazonia's environmental well-being was brought home once again by an event that occurred in June 1992, ironically during the Earth Summit. An alleged episode of debauchery involving an internationally known Native Brazilian activist received sensational coverage by the press. The population at large already had been exposed to the information that certain Indian groups were given to conspicuous consumption, paid for by selling off their reservations' natural resources. Something of a backlash against the rights of Native Brazilians was stirred up, serving the objectives of powerful interests that aspired to exploit the tribal lands: ranchers, loggers, hydropower developers, miners – not to mention all those who beat the drum of national security.

Appended to the 1988 constitution proper is an article providing for its revision five years after promulgation. This clause opened the way for a startling amount of political manoeuvring aimed at repealing or watering down the protection so recently enacted in favour of

Figure 6.15 **Development of environmental awareness at the grass roots, and the ensuing impatience with what is perceived as the faineancy of government, may be illustrated by the message on the T-shirt of this young woman encountered in 1991 in a small Amazon riverbank town. These are the harsh words levelled at the politicos in the nation's capital:**

Animals of Amazonia (becoming extinct)
Animals of the Pantanal* (becoming extinct)
– Those in Brasília are well, thank you

*A vast wetland in west-central Brazil, known for the abundance and diversity of its fauna.

the environment and indigenous people. Among the 17,246 revisionary proposals presented by lawmakers in Brasília, a number reflected such intentions, usually encrypted in high-minded concern for the "national good."

Take the attempt to deprive Native Brazilians of land officially recognized as theirs. It rested on three major contentions: that the reservations represented a disproportionally large area for a small number of Indians,[38] that they prevented the economic use of resources vital to the nation, and that they imperilled Brazilian sovereignty over the Faixa de Fronteira. The then Minister for the Environment and Amazônia Legal, Rubens Ricupero, in an incisive piece on the op-ed page of the influential *Jornal do Brasil*, challenged these "unfounded arguments" (Ricupero, 1994). The former ambassador to the United States disputed the claim that the land attributed to the Native Brazilians is unreasonably extensive, finding it "ironic, to say the least, in the country of the *latifundio* par excellence, where owners of ranches larger than European countries are not rare." And he asked: "Does anybody believe that if the reservations were extinguished, [their holdings] would be distributed to landless farm people?" Addressing the other allegations, Ambassador Ricupero pointed out that nothing in the constitution prevented the utilization of the reservations' natural resources, with Indians sharing in the benefits; and, regarding the issue of sovereignty, that the law had always allowed for intervention in the tribal lands, in the case of a foreign threat – something which, he noted, has never materialized.

The outcome of the constitutional revision in 1994 may itself serve here as the final illustration of unpredictability. Congress, shaken by hearings on corruption involving a number of legislators, frequently immobilized by lack of quorum, and driven by the politics of an election year, managed to approve, within the prescribed deadline, no more than six amendments, having essentially failed to carry through the announced overhaul.

Conclusions

The countless imponderables, only briefly exemplified in this paper, that will determine the future of Amazonia's waters and wetlands, suggest the need for a conceptual framework within which to attempt the identification and evaluation of a whole spectrum of uncertainties. Such an analysis is a "critical component" of all risk assessments (Kimerle and Smith, 1993), and, therefore, basic to decision-making. The purpose of a prospective identification of hazards – combined with a postmortem of past mistakes – is to assist in taking stock of potential problems before they balloon into full-fledged, unmanageable crises. Clearly, such a purpose would be defeated by a consistently optimistic "best-case scenario" approach, in which the expectation always is that "solutions will arrive in time" (Cavalcanti, 1972).

It is true that, sometimes, when uncertainties regarding the effects of a particular policy finally give way to observed facts, an unexpectedly favourable outcome is revealed.[39] An example, of a physico-biotic kind, comes from an opencut bauxite mine near the Trombetas River. It would be hard to imagine a more discouraging site for re-

161

vegetation than the once-forested terrain, from which the ore has been strip-mined. Yet different treatments, selected by trial and error, have been used in an attempt to establish native and exotic species. There is considerable spatial variation in the degree of success obtained, apparently a function of the methods used in removing the overburden, excavating the ore, and restoring the surface (Pereira and Knowles, 1985; Ferraz, 1991; Ruivo et al., 1991). Nevertheless, it has been surprising and encouraging to observe, in the course of successive visits, that deer and birds have returned to the revegetated area. Whether the closed nutrient cycling typical of the rain forest can be re-established in a reasonable length of time, once it has been broken, remains to be seen.

That public opinion concerning Amazonian environments and native peoples is divided and in a state of flux adds to the uncertainties regarding the region's waters and wetlands and leaves little ground for complacency. At this point, the unequivocal positions taken at a high level of career officialdom by Ambassadors Azambuja and Ricupero assume special significance. To the extent that reality catches up with, rather than falls further behind, their statesmanlike affirmations, prospects improve of a new stature for Brazil in terms of earth stewardship. And of more sanguine expectations for irreplaceable ecosystems.

Acknowledgements

The paper is part of a research project dealing with the Brazilian humid tropics. In the course of this long-term endeavour, financial support for various aspects of the study has been received from the National Science Foundation; the joint Committee on Latin American Studies of the Social Science Research Council and the American Council of Learned Societies; the John Simon Guggenheim Foundation; and the University of California at Berkeley (Center for Latin American Studies and Committee on Research).

I am indebted to Carlos A. Nobre, Instituto Nacional de Pesquisas Espaciais, for the computation, at my request, of average rainfall over the Brazilian Amazon; to Marciana Leite Ribeiro, of the same Institute, for publications and references; to Ingrid Radkey, BioSciences Library, UCB, for help in the retrieval of pertinent literature; to Steve Schwartzman, Environmental Defense Fund, for sharing updated information on amendments to Brazil's 1988 Constitution; to John Cadman, Eduardo de F. Madeira, and co-workers, Eletronorte, Brasília, as well as to E. G. M. Cesar, Projeto de Hidrologia e Climatologia da Amazônia, Belém, for hydrological, climatological, and other data; to Portobrás, Manaus, for successive updates of raw data from the stream gauge on the Rio Negro; to Geraldo de Macedo Pinheiro, for his help, over the years, in obtaining information from sources in Manaus; to the late Antonio Vizeu da Costa Lima and his family, for hospitality and assistance during many field seasons in Pará state; to Oliver H. Knowles, for his guidance during my visits to the Mineração Rio Norte, on the Trombetas River; to Tadeu Veiga, for his good offices in Brasília; to Zhong Gongfu, Guanzhou, for accompanying me on visits to the Zhu Jiang delta and for introducing me to the intricacies of the dyke-and-pond system; to Orman Granger, for giving me the benefit of his knowledge of meteorological and climatological literature. I thank Elmer Prata Salomão, Director of the Departamento Nacional da Produção Mineral, Brasília and the Instituto Nacional de Pesquisas da Amazônia, Manaus, for logistic support.

Very special thanks are due to David R. Brillinger, who has given generously of his time and statistical expertise in the trend analysis of the water stage data.

Finally, it is a pleasure to acknowledge my gratitude to my wife, Carolina da Silveira Lobo Sternberg, for her untiring support and collaboration in all phases of the undertaking. The paper benefited stylistically from constructive comments by Herbert G. Baker and James J. Parsons.

Credit for the cartographic work goes to Adrienne Morgan and Tim Eisler.

Notes

1. According to Brazilian usage, the designation Rio Amazonas is applied to the main stem below the mouth of the Rio Negro; upstream, as far as the border between Brazil and Peru, the river is named Solimões; and, beyond that, Marañon. In this paper, Amazon River or, simply, Amazon, is used to designate the Marañon–Solimões–Amazonas continuum; and Amazonas River or Amazonas, to specify the section below the embouchure of the Negro. The name Amazonia (*adj.* Amazonian) is used variously: to designate a "natural" region, closely identified with the rain forest; as equivalent to the official "North Region," a politico-administrative division that comprises the states of Rondônia, Acre, Amazonas, Roraima, Pará, Amapá, and Tocantins; and, finally, to define an operational region, "Amazônia Legal," which, in addition to these states, includes Mato Grosso and part of Maranhão (Brasil, 1992).

2. Such an outflow is equivalent to more than four times the mean flow of the Congo, and to about ten times that of the Mississippi. It accounts for between 15 and 20 per cent of all fresh water passed into the world's oceans.

3. On the *campo cerrado* (*cerrado*, for short), as the savanna woodlands and associated grasslands of Brazil are called, see chapter 5 in Cole, 1986.

4. According to a recent computation that used data from 168 stations keyed to a 2° latitude–longitude grid (Nobre, 1992).

5. There are now attempts, using satellite images, to quantify the sediment concentration of waters by their reflectance (Mertes, Smith, and Adams, 1993).

6. Because the Amazon basin is asymmetric in relation to its axis, a smaller part of its catchment lies north of the equinoctial line; furthermore, much of this area is actually subject to an equatorial rather than a tropical rainfall regime. The annual rise and fall of the water in the lower Amazon is, thus, most clearly influenced by the markedly seasonal discharge of its far-flung southern tributaries.

7. Mertes (1993) calculates that, depending on the magnitude of the inundation, approximately 60 to 80 per cent of the main stem floodplain in Brazil is influenced *directly* by the overflow from the Solimões–Amazonas. According to her analysis, the area thus affected in the reach between Vargem Grande and Óbidos amounts, on average, to *c.* 40,000 km^2.

8. Emílio Goeldi (after whom the famous Museu Paraense in Belém was later named), having travelled upriver in the early years of the century, is reported to have remarked on the dissemination of malaria by steamboats plying the waters from Belém to the upper Amazon. Although this region was a "paradise" for the vector, in the absence of the plasmo-

dium the disease is said to have been unknown, becoming endemic in the latter part of the nineteenth century (Lima, 1937).

9. For a pedological study of archaeological black earth in the region of Oriximiná, Pará, see Kern, 1988.

10. See, for instance, Roosevelt, 1993.

11. Despite official protection by law, illegal capture of the manatee continues. See *Sirenews*, 1991a and 1991b.

12. The International Union for the Conservation of Nature and Natural Resources lists *Podocnemis expansa* as in danger of extinction and *Trichechus inunguis* as vulnerable (IUCN, 1990). This means, according to IUCN categories, that, if the causal factors continue operating, the giant river turtle is unlikely to survive, while the manatee is likely to move into the endangered category in the near future.

13. Local subsidence may have played a role in producing exceptionally low-lying sections in the recently established Mamirauá ecological station, situated within more than one million hectares of continuous wetlands, whose forests have been described by Ayres (1993) in the first volume of a promised series of studies concerning the reserve.

14. A vast area targeted for special government incentives, located north of parallel 8°S and between the Amazon, Xingu, and Parnaíba rivers, covering part of the states of Pará, Tocantins, and Maranhão.

15. See also the special issue of *Pará Desenvolvimento* (1987), devoted to the question of charcoal and iron smelting in Amazonia.

16. It has been said that the Cali cartel, dominant in the global cocaine trade since the demise of Pablo Escobar of the Medellín cartel, is preparing the transfer of some of its processing laboratories to Brazil (Adams, 1993).

17. A recent survey of Brazil's fluctuating population of garimpeiros put their number at some 300,000 (400,000, if the temporarily inactive are included). Those operating in Amazonia were estimated at 180,000 (Brasil, 1993c).

18. In mid-1994, while a number of dragas had been moved to other rivers and many had been abandoned as rusting scrap-iron on the banks of the Madeira, some garimpeiros attempted to dredge the rich, and virtually unworked, environmentally protected 5-km stretch in front of Porto Velho.

19. In only partial settlement of charges brought by Alaskan residents and fishermen, seeking billions of dollars in damages, the Exxon Corporation in July 1994 agreed to pay US$20 million to native villagers who claim that the spill ruined their hunting grounds. Subsequently, a Federal Court jury awarded a $5 billion punitive award to 34,000 fishermen and other Alaskans (*New York Times*, 1994).

20. A recent and succinct statement regarding the status of the project in Brazil: "no plans are under way, in conjunction with neighbouring countries, for the connection of hydrographic basins" (Brasil, 1993a). A symposium entitled "Linking the Great Rivers of South America," held on 12 March 1993 in Washington DC under the auspices of the Inter-American Development Bank, was, according to several participants, an exercise in futility.

21. See the special issue of *Amazoniana* (1993) devoted to Careiro Island.

22. Similarly, in some wetland areas of China, such as the delta of the Zhu Jiang, an artificial ecosystem of millenary tradition incorporates the water of the saturated land in a productive form of land use (Ruddle et al., 1983; Zhong Gongfu, 1989, 1990).

23. The "uncertainties" discussion group of a workshop dealing with scientific issues in risk assessment recently identified three general categories of uncertainty that affect all assessments. They are, with excerpted examples, as follows: (1) measurement uncertainties, e.g. insufficient observations, difficulties in making physical measurements; (2) conditions of observation, e.g. spatiotemporal variability in climate and ecosystem structure; (3) inadequacies of models, e.g. lack of, or insufficient, knowledge concerning underlying mechanisms. The consensus of the group was that the third category of uncertainties was often the most important (Kimerle and Smith, 1993).

24. See, for instance, Phillips and Gentry (1994), who suggest a possible link between increased turnover in tropical forests and CO_2 buildup.

25. The slaughter took place on 14 August 1993, on Venezuelan soil, near the border. Figures for the number of Indians massacred range from 16 to 100 (RAN, 1993).

    A combined operation of the Venezuelan National Guard and Air Force that surrounded 136 Brazilian garimpeiros in 1994, killing one and wounding several others, gave rise to a minor diplomatic crisis (*O Globo*, 1994a). Meanwhile, the Colombian army deported 300 Brazilian gold miners (*O Globo*, 1994b) and, as a result of lengthy negotiations, Surinam is said to have repatriated another group of imprisoned garimpeiros.

26. In two very similar single-page statements, one focusing on Amazonia, the other on Central America, Uhl and Parker (1986a, 1986b) attempt to establish a ratio between tonnage of hamburger meat produced and area of rain forest converted to pasture. The underpinning calculations were admittedly crude: the authors recognize "that values might range from half to double those used in their papers." Subsequently, Goodland (1990) picked up the "hamburger connection" and, extrapolating from these calculations, concluded that "the Brazilian government could have acquired nearly two metric tons of foreign beef for the same amount of capital it spent subsidizing the production of 1 metric ton of Amazon beef." Without underwriting the assumptions and computations of these speculative papers, the essential point remains valid, namely that "the amount of rainforest for even a simple hamburger is not trivial" (Uhl and Parker, 1986b).

27. The ubiquitous intrusion of the political into the scientific sphere was recently illustrated, in connection with the carbon cycle, by a scientist at the Australian National University: "There is the political angle – you might want to discover a substantial CO_2 sink in your region if this can be used to offset industrial emissions of CO_2; on the other hand, this may bring with it restrictions on land use with concomitant economic penalties" (Taylor, 1993).

28. Repeated attempts to lay hands on Amazonia, made by Leopold II, King of the Belgians (best known for his appropriation of the Congo), have only recently come to light (Sternberg, 1988a).

29. Vice-President (at the time Senator) Al Gore (1992), criticizing the way "the World Bank, the International Monetary Fund, regional development banks, and national lending authorities" determine the kinds of assistance given, wrote:

    the World Bank should halt the funds that subsidize the building of roads through the Amazon rain forest as long as there are no credible safeguards to stop what has been until now the primary use of such roads: providing direct access to the heart of the forest for chain saws and torches.

    However, closer to home, one candidate for the 1994 presidential election in Brazil made the controversial highway link of Acre state to the Pacific Ocean a priority issue in his campaign (*A Gazeta*, 1994).

30. According to the latest published farm census (1985), holdings having more than 1,000 hectares constitute less than one per cent of the number of agricultural operations in Brazil, but occupy 43.73 per cent of the nation's farmland. By contrast, farms with less than 10 hectares represent 52.83 per cent of all agricultural units, but total only 2.66 per cent of Brazil's agrarian space (Brasil, 1990). Meanwhile, the increasing militancy of an impatient landless population ("invade, resist, and produce") is translated into a growing number of *invasões* (seizures of property) by the *sem terra*, making for potentially explosive situations (*Jornal do Comércio* 1994).

31. The matter was given a popular treatment by Rifkin (1992). Note, however, a recent poll by Louis Harris and Associates, Inc. (1993), who have been monitoring US health habits since 1983. The new survey points to a current relaxation in the avoidance of fat and cholesterol. As the pollsters conclude, "there is nothing inevitable about progress."

32. See, for instance, Gleick, 1993.

33. With water essential for the survival of human societies, the issue of its degradation could come to assume something of an emotional charge. Persons yielding to the foreboding of a quasi-apocalyptic thirst, and moved by an instinct of self-preservation, might generate apprehensions reminiscent of the unjustified oxygen "scare" of the 1970s. At that time, the misrepresentation in the media of a statement by a well-known scientist raised the spectre of a critical decrease in atmospheric oxygen, supposed to result from destruction of the "lung of the world" – an entirely inappropriate metaphor for the Amazon forest which still surfaces occasionally. The resulting outcry raised hackles in Brazil, because it implied that sovereign decisions concerning Amazonia should be constrained by the obligation to preserve an essential component of the earth's life-support system (Sternberg, 1980, 1986a, 1987c).

34. Nevertheless, in April 1994, the Itamar Franco administration made the startling announcement that it was about to plunge headlong into a two-billion-dollar scheme to divert water from the São Francisco River to the Nordeste. Construction was to begin before the national elections in October, and the first phase of the project was to be inaugurated by year's end. Involving short-term, high-interest loans, the undertaking, for which detailed technical studies – if they exist – were not made public, came under fire from several quarters. Some of the criticism of the "pharaonic" enterprise (*Folha de São Paulo*, 1994a) even originated within the administration, coming, for instance, from the National Department of Waters and Electric Energy (Paula and Fechine, 1994), and the then Finance Minister Rubens Ricupero (*Folha de São Paulo*, 1994b). In mid-August, after much controversy and a considerable scaling down of the plan, imposed by financial realities, Franco interrupted the proceedings, just as the public bidding phase was about to begin (Freitas, 1994).

35. Ghillean Prance, director of the Royal Botanic Garden at Kew, aligns himself with this approach and, in fact, is actively working in Britain with the private sector to promote the manufacture of products based on the sustained harvest of non-wood forest resources (Prance, 1990). For several perspectives on alternatives to deforestation in Amazonia, see, for instance, Anderson, 1990.

36. On the growth of the Brazilian environmental movement, see, for example, Goldstein, 1990; and Kohlhepp, 1991.

37. Concerning this premise, see, in the context of the Yanomami, Birraux-Ziegler, 1989–1990.

38. With Minister of Justice, Colonel Jarbas Passarinho, arguing that a 1984 study, the basis for delimitation of the Yanomami lands, was outdated, President Collor in 1991 ordered the long-delayed demarcation to be put on further hold, pending a census of the indigenous population of the area. In this respect, José Goldemberg, then Minister of Education, surmised that a reserve of 9.4 million hectares was excessive for the then surviving tribespeople (*O Globo*, 1991). Given the increased mortality and general deterioration that afflicts this tragically victimized group following contact with miners and other invaders of their territory, the ratio of Indians to land can be expected to decrease further, and faster. Nevertheless Collor, probably with an eye to the financial assistance he desired from industrialized countries, reversed his decision and granted the dwindling Yanomami population permanent rights to its tribal lands.

39. A succinct, decidedly upbeat, report on some "good things" in Amazonia is provided by Smith (1992).

References

A Crítica [Manaus]. 1988a. "Ação popular contra o desastre no rio Urucu." 4 August.

———. 1988b. "Confirmado vazamento no Urucu." 27 August.

———. 1988c. "Navezon assume culpa no acidente ecológico." 28 August.

————. 1988d. "Assustador o impacto do desastre no Urucu." 30 August.

————. 1988e. "Procuradoria processa Navezon por poluição." 2 September.

A Gazeta [Rio Branco, Acre]. 1994. "Quércia volta ao Acre para defender ligação." 5 June.

Acuña, C. de. 1942. *Nuevo descubrimiento del gran río del Amazonas, por el P. Cristobal de Acuña, al cual fué por la provincia de Quito el año de 1639; publicación dirigida por Raúl Reyes y Reyes*. Biblioteca Amazonas 4. Imprenta del Ministerio de Gobierno, Quito, Ecuador.

Adams, D. 1993. "Gentler war on cocaine cartel." *San Francisco Chronicle*, 27 December.

Amazoniana. 1993. Special issue devoted to Careiro Island, 12(3/4).

Anal, 1773. Record of events for the year 1773 presented to the City Council of Vila Bela. In G. Freyre, 1968. *Contribuição para uma sociologia da biografia: o exemplo de Luiz de Albuquerque, governador de Mato Grosso no fim do século XVIII*, vol. 1. Academia Internacional da Cultura Portuguesa, Lisbon.

Anderson, A.B. (ed.). 1990. *Alternatives to deforestation: steps toward sustainable use of the Amazon rain forest*. Columbia University Press, New York.

Anon. 1984. Personal communication.

Ayres, J.M. 1993. *As matas de várzea do Mamirauá: médio Rio Solimões*. Conselho Nacional de Pesquisas, Programa do Trópico Úmido, Sociedade Civil Mamirauá, Brasília, DF.

Azambuja, M.C. de. 1990. IV Seminar on Formulation and Analysis of Foreign Policy, Brasília, December 1990. In Ministry of External Relations, General Secretariat for Foreign Policy, Division for the Environment, "Brazilian positions on environment and development" (Brasília, mimeo. 1991), p. 9.

Bahri, S. 1992. "L'Agroforesterie, une alternative pour le développement de la plaine alluviale de l'Amazone – l'exemple de l'île de Careiro." Thèse de Doctorat, Université des Sciences et Techniques du Languedoc, Université de Montpellier II.

Barrett, S.C.H. [1975]. "Report on the weeds of cultivated rice at Jari, Lower Amazon." Department of Botany, University of California at Berkeley, mimeo.

Bastos, J.B. dos S. 1988. "Depósito de ouro do Rio Madeira, Rondônia." In C. Schobbenhaus and C.E. Silva Coelho (eds.), *Principais depósitos minerais do Brasil: III – Metais Básicos não-ferrosos, ouro e alumínio*. Ministério das Minas e Energia, Brasília.

Bemerguy, R.L., and J.B.S. Costa. 1991. "Considerações sobre a evolução do sistema de drenagem da Amazonia e sua relação com o arcabouço tectônico-estrutural." *Boletim Museu Paraense E. Goeldi* (Ciências da Terra) 3: 75–97.

Birraux-Ziegler, P. 1989–1990. "Protection de la nature et indigénisme: quelques réflexions à propos des droits territoriaux des Yanomami du Venezuela et du Brésil." *Schweizerische Amerikanisten-Gesellschaft Bull.* 53/54: 99–108.

Bonalume, R. 1990. "Ecologist appointed to environment post." *Nature* 344: 96.

Boudeville, J.R. 1957. "Contribution à l'étude des pôles de croissance brésiliens: une industrie motrice – la sidérurgie du Minas Gerais." *Cahier ISEA*, sér. F, n° 10.

————. 1973. "Pôles de développement et pôles de croissance brésiliens au XXᵉ siècle." In CNRS, *L'Histoire quantitative du Brésil de 1800 à 1930*, Paris, Colloques Internationaux du CNRS 543: 433–439.

Brasil. 1972. "Conferência das Nações Unidas sobre o Meio Ambiente: o Brasil e a preparação da conferência de Estocolmo." Ministerio das Relações Exteriores, Brasília, mimeo.

————. 1990. *Censos econômicos 1985, Censo agropecuário*. Fundação Instituto Brasileiro de Geografia e Estatística – IBGE, Rio de Janeiro, 1.

————. 1991. *Coordenação do Relatório Nacional do Brasil para a CNUMAD-92*. Comissão Interministerial para a preparação da Conferência das Nações Unidas sobre o meio ambiente e desenvolvimento – CIMA, Brasília, DF.

————. 1992. *Anuário Estatístico 1992*, Fundação Instituto Brasileiro de Geografia e Estatística – IBGE, Rio de Janeiro.

————. 1993a. Consulate General of Brazil in San Francisco, California, Reply to a request for information.

————. 1993b. *República Federativa do Brasil: Constituição 1988*, Senado Federal, Centro Gráfico, Brasília.

————. 1993c. *Levantamento nacional dos garimpeiros: relatório analítico*, Série Tecnológica Mineral n° 45, Departamento Nacional da Produção Mineral, Brasília.

Bremer, H. 1971. *Flüsse, Flächen- und Stufenbildung in den feuchten Tropen*, Würzburger geographische Arbeiten/Mitteilungen der Geographischen Gesellschaft 35, Würzburg.

————. 1973. Der Formungsmechanismus im tropischen Regenwald Amazoniens, *Z. Geomorph*, N. F., Suppl. 17: 195–222.

Brillinger, D.R. 1988. "An elementary trend analysis of Rio Negro levels at Manaus, 1903–1985." *Rev. Bras. de Probabilidade e Estatística* 2: 63–79.

Brown, L.R. 1993. "Meat production up slightly." In L.R. Brown, H. Kane, and E. Ayres (eds.), *Vital signs 1993: the trends that are shaping our future* (Worldwatch Institute, Norton, New York), 30–1.

Brown, C.B. and W. Lidstone. 1878. *Fifteen thousand miles on the Amazon and its tributaries*. Edward Stanford, London.

Budweg, F.M.G. 1981. "Irrigation for Brazil's polígono das secas." *Water Power & Dam Construction* 33 (8): 20–2.

Camargo, F.C. 1958. "Report on the Amazon region." In UNESCO, *Problems of humid tropical regions* (Paris), 11–23.

Caputo, M.V. 1984. *Stratigraphy, tectonics, paleoclimatology and paleogeography of northern basins of Brazil*. University Microfilms International, Ann Arbor.

Carneiro, F.G. 1993. "Ecologia/economia: um casamento perfeito," *Conjuntura Economica* 74 (4): 70–1.

Carvajal, G. de. 1942 [1541–1542]. *Relación del nuevo descubrimiento del famoso Río Grande que descubrió por muy gran ventura el Capitán Francisco de Orellana: Transcripciones de Fernández de Oviedo y Dn. Toribio Medina y estudio crítico del descubrimiento; Publicación dirigida por Raúl Reyes y Reyes*. Biblioteca Amazonas 1. Quito, Ecuador.

Castro, M.B., B. Albert, and W.C. Pfeiffer. 1991. "Mercury levels in Yanomami Indians hair from Roraima Brazil." In *International Conference Heavy Metals in the Environment* (Edinburgh), 1, 367–70.

Cavalcanti, J.C. 1972. "Discurso pronunciado pelo Senhor Ministro do Interior…, chefe da delegação do Brasil à conferência das Nações Unidas sobre o meio ambiente, na sessão inaugural da mesma conferência." Stockholm, 6 June, mimeo.

Cavalcanti, M. de B. 1967. *Da SPVEA à SUDAM (1964–1967)*. Imprensa da Universidade do Pará, Belém.

CEM [Centro de Estudos Migratórios]. 1986. *Migrações no Brasil: o peregrinar de um povo sem terra.* Edições Paulinas, São Paulo.

Chatterjee, I.B. 1973. "Evolution and the biosynthesis of ascorbic acid." *Science* 182: 1271–72.

Coatney, G.R., W.E. Collins, McW. Warren, and P.G. Contacos. 1971. *The primate malarias.* US Department of Health, Education and Welfare, Bethesda.

Coelho, C.E. da S. 1986. "Depósitos de ferro da Serra dos Carajás, Pará." In C. Schobbenhaus and C.E. da S. Coelho (eds.), *Principais depósitos minerais do Brasil* (Departamento Nacional da Produção Mineral, Brasília), vol. 2, 29–64.

Cole, M.M. 1986. *The savannas; biogeography and geobotany.* Academic Press, London.

Companhia do Jari. 1988. Letter from the President of the Conselho de Administração, Augusto Antunes, and the Director-President, José C. Cavalcanti, to Minister Jader Barbalho, Ministério da Reforma Agrária. Rio de Janeiro, 26 February.

COPEGRO [Cooperativa dos Garimpeiros de Rondônia Ltda]. 1989. *Ofício* N° 007 to the President of Rondonia's Federação do Comércio, Porto Velho, 14 April.

Costa, F. de A., C. do S.F. de Senna, E. da S. Pereira, and D.C. Kern. 1986. "Levantamento arqueológico na área da UHE Cachoeira Porteira: relatório global," Museu Paraense E. Goeldi (Arqueologia), Belém, mimeo.

Costa, M.L. da. 1993. Personal communication by letter, Belém, 1 March.

Coutinho, J.M. da S. 1868. "Sur les tortues de l'Amazone." *Bulletin de la Société Impériale Zoologique d'Acclimatation.* 2nd ser. 5: 147–66.

Coy, M. 1988. *Regionalentwicklung und regionale Entwicklungsplanung an der Peripherie in Amazonien.* Tübinger Beiträge zur Geographischen Lateinamerika-Forschung 5. Geographisches Institut der Universität Tübingen, Tübingen.

Curtin, T.B. 1986a. "Physical observations in the plume region of the Amazon River during peak discharge – II. Water masses." In C.A. Nittrouer and D.J. DeMaster (eds.), *Sedimentary processes on the Amazon continental shelf, Continental Shelf Research* 6 (1/2): 53–71.

————. 1986b. "Physical observations in the plume region of the Amazon River during peak discharge – III. Currents." In C.A. Nittrouer and D.J. DeMaster (eds.), *Sedimentary processes on the Amazon continental shelf, Continental Shelf Research* 6 (1/2): 73–86.

Curtin, T.B., and R.V. Legeckis. 1986. "Physical observations in the plume region of the Amazon River during peak discharge – I. Surface variability." In C.A. Nittrouer and D.J. DeMaster (eds.), *Sedimentary processes on the Amazon continental shelf, Continental Shelf Research* 6 (1/2): 31–51.

Devol, A.H., J.E. Richey, W.A. Clark, S.L. King, and L.A. Martinelli. 1988. Methane emissions to the troposphere from the Amazon floodplain. *Journal of Geophysical Research* 93, D2: 1583–92.

Dias, R. 1993. Personal communication by letter, Porto Velho, 22 June.

DNAEE/DCRH [Departamento Nacional de Águas e Energia Elétrica/Divisão de Controle de Recursos Hídricos]. 1983. *Transposição das águas do São Francisco e Tocantins para o semi-árido nordestino: avaliação preliminar.* Brasília.

Dourojeanni, M. 1992. "Environmental impact of coca cultivation and cocaine production in the Amazon region of Peru." *Bulletin on Narcotics* 44 (2): 37–53.

Ducke, A. 1946. *Plantas de cultura precolombiana no Amazônia Brasileira ... notas sôbre as espécies ou formas espontâneas que supostamente lhes teriam dado origem.* Boletim Técnico Instituto Agronômico do Norte 8, Belém.

―――. 1949. "Ávores Amazônicas e sua propagação." *Boletim Museu Paraense E. Goeldi* 10: 81–92.

Dumont, J.F. 1993. "Lake patterns as related to neotectonics in subsiding basins: the example of the Ucamara Depression, Peru." *Tectonophysics* 222: 69–78.

Dunn, F.L. 1965. "On the antiquity of malaria in the western hemisphere." *Human Biology* 37: 385–93.

―――. 1993. "Malaria." In Kenneth F. Kiple (ed.), *The Cambridge world history of human disease* (Cambridge University Press, Cambridge), 855–62.

Eletrobrás. 1992. *Plano 2015, Projeto 4. Oferta de energia elétrica, tecnologias, custos e disponibilidades. Subprojeto Fontes alternativas de energia solar, eólica, xisto, oceânica, hidrogônio, resíduos orgânicos, turfa e linhito.* Eletrobrás, Rio de Janeiro.

Fabricant, Florence. 1993. "Top chefs try to develop a taste for Amazon fish." *The New York Times*, 21 July.

Falesi, I.C. 1967. "O Estado atual dos conhecimentos sôbre os solos da Amazônia brasileira." In H. Lent (ed.), *Atas do Simpósio sôbre a Biota Amazônica*, (Conselho Nacional de Pesquisas, Rio de Janeiro), 1, 151–68.

Fearnside, P.M. 1993. "Deforestation in Brazilian Amazonia: the effect of population and land tenure." *Ambio* 22: 537–45.

Ferrando, G. [1515]. "Testigo de García Ferrando." In C. Fernández Duro, *De los Pleitos de Colon II*, Colección de documentos inéditos relativos al descubrimiento, conquista y organización de las antiguas posesiones españolas de Ultramar, 2da serie (Real Academia de la Historia, Madrid, 1894), 186–90.

Ferraz, J. 1991. *Diagnóstico do comportamento do reflorestamento realizado na mina Saracá IV (Porto Trombetas – PA) entre 1981–1987.* INPA/CPST, Manaus, 1.

Ferreira, A.R. 1971. *Viagem filosófica pelas capitanias do Grão Pará, Rio Negro, Mato Grosso e Cuiabá 1783–1792. Iconografia, vol. 2 – Zoologia.* Conselho Federal de Cultura, Rio de Janeiro.

―――. 1972. *Viagem filosófica pelas capitanias do Grão Pará, Rio Negro, Mato Grosso e Cuiabá 1783–1792. Memórias: Zoologia, Botânica.* Conselho Federal de Cultura, Rio de Janeiro.

Fittkau, E.J., U. Irmler, W.J. Junk, F. Reiss, and G.W. Schmidt. 1975. "Productivity, biomass and population dynamics in Amazonian water bodies." In F.B. Golley and E. Medina (eds.), *Tropical ecological systems, trends in terrestrial and aquatic research.* Springer Verlag, Berlin/New York, 289–311.

Flannery, K.V. (ed.). 1982. *Maya subsistence studies, in memory of Dennis E. Puleston.* Academic Press, New York.

Folha de São Paulo. 1989. "Coname quer revisão do 'Nossa Natureza'." 6 May.

―――. 1994a. "Nordeste terá obra faraônica contra a sêca." 28 April.

―――. 1994b. "Governo decide gastar em megaobra." 24 July.

Freitas, J. de. 1994. "O negócio secou." *Folha de São Paulo*, 16 August.

Fundação Padre Leonel Franca. 1988. *Atlas do potencial eólico nacional*, vol. 1. Centrais Elétricas Brasileiras S.A./Eletrobrás, Rio de Janeiro.

Furtado, L.G. 1992. "Preliminary notes on conceptual aspects of the analysis of fishing in the Baixo Amazonas." In A.C.S. Diegues (ed.), *Tradition and social change in the coastal communities of Brazil: a reader of maritime anthropology* (Universidade de São Paulo, CEMAR [Center of Maritime Cultures], São Paulo), 66–79.

Fyfe, W.S., B.I. Kronberg, O.H. Leonardos, and N. Olorunfemi. 1983. "Global tectonics and agriculture: a geochemical perspective." *Agriculture, Ecosystems and Environment* 9: 383–99.

Gentry, A.H., and J. López-Parodi. 1980. "Deforestation and increased flooding of the upper Amazon." *Science* 210: 1354–6.

———. 1982. A reply to C.F. Nordin and R.H. Meade's commentary on "Deforestation and increased flooding of the upper Amazon". *Science* 215: 427.

Gessner, F. 1959. *Hydrobotanik, Die Physiologischen Grundlagen der Pflanzenverbreitung im Wasser*. VEB Deutscher Verlag der Wissenschaften, Berlin, 2.

Gibbs, R.J. 1967. "Amazon River: environmental factors that control its dissolved and suspended load." *Science* 156: 1734–7.

———. 1970. "Mechanisms controlling world water chemistry." *Science* 170: 1088–90.

Gibbs, R.J., and L. Konwar. 1986. "Coagulation and settling of Amazon River suspended sediment." In C.A. Nittrouer and K.J. DeMaster (eds.), *Sedimentary processes on the Amazon continental shelf, Continental Shelf Research* 6 (1/2): 127–49.

Gleick, P.H. 1993. "An introduction to global fresh water issues." In P.H. Gleick (ed.), *Water in crisis: a guide to the world's freshwater resources* (Oxford University Press. New York), 3–12.

Goldstein, K. 1990. "The Brazilian environmental movement." Undergraduate thesis in Politics/Latin American Studies, Princeton University, mimeo.

Goodland, R. 1990. "Environmental sustainability in economic development – with emphasis on Amazonia." In R. Goodland (ed.), *Race to save the tropics, ecology and economics for a sustainable future* (Island Press, Washington, DC), 171–89.

Gore, A. 1992. *Earth in the balance: ecology and the human spirit*. Houghton Mifflin Company, Boston.

Gottsberger, G. 1978. "Seed dispersal by fish in the inundated regions of Humaitá, Amazonia." *Biotropica* 10, 3: 170–83.

Goulding, M., 1980. *The fishes and the forest: explorations in Amazonian natural history*. University of California Press, Berkeley.

Gourou, P. 1982. *Terres de bonne espérance; le monde tropical*. Plon, Paris.

Harrison, P.D., and B.L. Turner II (eds.). 1978. *Pre-Hispanic Maya agriculture*. University of New Mexico Press, Albuquerque.

Heriarte, M. c. 1662. *Descriçam do Estado do Maranham, Para Corupa, Rio das Amazonas*. Faksimile-Ausgabe aus den MSS 5880 and 5879 der Österreichischen National-Bibliothek, Wien. Einleitung Karl Anton Nowotny, Wien, Akademische Druck- u. Verlagsanstalt Graz/Austria, 1964.

Hilde, J. 1989. "Garimpciros são blefados: dragas." *O Estadão do Norte* [Porto Velho], 3/4 September.

Hoffman, J.S. 1984. "Estimates of future sea level rise." In M.C. Barth, J.G. Titus, and W.D. Ruckelshaus (eds.), *Greenhouse effect and sea level rise: a challenge for this generation* (Van Nostrand Reinhold, New York), 79–103.

Howard-Williams, c. and W.J. Junk. 1977. "The chemical composition of Central Amazonian aquatic macrophytes, with special reference to their role in the ecosystem." *Archiv für Hydrobiologie* 79: 446–64.

Huber, J. 1909. "Mattas e madeiras amazonicas." *Boletim Museu Paraense E. Goeldi* 6: 91–225.

Humboldt, A. de, and A. Bonpland. 1820–1822. *Voyage aux régions equinoxiales du*

Nouveau Continent fait en 1799, 1800, 1801, 1802, 1803 et 1804, vols. 6 and 7 (1820), 8 (1822). Chez N. Maze, Libraire, Paris.

IUCN [International Union for Conservation of Nature and Natural Resources]. 1990. *Red Data Book*. IUCN, Gland, Switzerland.

Janzen, D.H. 1988. "Tropical ecology and biocultural restoration." *Science* 239: 243–4.

———. 1991. "How to save tropical biodiversity." *American Entomologist*, Fall, 159–71.

Johns, W.E., T.N. Lee, F.A. Schott, R.J. Zantopp, and R.H. Evans. 1990. "The North Brazil Current retroflexion: seasonal structure and eddy variability." *Journal of Geophysical Research* 95: 22,103–22,120.

Jornal do Comércio [Manaus]. 1991. "Frota questiona postura de Mestrinho sobre a ecologia." 16 August.

———. 1994. "Ação de Sem-Terras preocupa governo." 31 May.

Joyce, C. 1991. "Prospectors for tropical medicines." *New Scientist* 19: 36–9 and 42.

Junk, W.J. 1970. "Investigations on the ecology and production-biology of 'Floating meadows' (Paspalo-Echinochloetum) on the Middle Amazon, Part I: The floating vegetation and its ecology." *Amazoniana* 2: 449–95.

———. 1973. "Investigations on the ecology and production-biology of 'Floating meadows' (Paspalo-Echinochloetum) on the Middle Amazon, Part II: The aquatic fauna in the root zone of floating vegetation." *Amazoniana* 4: 9–102.

———. 1985a. "Temporary fat storage, an adaptation of some fish species to the waterlevel fluctuations and related environmental changes of the Amazon River." *Amazoniana* 9: 315–51.

———. 1985b. "The Amazon floodplain – a sink or source for organic carbon?" *Mitt. Geol.-Paläont.* Inst. Univ. Hamburg. SCOPE/UNEP Sonderband 58: 267–83.

Kern, D.C. 1988. "Caracterização pedológica de solos com terra preta arqueológica na região de Oriximiná – Pará." Thesis presented for Master's degree in Soils, School of Agronomy, Federal University of Rio Grande do Sul, mimeo.

Kerr, W.E., F. de J. Campos, and M.J.B. Barros. 1986. "Notas sobre os recursos naturais da horticultura na Amazonia." In Empresa Brasileira de Pesquisa Agropecuária, *Anais 1° Simp. Trop. Úmidos* 6: 451–6.

Kimerle, R., and E.P. Smith. 1993. "Uncertainty." In National Research Council, *Issues in risk assessment* (National Academy Press, Washington, DC), 327–9.

Kohlhepp, G. 1987. "Herausforderungen von Wissenschaft und regionaler Entwicklungspolitik. Überlegungen zur zukünftigen Entwicklung Amazoniens." In G. Kohlhepp (ed.), *Brasilien: Beiträge zur regionalen Struktur- und Entwicklungsforschung* (Tübinger Beiträge zur Geographischen Lateinamerika-Forschung, Tübingen), 1, 303–18.

———. 1991. "Umweltpolitik zum Schutz tropischer Regenwälder in Brasilien: Rahmenbedingungen und umweltpolitische Aktivitäten." *Konrad Adenauer Stiftung, Auslands-Informationen* 7: 1–23.

La Condamine, C.M. 1745. *Relation abrégée d'un voyage fait dans l'intérieur de l'Amérique Méridionale, depuis la Côte de la Mer du Sud, jusqu'aux Côtes du Brésil & de la Guiane, en descendant la rivière des Amazones*. Chez la Veuve Pissot, Paris.

Le Cointe, P. 1903. "Le bas Amazone." *Annales de Géographie* 12: 54–66.

———. 1922. *L'Amazonie brésilienne*, vol. 1. Augustin Challamel, Paris.

————. 1935. "Les crues annuelles de l'Amazone et les récentes modifications de leur régime." *Annales de Géographie* 44: 614–19.

————. 1945. *O estado do Pará: a terra, a água e o ar.* Companhia Editora Nacional, São Paulo.

————. 1948. "As grandes enchentes do Amazonas." *Boletim Museu Paraense E. Goeldi* 10: 175–84.

Lettau, H., K. Lettau, and L.C.B. Molion. 1979. "Amazonia's hydrologic cycle and the role of atmospheric recycling in assessing deforestation effects." *Monthly Weather Review* 107: 227–38.

Lima, [J.F. de] A. 1937. *Amazônia: a terra e o homen.* 2nd edn, Companhia Editora Nacional, Brasiliana, Rio de Janeiro. First published 1933.

Lima, R.R. 1956. *A agricultura nas várzeas do estuário do Amazonas,* Boletim Técnico 33, Instituto Agronômico do Norte, Belém.

Lochead, W. 1798. "Observations on the natural history of Guiana." *Transactions of the Royal Soc. of Edinburgh* 4, 2: 41–63.

Lopes, D.F., and M. I. da Silveira. 1990. "Estudos arqueológicos em Carajás: considerações sobre a ocupação pré-cerâmica nas grutas da Serra Norte." Museu Paraense E. Goeldi, Belém, mimeo.

Louis Harris & Associates, Inc. 1993. "Healthier lifestyles trend goes into reverse [sponsored by Baxter International]." *The Harris Poll* 19.

Lowe-McConnell, R.H. 1967. "Factors affecting fish populations in Amazonian waters." In H. Lent (ed.), *Atas do Simpósio sôbre a Biota Amazônica* (Conselho Nacional de Pesquisas, Rio de Janeiro), 7, 177–86.

L'vovich, M.I. 1979. *World water resources and their future.* American Geophysical Union, Washington, DC.

Magalhães, M.P. 1993. *O tempo arqueológico.* Museu Paraense E. Goeldi, Belém.

Mahar, D., 1989. *Government policies and deforestation in Brazil's Amazon region.* Working Paper 7. World Bank, Washington, DC.

Malm, O., M.B. Castro, W.R. Bastos, F.J.P. Branches, C.K. Zuffo, and W.C. Pfeiffer. 1993. "Mercury levels in fish samples from different goldmining areas, Amazon, Brazil." In *International Conference Heavy Metals in the Environment* (Toronto), 2: 96–9.

Marlier, G., 1967. "Hydrobiology in the Amazon Region." In H Lent (ed.), *Atas do Simpósio sôbre a Biota Amazônica* (Conselho Nacional de Pesquisas, Rio de Janeiro), 3, 1–7.

Martinelli, L.A., J.R. Ferreira, B.R. Fosberg, and R.L. Victoria. 1988. "Mercury contamination in the Amazon: a gold rush consequence." *Ambio* 17: 252–4.

Mayer, E.W., D.R. Blake, S.C. Tyler, Y. Makide, D.C. Montague, and F.S. Rowland. 1982. "Methane: interhemispheric concentration gradient and atmospheric residence time." *Proceedings National Academy of Sciences* 79: 1366–70.

Meade, R.H., C.F. Nordin, Jr., and W.F. Curtis. 1979. "Sediment in Rio Amazonas and some of its principal tributaries during the highwater seasons of 1976 and 1977." In Associação Brasileira de Hidrologia e Recursos Hídricos, *Anais 3° Simpósio Brasileiro de Hidrologia,* 2: 472–85.

Meade, R.H., T. Dunne, J.E. Richey, U. de M. Santos, and E. Salati. 1985. "Storage and remobilization of suspended sediment in the lower Amazon River of Brazil," *Science* 228: 488–90.

Mertes, L.A.K. 1993. Personal communication.

Mertes, L.A.K., M.O. Smith, and J.B. Adams. 1993. "Estimating suspended sediment concentrations in surface waters of the Amazon River wetlands from Landsat images." *Remote Sens. Environ.* 43: 281–301.

MINTER [Ministério do Interior]. 1976. *Programa de polos agropecuários e agrominerais da Amazônia: POLAMAZÔNIA.* Secretaria Geral, Secretaria de Planejamento e Operações, Brasília.

Muller-Karger, F.E., C.R. McClain, and P.L. Richardson. 1988. "The dispersal of the Amazon's water." *Nature* 333: 57–9.

Muller-Karger, F.E., and R.J. Varela. 1989/1990. "Influjo del Río Orinoco en el Mar Caribe: observaciones con el CZCS desde el espacio." *Memoria de la Sociedad de Ciencias Naturales La Salle* 49/50: 361–390.

Netherlands, Ministry of Agriculture, Nature, Management and Fisheries, Department of Information and External Relations. 1990. *Nature policy plan of the Netherlands in outline.* November.

——. 1993a. *Structure plan for the rural areas in the Netherlands: essentials.* January.

——. [Benno Bruggink]. 1993b. "Background information on the development of Dutch nature areas, including plans to develop marshlands. March; mimeo.

New York Times. 1994. "Long shadow of the Exxon Valdez," 21 September.

Nittrouer, C.A. and D.J. DeMaster. 1986. "Sedimentary processes on the Amazon continental shelf: past, present and future research." In C.A. Nittrouer and D.J. DeMaster (eds.), *Sedimentary processes on the Amazon continental shelf, Continental Shelf Research* 6(1/2): 5–30.

Noble, E.R., G.A. Noble, G.A. Schad, and A.J. MacInnes. 1989. *Parasitology: the biology of animal parasites.* Lea & Febiger, Philadelphia.

Nobre, C.A. 1992. "Media da precipitação total anual da Amazonia calculada em grades de 2 × 2 (lat × long) de 2N–10S e 48W–74 e de 10S–14S e 48W–70W." Personal communication.

Nordin, C.F., Jr., and R.H., Meade. 1986. "The Amazon and the Orinoco." In *McGraw-Hill Yearbook of Science and Technology* (McGraw-Hill, New York), 385–90.

Odebrecht Informa. 1993. "Commitment to conservation: The creation of Odebrecht Tecnologia Ambiental combines the Companies' experience to provide new business opportunities." *Odebrecht Informa* 19: 22–3.

O Globo [Rio de Janeiro]. 1991. "Reserva yanomâmi depende de estudo." 2 November.

——. 1994a. "Venezuela e Brasil já têm acordo sobre garimpeiros." 17 April.

——. 1994b. "Colômbia deporta 300 garimpeiros brasileiros." 23 April.

O Liberal [Belém]. 1989. "Lago Grande de Monte Alegre foi transformado em uma baía." 13 August.

——. 1991. "Repórter 70." 27 July.

Palmatary, H.C. 1939. "Tapajó pottery." *Ethnol. Studies* (Göteberg), 8.

——. 1960. *The archaeology of the lower Tapajós valley, Brazil.* American Philosophical Society, Philadelphia.

Panero, R. 1967. "On the use of low dams as a possible stimulant to South American development." Hudson Institute 788-RR, Croton-on-Hudson, New York.

——. 1969. "A dam across the Amazon." *Science Journal* (London), September, 56–60.

Pará Desenvolvimento. 1987. *O carvão vegetal e a indústria siderúrgica na Amazonia*, Special issue of *Pará Desenvolvimento*, IDESP 22, July–December.

Paula, I. de, and Y. Fechine. 1994. "São Francisco é pivô de guerra eleitoral." *O Globo* (Rio de Janeiro), 12 June.

Penna, C.R.G.M. 1989. "A Amazonia e a xenofobia." *Jornal do Brasil* (Rio de Janeiro), 14 March.

Pereira, F.S., and O.H. Knowles. 1985. "Recuperação das áreas mineradas pela Mineração Rio do Norte em Porto Trombetas, Pará." In *Anais do I Congresso Brasileiro de Mineração* (Brasília), 4, 170–85.

Pessoa, D. 1989. "Referências para uma avaliação." In D. Pessoa and O. Galindo (eds.), *Transposição do Rio São Francisco: a dimensão sócioeconômica* (Fundação Joaquim Nabuco, Recife), 211–28.

Peters, C.M., A.H. Gentry, and R.O. Mendelsohn. 1989. "Valuation of an Amazonian rainforest." *Nature* 339: 655–56.

Pfeiffer, W.C., O. Malm, C.M.M. Souza, L.D. Lacerda, E.G. Silveira, and W.R. Bastos. 1991. "Mercury in the Madeira River ecosystem, Rondônia, Brazil." *Forest Ecology and Management* 38: 239–45.

Pfeiffer, W.C., L.D. Lacerda, W. Salomons, and O. Malm. 1993. "Environmental fate of mercury from gold mining in the Brazilian Amazon." *Environmental Reviews* 1: 26–37.

Phillips, O.L., and A.H. Gentry. 1994. "Increasing turnover through time in tropical forests." *Science* 263: 954–8.

Picanço J. 1993. *Wind energy in Brazil and in the state of Ceará*. Companhia Energética do Ceará (COELCE), Fortaleza.

Pimentel, T.M. 1986. "O primeiro sucesso na Amazonia." *Brasil Mineral* 36: 104–9.

Pinto, J.M. 1966. *Aspectos econômicos da juta na Amazonia*. Cadernos da Amazonia 7. Instituto Nacional de Pesquisas Amazônicas, Manaus.

Plowman, T. 1981. "Amazonian coca." *Journal of Ethnopharmacology* 3: 195–25.

Prance, G. 1990. "Fruits of the rainforest." *New Scientist* 125 (1699): 42–5.

Projeto RADAMBRASIL. 1978. Folha SA.20 Manaus: geologia, geomorfologia, pedologia, vegetação e uso potencial da terra. Levantamento de Recursos Naturais, 18, Departamento Nacional da Produção Mineral, Rio de Janeiro.

RAN [Rainforest Action Network]. 1993. "The Yanomami: an ongoing massacre." *World Rainforest Report* (San Francisco) 10, October–December, 3.

Räsänen, M. 1991. *History of the fluvial and alluvial landscapes of the western Amazon Andean forelands*. Annales Universitatis Turkuensis, Sarja-Ser. A, II. Biologica–Geographica–Geologica 75, Turku.

———. 1993. "La geohistoria y geología de la Amazonia Peruana." In R. Kalliola, M. Puhakka, and W. Danjoy (eds.), *Amazonia Peruana: vegetación húmeda tropical en el llano subandino* (Gummerus Printing, Jyväsjylä, Finland), 43–67.

Ricupero, R. 1994. "Brincando nos campos do Senhor." *Jornal do Brasil*, 2 January.

Rifkin, J. 1992. *Beyond beef: the rise and fall of the cattle culture*. Dutton, Penguin Books USA, New York.

Roberts, L. 1992. "Chemical Prospecting: hope for vanishing ecosystems?" *Science* 256: 1142–3.

Roberts, W.O., W.W. Kellog, C. Baes, G. Breuer, J.A. Laurmann, H. Meinl, J. Page, and I. Smith 1980. "Objectives of a climatic impact study program." In W. Bach, J. Pankrath, and J. Williams (eds.), *Interactions of energy and climate*, Proceeding

175

of an International Workshop held in Münster, Germany, 3–6 March 1980 (D. Reidel, Dordrecht), xxv–xxxiii.

Roche, M.A., C. Fernandez, A. Aliaga, J. Bourges, J. Cortes, J.-L. Guyot, J. Peña and N. Rocha. 1990. "Water and salt balances of the Bolivian Amazon." Symposium on Hydrology and Water Management of the Amazon Basin. Manaus, 5–9 August. UNESCO, mimeo.

Roosevelt, A.C. 1993. "Late Pleistocene/Early Holocene foragers in the lower Amazon." In *Resumos e Contribuições Científicas*, International Symposium on the Quaternary of Amazonia, Manaus, 8–13 November 1992 (Universidade Federal do Amazonas, Manaus), 13–16.

Roosevelt, A.C., R.A. Housley, M.I. da Silveira, S. Maranoca, and R. Johnson. 1991. "Eighth millenium pottery from a prehistoric shell midden in the Brazilian Amazon." *Science* 254: 1621–4.

Ruddle, K., J.I. Furtado, G.F. Zhong, and H.Z. Deng. 1983. "The mulberry dike-carp pond resource system of the Zhujiang (Pearl River) Delta, People's Republic of China, I – Environmental context and system overview." *Applied Geography* 3: 45–62.

Ruivo, M.L.P., M.E.C. Sales, and P.F.S. Martins. 1991. "Condições edáficas de um latossolo amarelo após a exploração mineral na Amazonia oriental." *Boletim Museu Paraense E. Goeldi* (Ciencias da Terra), 3: 25–42.

Ryther, J.H., D.W. Menzel, and N. Norwin. 1967. "Influence of the Amazon River outflow on the ecology of the western tropical Atlantic, I. Hydrography and nutrient chemistry." *Journal of Marine Research* 25: 69–83.

Salati, E., and P.B. Vose. 1984. "Amazon basin: a system in equilibrium." *Science* 225: 129–38.

Sampaio, F.X.R. de. 1825. *Diario da Viagem que em visita e correição das povoações da capitania de S. José do Rio Negro fez o ouvidor e intendente geral da mesma Francisco Xavier Ribeiro de Sampaio. No anno de 1774–1775*. Tipografia da Academia, Lisbon.

Sanford, R.L. Jr. 1987. "Apogeotropic roots in an Amazon rain forest." *Science* 235: 1062–4.

SAUHEB [Salvamento arqueológico Usina Hidrelétrica de Balbina]. n.d. [1989?] *Sítios arqueológicos*, [Sites in ink, on blueprint map at 1:200,000 by Eletronorte (Monasa/Enge-Rio)].

Simpson, D.R., and R.A. Sedjo. 1992. "Contracts for transferring rights to indigenous genetic resources." *Resources* (Resources for the Future) 109: 1–6.

Sioli, H. 1951. "Sôbre a sedimentação na várzea do Baixo Amazonas." *Bol. Tec. do Inst. Agron. do Norte* 24: 45–66.

———. 1975. "Tropical rivers as expressions of their terrestrial environments." In F.B. Golley and E. Medina (eds.), *Tropical ecological systems: trends in terrestrial and aquatic research* (Springer Verlag, New York), 275–88.

Sippel, S.J., S.K. Hamilton, and J.M. Melack. 1992. "Inundation area and morphometry of lakes on the Amazon River floodplain, Brazil." *Archiv für Hydrobiol.* 123 (4): 385–400.

Sirenews. 1991a. "Manatees still commercially exploited in Brazil." [excerpts from a report by Mônica Borobial]. *Sirenews*, Newsletter of the IUCN/SSC, 15: 6–7.

———. 1991b. "Manatee exploitation in Brazil: a reply" [by Ioni Colares, translated from the Portuguese]. *Sirenews*, Newsletter of the IUCN/SSC, 16: 5–7.

Smith, N.J.H. 1980. "Anthrosols and human carrying capacity in Amazonia." *Annals of the Association of American Geographers* 70: 553–66.

———. 1981. *Man, fishes, and the Amazon.* Columbia University Press, New York.

———. 1982. *Rainforest corridors: the Transamazon colonization scheme.* University of California Press, Berkeley.

———. 1992. "Despite grave losses of forest, some good things are happening in Amazonia." *Environmental Conservation* 19: 294–5.

Spix, J.B. von and C.F.P. von Martius. 1822–1831. *Reise in Brasilien auf Befehl Sr. Majestät Maximillian Joseph I. Königs von Baiern in den Jahren 1817 bis 1820*, M. Lindauer, Munich.

Spruce, R. 1908. *Notes of a botanist on the Amazon and Andes during the years 1849–1864.* Edited and condensed by A.R. Wallace. 2 vols. Macmillan, London.

SRAL – São Raimundo AgroIndustrial Ltda. n.d. [Prospectus], n.p.

———. 1984. "Projeto Arroz: informações básicas." mimeo, n.p.

Sternberg, H. O'R. 1950. "Vales tectônicos na planície amazônica?" *Rev. Bras. de Geogr.* 12: 511–34.

———. 1955. "Séismicité et morphologie en Amazonie brésilienne," *Ann. Géog.* 54, 97–105.

———. 1956. "A água e o homem na várzea do Careiro." Tese de concurso para a cátedra de Geografia do Brasil. Faculdade Nacional de Filosofia, Universidade do Brasil, Rio de Janeiro. Vol. 1, text; vol. 2, maps.

———. 1960. "Radiocarbon dating as applied to a problem of Amazonian morphology." In *Comptes Rendus 18ème Congrès International de Géographie* (International Geographical Union, Rio de Janeiro), 2, 399–424.

———. 1966. "Die Viehzucht im Careiro-Cambixegebiet, ein Beitrag zur Kulturgeographie der Amazonasniederung." In Heidelberge Studien zur Kulturgeographie, *Festgabe für Gottfried Pfeifer* (Franz Steiner Verlag, Wiesbaden), 171–97.

———. 1967. "Progrès techniques et décentralisation industrielle dans le paysage rural semi-aride du Nordeste." In *Actes du Colloque International sur "Les Problèmes agraires des Amériques Latines"*, Paris, 11–16 October 1965, Éditions du Centre National de la Recherche Scientifique, Paris.

———. 1970. Report to Ambassador Mario Gibson Barbosa, Minister of External Relations, 24 May.

———. 1975. *The Amazon river of Brazil*, Erdkundliches Wissen 40, Beihefte zur Geographischen Zeitschrift. Franz Steiner Verlag, Wiesbaden.

———. 1980. "Amazonien: Integration und Integrität." In D. Benecke, M. Domitra, and M. Mols (eds.), *Integration in Lateinamerika* (Wilhelm Fink Verlag, Munich), 293–322.

———. 1981. "Frontières contemporaines en Amazonie brésilienne: quelques conséquences sur l'environnement." In *Les phénomènes de "frontière" dans les pays tropicaux* (Institut des Hautes Études de l'Amérique Latine, Paris), 177–200.

———. 1986a. "O 'Pulmão Verde'." *Geografia* (Rio Claro, SP) 11: 1–13.

———. 1986b. "Transformações ambientais e culturais na Amazonia: algumas repercussões sobre os recursos alimentares da região." In Empresa Brasileira de Pesquisa Agropecuária, *Anais 1° Simp. Trop. Úmidos* 6: 44–61.

———. 1987a. "Aggravation of floods in the Amazon River as a consequence of deforestation?" *Geografiska Annaler* 69A: 201–19.

———. 1987b. "'Manifest destiny' and the Brazilian Amazon: a backdrop to contemporary security and development issues." In *Proceedings of the Conference of Latin Americanist Geographers, Yearbook 1987*, 13: 25–35.

———. 1987c. "Life sciences and economic development in the Tropics – a holistic perspective." In D.O. Hall, M. Lamotte, and M. Marois (eds.), *The open research problems in the life sciences under tropical conditions* (A.A. Balkema Publishers, Rotterdam), 133–47.

———. 1988a. "Tentativas expansionistas belgas no Brasil: o caso 'Descalvados'." In *Livro de Homenagem a Orlando Ribeiro* (Centro de Estudos Geográficos, Universidade de Lisboa, Lisbon), vol. 2, 655–67.

———. 1988b. "Gegenwärtige Siedlungsfronten im brasilianischen Amazonien: Gedanken zur Umweltzerstörung." *Geographische Rundschau* 40: 42–9.

Sternberg, H. O'R., and R.J., Russell. 1952 [1957]. "Fracture patterns in the Amazon and Mississippi valleys." In *Proceedings, VIIIth General Assembly – XVIIth Congress* (International Geographical Union, Washington, DC), 380–5.

Swap, R., M. Garstang, and S. Greco. 1992. "Saharan dust in the the Amazon Basin." *Tellus* 448: 133–49.

Talbot, R.W., M.O. Andreae, H. Berresheim, P. Artaxo, M. Garstang, R.C. Harriss, K.M. Beecher, S.M. Li. 1990. "Aerosol chemistry during the wet season in central Amazonia: the influence of long-range transport." *Journal of Geophysical Research* 95 (D10): 16,955–69.

Taylor, J. 1993. "The mutable carbon sink." *Nature* 366: 515–16.

Teixeira, E. 1989. "Sarney pede reação militar contra ameaças à Amazônia." *Jornal do Brasil* (Rio de Janeiro), 18 March.

Torroni, A., T.G. Schurr, M.F. Cabell, M.D. Brown, J.V. Neel, M. Larsen, D.G. Smith, C.M. Vullo, and D.C. Wallace. 1993. "Asian affinities and continental radiation of the four founding Native American mtDNAs." *Am. J. Hum. Genet.* 53: 563–90.

Torroni, A., J.V. Neel, R. Barrantes, T.G. Schurr, and D.C. Wallace. 1994. "Mitochondrial DNA 'clock' for the Amerinds and its implications for timing their entry into North America." *Proc. Nat. Acad. Sci. USA* 91: 1158–62.

Turner B.L. II and W.M. Denevan. 1985. "Prehistoric manipulation of wetlands in the Americas: a raised field perspective." In I.S. Farrington (ed.), *Prehistoric intensive agriculture in the tropics*, British Archaeological Reports, International Series 232, Oxford.

Uhl, C. and G. Parker. 1986a. "Our steak in the jungle." *BioScience* 36: 462.

———. 1986b. "Is a quarter-pound hamburger worth a half-ton of rainforest?" *Inter-Ciência* 11 (5): 210.

Varnhagen, F.A. de. 1927. *Historia Geral do Brasil*, vol. 1. Companhia Melhoramentos, São Paulo.

Veen, J. van. 1962. *Dredge, drain, reclaim: the art of a nation*. Martinus Nijhoff, The Hague. 5th ed.

Veiga, T. 1993. Personal communication by letter, Brasilia, 13 April.

Vieira, A. 1659. "Carta ao Rei Afonso VI, Maranhão 28 November 1659. In J.L. Azevedo (ed.), *Cartas do Padre Antonio Vieira* (Imprensa da Universidade de Coimbra, Coimbra, 1925–1928), vol. 1, 549–71.

Wallace, A.R. 1853. *A narrative of travels on the Amazon and Rio Negro, with an account of the native tribes, and observations on the climate, geology, and natural history of the Amazon Valley*. Reeve and Co., London.

Wallace, D.C., and A. Torroni. 1992. "American Indian prehistory as written in the Mitochondrial DNA: a review." *Human Biology* 6 (3): 403–16.

Went, F.W., and N. Stark. 1968. "The biological and mechanical role of soil fungi." *Proc. Nat. Acad. Science USA* 60: 497–504.

Wigley, T.M.L., and S.C.B. Raper. 1992. "Implications for climate and sea level of revised IPCC emissions scenarios." *Nature* 357: 293–300.

Wood, C.S. 1975. "New evidence for a late introduction of malaria into the New World." *Current Anthropology* 16: 93–104.

Zhong, G.F. 1989. "The structural characteristics and effects of the dyke-pond system in China." *Outlook on Agriculture* 18: 119–23.

———. 1990. "The types, structure and results of the dike-pond system in South China." *GeoJournal* 21: 83–9.

7

A fragile capitalism in a fragile environment: Entrepreneurs and state bureaucracies in the free zone of Manaus

Roberto Motta

1 Introduction

Try to imagine the city of Manaus. It is a kind of island right in the middle of the Amazonian forest, far from every other city or town, thousands of kilometres away from the industrialized core of Brazil (São Paulo, Rio de Janeiro, Belo Horizonte, Porto Alegre, and nearly all that lies around and between these cities). It is also distant from Brazil's other underdeveloped, but densely settled region, the Nordeste (North-East), where the cities of Recife, Salvador, and Fortaleza, among the largest cities in Brazil, are located. Brazil has never quite known what to do with Amazonia, an immense territory, comprising about 5,000,000km², nearly 58 per cent of the whole area of the country.[1] Yet the region is inhabited by fewer than 10 million people, about 7.5 per cent of the whole national population.

With the exception of the fairly recent discovery of gold fields, both in the extreme north and the extreme south of the Amazon, and the iron ores of the Grande Carajás project, Amazonia has not revealed a spectacular richness in mineral resources. Despite a debate that lingers on (Motta, 1985), its soils are inappropriate for the kind of plantation agriculture which, since the early sixteenth century, has characterized, for instance, the humid coast of north-eastern Brazil.

180

The area, therefore, had only marginal utility of for the kind of international economy that begins to take shape with the European discovery of the Orient and the Americas. It is not, after all, too surprising that Portugal, with little military might and scant manpower, was able to seize and hold it, penetrating westward up to the present border between Brazil and Peru. All of the area west of the present-day city of Belém (very near the mouth of the Amazon River) had been attributed to Spain by the Treaty of Tordesillas, signed by the representatives of the Castilian and Portuguese kings in 1494. The Spaniards, however, were much too busy elsewhere, and thus the Portuguese with little difficulty were able to expel the missionaries dependant upon the Crown of Castille, while enslaving all the Indians – pagan as well as Christian – they found on their way (d'Ans, 1982). With only minor adjustments,[2] the boundaries of Luso-Brazilian Amazonia have not changed since the Treaty of Madrid was signed in 1750 by Spain and Portugal, recognizing the *faits accomplis* in South America. During the eighteenth and most of the nineteenth centuries, that huge area, belonging from 1822 onward to independent Brazil, had no other use than that of serving as a vast reservoir of drugs, spices, and rare woods. An exception was its easternmost end, due east of Belém, where some crops were grown. Population density was very low. Thus, in 1872 the combined population of the two Amazonian states, Pará and Amazonas, with a total area of 4,200,000km², did not exceed 329,000 persons.

Things were drastically altered by the rubber boom, which brought untold wealth at least to the big landowners and traders who came to settle in the area (Weinstein, 1986). The cycle peaked between 1890 and 1910. The rubber tree (*Hevea brasiliensis*, Portuguese *seringueira*) grew wild in the Amazonian forest and, at the time, only there. Discovery of the vulcanization process by Charles Goodyear in 1839 had made possible the industrial use of rubber as it is known today. The Amazonian boom peaked with the so-called bicycle craze, only to decline when the supply of Amazonian rubber proved unable to meet the demand of the growing automobile industry, which represented the greatest incentive for the establishment of rubber plantations in South-East Asia. The handsome *fin-de-siècle* architecture of Manaus, the opera house, the public market, and other fine buildings, still bear witness to the opulence of that period. By 1925 it had gone with the wind: *Hevea brasiliensis*, after a stage in the Kew Gardens of London, had been transplanted to the now independent countries of Malaysia, Singapore, Indonesia, and Viet Nam, where it was cultivated in large, well-organized plantations. These, due either to ecological reasons, or to the lack of a qualified and abundant supply of manpower or both, were never successfully adopted in the Amazon.

The forty years that elapsed between 1925 and 1965 were, in spite of some public and private initiatives, a period of stagnation in the economic history of Brazilian Amazonia, which did not experience the outbursts of industrialization and modernization that characterized other areas of Brazil during the same period. Like the northeastern region – although completely different from it in ecological and demographic terms – the Amazon lagged behind the main trend of Brazilian development. Hence the creation of a system, indeed of several systems, of tax incentives in order to attract investments into the area. Their detailed description is beyond the scope of the present paper. I will limit myself to the fiscal legislation that really mattered to western Amazonia, or at least to the state of Amazonas, its capital city, Manaus, and immediate environs, and brought about extensive changes of an economic, demographic, social, and cultural kind. I refer to the legislation enacted early in 1967, creating the Free Trade Zone of Manaus (Zona Franca de Manaus).

Let us keep in mind that Brazil follows a protectionist policy (Mahar, 1979). Foreign-made goods are subject to taxation, often heavy taxation, on entering the country. The essence of the Zona Franca system consists of import duty exemptions, given both to certain kinds of finished goods to be sold in the city of Manaus and only there, and to semi-finished goods or component parts, to be further worked on or assembled in the industrial sector of the free trade area and then re-exported elsewhere in Brazil. The final product is again exempt from duties in proportion to the value added to it in Manaus: the so-called *imposto sobre produtos industrializados* (tax on industrialized products – really a value-added tax) does not apply, either, to goods finished or assembled in the area.[3] These provisions, however, have several strings attached. In order to benefit from them, industrial investments must have been approved by a special agency of the Brazilian Federal Government, the Superintendência da Zona Franca de Manaus, generally known by the acronym "Suframa." This is the source of the powers of the state bureaucracies of the Zona Franca.

A second and more important stipulation was created in 1976, with the introduction of an annual ceiling on all imports into the area. Conceived as a general deterrent to the depletion of hard currency through the expansion of imports, this ceiling may, and does, vary according to the year. This second proviso applies less to the ceiling itself than to its distribution to the Zona Franca's individual firms, both industrial and commercial. The quotas are allocated *in situ* by the top echelons of Suframa. As we are about to see, the importance of Suframa lies, to a very large extent, in its quota-distributing power, and its head, the Superintendent (*Superintendente*), can be defined, for most practical purposes, as the man who controls the quotas.

The Zona Franca represents, therefore, a deliberate attempt to create a modern industrialized enclave in the equatorial forest. The rationale was that backward and forward linkages associated with that focus of growth would, in due time, diffuse development throughout all of the region. The goal of this paper is not the evaluation of the Zona Franca from an economic standpoint, but rather the discussion of some of the anthropological issues connected with that form of induced development. First is the problem of the origin, or recruitment, of entrepreneurs in a setting such as that of the Zona Franca de Manaus – a classical problem of economic anthropology and economic sociology. A second issue to be discussed relates to the role of the federal and state bureaucracies in the installation and management of the Free Trade Zone.

2 Methodological remarks

Although I had visited Manaus and the Amazon several times for scholarly purposes between 1979 and 1986, fieldwork for the research on entrepreneurs and bureaucrats was actually done in the first semester of 1987. As an anthropologist, I adopted, above all, a typically anthropological methodology. I conducted a series of open, in-depth, formal and informal interviews with entrepreneurs and members of the highest echelons of the federal and state bureaucracies (mainly at Suframa and at one of its subsidiaries, Fucapi, the acronym for the Fundaçao Centro de Análise da Produção Industrial, or Foundation Centre for Industrial Production Analysis).[4] My goal was to understand the basic structures underlying the opinions of the persons interviewed on the subject of "being an entrepreneur in Manaus."[5]

However, I was aware of a basic principle of the social sciences methodology (all the more relevant in a research setting involving so many vested interests of an economic and political kind): people's utterances serve as often to veil their real thoughts as to bare them.[6]

Therefore, in my effort to understand the deep structures underlying not only the speech, but also the behaviour of my respondents, I often resorted to what may be called the method of internal and external dissonances. By internal dissonances I mean those which occur in the speech of a single individual, in the form of inconsistencies, hesitations, superfluous reiterations, retractions, lapses, and other signs of discrepancy between, on the one hand, the apparent meaning of individual's utterances and, on the other, the person's behaviour and thoughts (the latter discerned through behaviour). External dissonances are those that become manifest when the researcher compares the utterances of two or more respondents judged to be of similar social and economic status (thus presumably sharing the same interests), interviewed on the same subject.

I also made use of written sources. Here I refer less to the rich literature available about Amazonian problems (Benchimol, 1977; d'Ans, 1982; Ferreira Reis, 1972; Mahar, 1979; Mendes, 1974; Wagley, 1974; Weinstein, 1986), than to the documentation available in the archives of Suframa, Fucapi, the Commercial Association (Associação Comercial) of Manaus, and other institutions. Thus, I obtained access to the full text of Resolution no. 023/87, signed by the Superintendent of Suframa, distributing the import quotas for fiscal 1987. I also gained access to the files of every firm registered in the Zona Franca area (indeed in the whole of the western part of Brazilian Amazonia). The combined reading of Resolution no. 023/87 and the Suframa files greatly helped me in my attempt to answer, at least in part,[7] the question "who gains and who loses with the creation of the Free Trade Zone of Manaus?"

3 A theoretical excursus

As I conceived it, an investigation of the economic élites of the Zona Franca should mainly focus on the cultural characterization of the entrepreneurs involved. The basic query of this essay can, therefore, be formulated as follows. What is it that, in the social and cultural background of certain persons or groups, renders them more, or less, motivated and/or more, or less, capable to play an entrepreneurial role in the Free Trade Zone of Manaus?

The question poses one of the basic problems of the anthropology (and the sociology) of economic activity. It is, for instance, one of the central issues of the economic, sociological, and historical essays of Max Weber. This German author saw the problem of the energizing forces of modern capitalism as one less of the actual origin of the sums available for investment than of the development of a spirit of capitalistic entrepreneurship. Where that "spirit" is able to unfold its virtualities, it will bring about its own capital and money supply, rather than the other way round. The entrepreneur is, thus, for Weber, the bearer of the spirit of capitalism, characterized, above all, by a rational approach to the factors of economic production and by the achievement motivation (McClelland, 1951; Weber, 1988). It can also be said, in spite of the restrictions Weber formulates concerning this trait, that the spirit of capitalism is also characterized by the acquisition motivation, the tendency toward an unlimited expansion of both capital and profits.

Similarly, for another German theoretician of entrepreneurship, Werner Sombart, the process of development is a function of the presence, within a given area, of a group possessing some abilities basically of a cultural kind. The entrepreneurial mind must combine method, persistence, acquisitiveness, and more of the like. Even more important, the entrepreneur ought to be imbued with "that revolutionary, Faustian, European[8] spirit, that gave birth to the cultural period in which we live ... The basic characteristic of that mentality lies in the conception that theory and practice are inseparable" (Sombart, 1946: 162–3). Let us beware, nevertheless, that, at least for Sombart, entrepreneurship requires no ethical qualification. "The needs of the community are important for the economic utilization of a discovery only in so far as it can bring a profit to the entrepreneur" (Sombart, 1946: 106).

A third author, Joseph Schumpeter, considered the entrepreneur along the same lines as Sombart, as the main actor in the process of economic development, since he is basically the introducer of innovations into actual economic practice. Schumpeter's concept of entrepreneurial action is a rather broad one, since innovation, according to him, can assume five different forms: (1) the introduction of a new commodity or of a new service; (2) the introduction of a new method of production or trade; (3) the opening of a new market; (4) the discovery of a new source of raw materials or semi-finished goods; and (5) the restructuring of a sector or branch of industry or commerce, leading, for instance, to the creation or elimination of monopolies (Brandão Lopes, 1965; Oliveira Mota, 1964; Schumpeter, 1934).

The anthropological and sociological issue of entrepreneurship is connected with ethnic and religious variables. Thus, one of the central questions of Max Weber's famous essays on the "spirit of capitalism" is why certain ethnic and confessional groups, compared to other groups of the same kind, exhibit a greater or a lesser propensity toward entrepreneurship. It is well known that for him the causation of modern capitalist development should be mainly ascribed to the "Protestant ethic" or, more precisely, to the inner-worldly asceticism of Calvinism and the Baptist sects. Weber, however (far more so than Sombart), drew a sharp distinction between a "rational" capitalism, associated, according to him, with the "Protestant ethic" and representing a historical phenomenon with clear-cut limits in both time and space, and a speculative capitalism, with its own entrepreneurs, associated, as he says, "nowadays as always," with international trade. The ever-clairvoyant Weber also drew attention to the links between speculative entrepreneurs – often recruited from among specific ethnic and religious groups – and such fiscal privileges as may be granted by princes and heads of government (Weber, 1988).

Irrespective of the ethnic and religious implications of the Weberian analysis, the distinction between a rationally innovative and a rather speculative entrepreneurial motivation will be adopted as the basis of one of the central hypotheses of this paper, namely the speculative character of much of the capital invested in the Free Trade Zone of Manaus and its links – mainly in commercial investments – with the "pariah capitalism" (another Weberian expression) of what I here call the "international of the free ports"[9] with its peculiarities of an ethnic and religious kind.[10]

4 Entrepreneurs and bureaucrats

I have already alluded to the utmost importance of the role of the state bureaucracies in the Manaus Free Trade Zone, meaning the Brazilian federal state bureaucracies – basically Suframa and subsidiaries – and not (unless otherwise stated) the bureaucracies of the State of Amazonas. As is well known, in situations of retarded economic development the state and its bureaucracies tend to assume some of the functions that otherwise devolve upon private enterprise. And the economic role of the state is all the more important in Brazil due to the omnipresence, throughout the whole history of both Brazil and its motherland, Portugal, of what Brazilian sociologist Raymundo Faoro has termed the "bureaucratic estate" (*estamento burocrático*), which commands

... both the civil and the military branches of the public administration, seizing and leading the economic, financial, and political spheres. In the economic field, going well beyond the regulative function accorded to it by the ideology of liberalism, surpassing even the system of regulated concessions, the bureaucratic estate assumes the direct management of enterprises. Acting directly upon the economy or using incentives are but alternative means to reach the same goals. (Faoro, 1979: 738–9)

Indeed, the Free Trade Zone of Manaus can be described as a condominium of private entrepreneurs and state bureaucrats, each side receiving, in a direct or an indirect way,[11] a share of the profit generated by the industrial and commercial activities of the economic enclave. This is why I suggest that the concept of Oriental, or hydraulic, despotism, as formulated by Karl Wittfogel (1957, 1968), be adopted for the understanding of some of the basic features of the Zona Franca. I use the concept in a very broad sense, as Wittfogel himself understood it. Thus he considered the Inca empire, located on the Andean plateau, as "a purely Oriental society".[12] Conversely, many societies which are located in the Orient from a purely geographic point of view have nothing in common with despotism as understood by Wittfogel.

Although the historical prototypes of Oriental despotism are derived from the hydraulic societies of ancient Egypt, Mesopotamia, China, and others, its main characteristic consists less of the presence of public works on a grandiose, pharaonic scale, not missing in Brazil as a whole or in Brazilian Amazonia, than of the role of the large state bureaucracies. Although these do not own the means of economic production, they nevertheless exert, or share, control over the basic economic activities of the society. Either through the management of some essential resource (such as water) or through regulations, incentives, restrictions, and the like, state bureaucracies are able to appropriate a significant part of the wealth – or of the "surplus value," if one prefers this expression – generated in the same society. In point of fact, the concept of "Oriental despotism" might well be used for the understanding not only of the Free Zone of Manaus with its controlling bureaucracies at Suframa and Fucapi, but also the North-East of Brazil (where state bureaucrats have as one of their basic tasks the management of hydric resources in the strict sense), and even Brazilian society as a whole.

The preceding considerations can be summed up in the two following hypotheses:

1. The hypothesis of a "pariah capitalism," that is, the expectation that entrepreneurial activity in the Manaus Free Trade Zone has a largely speculative character, taking advantage of the system of tax incentives offered by the government and being associated with ethnic and religious groups who tend to play a peripheral role in the general context of world trade (East Indians of certain castes and certain regional origins, South-East Asians, Middle Eastern Jews and Arabs, etc.). This would seem to constitute a typical case of what Max Weber called speculative capitalism, turned, as he said, toward "irrational and political opportunities of gaining a profit" and opposed to "the rational organization of the enterprise oriented toward a real market" (Raphaël, 1982; Weber, 1988);

2. The hypothesis of the "hydraulic," or bureaucratic, despotism, that is, the expectation that there exists, in the Free Trade Zone of Manaus, an élite of state bureaucrats which is more than merely functional to the task of planning, regulating, and managing the economic activity of the enclave. In a direct or indirect way, this bureaucratic élite is able to appropriate part of the profit generated by commerce and industry in the area.

Whereas these were my two major research interests in Manaus, I did not disregard a few other relevant topics. Thus, entrepreneurship appeared to have not only a "speculative" rather than, in the Weberian sense of the word, a "rational" character, but it also tended to be represented in the area by the local managers of firms with headquarters elsewhere in Brazil, or abroad, and therefore wielding a rather limited power to take major decisions. Sheer speculative entrepreneurship appeared to be more typical of the enclave's commercial sector and merely managing, surrogate entrepreneurs were mainly found in the industrial sector. Yet these two categories are by no means mutually exclusive.

I was also very much interested in the mechanisms and subtleties of the formal and informal decision-making process in the Free Trade Zone concerning, first and foremost, the allocation of import quotas to both trading and manufacturing enterprises. This power seems to be essentially vested in the person of the Superintendent and his immediate assistants. Indeed, since the establishment in 1976 of a ceiling of importations into the enclave, this official has acquired an almost imperial importance. Nevertheless, as the "hydraulic despotism" in the Zone is, after all, tempered by an abundant legislation that emanates from the central Brazilian government (and even to a certain extent from the government of the state of Amazonas) and the procedural labyrinth that derives from it, one can easily understand that the office of the Superintendent is subject to the influence of persons and groups capable of making good use of laws, regulations, and subterfuges of several kinds.

I never forgot the biggest query of all. Who, in the end, profits from the Free Trade Zone? What persons, groups, strata, social classes are actually the beneficiaries of the incentive system of Manaus? A definitive answer to this all-important question far surpasses the scope of my research. But the data I could gather do provide me with the elements of what is perhaps more than a mere tentative answer to that big riddle. I will return to it.

5 Findings

The pariah capitalism

In a general way, the research findings have confirmed the hypothesis of the "pariah capitalism," in which entrepreneurs are recruited from among certain ethnic or religious groups that are typically peripheral in the context of international commerce. Indeed, here we face a characteristic trait of the economic history of Luso-Brazilian Amazon. As stressed by many of my respondents, there always were in the region, even previous to the rubber boom, entrepreneurs of Sephardic, Lebanese, recent Portuguese, or other origins, who filled the gap caused by the absence, or the weakness, of a native bourgeoisie of traders and manufacturers. However, these migrant entrepreneurs have often been rapidly assimilated into their new society, thereby losing, or tending to lose, touch with their countries and groups of origin. Thus, some of my informants made a point of drawing my attention to the fact (at least according to them) that the westernmost state of Acre is completely ruled, both economically and politically, by descendants of Syrian and Lebanese immigrants. The state of Amazonas, on the other hand, has fallen, according to the same sources, under the power of *caboclos* (among them the governor of the State himself), that is, Brazilians of mixed Portuguese and Amerindian ancestry. My informants added that both entrepreneurs and bureaucrats (often Brazilians from other regions) had to adjust to "those people" more than they would really like. But it is true that

189

ethnic terms in the Amazon, like *caboclo*, *Português*, *Paulista* (a native of São Paulo State), and others, are frequently used with the vaguest of meanings.

Concerning immigrant entrepreneurs in the Amazon (especially commercial ones) I had reached my conclusions independently from, but in agreement with, Barbara Weinstein, who writes, referring to Pará, that:

The Paraense elite had a long tradition of assimilating diverse individuals from Europe or other parts of Brazil ... As older, more established firms dissolved or collapsed, enterprising Syrian, Lebanese, and Jewish immigrants rushed in to fill the vacuum, eventually coming to exercise a near complete control over the Brazilian nut trade. By 1920, two Sephardic Jews could be counted among the leading officials of Pará's commercial association and another Paraense of Jewish extraction operated one of Belém's biggest export houses ... Bringing with them entrepreneurial skills and a bit of cash, Pará's Levantine and European immigrants succeeded in capitalizing on the few financial opportunities that a depressed economy offered. (Weinstein, 1986: 259–260)

Nearly all of my informants declared that at least 90 per cent of the industrial entrepreneurs of Manaus[13] came from outside the Amazon, being mainly Paulista.[14] The percentage of non-Amazonians is smaller in the commercial sector of the Free Trade Zone, and yet it is there that the presence of the "pariah capitalism," often connected to the "international of the free ports," is more keenly felt. There were, in early 1987, ten East-Indian-owned businesses in Manaus[15] – a phenomenon unknown elsewhere in Brazil.

In spite of much talk one hears in Manaus about the Free Trade Zone being nothing but "a consortium of Paulistas and Japanese," one sees no Japanese merchants in Manaus. One of my interviewees explained this in the following way: "The Japanese, sir? Here in the Amazon they are only gardeners and even so, you know, the climate, the soil do not help them at all." Yet in no way did this prevent the same informant, as well as several others during formal and informal contacts, from adding that the "real currency" of the Zona Franca was not even the United States dollar, but the Japanese yen.

It appears safe to conclude that there exists in Manaus a kind of "pariah capitalism" such as understood by Weber (1952) and even by Marx. This is made evident above all in the commercial sector by the high proportion of entrepreneurs belonging to ethnic minorities, who benefit from the often family-based links with the "international of the free ports" and from the experience and know-how they have acquired in other areas. Yet one should not belittle the presence, the activities, or the profits of the "native"[16] entrepreneurs, especially in the commercial sector. Everything leads me to believe that a whole series of "backward and forward linkages" (Hirschman, 1958) benefited the commerce of Manaus even when not directly turned to the importation of foreign goods.

According to the respondents there would have been, in the whole history of the Free Trade Zone, only one clearcut instance of a "native" turned into a successful industrial entrepreneur. Yet, my informants continued, even this person, either for personal reasons or because he could no longer bear the way in which Suframa constantly persecutes all manifestations of local entrepreneurial talent, eventually moved to southern Brazil, taking his capital along with him. Recent immigrants, however (either from abroad or from elsewhere in Brazil), tend to describe the "native"[17] as lacking in capital, initiative, know-how, and other requirements for a successful entrepreneurial career.

Whatever the boasts or complaints of both outsiders and "natives" (whose basic economic interests are not necessarily antagonistic), considering the low level of capital accumulation in Amazon, the Zona Franca model could not succeed without the resources of foreign and Paulista entrepreneurship, attracted to the area by generous tax incentives. The ideological justifications, revindications, or explanations of the several kinds of entrepreneurs (or of their surrogates) are not always to be taken at face value.

Bureaucratic despotism

A much larger investigation would be required to analyse the composition, attributions, recruitment system, and performance of the bureaucracies associated with Suframa, its subsidiaries, like Fucapi, and other agencies, both on the national and on the Amazonas State level, including the several institutes that each claim to be the sole, or at least the main, agency legally entitled to do research in the Amazon valley. This is certainly a task which should be accorded top priority; however, here I will concentrate on the powers attributed by my respondents to the Superintendent of Suframa (surrounded, as already remarked, by a quasi-imperial aura) and his immediate assistants.

Keeping in mind the maze of laws, decree-laws, decrees, resolutions, and the like (Brazilian administrative procedure is full of complexities and subtleties), we need not be amazed that the Superintendent and his assistants indeed have a great latitude in granting, denying, speeding, and delaying. However, as previously remarked, no other attribute of the Superintendent seemed to be more important for my interviewees, as, indeed, for every cognizant Manauara (the Amazonian Portugurse term for inhabitants of Manaus), than his authority over distributing importation quotas. There certainly are objective criteria for the exercise of that prerogative.[18] For the year 1987, these were stated in Resolution no. 050/87, signed by none other than the Superintendent himself. But everyone, even among the functionaries of Suframa, admitted to me that in spite of those criteria, or even because of them (since they are not always susceptible to a uniform interpretation), the Superintendent enjoys, to put it mildly, a considerable margin of discretion in dealing with quotas.

Thus, one of my respondents – whose opinions reflected the commercial, rather than the industrial, interest in the Free Zone – told me that, before the introduction of the quota system in 1976, the Superintendent of Suframa mattered so little that "he was not even invited to parties." But then, let us keep in mind that the main problem with quotas concerns their proportional allocation to commerce and industry. Industry has been given priority. Hence the anti-Suframa feelings of most tradesmen and the opposite reaction of most manufacturers.

When formally interviewed by me, the Superintendent himself reaffirmed that it was indeed the intention of Suframa to favour the industrial, rather than the commercial, sector of the Free Zone.[19] However, he added, I should not take too seriously the complaints of traders and should waste no tears upon them. In 1986, for instance, out of a total value of nearly one billion dollars represented by commerce in the Free Trade Zone of Manaus, no more than 10 per cent according to the Superintendent, derived from the importation and sale of foreign goods other than component parts of products assembled in Manaus itself.

In spite, or perhaps because, of its imperial aura, the post of Superintendent of Suframa (like other important posts in the bureaucracy of Suframa and its subsidiaries) is subject to a high rate of turnover, which is certainly associated with the complexities of the quota-distributing functions incumbent upon it. Although it has an appointive, rather than an elective, character, it ranks among the few topmost positions in the Brazilian administrative system and it carries with it far more effective power than that of Governor of the State of Amazonas.

6 The winners

Who, then, are the beneficiaries of the creation of the Free Trade Zone of Manaus? This question can be answered in a number of ways. I will turn first to the big importers.

From a document I was able to examine in the archives of Suframa (1987), I derived the data presented in table 7.1, describing the aggregate of import quotas attributed to the commercial sector in 1987, the total number of firms benefiting from them, the value of individual quotas, and the number of firms. Even in the absence of an elaborate statistical treatment of these data, table 7.1 permits a glimpse at the high concentration of profits.[20] Thus the fifteen topmost firms, representing no more than 4.2 per cent of all commercial firms in the Zone, get 35 per cent of the values of all quotas attributed to the commercial sector.[21] In the industrial sector, the total of importation quotas, affecting 154 firms, is five times as large as that of the commercial sector (US$456,220,000 and US$85,770,000, respectively). Table 7.2 shows the distribution of that total by the main industrial subsectors of the Free Trade Zone. Finally, Table 7.3 presents the twelve industrial enterprises whose importation quotas in 1987 reached or surpassed the amount of US$10m.[22]

Another way of answering the question about the winners in the Free Trade Zone is to see it as a consortium of interests, a kind of joint-stock company – Zona Franca, Inc. – whose great shareholders are: (1) transnational and transregional (Paulista) enterprises, which

Table 7.1 **Free Trade Zone of Manaus: Number of commercial firms by value of importation quotas, 1987**

Value of quotas (US$m)	Number of firms	%	Total of quotas (US$ '000)	%
1,000 or more	15	4.2	30,630	35.8
500–999	33	9.3	21,750	25.3
100–499	148	41.9	23,660	27.6
99 or less	158	44.6	9,730	11.3
Total	354	100.0	85,770	100.0

Source: Resolução 023/87, Gab. Sup. Suframa.

Table 7.2 **Free Trade Zone of Manaus: Importation quotas for industrial sector in 1987, distributed by subsectors**

Subsector	Importation quotas (US$'000)
Electronic	314,130
Watch-making	51,900
Cyclomotors	48,500
Optical	8,900
Other	32,790
Total	456,220

Source: Resolução 023/87, Gab. Sup. Suframa.

Table 7.3 **Free Trade Zone of Manaus: Industrial firms with importation quotas equal to or larger than US$10m in 1987**

Firms	Value of quotas (US$m)
Sharp do Brasil S.A.	32.0
Moto Honda S.A.	30.0
Evadim	25.0
Cape	20.0
CCE da Amazônia S.A.	19.5
Semp Toshiba S.A.	17.2
Gradient S.A.	17.0
Sanyo da Amazônia	14.2
Dismac S.A.	13.0
Philco da Amazônia S.A.	12.0
Philco Componentes S.A.	11.5
Philips da Amazônia S.A.	10.0
Total	221.4

Source: Resolução 023/87, Gab. Sup. Suframa.

stand out among the major beneficiaries from the tax incentive system of the Zone; (2) the "pariah" entrepreneurs, often linked with what I have called in this paper the "international of the free ports"; (3) local firms,[23] overwhelmingly commercial, which profit either from the tax incentives that still apply to the importation of finished goods or from the general economic impetus of the Zona Franca; and (4) the great state bureaucracies of Suframa and subsidiaries, as well as of other agencies at the federal level and – to a lesser extent – the local state level, who are the representatives of what I have called (borrowing from Karl Wittfogel) "Oriental" or "hydraulic" despotism.

A final query concerns the people of Manaus and of Amazonia.

Did they gain or lose with the creation of the enclave? A full answer to this all-important question requires far more data than I was able to gather. It certainly can be said that, as a consequence of the tax incentive system of Suframa, employment possibilities have greatly increased in the area of Manaus. But many observers – including several of my interviewees – stressed the artificial character of the Free Trade Zone, which is entirely dependent on the continuing good will of the Brazilian federal government.

There are also those who mourn the demise of the traditional society and the damage done to the environment. But a long time has already elapsed since the balance of egalitarian societies, in harmony with their milieu, was destroyed in the region. Considering the history of Amazonia since the intrusion of the Europeans, the Free Trade Zone of Manaus is perhaps not the worst of its many evils.

Notes

1. Figures concerning the area and population of the Amazon vary according to the way it is defined. The figure of 4,871,500km^2 refers to so-called "Amazônia Legal," which comprises the whole of the *Região Norte*, with the states of Pará, Amazonas, Acre, Amapá, Roraima, plus adjacent areas of the *Região Centro-Oeste*, with the state of Rondônia and parts of Mato Grosso and Goiás, plus a chunk of the North-East, with the state of Maranhão. The city of Manaus had in 1987 an estimated population of 1,100,000.
2. The biggest change in the limits of Brazilian Amazonia since the Treaty of Madrid was due, early in the twentieth century, to the conquest from Bolivia of the present Brazilian state of Acre, located in the far south-west of the region.
3. Although some of the tax incentives of the Suframa system apply to the whole of western Amazonia (with the states of Amazonas, Roraima, Acre, and Rondônia), investments have been overwhelmingly concentrated in the city of Manaus and its immediately surrounding area.
4. Excluding informal contacts, social gatherings, and the like (often an invaluable source of information), I conducted a total of 20 formal, in-depth interviews.
5. I tried to elicit as many data as possible on two special topics: the ethnic and cultural background of interviewees, and their relationship, as acting entrepreneurs, with the Free Trade Zone administration.
6. Of course, the very concept of a "real thought" is rather elusive and almost unreal. Why should some thoughts be more real than others? What I really understand by that expression are the guiding principles actually expressed in the behaviour of people. Indeed the ideal method of anthropology consists less in doing interviews than in observing the actual behaviour of social and cultural actors. However, circumstances often impose the adoption of methodological short cuts.
7. Of course financial benefits in the Free Trade Area also assume forms other than returns on invested capital: there are also the honoraria of consultants, lobbyists, and the like, as well as the salaries and gratuities of technicians, bureaucrats, public servants, etc.
8. Both Sombart and Weber, despite the apparent ethnocentrism of some of their statements, would certainly be ready to admit as "European" (in a very broad sense) North American, Japanese, and even some forms of South American entrepreneurship.

195

9. By this expression I mean, as the context of this paper has made clear, the commercial linkages, often reinforced by ethnic and kinship ties, between tradesmen in Manaus and their suppliers in Colón (Panama), Singapore, Hong Kong, etc. The study of these linkages would certainly represent an investigation of the highest interest for the anthropology and sociology of economic activity.

10. Just as a footnote to these theoretical remarks, let us also remark that Marx, a long time before Sombart and Weber and in spite of his thoroughly different conception of historical progress (since for him "the world of religion" is but "the reflex of the real world" of economic production), did not fail to note the connection between members of certain ethnic and religious groups and certain forms of economic activity. Thus, he speaks of the link between capitalism and Protestantism and mentions the presence of "Jews in the pores of Polish society" (Marx, 1967: 79).

11. Of course the gains of bureaucrats are not limited to their salaries and bonuses. To give just one example, they are also not infrequently recruited to top posts of private enterprises.

12. He adds: "The surplus production of this very strictly commandeered labour [in the Inca empire] went to the state, which applied it both to the reproduction of the material machinery of the state and to the maintenance of the court, and administrative officers, priests, and the military – *i.e.*, officialdom in its diverse categories. The situation here is completely transparent" (Wittfogel, 1968; 189).

13. They have in mind the recently arrived manufacturers, who came to Manaus after the establishment of Suframa and with its support. Traditional crafts are not contemplated in their answers.

14. In a very broad sense. There are Paulistas not only from São Paulo but from practically every Brazilian state, and even some European ones. Paulistas are overwhelmingly managers of local branches of multinational and multiregional firms.

15. Two (maybe three) four-star hotels, a supermarket, and some shops belonged to East Indian families, who had already started investing, in 1987, in the industrial sector as well. The links of these families of Sindhi roots with the East Indian diaspora found in Colón (Panamá), Singapore, Hong Kong, etc., would certainly constitute a fascinating research topic in its own right. According to one of my East Indian informants, his is a small community in Manaus, which, although it never fails to gather "on Independence Day, Constitution Day, Dewali," is rapidly being assimilated by the local society. My informant attributes this assimilation to the surprising absence of "a colour bar" in Manaus and to the influences of everyday life and of television programmes, mainly upon the young.

16. "Native," let it be stressed, no more than in the sense that they were already in the Amazon previous to the establishment, in 1967, of the Zona Franca system. To many of these entrepreneurs much of Weber's description of the "pariah community" would also apply. Keeping also in mind Marx's "Jews in the pores of Polish society," let us read the following quotation from a recent observer: "The so-called rubber economy gave rise to a strange pattern of interaction between the rural areas and the urban sector located in Manaus ... There was no money in the interior and rural produce was exchanged for all sorts of manufactured goods, including household appliances, machines, equipments, etc. Traders based in Manaus took part in this process by importing produce from the hinterland in exchange for everything that was required by the rather primitive latex [the raw material for industrial rubber] gathering economy. It is in the wake of this process that we hear of the great merchant firms of that time, such as I.B. Sabba, M.F. Sorfaty, J. Benzecry, O.F. Bauman, and Jacco Sabba" (Mourão, 1984: 17).

17. But then there are several kinds of "natives," as the "immigrants" are themselves aware. They are not likely to confuse the member of a family of traders of recent Portuguese or Middle Eastern origin with a *caboclo* whose parents lived by gathering latex in the jungle.

18. And this represents the whole difference between the power of the *Superintendente da Suframa* and those formerly wielded by the Mogul Emperors.

19. That tendency had already been observed by Mahar in his 1979 book: "Since the passage of

this legislation [creating quotas and a total ceiling of imports], Suframa has shown a marked preference for industry; during 1987, commerce was allocated only 76 million US dollars (23.8%) ... while industry was allocated 200 million (62.5%). During the pre-import restriction year of 1975 ... commerce imported 94 million US dollars (44.9%) and industry imported 100 million (47.8%) of 210 million US dollars total" (Mahar, 1979; 153).

20. Supposing, of course, that the higher the value of a quota attributed to a firm, the bigger the final profit of that firm.

21. Of course table 7.1 is very far from telling us the whole story. It tells us nothing about individual shareholders. I did have access to documents listing every individual owner or co-owner of every firm registered at Suframa, but I did not have the resources, the time, or the institutional support required for a detailed investigation on individual ownership in the Zona Franca.

22. The mere inspection of names listed in table 7.3 indicates the importance in Manaus of investments by multinational and multiregional enterprises, locally represented by what I have called in this paper "surrogate entrepreneurs."

23. "Local" meaning those enterprises which were already installed in Manaus previous to the creation of the Free Zone. Locals often exhibit a somewhat ambiguous attitude toward the Zona Franca, Suframa, and the Superintendent. Thus, one of their representatives, who happened to be one of the most respected tradesmen of traditional Manaus, had a very negative discourse concerning the tax incentive system and the way it was implemented. Yet he added: "I sell to prosperity and I eat from the cake." Then why the negative speech? First, because of what he sees as the inequities of the quota-distributing process. Second, and probably more important, because, in spite of what he may have gained in absolute economic terms with creation of the Free Trade Zone, he, and others like him, who used to constitute *la crème de la crème* of the local society, have suffered a relative loss with the coming into the area of foreign and Paulista firms and of the huge state bureaucracies which the older élites can no longer control.

References

Ans, André-Marcel d'. 1982. *L'Amazonie péruvienne indigène*. Payot, Paris.

Benchimol, Samuel. 1977. *Amazônia*. Editora Umberto Caldeirão, Manaus.

Brandão Lopes, Juarez. 1965. *Empresário industrial e desenvolvimento econômico no Brasil*. Difusão Européia do Livro, São Paulo.

Faoro, Raymundo. 1979. *Os donos do poder: Formação do patronato político brasileiro*. Globo, Porto Alegre.

Ferreira Reis, Arthur César. 1972. *A Amazônia e a cobiça international*. Companhia Editora Americana, Rio de Janeiro.

Hirschman, A.O. 1958. *The strategy of economic development*. Yale University Press, New Haven, CT.

Mahar, Denis J. 1979. *Frontier development policy: A study of Amazonia*. Praeger, New York.

Marx, Karl. 1967. *Capital*. International Publishers, New York.

McClelland, David. 1951. *The achieving society*. Princeton University Press, Princeton.

Mendes, Armando. 1974. *A invenção da Amazônia*. Universidade Federal do Pará, Belém.

Motta, Roberto (ed.). 1985. *A Amazônia em questão*. Massangana, Recife.

Mourão, Assis. 1984. "Artigos sobre a Zona Franca de Manaus veiculados no jornal *A Notícia*. Mimeo, Manaus.

Roberto Motta

Oliveira Mota, Fernando. 1964. *Manual do desenvolvimento econômico*. Fundo de Cultura, Rio de Janeiro.

Raphaël, Freddy. 1982. *Judaïsme et capitalisme*. Presses Universitaires de France, Paris.

Schumpeter, Joseph. 1934. *The theory of economic development*. Harvard University Press, Cambridge, MA.

Sombart, Werner. 1946. *El apogeo del capitalismo*. Fondo de Cultura Económica, México, DF.

Suframa. 1987. *Quotas individuais de importação*. Conforme resolução 023/87, 27 February 1987.

Wagley, Charles (ed.). 1974. *Man in the Amazon*. University of Florida Press, Gainesville.

Weber, Max. 1952. *Ancient Judaism*. The Free Press, New York.

———. 1988. *Die Protestantische Ethik und der Geist des Kapitalismus*. Gesammelte Aufsätze zur Religionssoziologie, Band I, 9. Auflage, J.C.B. Mohr (Paul Siebeck) Verlag, Tübingen.

Weinstein, Barbara. 1986. *The Amazon rubber boom 1850–1920*. Stanford University Press, Stanford, CA.

Wittfogel, Karl A. 1957. *Oriental despotism*. University of Yale Press, New Haven, CT.

———. 1968. "The theory of oriental society." In Morton H. Fried (ed.), *Readings in anthropology*, vol. II (Cultural Anthropology) (Crowell, New York), 179–200.

Part III
The Peruvian Amazon

8

Aquatic and land fauna management among the floodplain ribereños of the Peruvian Amazon

Mario Hiraoka

1 Introduction

In studying the small-scale farmers' economy, social scientists and development planners have tended to place undue emphasis on the role of agriculture. Development planners, attempting to improve the economic lot of the rural poor, have focused their attention mainly on increasing the output of the farming sector. Production and productivity increases have been sought in instruments like improvements in transportation and communication, access to technical knowledge and credit, and the application of science and technology in cultivation procedures (Hecht, Anderson and May, 1988).

More recently, with an increase in ecologically oriented studies which emphasize a holistic approach to viewing human societies, attention has begun to be focused on the adaptation of traditional management practices as an alternative model for improving the living standards of small-scale farmers. The emphasis on indigenous practices is beginning to uncover hitherto unknown aspects of land use. For example, the "discovery" of managed successional forests among the tribal and non-tribal groups in Amazonia has shed new light on the dynamics of swidden farming (Alcorn, 1984; Anderson, 1988; Denevan and Padoch, 1988; Hiraoka, 1986; Padoch et al.,

1985; Posey, 1983; Posey and Balée, 1989). The extraction of economically valuable products from the successional flora is another example (Anderson, 1990; Hecht, Anderson and May, 1988). Likewise, fishing and hunting are also important economic activities practised by many small-scale farmers, yet the contribution of these activities to the overall economy of the peasants has received limited attention. Fishing and hunting provide essentially all the animal protein requirements for many peasant groups (Nietschmann, 1973). Aquatic and land fauna are also major generators of cash income to peasants. Thus, the new directions not only indicate the diverse and complex nature of peasant economies but also point out that traditional management systems may offer important rural development alternatives.

Aside from offering new insights into the small-scale farming economy, the focus on indigenous economic activities contributes to the knowledge of sustainable resource management. Although largely unsubstantiated, ecological disruptions are believed to be minimized under traditional practices, because of the people's long association and familiarity with local ecosystems.

In this study, attention is directed to the understanding of the fishing and hunting activities practised by a group of peasant farmers in Amazonia. The specific objectives are: (1) to evaluate the role of fishing and hunting in producing food and income; (2) to outline the spatial context within which the activities occur; (3) to relate the changes in the faunal population resulting from ecological disruptions associated with cash cropping; and (4) to emphasize the importance of incorporating non-crop activities in rural development projects.

Information was collected among the Amazonian peasants of north-eastern Peru between 1981 and 1987. In addition to several short visits, a year-long stay in a village along the Amazon River (1983/1984) enabled me to record an annual cycle of faunal management. In addition to the changing patterns of fishing and hunting that accompanied the fluctuations in river level, data on harvests, sites, efforts, and harvested species were kept on selected households.

2 The ribereños of San Jorge

The contemporary inhabitants of riparian Amazonia, known as *ribereños* in Peru, consist of a mélange of ethnic groups that includes detribalized natives, mestizos, and European descendants. The actual mix may vary according to the location and history within the basin

(Padoch and de Jong, 1990; Parker, 1985). The majority of the ribereños in the Peruvian north-east consists of mestizos and detribalized Amerindians.

The subsistence techniques of the ribereños inhabiting the shores of white-water rivers are relatively homogeneous. Farming is the major focus, but fishing, hunting, extraction of forest products, and waged labour are also integral economic pursuits of the river people. The primary dietary staples are sweet manioc and plantains. Over sixty other plants are raised, including maize, rice, cow pea, and a number of fruits and vegetables (Hiraoka, 1985). At San Jorge and elsewhere on the floodplains, the ribereños recognize a large number of biotopes. Crop cultivation is based on minute familiarity with these biotopes. Several biotopes are managed simultaneously, each producing a number of differing crops (Denevan, 1984). Judging from historical accounts, the resource perception and management systems appear to be strongly aboriginal in nature, despite almost five centuries of European cultural and biological intermixing. As is seen below, techniques and tools associated with fishing and hunting among the ribereños also remain essentially native in origin.

3 The Amazon floodplain in north-east Peru

The data was collected at San Jorge, an Amazon floodplain community of 250 inhabitants, located 45 km to the south and upriver from Iquitos (fig. 8.1). In the vicinity of Iquitos, a regional service centre of 300,000 people, the floodplain measures between 15 and 25 km in width. The low-lying terrain is composed of fine sediments eroded and transported from the recently uplifted Andean mountains and fluvially deposited mostly during the Quaternary. Locally, the floodplain is called *bajo*. A slightly higher land of Tertiary origin rises 5–40 m above the water level and forms the floodplain borders. The higher ground is named *altura*. The Amazon meanders within the soft sediments, forming single to multiple channels (fig. 8.2).

The floodplain ecosystem consists of varied landforms and aquatic surfaces sculptured by the river. These include the natural levees (*restingas*), mud and sand bars (*barreales* and *playas*), backswamps (*tahuampas*), palm swamps (*aguajales*), lakes (*cochas*), side channels (*caños*), and the trunk river. Excepting the river, the multiple surfaces are covered with diverse vegetation that ranges from palm forests and floodforests to grasses and aquatic macrophytes. The combination of differing land/water and floral associations provide rich

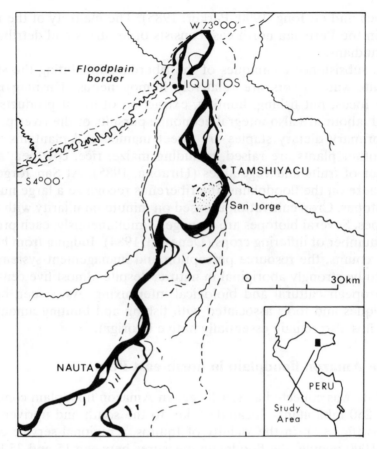

Figure 8.1   **Study site. The village of San Jorge is located on the Amazon floodplain, south of Iquitos.**

habitats for animals and fish. The floodforest on the natural levees extends as a narrow band along the Amazon. The extensive swamps of *aguaje* (*Mauritia flexuosa*) palms occupying the interior of the floodplain, the lake shores, and, above all, the successional flora in differing stages of growth are the primary hunting grounds for the San Jorginos.

4 Ribereño hunting

Hunting, along with fishing, constitutes an integral part of ribereño livelihood. The bulk of the San Jorginos' animal protein and a portion of their cash income derive from the two activities. Game is pre-

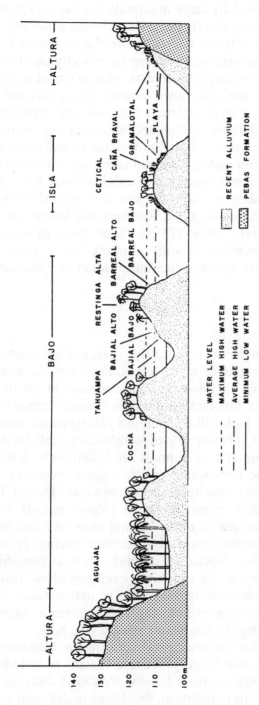

Figure 8.2 **Cross-section of the Amazon floodplain in the vicinity of the study site.**

ferred to fish, especially large mammals like tapir (*Tapirus terrestris*), deer (*Mazama americana*), peccaries (*Tayassu pecari*), and rodents such as capybara (*Hydrochoerus hydrochaeris*), paca (*Agouti paca*), and agouti (*Dasyprocta* spp.). However, scarcity due to over-harvests in the past, unreliability of harvests, and seasonal availability cause the inhabitants to seek the more dependable and abundant fish.

The floodplain, with its nutrient-rich soils and varied biotopes offer a variety of faunal niches and an abundance of food sources. The multiple habitats supported a dense and varied faunal population, but the ease of access from water, external demands for meat and pelt, the slow breeding of some species, and efficient tools have drastically reduced their population within the last two centuries (Hiraoka, 1990; Pierret and Dourojeanni, 1966; Redford and Robinson, 1987; Smith, 1974, 1985; Villarejo, 1979: 173–9). Game meat procurement among contemporary ribereños is still common, but it plays a decidedly minor role in their diet and income production (Bodmer, Fang, and Ibañez, 1988).

Hunting sites

Land fauna is sought throughout the year, but game sites vary in response to changes in river water levels. For example, during the flood season, mid-March to mid-May, game is sought on the levee tops. When most of the low-lying floodplain terrains become underwater, the non-arboreal fauna like armadillo (*Dasypus novemcintus*), tapir, agouti, paca, and tortoise (*Testudo tabulate*) seek food and protection on dry terrain. These animals are killed with shotguns and machetes. When the floodwater recedes, game becomes dispersed on the diverse habitats, and harvests become less efficient. Between August and November, game like coati (*Nasua nasua*), tortoise, tapir, and agouti are sought in mass fruiting sites like the Mauritia palm forests. The dry forest floors also become hunting grounds between July and December. Nocturnal animals, such as armadillo and paca, are harvested during the moonless evenings along trails opened in the forest. Game inhabiting the shores of oxbow lakes and floodplain streams, e.g., capybara and caiman (*Melanosuchus niger*), are killed occasionally during the low-water season (fig. 8.3).

The most productive sites, however, are the human-altered tracts. The ribereños of San Jorge practise a variant of swidden-agroforestry on the flood-free natural levees. *Restingas altas*, or high levees, are rarely subject to inundation. Swiddens in different stages of man-

Figure 8.3 **Rodents comprise the largest share of game killed in the long-inhabited portions of the floodplain.**

agement, agroforests, and diverse successional floral communities are found on these restingas. The abundant food sources, including culti-vated and protected plants like rice, maize, manioc, taro, yam, bana-nas, papaya, guava (*Inga* spp.), peach palm (*Bactris gasipaes*), and yarina (*Phytelephas macrocarpa*), attract a large number of avian, arboreal, and land fauna (table 8.1). The low but dense shrubs and trees, and the partially decomposing logs and branches, offer protec-tive cover, nesting dens, and abundant microfauna for food as well. Among the diverse game species visiting or inhabiting the human-altered habitats, armadillos, agouti, paca, opossum (*Didelphis marsu-pialis*), and small rodents locally known as *ratón/sacha cuy* (*Proechi-mys brevicauda*), comprise the main sources of animal proteins (fig. 8.4). These animals, as pointed out by Irvine (1987) and Linares (1976), have been long associated with swidden gardens and other regrowth stands. The relative abundance of game, especially ro-dents, is the result of human management. Efforts are directed to-wards enriching the food sources through cropping and protection of native fruit trees. In some cases, fruit trees, e.g., ubos (*Spondias mombim*) are protected, or groves of peach palm are planted to at-tract game. Another technique is to remove the adult game popula-tion. This improves the sub-adult survival rates for territorial species

207

Table 8.1 **Game species harvested in human-altered habitats (San Jorge), 1 June 1983–31 May 1984**

Scientific name	Local name	English name	Number killed
Accipitridae			
Sipzaetus tyrannus	gavilán		1
Alligatoridae			
Melanososuchus spp.	lagarto	cayman	12
Anatidae	pato	ducks	1
Ardeidae	garza	heron, egrets	6
Carnivora			
Nasua nasua	achuni	coati	31
Panthera spp.	achuni puma		2
Columbidae			
Columba spp.	paloma de monte	pigeons, doves	37
Columba sp.	torcaz	pigeons	3
Cracidae			
Penelope jacquacu	pucacunga	guan	1
Ortalis gutata	manacaraco		6
Mitu mitu	paujíl	curassow	2
Edentata			
Dasypus novemcintus	carachupa	armadillo	17
Bradypus tridactylus	pelejo	three-toed sloth	1
Marsupialia			
Didelphis marsupialis	zorro	opossum	3
Pelomeducidae			
Podocnemis expansa	charapa	river turtle	1
Podocnemis unifilis	taricaya	river turtle	2
Perissodactyla			
Tapirus terrestris	sacha vaca	tapir	1
Primates			
Saguinus spp.	pichico		6
Saimiri sciureus	fraile		2
Rallidae			
Aramides cajanea	unchala		3
Rodentia			
Agouti paca	majás	paca	39
Dasyprocta spp.	añuje	agouti	34
Myoprocta pratti	punchana	acouchy	18
Holochilus sciureus	zambona	rice-rat	45
Hydrochoerus hydrochaeris	ronsoc	capybara	6
Proechimys spp.	sacha cuy	forest rat	791
Sciureus spp.	pichico	squirrels	26
Testitudinidae			
Geochelone spp.	motelo	tortoise	13
Tinamidae			
Crypturellus untulatus	panguana	tinamou	4
Tinamus major	panguana	tinamou	2

No. of households where data was collected = 12.

Figure 8.4 ***Proechimys brevicauda* is one of the most reliable sources of animal protein from the anthropic forests.**

like the agouti, paca, and ratón (Emmons, 1982, 1990; Smythe, 1978). Although less numerous, mammals like deer (*Mazama americana*), porcupine (*Coendou bicolor*), and various birds are also associated with the ribereño gardens.

Collectively known as *purmeros*, these animals live in a symbiotic relationship with the peasants. The purmeros, although available throughout the year in the new and old gardens, show fluctuations in their populations according to seasons. Peak harvests occur during the high-water season, as pointed out above. The capture of purmeros, especially the small *Proechimys*, has been overlooked in the literature. This largely invisible activity is carried out by women and children, and it contributes significantly to ribereño household protein intake.

In sum, it is possible to state that hunting is carried out in practically all floodplain habitats, but specific harvest sites vary during the year, reflecting factors like ripening season of particular feed sources, ground conditions, and productivity of fishing activities. The example of San Jorge also indicates that numerous birds and mammals are killed, but the focus is mainly on purmeros of the restingas.

209

Hunting tools and techniques

Unlike fishing, where a variety of tools and techniques is employed, and with which much folklore is associated, ribereño hunting is unceremonious and involves few tools and simple techniques. Four tools are used to harvest the animals: shotgun, deadfall trap, bird trap, and spear or harpoon. On occasion, a paca or agouti may be killed with a deadfall trap, but most of the larger rodents and other mammals are harvested with the shotgun. In 1984, ten out of a total of 34 households in San Jorge owned a shotgun. Those who do not possess a firearm often borrow one from a friend or relative. In exchange for its use, the hunter supplies the ammunition and the meat is divided equally with the owner.

Several strategies are employed in harvesting game with the shotgun. Opportunistic hunting is the most common. The firearm is often carried along to the sites of economic activities, especially when evidence of animal presence, e.g. crop feeding, faecal remains, and burrowing, have been noticed during previous forays. Active pursuit is practised when chances of game kills are high. *Restingueo* or restinga hunting, for example, is done during the flood season, when game is frequently spotted in the restricted dry ground. Platform or scaffold hunting is common during periods of mass fruiting: animals are killed from temporary platforms built near feeding sites, such as around the base of a fruit tree, or along pre-cleared trails. Another technique is to set the firearm in the proximity of a salt lick and to activate it with a trip wire.

The most common instrument of animal harvest is the trap. Deadfall traps using fresh banana stalks or tree trunks, and baited with garden crops like maize, manioc, or peach palm fruit, are set in different parts of the agroforest and successional growth (fig. 8.5). At San Jorge, 52 per cent of the households used this tool at least once during 1984. Small game like agouti, yulilla (*Anodus elongatus*), unchala (*Aramides cajanea*), monkeys, and sacha cuy are trapped. Between 25 and 35 of the easily made traps are set by each household. As catches decline rapidly after 15–20 days in a given area, traps are moved to new locations. The practice of hunting zone rotation, which enables game population recovery, is also reported from other parts of Amazonia (Balée, 1985). Baiting is done in the early evening and it is one of the children's chores to check the traps the following morning. Grain crops in the swidden phase of a garden attract numerous birds and small rodents, and many of them are captured with pyramidal

Figure 8.5 **The easily-built deadfall traps, baited with tubers and agroforest fruit, are one of the most efficient hunting tools to harvest small rodents and birds.**

bird traps made by tying twigs and vines. The simple instruments, also built and managed by women and children, are easy to handle and contribute meat to the household in a minor but continuous manner.

Metal-tipped harpoons are used mainly to kill caymans. They are hunted from canoes at night in the floodforests and lakes, especially during the high-water season.

As the hunting tools and techniques suggest, and the historical records corroborate, floodplain hunting does not appear to have been as important an activity as on the interfluvial terrain. There, the absence of reliable sources of fish forced the inhabitants to rely on land fauna as their main source of animal proteins.

Harvest yield and composition

During the 1983/1984 field season, the control group harvested an average of 86.2 kg per household. The meat came from most biotopes, but the most productive were the agroforests and successional communities, where 75 per cent of the kills occurred. As might be expected, returns were greatest during the flood season (February–

211

May), when 68 per cent of the land fauna were caught. Of the total catch, 47.8 per cent consisted of small game, i.e., purmeros like agouti, armadillo, paca, and small rodents, and birds like dove (*Columba* spp.), pucacunga (*Penelope jacquacu*), and unchala (*Aramides cajanea*). Average returns to labour are comparable to those on fishing, i.e. 1.1 kg/hr. However, the relatively high productivity results mainly from the ribereños' emphasis on small purmeros, abundant in the vicinity of settled areas. Occasionally a tapir, deer, or peccary may be killed, but this are so rare and unreliable an occurrence that there is no riverine settlement in the Iquitos area that specializes in ungulate hunting.

Wild meat, especially that of agouti, armadillo, and paca, finds a ready market in Iquitos, but, as the supply is not sufficient to meet village needs, most of the game is consumed locally. Reflecting the scarcity and the craving of the inhabitants for game meat, most animals end up on the table.

5 Fishing

The floodplains of Amazonia have supported a large and dense population since prehistoric times (Denevan, 1976; Roosevelt, 1989, 1991). High demographic density was enabled by the rich edaphic resource and by the abundant fisheries. To this day, the ribereños rely on fish to fulfil most of their amino acid needs. On the floodplains, fishing plays a role comparable to farming. As in agriculture, it supplies one of the vital ingredients of food intake, and it also contributes to producing cash. As such, every household is engaged in the activity during most of the year.

As with farming, there are a number of cultural controls influencing the exploitation rates, harvest location, and consumption patterns of fish. For example, until recently, the two lakes within the bounds of San Jorge, Ahuasi Cocha and Cocha de Mangua, were believed to be inhabited by *yacu maman*, the "mother of the lake." This supernatural being discouraged fishing with nets and canoes, thus assuring the local inhabitants with a sustained supply of fish (Galvão, 1955: 98). The feeding behaviour, taste, odour, and appearance of fish, in association with belief in supernaturals, developed into taboos. These culturally conditioned avoidances led to the exclusion of the atinga (*Symbrancus marmuratus*), electric eel (*Electrophorus electricus*), canero (*Cetopsis* spp.), carachama maman (*Hemiancystrus arenarius*), and dolphin (*Inia geoffrensis*) from the edible species list.

Although women sometimes fish with poles, the task of procuring fish has been predominantly a man's activity. Touching or crossing over the fishing equipment and canoes by women, especially those in menstruation, are thought to bring bad luck. Ritual purification of the fisherman's body, tools, and canoes with *ajo sacha* (*Monsoa alliacea*) to assure a good catch, as well as other practices, have traditionally played important roles in ribereño fishing. Activities associated with fishing have contributed also to maintaining solidarity among the inhabitants. Solitary fishing is possible when using projectiles like gigs and harpoons, but the use of nets and trotlines is commonly done in pairs. Larger groups, consisting of five to six members, are common during the *mijanos* or periods of fish migration. These groupings fulfil not only an economic objective but also social needs. As the fishing does not take place continuously, the moments in between are spent in socialization. San Jorge is situated on a broad stretch of the floodplain containing extensive tahuampas and cochas rich in fishing grounds. During the mijanos, ribereños without access to such terrain flock in selected segments of the shore where fish are exiting from the floodplain and moving upstream close to the banks. Seasonal concentration of people on such sites offers opportunities to re-establish contacts with people from neighbouring villages. Household fish is not continuously available because of fluctuating day-to-day yields. Moreover, the demands of other chores do not allow daily fishing. Since fish is a desirable item, the product is continuously exchanged between households and serves to maintain social bonding. Fishing, then, does much more than provide income and a balanced diet to the dwellers. It is an integral element of ribereño livelihood.

Fish habitats

Floodplain inhabitants occupy productive and varied aquatic environments, where fish is available practically all year round. The shallows along the Amazon, such as the mud and sand bars, the floodplain lakes, and the lesser streams, serve as the primary fishing sites.

Fisheries in Amazonia are characterized by a diversity of species. The described species alone number over 1,400, thus making the basin the largest in speciation of any drainage system in the world. Of these, approximately 92 per cent are composed of siluroids (44 per cent), characoids (42 per cent), and cichlids (6 per cent). The large number of species is attributed to a number of factors, including: (*a*) geologic and climatic stabilities, especially the absence of oceanic

213

transgressions and major climatic changes within the recent past; (*b*) the existence of a variety of ecological niches and habitats; (*c*) separation of fish population through physical and chemical barriers like waterfalls, rapids, and differences in hydrochemistry; and (*d*) genetic flexibility favouring mutations (Junk, 1983: 64–7; Rodriguez and Lewis, 1990).

The Amazonian waters, especially those with headwaters in the Andean mountains, generally called white-water rivers, are well-known for a large aquatic biomass (Junk and Furch, 1985). This abundance results from the interplay of several biophysical factors, including climate, geological history, landforms, flora, and hydro-chemistry. The study area receives an average annual precipitation of 2,800 mm. The distribution is uneven. The period of least rain is between August and October, when monthly means decline to 170 mm. During the peak months, February–April, the monthly totals average 340 mm. This seasonality of rains corresponds approximately with that of the headwater areas of the Amazon River and its major southern tributaries. In spite of the seasonality, the abundant rains actively cut down the geologically recent, alkaline-rich ranges, and transport the dissolved and suspended salts to the low-lands. The combination of nutrient-rich water, warm temperatures, and aeration of water through turbulent currents produces an abundant biotic community of phytoplankton and aquatic vegetation, the support base for the aquatic faunal chain.

Although the aquatic environment is favourable, the large fish biomass is also the outcome of a series of adaptations developed for the floodplain ecosystem. Ability to feed on nutritious food is one. During high water, while the nutrient-rich water nourishes the floodforest, the fish enter to consume seeds, nuts, and fruit being shed from the flora. Others feed on vegetation detritus, pollen, insects, algae, fungi, and leaves and roots of aquatic vegetation. The numerous shallow water bodies of the floodplain seasonally support a large fish population, yet the environment is not conducive to year-round subsistence for many species. When the exchange of water with the river is severed during the low-water season, the depressions become cut off from the main channel. An oxygen deficiency develops in the ta-huampas and cochas. Unlike the Amazon, where the churning water mixes the oxygen, its production by phytoplankton is reduced in the stagnant water bodies under the shade of the floodforest.

Concurrently, the bacteria and fungi that decompose the sunken organic matter are also consuming oxygen. Commonly, thus, an oxygen deficiency exists at 2–3m below the surface. To cope with such an environment, the non-migrating floodplain fish have developed a number of adaptive mechanisms. The thin skin among some species serves to absorb additional oxygen. In the case of gamitana (*Colossoma macropomum*), their thick lips serve to ingest the near-surface oxygen. The bottom-feeding carachama (*Pterygoplichthys multiradiatus*) and other catfishes surface periodically to gulp air and absorb the oxygen through their digestive tracts. In addition to the gills, the *Arapaima gigas* solves the anaerobic situation by having oxygen-absorbing bladders (Junk, 1983; Lowe-McConnell, 1977). Other fish migrate during high-water into the floodforest to avail themselves of the abundant food and to gain extra fat, to be expended upon return to the main channel. Some have solved the food scarcity problem through omnivorous behaviour, consuming plankton, fruit, and seeds.

Although our understanding of Amazonian ichthyofaunal behaviour is still imperfect, findings thus far suggest that their numbers are intricately tied in with the seasonal changes in water level, and the multiple micro-terrains and flora of the floodplain.

Groups of fish

There are essentially three groups of fish in the Amazon: the migrating characins, the channel siluroids that prey on the migrating fish, and the floodplain fish (Goulding, 1981). The familiarity with the food, migration, and reproduction habits among the ribereños assure a continuous supply of this protein source for the inhabitants. As a group, the characoids are the most consumed by the riverine people. These fish remain in the numerous floodplain water bodies until the floodforest is seasonally filled with the turbid water. Two or three weeks after the floodplain is linked with the main channel, characins like boquichico (*Prochilodus nigricans*), lisa (*Schyzodon fasciatus*, *Leporinus* spp.), and yahuarachi (*Gasterotomus latior*) form schools and enter the white water-river. These mijanos are caught as they move out of the floodplain (fig. 8.6). Large channel siluroids that feed on the characins are the second group of prized fish. Among the zúngaros or large catfish, the most important are the dorado (*Brachiplastystoma flavicans*), saltón (*Brachiplastystoma filamentosum*), tigre zúngaro (*Pseudoplastystoma tigriinum*), and doncella (*Pseudoplastystoma fasciatum*). The large catfish are caught primarily for the urban market of Iquitos. Often referred to as *pejes negros* (black fish), fish like acarahuazu (*Astronotus ocellatus*), carachama

Figure 8.6   **As a group, characins provide the bulk of the fish caught by the ribere-ños.**

(*Plecostumus* spp.), fasaco (*Hoplias malabaricus*), bojurqui (*Cichlasoma* spp., *Arquidens* spp., *Acaronia* spp., *Geophagus jurapari*), and paña (*Serrasalmus* spp.) reside mainly in the depressions. These are caught mostly during the low-water season, when they become concentrated in the shrinking bodies of water. The black fish have traditionally been exploited for domestic consumption.

Fishing sites

Fishing sites are to a large degree determined by the water level in the Amazon. For example, after the floodplain depressions become connected with the main channel, mijanos begin in late March. For the next seven or eight weeks, as different schools of migrating fish move out from the floodplain, fishermen capture their prey with cast nets by positioning them at the edge of the main channel. Gill nets are tied to the floodforests nearby. During the season, yields may average 7–8 kg/hr, far above the annual mean of 1.4 kg/hr. Large-scale participation among the menfolk is the result of several factors. Although market prices for fish are depressed during the season because of oversupply, the returns on labour are so rewarding that the activity is still attractive. Lack of alternate work on account of inundation is also a factor. The activity is strenuous, but it offers an opportunity for socialization. The outlets of floodplain streams are also sites for placement of bottom trotlines and volantin, hand-cast lines intended to capture the channel siluroids.

With the end of mijanos by late May, and the river returning to its channel, the main locus of fishing becomes the river banks. Here, fishing is not efficient because the water volume is still large and the fish are dispersed in the river. A variety of equipment is employed. Quiet pools on the lee of currents where gramalote (*Paspalum* spp.) grass and other floating meadows are found, or sites with accumulation fishing, *solterito* or short line and hook devices tied to nearby flora, gigs and spears of various types, and cast nets are used. Output averages about 1.0 kg/hr and the catch consists of varied species. Fishing is no longer the sole activity. As the different bottomlands, such as, sand and mud bars, and low levees are uncovered, several tasks await the ribereños. Aquatic protein capture becomes relegated to young boys. If adults participate, it is done in the early morning hours or in between farming chores.

The continuously diminishing flow of water exposes an increasingly large proportion of flood zone by July. Floodplain lake and stream levels decrease rapidly, restricting the habitat of pejes negros. The choice of multiple fishing biotopes imply a variety of species, so that the ribereños can, to a certain degree, select the desired ones. For example, the acarahuazu are caught in the oxbow lakes, while the palometas (*Mylossoma duriventris*), prized for the fat stored in their undersides, are fished in the Amazon. The carachamas are caught in the floodplain streams. To add diversity to the diet, river turtles like taricaya (*Podocnemis unifilis*) or charapa (*Podocnemis expanse*) and their eggs, laid on the sandy beaches, may be occasionally harvested.

Between August and October, when the river level is lowest, the opacity of the water diminishes with less sediment transport. Debris in the channels and depressions become visible. Therefore, cast nets and gill nets are used on the playas (fig. 8.7). With output averaging 1.2 kg/hr, the season is not especially productive, but catches are reliable.

217

Figure 8.7 **Among the nets, the cast net is widely used among the ribereños of the north-eastern Peruvian Amazon.**

As the water begins to rise again in November, channel fishing becomes unpredictable and unreliable. Netting continues in the Amazon, but when that fails, ribereños seek their prey in the floodplain depressions. Yields oscillate around 1.0 kg/hr, and this lower productivity is due in part to the use of less efficient pole fishing.

The period of greatest fish scarcity occurs between late December and March. As the river swells and gradually engulfs the floodplain, the fish disperse into the floodforests. Until most of the low-lying terrain is submerged, hunting for mammals is not highly efficient either. In the absence of productive sites, fishing is attempted in various locations using varied tools. Some venture beyond the community bounds, into lakes three to four hours from the village. Controlled use of piscicides like barbasco (*Lonchocarpus nicou*), sacha barbasco (*Lonchocarpus* spp.), huaca (*Clibadium silvestre*), and catáhua (*Hura crepitans*), although illegal, is practised in portions of the floodplain streams, oxbow lakes, and vegetated sites along the main channel (fig. 8.8) (Acevedo-Rodriguez, 1990: 3). In addition to the pole, nets and trotlines are used in the tahuampas. Projectiles like the gig and spear and hand lines are also employed. The difficulty of catch is reflected in the low productivity. Returns for the sample group aver-

Figure 8.8 **Piscicides, especially barbasco, are sometimes used when nets, gigs, and other tools are unproductive.**

aged less than 1.0 kg/hr between December and March. Yields for March, with the lowest catch, averaged 0.6 kg/hr.

The foregoing suggests that fishing along the Amazon is an activity well defined in both time and place. To ensure a continuous supply of fish, ribereños have to have a detailed knowledge of fishing behaviour and the floodplain ecosystem. To gain such a familiarity, individuals are initiated into the various fisheries activities by the age of five or six, when they begin to accompany their elders in local fishing outings. Gradually, the young learn that the activity is analogous to farming in the region, that is, that it consists of an integrated management of a number of distinct biotopes for a successful year-round supply of fish.

On an annual basis, the ribereños of San Jorge expend between 22 and 30 per cent of their food-getting efforts in fishing, i.e. between 550 and 690 hours per year. This input produces between 770 and 966 kg/yr per household, resulting in an estimated harvest of 22–30 mt/yr of fish from the resource zones available to the villagers. In contrast to the fisheries at Itacoatiara, in the Brazilian Amazon, where a considerable part of the catch is destined for sale, both the total output and the productivity of the San Jorge peasants are low (Smith, 1981). However, the figures from San Jorge are comparable to those of other semi-subsistence ribereños of the Peruvian Amazon (Bergman, 1980: 235). Limited yields among the ribereños are obviously related to their techniques and tools. At the time of fieldwork in 1984, there were only 24 cast nets and eight gill nets in the village. The rest of the equipment consisted mainly of relatively inefficient, traditional, and simple equipment like gigs, harpoons, and poles. Inability to purchase motorized boats and large nets precludes the San Jorginos from venturing into the more productive floodplains of the lower and middle Ucayali, or from increasing the catch during the mijanos. However, as is true also among other riverine communities of Amazonia, fish is available practically all year round and it can be expected to be caught on a reliable basis. This reliability is the result of a combination of factors. Protection of floodforests and tahuampas from deforestation, communal control and limited access of outsiders to inland water bodies such as lakes and floodplain streams, the existence of conservation-oriented folklore, emphasis on extraction of minor forest products, and restricted potential for the sale of fish in the past served as important mechanisms for conserving fisheries.

6 Distribution and consumption

Fish is viewed as a source of food and income by contemporary ribereños. Between 65 and 75 per cent of the catch is consumed locally. As is true in most peasant societies, food serves both social and economic functions. Food sharing among a well-established network of friends and relatives is one of the means for cementing social bonds among the ribereño villagers. The scarcity of fish, especially during the December–March period, makes the product an especially valuable item. Gifts of fish during the season of scarcity are remembered and reciprocated among the villagers. Aside from its social relevance, the partitioning of fish has a practical purpose: since preservation is difficult, reciprocation of supply serves to equalize its year-round availability. Fish is often "borrowed" when other pressing activities like crop harvests or wage labour, or the absence of key family members, preclude fishing. Increasingly, such debts are paid in store-bought goods or cash at a later date.

Several forms of fish preservation are practised to increase continuous supply. The bottom-feeding carachamas, able to withstand high water temperatures and low dissolved oxygen in the water, are kept alive in canoes and plastic or aluminum containers for as long as a week. Nylon nets and caña brava (*Gynerium sagitatum*) stalks are used to prepare small corrals called *rapisheos* to keep the fish alive. Smoke and salt are commonly employed to preserve fish for a few days. The only form of long-term storage practised among the ribereños is to salt and sun-dry the catch. This method enables the fish to be preserved for several months. Although the techniques are known, ribereños rarely practise them consistently. The preference for freshness and regular availability appear to mitigate against preserving the product.

A portion of the fish is destined for the market. During the study period, 25–35 per cent of the catch was sent to Iquitos, but the marketing period and species were well defined. Over 90 per cent of the fish sold from San Jorge was caught during the months of April, May, and July, the main period of mijanos. Among the fish sold, 86 per cent was accounted for by characins like lisa, palometa, boquichico, and carachama. The rest consisted of siluroids, especially dorado and saltón. The significance of fisheries for income generation varied during the year, but its sale accounted for less than 10 per cent of the ribereños' income. During the April–July period, when outside employment and agricultural revenues are limited, fish sales may represent 50–60 per cent of the cash receipts. The capture of ornamental fish for exports was important for a short period in the 1970s at San Jorge. However, the harvest of *piabas*, as the ornamental fish are collectively called, involved few individuals and was limited to the low-water season. The seasonal nature of revenues and the depletion of stock from the neighbouring waters led to the abandonment of this pursuit.

Fishing is likely to continue as a minor income-generating activity into the near future. Increased output is unlikely as conservation-oriented practices are progressively abandoned among the residents and commercial fishermen from Iquitos continue to increase the pressure on the resource with unsustainable practices. Already large catfishes are rare, and choice species like *Arapaima gigas* and *Mylossoma* and *Colossoma* spp. have virtually disappeared from the San Jorge area.

Fish, however, play a major role in the diet of the riverine people. Ichthyofauna are relied on as the main source of animal protein for several reasons. Every household keeps between ten and thirty fowl, but they are raised mainly for sale. Land fauna is insufficient to meet all the animal protein needs on a year-round basis. Cattle and water buffalo meat is unavailable in the village.

7 Changes in fisheries

As is occurring elsewhere along the Amazon, a number of internal and external factors are changing the local fish population and the fish-dominated diet. Rapid regional population growth, especially among the rural people and the urban poor, is placing increasing demands on inexpensive fish-derived protein sources.

Use of new technologies and tools by both the local people and the commercial fishermen is hastening the decline of some species. New forms of land use, competing directly with the habitats of important ichthyofaunal species such as *Arapaima gigas*, *Colossoma* spp., and *Plagioscion* spp., are contributing to their decrease. With increased participation in the market economy, more attention is devoted to saleable species. The breakdown of traditional beliefs, myths, and lore that served to protect aquatic fauna and their habitats is causing the inhabitants to re-evaluate their resource base, often leading to accelerated harvests. The long-term trend does not seem promising. Species composition is becoming streamlined because those species requiring specialized habitats, having limited initial stock, and undergoing selected removal to supply market demands are reduced or eliminated.

The ribereños' fish-based diet shows signs of alteration. With the expansion of cash cropping, an increasing proportion of the inhabitants' time is taken up by agriculture. The detraction of time from fishing seems to be responsible for a slow shift to the consumption of more abundant but less desirable species and lesser per capita intake. Average fish consumption in 1983, the period before rice began to be cultivated for the market by the majority, was 130 g/capita/day. By 1987, the consumption had declined to 94 g/capita. To make up for the shortage, people increasingly resort to purchased items like canned sardines and meat. But as the terms of trade are usually unfavourable to the farmers, animal protein intake declines. A contributing factor is in the change in perception of desirable food. As middle-class urban values diffuse to the riparian communities, the multiple species making up the bulk of the small fish consumed by the ribereños are slowly equated with poverty and low social status. The response has been an increase in the consumption of processed foods, including larger fish like gamitana (*Colossoma macropomum*), paco (*Piaractus brachypomum*), and paiche in salted and dried form. The ecological changes associated with increased extraction of forest products and with the expansion of farming within the floodplain are also responsible for alteration in the amount of fish harvests.

8 Conclusion

San Jorge illustrates the importance of non-agricultural activities in the overall livelihood of Amazonian peasant communities. Aside from contributing to sustenance and to income generation, fishing and hunting play significant roles in the regional economic, social, and ecological stabilities. Mechanisms to maintain inter- and intra-community ties, such as socialization opportunities during the mijanos and partitioning of surplus fauna, are integral parts of the activities. Myths, taboos, and folklore associated with faunal management also serve as crucial elements in maintaining floodplain ecological balance.

It seems appropriate that students of rural economies, especially small-scale farmers, direct attention to non-farm activities for a better understanding of social and economic patterns. Likewise, rural development planning aimed at improving the lot of family farmers has to incorporate not only plans to improve crop production and productivity, but also other complementary activities that may offer valuable information about economically and ecologically sustainable management practices. Increased familiarity with indigenous fishing and hunting activities, in conjunction with a better understanding of the natural history of economically valuable species, may serve to devise wildlife management procedures suited to supplying households with the needed animal proteins and complementing household incomes while maintaining the existing faunal population.

Acknowledgements

The author would like to acknowledge the Museu Paraense Emílio Goeldi-CNPq, the National Geographic Society, the Pennsylvania State System fo Higher Education, and the Millersville University Academic Grants Committee for their financial assistance. He is also indebted to M. Chibnik, C. Padoch, and M. Pinedo V. for valuable insights and discussions over the years on the ribereños of Peru.

References

Acevedo-Rodriguez, P. 1990. "The occurrence of piscicides and stupefactants in the plant kingdom." In G.T. Prance and M.J. Balick (eds.), *New directions in the study* of plants and people (Advances in Economic Botany 8, New York Botanical Garden, New York), 1–9.

Alcorn, J.B. 1984. "Development policy, forests, and peasant farms." *Economic Botany* 38 (4): 387–409.

Anderson, A.B. 1988. "Use and management of native forests dominated by acai palm (*Euterpe oleracea* Mart.) in the Amazon estuary." In M.J. Balick (ed.), *The palm – tree of life: Biology, utilization and conservation* (Advances in Economic Botany 6, New York Botanical Garden, New York), 144–54.

————. (ed.). 1990. *Alternatives to deforestation: Steps toward sustainable use of the Amazon rainforest*. Columbia University Press, New York.

Balée, W. 1985. "Ka'apor ritual hunting." *Human Ecology* 13 (4): 485–510.

Bergman, R.W. 1980. *Amazon economics: The simplicity of Shipibo Indian wealth*. Dellplain Latin American Studies, No. 6. University Microfilms International.

Bodmer, R.E., T.G. Fang, and L.M. Ibañez. 1988. "Ungulate management and conservation in the Peruvian Amazon." *Biological Conservation* 45: 303–10.

Denevan, W.M. 1976. "The aboriginal population of Amazonia." In W.M. Denevan, (ed.), *The native population of the Americas in 1492* (University of Wisconsin Press, Madison), 205–35.

————. 1984. "Ecological heterogeneity and horizontal zonation of agriculture in the Amazon floodplain." In M. Schmink and C.H. Wood, (eds), *Frontier expansion in Amazonia* (University of Florida Press, Gainesville), 311–36.

Denevan, W.M., and C. Padoch. 1988. *Swidden-fallow agroforestry in the Peruvian Amazon*. Advances in Economic Botany 5, The New York Botanical Garden, New York.

Emmons, L.H. 1982. "Ecology of *Proechimys* in southeast Peru." *Tropical Ecology* 23: 280–90.

————. 1990. *Neotropical forest mammals: A field guide*. University of Chicago Press, Chicago.

Galvão, E. 1955. *Santos e visagens*. Companhia Editôra Nacional, São Paulo.

Goulding, M. 1981. *Man and fisheries in an Amazonian frontier*. W. Junk, The Hague.

Hecht, S.B., A. B. Anderson, and P. May. 1988. "The subsidy from nature: Shifting cultivation, successional palm forests, and rural development." *Human Organization* 47 (1): 25–35.

Hiraoka, M. 1985. "Floodplain farming in the Peruvian Amazon." *Geographical Review of Japan* B58: 1–21.

————. 1986. "Zonation of mestizo farming systems in northeast Peru." *National Geographical Research* 2: 354–71.

————. 1990. "The role of swidden fallow in the provision of game: Examples from the Peruvian Amazon." Paper presented at the Annual Meeting of the Association of American Geographers, Toronto, 18–22 April.

Irvine, D. 1987. "Resource management by the Runa indians of the Ecuadorian Amazon." Ph.D. dissertation, Department of Anthropology, Stanford University.

Junk, W.J. 1983. "As águas da região amazônica." In E. Salati, H.O.R. Schubart, and A.E. Oliveira, (eds.), *Amazônia, desenvolvimento, integração, e ecología* (Editôra Brasiliense–CNPq, São Paulo), 45–100.

Junk, W.J., and K. Furch. 1985. "The physical and chemical properties of Amazonian waters and their relationship with the biota." In G.T. Prance and T.E. Lovejoy (eds.), *Key environments: Amazonia* (Pergamon Press, New York), 3–17.

224

Linares, O. 1976. "Garden hunting in the American tropics." *Human Ecology* 4: 331–49.

Lowe-McConnell, R.H. 1977. *Ecology of fishes in tropical waters*. E. Arnold, London.

Nietschmann, B. 1973. *Between land and water: The subsistence ecology of the Miskito Indians in Nicaragua*. Seminar Press, New York.

Padoch, C., J. Chota Inuma, W. de Jong, and J. Unruh. 1985. "Amazon agroforestry: A market-oriented system in Peru." *Agroforestry Systems* 3: 47–58.

Padoch, C., and W. de Jong. 1990. "Santa Rosa: The impact of the minor forest products trade on an Amazonian place and population." In G.T. Prance and M. Balick (eds.), *New directions in the study of plants and people* (Advances in Economic Botany 8, New York Botanical Garden, New York), 151–58.

Parker, E.P. 1985. "The Amazon caboclo: An introduction and overview." In *The Amazon caboclo: Historical and contemporary perspectives* (Studies in Third World Societies 32. College of William and Mary, Dept. of Anthropology, Williamsburg), xvii–li.

Pierret, P.V., and M.J. Dourojeanni. 1966. "La caza y la alimentación humana en las riberas del Rio Pachitea, Peru." *Turrialba* 16 (3): 271–7.

Posey, D.A. 1983. "Indigenous ecological knowledge and development of the Amazon." In E. Moran (ed.), *The dilemma of Amazonian development*, Westview Press, Boulder.

Posey, D.A., and W. Balée (eds.). 1989. *Resource management in Amazonia: Indigenous and folk strategies*. Advances in Economic Botany 7. New York Botanical Garden, New York.

Redford, K.H., and J.G. Robinson. 1987. "The game of choice: Patterns of Indian and colonist hunting in the Neotropics." *American Anthropologist* 89 (3): 650–67.

Rodriguez, M.A., and W.M. Lewis. 1990. "Diversity and species composition of fish communities of Orinoco floodplain lakes." *National Geographical Research* 6 (3): 319–28.

Roosevelt, A.C. 1989. "Lost civilizations of the Lower Amazon." *Natural History* 66: 74–83.

———. (1991). *Mound builders of the Amazon: Geophysical archaeology on Marajó Island, Brazil*. Academic Press, New York.

Smith, N.J.H. 1974. "Destructive exploitation of the South American turtle." *Yearbook of the Association of Pacific Coast Geographers* 36: 85–102.

———. 1981. *Man, fishes, and the Amazon*. Columbia University Press, New York.

———. 1985. "The impact of cultural and ecological changes on Amazonian fisheries." *Biological Conservation* 32: 355–73.

Smythe, N. 1978. *The natural history of the Central American agouti*. Smithsonian Contributions to Zoology, no. 257. Smithsonian Institution Press, Washington, DC.

Villarejo, A. 1979. *Así es la selva*, 3rd edn. CETA, Iquitos.

225

9

Subsistence- and market-oriented agroforestry in the Peruvian Amazon

Christine Padoch and Wil de Jong

1 Introduction

In recent years, researchers have demonstrated that indigenous Amazonians have a profound knowledge of agricultural soils, useful plants and animals, and productive agricultural and forestry techniques (Boom, 1987; Clay, 1988; Denevan and Padoch, 1988; Dufour, 1990; Posey, 1982, 1984, 1985; Prance, 1984; Vickers and Plowman, 1984; and others). Many of these researchers have suggested that indigenous knowledge and technologies can be incorporated into the planning of contemporary agricultural and forestry efforts in Amazonia. Data showing traditional practices to be economically attractive alternatives for recent colonists and other non-indigenous people who need and want market goods are, however, still very scarce. The paucity of demonstrated economic potential is among the most important factors that have recently prompted some experts to question the usefulness of indigenous patterns in future economic development (Redford, 1990).

Increased interest in studying the resource use patterns of indigenous or long-resident, but non-tribal communities of Amazonia, such as Peru's ribereños (de Jong, 1987; Hiraoka, 1985a, 1985b, 1986, 1989; Padoch and de Jong, 1987, 1989, 1990; Padoch et al.,

1985) or the caboclos of Brazil (Anderson et al., 1986; Parker, 1985) may help fill this gap in the discussion of development alternatives for the region. These populations usually participate more actively in local and even export markets than do most tribal peoples, and have needs and expectations that more closely reflect national norms.

Ribereño and caboclo resource use practices show clearly that these frequently ignored people are inheritors as well as adapters of indigenous traditions. Examination of many traditional swidden-fallow agroforesty practices in the Department of Loreto, Peru, provides several examples of how indigenous patterns have been adapted to the market-oriented economy of ribereño villagers (Denevan and Padoch, 1988; Padoch and de Jong, 1987, 1989).

2 Traditional agroforestry in north-eastern Peru

Amazonian agroforestry systems include a diversity of production patterns, ranging from the most subtle manipulation of largely natural forests to increase their economic yields, to the creation and maintenance of near-monocultural commercial orchards (Hecht, 1982; Padoch and de Jong, 1989; Padoch et al., 1985). Many, although not all, of these systems are cyclic and are based on an alternation of intensively cultivated swiddens and less intensively managed fallows. Swidden-fallow use by tribal peoples has been studied in several parts of the Amazon Basin, including areas in Ecuador (Irvine, 1985) and Brazil (Dufour, 1990; Posey, 1982).

We conducted studies on agroforestry in the Department of Loreto, Peru, between 1981 and 1983 as part of a cooperative programme of research between the University of Wisconsin (USA) and the Universidad Nacional de la Amazonía Peruana, and in 1984 and 1985 as participants in a research programme of the Instituto Nacional de Investigacíon y Promoción Agrícola. In this paper, we report on two examples of swidden-fallow agroforestry systems: one typical of a community of tribal Bora Indians, the other a pattern found in the ribereño village of Tamshiyacu. These examples share some characteristics. Both begin as swidden fields, both involve quantitative and qualitative changes in management practices, and both exhibit major shifts over time in species composition and production. However, major differences between the two are also notable, particularly in the diversity, quantity, and destination of the species produced, and in the intensity and quality of their management.

The types that we present are only two of a large variety of swid-

227

Figure 9.1   **Area of study in the Department of Loreto, north-eastern Peru, showing locations of the Bora community of Brillo Nuevo and the ribereño village of Tamshiyacu. (Map drawn by Carol Gracie, adapted from Padoch and de Jong, 1987.)**

den-fallow agroforestry patterns found in the region and should not be considered typical of the Department of Loreto. After presenting and comparing these examples of traditional resource use practices, we shall attempt to point out several aspects of these systems that may prove useful in planning for enhanced agricultural and forestry production in the humid tropics.

3 Swidden-fallow agroforestry among the Bora Indians

The Bora community of Brillo Nuevo is located along the Yagua-syacu River, a tributary of the Ampiyacu River, which itself joins the Amazon around the town of Pebas, 120 km north-east of Iquitos (fig. 9.1). Much of the village territory of Brillo Nuevo is still covered by mature humid tropical forest, although considerable areas of secondary forest, swiddens, and small pastures are found near the settlement. Climatically the area is characterized by consistently high temperatures (around 26°C throughout the year), high humidity, and rainfall averaging almost 3,000 mm per year. (See Denevan and Padoch, 1988, for a more detailed description of the area.) The residents of Brillo Nuevo were brought to the present site by a *patrón* from neighbouring Colombia in 1934. While contemporary Bora use market products and have become assimilated to varying degrees into Peruvian society, their subsistence activities still largely reflect traditional practices. Bora resource use in their homeland closely resembles Brillo Nuevo patterns (Centlivres et al., 1975; Gasché, 1980). The considerable distance of the village from Iquitos, the major regional market, and the difficulty of using boats in the Yaguasyacu river during low water, makes it difficult for most Brillo Nuevo residents to participate actively in local markets.

Bora farmers make new agricultural fields in old forests as well as in secondary forest. Like most Amazonian terra firme farmers the Bora follow a cycle that begins with the cutting, drying, and burning of a forest plot between 0.5 and 1 ha in size. Any valuable species found in the original forest cover, including fruit trees, palms used for fibre, thatching, or construction, and important timber trees are usually spared.

Initial planting includes a variety of crops, but manioc (*Manihot esculenta*), the dietary staple, predominates in new swidden fields. The number of crop species planted varies from field to field. Some swiddens are planted with very few species, others with a large variety. Planted species usually include annuals and perennials. The latter often are species of fruit trees, but other woody species such as coca (*Erythroxylum coca*), or barbasco (*Lonchocarpus* spp.), which is used as a fish poison, are frequently also present.

Bora farmers distinguish between the agricultural phase, in which their fields yield manioc, and which lasts for about two years, and the following phase, in which fields are less actively managed. This second phase begins the transition from the swidden to the swidden-fallow stage. While this transition is occurring in one holding, the Bora cultivator is often already clearing other sites to plant new annual crops. Thus a farmer manages several plots at the same time: swidden fields producing annual crops, other fields just passing into the fallow stage, and still others in the mature forest-fallow phase.

The assemblage of plant species present in a Bora swidden fallow is often very diverse and changes considerably during its life cycle. The pre-existing fruit and other economically important forest trees that were originally spared are often present later in the managed fallow field. Many plants that appear spontaneously from coppicing stumps, or that sprout from seeds, are of use to the owner and may also be left untouched or may even be actively protected. In fact, weeding is often directed toward aiding the growth of valuable "weed" species, as well as the protection of planted crops. Still other individual plants are the result of natural reseeding by planted species. Thus, deliberate planting is only one of many pathways by which a particular individual plant may find itself in a Bora swidden fallow at any particular stage.

The swidden-fallow fields that result from the interaction of these complex processes often include a large variety of useful plants. Denevan and Treacy (1988: 17–18), for instance, found a Bora field, five years after it was first planted, that featured a small, unproductive manioc patch. Six of the other twelve originally planted crops were, however, still yielding well and were frequently harvested. The outer edges of the field were not being actively weeded any more, and secondary vegetation had encroached considerably. This invading vegetation, however, also contained many useful species. Handicraft materials and medicinal species were abundant in this zone, while several trees useful for construction were nearing harvestable size.

Weeding and protection of plants in many Bora swidden fallows continue for at least twelve years after their first planting. One nine-year-old fallow sampled at Brillo Nuevo still included five cultivated fruit species as well as coca; all but the last of these were represented by only a few individuals. Together with these planted trees numerous useful – protected but not planted – species were found, including such valuable construction timbers as tropical cedar (*Cedrela odorata*).

Bora swidden-fallow management techniques result in fields with a very patchy pattern. While overall management of a plot may decrease with time, limited areas may continue to be actively cleared for many years. In older fields the cultivated area shrinks rather than being totally abandoned. Even when a forest canopy covers the entire plot, old fallow areas still yield fruits or other useful materials. During occasional visits farmers will often clear a few lianas or other plants which threaten to interfere with economically valuable species. Even after twenty years cultigens may still be harvested. One such field that was studied included three cultivated fruit species and another 53 useful native forest species. These included species used as construction materials, medicines, and foods, and in basket-making, salt-making, and extraction of pitch.

Swidden-fallow fields located at larger distances from the village attract a variety of forest animals that come to feed on the fruits of the planted and protected trees. In certain seasons animals appear in fallow fields in higher numbers than in the surrounding forest. The swidden-fallow fields then become important hunting sites, especially abundant in fruit-eating monkeys and large rodents.

Although the general pattern we described above is fairly common among Brillo Nuevo farmers, numerous geographical, cultural, ecological, personal, and purely chance factors give rise to variations in the composition of a swidden fallow. Among important variables that contribute to this diversity are: the age of the original vegetation as well as its previous use, the distance of the field from the village, other fields the owner farms, soil conditions, drainage, slope, and aspect of the site.

Although each Bora swidden fallow differs in exact species composition from every other, most older fields are rich in useful plants. In the fallows that were sampled at Brillo Nuevo, a total of 133 useful species were identified. The Bora swidden-fallow agroforestry pattern, characterized by a high diversity of species, appears appropriate for a population that seeks to satisfy a wide variety of its daily needs through harvesting its own fields and forests. With little access to markets, the Bora cannot and do not specialize in the production of any particular plant species. Rather, they seek to produce a little of many different things. This pattern, which may have been typical of Amazonian communities in the past, is not a universal strategy among the rural folk of the Department of Loreto.

4 Market-oriented agroforestry in Tamshiyacu

The town of Tamshiyacu, located 30 km upstream from Iquitos, is known as one of the most important native fruit-producing areas in the region. The two principal products marketed by Tamshiyaquinos, pineapples and umarí (*Poraqueiba sericea*), are cultivated within a well-designed, market-oriented agroforestry system. The two products are harvested at different phases of this system. Although Tamshiyacu farmers do grow products destined for household consumption, a market emphasis pervades virtually every phase of this particular agroforestry system. (For more detailed information on Tamshiyacu agriculture see de Jong, 1987; Hiraoka, 1986; Padoch et al., 1985.)

In contrast to the Bora, the people of Tamshiyacu are not officially recognized as Indians, that is, natives of the region, although few if any Tamshiyaquinos are recent arrivals. They belong to a large group of Amazonians known locally as ribereños (Padoch, 1988), who are largely offspring of detribalized natives and immigrants who arrived during or soon after the great Rubber Boom of the turn of the century. This largest group of rural people in the lowland Peruvian Amazon has gone surprisingly unnoticed by scientists.

Tamshiyacu is one of the larger towns in the area, and the majority of its approximately 2,000 inhabitants are farmers who frequently visit Iquitos and its markets. Transportation is provided by *colectivos* (river buses), several of which leave the village for the city early in the morning, or pass by from upstream and stop at the village dock. Many producers, however, choose not to make the trip themselves but sell their products to middlemen in the village itself.

In Tamshiyacu, which is both more populous and longer-settled than Brillo Nuevo, mature forest is found at a greater distance from the community centre. Tamshiyacu farmers, like the Bora, begin the swidden-fallow agroforestry cycle by clearing patches of forest, both primary and secondary. As in Brillo Nuevo, valuable forest species including palms and fruit trees may be spared. However, in contrast to the practice of Bora farmers and other tribal shifting cultivators, part of the cut and slashed vegetation is not burned in the field but is turned into charcoal for sale in Iquitos. Sites where charcoal is made are then often reserved for the planting of nutrient-demanding crops.

Most of the crop species planted in Brillo Nuevo can also be found in Tamshiyacu fields. In the town, however, the selection of cultigens, and especially the quantity planted of any species, is determined more by recent and expected urban market price trends than by household needs. The first crops to be harvested are manioc and plantains, which are also planted first. Both these crops, meant for market and household consumption, are commonly replanted after the first harvest. The planting of a field is, however, a complex process that continues for a over a year or more. After manioc and plantains, other annuals and several perennials are planted. The timing of many plantings depends on the availability of seeds or seedlings.

However, a field may already show a large diversity of crops at an early stage. After about two years, manioc and plantain production is phased out and pineapples start producing in quantity. At this point, the fields change primarily into cash crop plantations. Pineapple is harvested until the fourth year. By then, tree crops have come into prominence.

Apart from umarí (*Poraqueiba sericea*), trees commonly planted in agroforestry fields are fast-growing but short-lived species such as cashew (*Anacardium occidentale*), uvilla (*Pourouma cecropiaefolia*), and caimito (*Pouteria caimito*). The production of these fruits starts early and does not last very long; their productive life is from two to six years. Together with pineapple these fruits provide cash income during the transition stage from swidden to mature fruit orchard. Once production of these species has declined, umarí, a much-favoured fruit in the Iquitos market, becomes the pre-eminent product. An umarí stand normally yields for at least thirty years, although examples of sixty-year-old umarí orchards can be found. Yields of up to 80,000 fruits per hectare of umarí orchard are not unusual. A second important cash crop species in older orchards is Brazil nuts (*Bertholletia excelsa*). This long-lived tree crop has traditionally been planted in small quantities, although farmers now are increasingly including this crop in their fields.

Although total labour input declines when fields become older, Tamshiyacu farmers clean their field thoroughly as long as they are being harvested. In the swidden stage, while manioc is in production, weeding and harvesting are done frequently. When pineapple becomes the principal crop, fields continue to be weeded once or twice a year. However, as perennials take over, weeding changes in intensity. The more careful weeding in early swiddens gives way to a more rapid slash weeding in older fields. The shade provided by the fruit trees allows for more open understorey in older fields and a much faster weeding. Some cleaning, however, remains essential even in old fields, since umarí fruits must be gathered when they fall to the ground. Although several naturally occurring fruits or other useful species may survive the periodic weeding of an umarí orchard, Tamshiyacu agroforesters commonly protect or encourage far fewer forest species than do the Bora.

After thirty years or so, production in many umarí fruit orchards declines. The stand is then cut, with many of the umarí trees made into charcoal. Brazil nut trees, however, are not felled since they continue to fruit for a much longer time. After cutting, the umarí field may be fallowed for five to ten years, but it is not unusual to see farmers plant new swiddens immediately, and begin the cycle again.

Although we have presented a generalized picture of agroforestry in Tamshiyacu, individual differences among farmers, their fields, and the management techniques they employ are notable. Some farmers never use forest slash to make charcoal, some never convert annual crop fields to perennial-dominated orchards, some market most of their produce, others market little. Furthermore, it must be pointed out that many residents of Tamshiyacu engage in other economic pursuits. Some have diverse agricultural holdings in the Amazon floodplain (Hiraoka, 1986). Most farmers are also hunters, fishermen, occasional waged labourers, or even market vendors. The majority of Tamshiyacu farmers, however, obtain the bulk of their income from selling cultivated fruits from agroforesty fields (Padoch, 1988). While incomes vary enormously, Tamshiyacu producers as a group are exceptional in the level of incomes they report from sales of agroforestry products. Owners of large umarí orchards have incomes several times the Amazonian average. Yearly household incomes of approximately US$5,000 were enjoyed by several Tamshiyacu umarí producers, a level few other rural residents of the region ever reach.

5 Conclusions and recommendations

We have presented descriptions of agroforestry practices found in two communities in the Peruvian Amazon. One of our sample villages is inhabited by members of a tribal group, the other is a settlement of non-tribal, but none the less largely indigenous Amazonians known as ribereños. The Tamshiyacu and the Bora systems show some obvious similarities; ribereño practices should quite clearly be considered a transformation and adaptation of indigenous tribal patterns. However, the two systems described differ dramatically as well. In Tamshiyacu, production in older fields becomes highly specialized, reflecting the relatively easy access the town's farmers have to the Iquitos market. Brillo Nuevo farmers, on the other hand, do not have the same market opportunities. Their system is much more generalized, diverse in species, and successful in satisfying the many needs of farmers in an area far from markets.

The differences in species composition and production between the two Amazonian settlements largely reflect differences in management. Tamshiyacu orchards are managed more intensively over a longer period, while Bora farmers allow, even encourage, more forest vegetation in their ageing fallows.

While the choice to specialize does help Tamshiyacu farmers frequently to earn high incomes, it also has drawbacks. In years of particularly high umarí production throughout the Iquitos region, a considerable part of the harvest cannot be sold and farmers are not adequately compensated for their labour investments. To date, no suitable process for preserving the bland, oily pulp of the umarí fruit has been developed and all fruit must be consumed fresh.

We have noted that the two descriptions given here are not an exhaustive summary of agroforestry types found in the lowland Peruvian Amazon. Our research indicates that agroforestry systems in the Peruvian Amazon are widespread and greatly varied (see Padoch and de Jong, 1987). There is no one Amazonian agroforestry system. Local patterns of swidden-fallow agroforestry are highly flexible, adaptable to various environmental and economic conditions. The examples that we have presented are also highly dynamic. Active experimentation occurs in both communities, as farmers attempt to accommodate their agroforestry practices to changing environmental and economic conditions.

In focusing much of our discussion on the market-oriented system of Tamshiyacu, we would particularly like to emphasize the need to study the traditional systems of non-tribal communities. These forgotten villages of the Peruvian Amazon (and of other Amazonian states) often present useful models to resource use planners. Yet it is the remote, tribal communities that have been given more attention. Most ribereños or mestizos living within a day's travel of Iquitos participate more actively in market trade than do natives on small isolated tributaries. Rather than using such tribal systems as models, and speculating on how these might serve the Amazonian who is heading toward increased market involvement, ribereño patterns may offer a more accessible model.

Our investigations in the Iquitos area have pointed out the great importance of market access and market demand in determining the configuration of a particular agroforestry system. The example taken from Tamshiyacu demonstrates conclusively that swiddeners can and do respond strongly to market opportunities. However, the market of Iquitos, like many tropical regional markets, is limited and often cannot consume even the yields that are produced. Research and extension in agroforestry systems must be accompanied by sound economic knowledge and advice. If the small farmers of Iquitos and similar regions elsewhere are to be encouraged to augment their production of fruits and other agroforestry products, they must also be presented with opportunities for processing and extraregional export of those products.

References

Anderson, A.B., A. Gely, J. Strudwick, G.L. Sobel, and M.G.C. Pinto. 1986. "Um sistema agroflorestal na várzea do estuário amazónico" (Ilha das Oncas, Municipio de Barcarena, Estado do Pará). *Acta Amazonica* 15 (1–2): 195–224.

Boom, B. 1987. *Ethnobotany of the Chacobo Indians, Beni, Bolivia.* Advances in Economic Botany 4. New York Botanical Garden, New York.

Centlivres, P., J. Gasché, and A. Lourteig (eds). 1975. *Culture sur brulis et évolution du milieu forestier en Amazonie du Nord-ouest.* Musée d'Ethnographie, Geneva.

Clay, J.W. 1988. *Indigenous peoples and tropical forests.* Cultural Survival Report 27. Cambridge.

De Jong, W. 1987. "Organizacíon del trabajo en la Amazonía peruana: El caso de las sociedades agrícolas de Tamshiyacu." *Amazonía Indígena* 7 (13): 11–17.

Denevan, W.M., and C. Padoch (eds.). 1988. *Swidden-fallow agroforestry in the Peruvian Amazon.* Advances in Economic Botany 5. New York Botanical Garden, New York.

Denevan, W.M., and J.M. Treacy. 1988. "Young managed fallows at Brillo Nuevo." In Denevan and Padoch, 1988, 8–46.

Dufour, D.L. 1990. "Use of tropical rainforests by native Amazonians." *BioScience* 40 (9): 652–59.

Gasché, J. 1980. "El estudio comparativo de los sistemas de cultivo nativos y su impacto sobre el bosque amazónico." In *Consulta científica subregional sobre las actividades de corte y quema en el ecosistema de bosque tropical* (Man and the Biosphere Programme, Iquitos), 61–74.

Hecht, S.B. 1982. "Agroforestry in the Amazon Basin: Practice, theory and limits of a promising land use." In S.B. Hecht, (ed.), *Amazonia: Agriculture and land use research* (CIAT, Cali), 331–71.

Hiraoka, M. (1985a). "Mestizo subsistence in riparian Amazonia." *National Geographic Research* 1: 236–46.

———. 1985b. "Changing floodplain livelihood patterns in the Peruvian Amazon." *Tsukuba Studies in Human Geography* 3: 243–75.

———. 1986. "Zonation of mestizo riverine farming systems in northeast Peru." *National Geographic Research* 2: 354–71.

———. 1989. "Agricultural systems on the floodplains of the Peruvian Amazon." In J. Browder (ed.), *Fragile lands of Latin America* (Westview Press, Boulder), 75–99.

Irvine, D. 1985. "Succession management and resource distribution in an Amazonian rainforest." Paper presented at meeting of the American Anthropological Association, Washington, DC.

Padoch, C. 1988. "People of the floodplain and forest." In J.S. Denslow and C. Padoch, (eds.), *People of the tropical rain forest* (University of California Press, Berkeley and Los Angeles), 127–40.

Padoch, C., and W. de Jong. 1987. "Traditional agroforestry practices of native and ribereño farmers in the lowland Peruvian Amazon." In H.L. Gholz, (ed.), *Agroforestry: Realities, possibilities, and potentials* (Martinus Nijhoff, Dordrecht), 179–94.

———. 1989. "Production and profit in agroforestry: An example from the Peruvian Amazon." In J. Browder, (ed.), *Fragile lands of Latin America* (Westview Press, Boulder), 102–14.

———. 1990. Santa Rosa: "The impact of the minor forest products trade on an Amazonian place and population." In G.T. Prance and M. Balick (eds.), *New directions in the study of plants and people* (Advances in Economic Botany 8, New York Botanical Garden, New York), 151–8.

Padoch, C., J. Chota Inuma, W. de Jong, and J. Unruh. 1985. "Amazonian agroforestry: A market-oriented system in Peru." *Agroforestry Systems* 3: 47–58.

Parker, E.P. (ed.). 1985. *The Amazon caboclo: Historical and contemporary perspectives*. Studies in Third World Societies 32. College of William and Mary, Dept. of Anthropology, Williamsburg.

Posey, D.A. 1982. "Keepers of the forest." *Garden* 6 (1): 18–24.

———. 1983. "Indigenous ecological knowledge and development of the Amazon Basin." In E. Moran (ed.), *The dilemma of Amazonian development* (Westview Press, Boulder) 225–57.

———. 1984. "A preliminary report on diversified management of tropical forest by the Kayapo Indians of the Brazilian Amazon." In G.T. Prance and J. Kallunki (eds.), *Ethnobotany in the neotropics* (Advances in Economic Botany 1, New York Botanical Garden, New York), 112–26.

———. 1985. "Indigenous management of tropical forest ecosystems: The case of the Kayapo Indians of the Brazilian Amazon." *Agroforestry Systems* 3: 139–58.

Prance, G.T. 1984. "The use of edible fungi by Amazonian Indians." In G.T. Prance and J. Kallunki (eds.), *Ethnobotany in the Neotropics* (Advances in Economic Botany 1, New York Botanical Garden, New York), 127–39.

Redford, K.H. 1990. "The ecologically noble savage." *Cultural Survival Quarterly* 15 (1): 46–8.

Vickers, W.T., and T. Plowman. 1984. "Useful plants of the Siona and Secoya Indians of eastern Ecuador." *Fieldiana*: Bot., N.S. 15: 1–63.

10

Local management of forest resources in a rural community in north-east Peru

Miguel Pinedo-Vasquez, Daniel Zarin, and Peter Jipp

1 Introduction

Indigenous systems of natural resource management in the Amazon Basin have led outside observers to judge the productivity and sustainability of those systems in dramatically different ways. Two opposing points of view about the sustainability of forest management systems are prevalent in the available literature. One group of analyses describes indigenous forest management as primitive, unproductive, and unsustainable (e.g. Benedict, 1959; Redfield, 1953). Those analyses reinforced the biases of many of the region's urban-based politicians and bureaucrats, who often choose to neglect the interests of distant rural Amazonians. More recent analyses tend to depict traditional forest management techniques as blueprints for optimal use of available resources (see, for example, Posey and Balée, 1989).

We believe that reality is neither as black nor as white as most of its interpreters portray it. Those who interpret particular places, peoples, and times generally do so more accurately than authors who write about the Amazon as if it were one homogeneous region. Indigenous methods of resource use are neither always unsustainable nor always sustainable. Rather, from a management perspective, such

238

systems can provide valuable insights, and valuable tools, for the planning and implementation of resource use and protection in different regions within the Amazon Basin.

In the region surrounding the city of Iquitos, in north-east Peru, indigenous systems of forest management are diverse and complex. Such systems have developed based upon the diversity of useful forest resources and the cultural diversity of the local populations.

None the less, overexploitation of highly valuable resources has always been a problem in the region. As early as the sixteenth century, for example, a report from the region mentions that native people had overhunted manatee (*Trichecus inunguis*) in the lakes and streams of the Marañon and Ucayali Rivers (Maroni, 1988). In other floodplain areas within the Amazon Basin, archaeological evidence suggests that overexploitation of fish and game resources by densely populated settlements forced Indian groups to migrate constantly from one location on the floodplain to another (DeBoer, 1981; Roosevelt, 1989).

2 Study area and objectives

During the summer of 1989, we conducted a study of forest resource management in the village of San Rafael, located two hours down the Amazon River from the city of Iquitos (figure 10.1). The village is one of many ribereño communities situated on the terra firme banks of the Amazon and its tributaries. In addition to the extraction of forest products, other important economic activities within the community include agriculture, fishing, hunting, temporary work in the cities, and the market exchange of cash and products both in the city and within the community itself. In the region generally, rural inhabitants depend on a wide range of extractive and productive economic activities (San Román, 1975; Hiraoka, 1985; Padoch, 1987).

In our study we examined different forest uses within the community as well as other human activities and their impacts on the sustainability of forest resource use. In particular, we addressed the following questions: (i) What forest types are present in the area? (ii) What products do members of the community extract from those forest types? (iii) How abundant are the economic resources of the forests? (iv) Are forest resources sustainably managed, or overexploited? (v) How does the community attempt to control the extraction and use of forest resources?

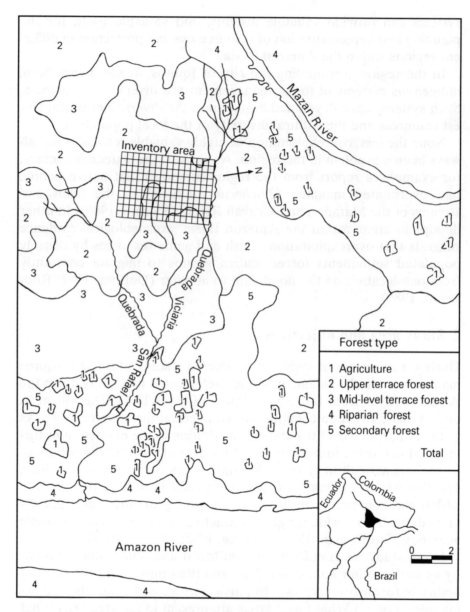

Figure 10.1 **Area of study, San Rafael, Iquitos, Peru.**

To answer these questions, we conducted questionnaires and personal interviews in each household in the community. We were aided by two local teachers. Additionally, we conducted a forest inventory, gathering information on the quantity, distribution, and uses of over two hundred tree species. The complete results of an ethnobotanical inventory are reported elsewhere (Pinedo-Vasquez et al., 1990).

3 Population dynamics

The population of San Rafael is descended from three indigenous groups: Cocama, Napo Quichua, and Lamista Quichua. A demographic census which we conducted in the community revealed that people from San Rafael continually move between the community and the city of Iquitos. Due to this constant migration, the total population in the community fluctuates throughout the year. The population of San Rafael is therefore divided into two groups: the permanent population, and the mobile population. The permanent population consists mostly of children and old people. The most mobile segment of the population are young people between the ages of 15 and 25.

During 1989 there were 333 permanent residents of San Rafael and a mobile population of an additional 124 (figure 10.2). Children (<15 years) constitute the largest segment (53 per cent) of the total population both in San Rafael and in other rural communities throughout the region (Ministerio de Educación, 1986). The number of perma-

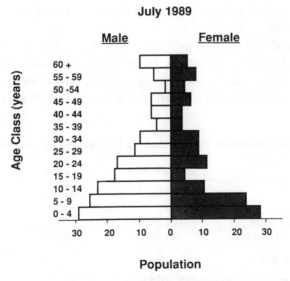

Figure 10.2 **Population pyramid, San Rafael, July 1989.**

nent residents between the ages of 15 and 25 is quite low, and the female population between the ages of 15 and 19 is extremely small. Many of these young women reside in Iquitos and make a living at domestic work. Thirty-one children (18% of the under-15 population) are being raised by their grandparents; these are the offspring of single mothers working and living in Iquitos. Similar results have been reported for other communities in the region (Chaumeil, 1984). The instability of rural populations, in particular the absence of young adults within the rural communities, is indicative of a lack of rural economic opportunities.

4 Distribution and use of terra firme lands in the community

With the exception of a narrow floodplain facing the Amazon River, San Rafael is located entirely on upland, terra firme, deposits. On the terra firme, lands are divided into three categories according to type and intensity of use: *chacras*, *purmas*, and *monte alto*. *Chacras* are swidden fields, generally planted with a succession of four crops: upland rice (*Oryza sativa*), cassava (*Manihot esculenta*), plantain, and banana (*Musa paradisiaca*). Prices for rice are set by the government, and credit is available for the production of all four crops (Chibnik, 1986; Hiraoka, 1988). The term *purma* includes a wide range of fallowed fields, from recently overgrown chacras to thirty-year-old successional forest. *Monte alto* are areas of older, intact forest. The use and distribution of land between the three categories is outlined in table 10.1.

An estimated 100.6 ha of agricultural fields (chacras) were planted and harvested in the community from January to July 1989, an average of 1.8 ha per household. The agricultural produce of San Rafael is either consumed locally or sold in the Iquitos markets (table 10.2).

Table 10.1 **Land distribution by household in San Rafael, Iquitos, July 1989**

	Monte alto	purmas	field
Total	303 ha	612 ha	100.6 ha
Total households	20	37	55.0
Average has/household	14.85 ha	16.54 ha	1.8 ha
% total household owned	38.1%	67.3%	100%

Total population: 333

Total land distribution by household: 1015.6 ha.

Table 10.2 **Production of four crops in San Rafael, Iquitos, July 1989**

Crops	hectares	planted (ha)	harvested (ha)	production	consumed	sold
Rice	16.3	11.3	5.0	12,600 kg	1,900 kg	10,700 k
Cassava	36.8	12.0	24.8	98,700 kg	62,900 kg	35,800 k
Plantain	34.0	21.5	12.5	5,970 r	1,905 r	4,065 r
Banana	13.5	11.0	2.5	250 r	110 r	140 r
Total	100.6	55.8	44.8	—	—	—

r = racemes

Rice is primarily sold in Iquitos. From a total of 12,600 kg of rice harvested between January and July 1989, only 1,900 kg (15 per cent) were consumed locally; the remainder was sold to government rice centres in Iquitos. Most of the plantain and banana grown in San Rafael is also marketed rather than consumed locally. Cassava, however, is primarily a subsistence crop; 63.7 per cent (98,700 kg) of the cassava produced between January and June 1989 was consumed locally. Per capita consumption of cassava, if we use the permanent population figure, is equal to about 1.6 kg per day.

Purmas cover a total area of 612 ha in San Rafael, representing 58.5 per cent of the total land area claimed by members of the community. Purmas are distributed among 37 households in the community. Recent arrivals in the community and the households of young couples generally do not claim purmas. Family and fictive kinship networks, however, often permit members access to their purmas. Fruits and construction materials are the most common economic products of purmas in San Rafael. With few exceptions these are used locally and do not enter into the market economy.

Elsewhere in the region, the management of fallows for marketed products is much more intensive than in San Rafael. In the town of Tamshiyacu, for example, Padoch et al. (1985) and Hiraoka (1986) have documented exceptional production of fallow products, principally a fruit called umarí (*Poraqueiba sericea*), for the Iquitos market. Padoch (1987) has also demonstrated the variability in resource use patterns both between and within ribereño villages, providing a good caveat for extrapolating results from one site to the entire region.

Historically, monte alto has belonged to the community as a whole. Retaining communal rights to non-agricultural land is an indigenous tradition in the region (Chaumeil, 1984). This tradition is recognized in Peru by the *Ley de Comunidades Nativas y de Desarrollo Agrario*

243

de las Regiones de Selva y Ceja de Selva, decreed by the government in 1973, which recognized the rights to land and resource tenure of tribal peoples. Non-tribal villages, including the hundreds of ribereño communities in the lowland Peruvian Amazon, are not extended rights of ownership to land or resources. Nonetheless, in 1984, an area of about 800 ha adjacent to the village of San Rafael was designated a forest reserve by the members of the community. The establishment of a reserve in San Rafael originated from a need to protect forest resources in monte alto from the extractive activities of outsiders, mainly timber companies. The formalization of the reserve in a communal assembly thus asserts a traditional regulatory mechanism as a response to a new necessity to protect forest resources from outside depredation. The extraction of forest resources from the reserve is regulated by written communal rules, although legal control of the land remains under the jurisdiction of the Ministry of Agriculture. Resources present in the reserve include latex, resins, fruits, medicinal products, timber, roundwood, and other construction materials.

In 1986, about 300 ha of monte alto was distributed among twenty heads of households in the oldest and largest families of the community. Land distribution was accomplished at a communal meeting which included representatives from the Ministry of Agriculture and the regional authorities. Each family received a temporary *certificado de posesión* which can be used as collateral for agricultural loans at the agrarian bank. Most of the families have requested loans for rice production. The distributed land is located along a path from an adjacent community on the Mazan River to San Rafael, on the Amazon River.

5 Traditional use of forest resources

Forest resources are utilized both for subsistence and for access to markets in Iquitos. Certain products are collected primarily from purmas, others from monte alto; many products are found in both land types. Because purmas are located closer to chacras and to village households, the intensity of forest product collection is greater there than it is in monte alto. Additionally, varying degrees of cultivation of useful species occur in purmas.

Both purmas and monte alto contribute roundwood and other building materials for house construction. For instance, 52 of the 55 households in San Rafael use palm leaves as roofing material. The frames of houses in the community are built entirely of locally extracted roundwood. Floors and walls are often constructed using

Table 10.3 **Species of roundwood (R) and other construction materials (Com) collected from purmas in San Rafael, Iquitos, July 1989**

No.	Common name	Scientific name	Family	R	Com
1	Atadijo	*Helicteres pentandra*	Sterculiaceae	x	x
2	Shapaja	*Scheelea cephalotes*	Palmae		x
3	Bombonaje	*Carludovica palmata*	Palmae		x
4	Purma caspi			x	
5	Yarina	*Phytelephas microcarpa*	Palmae		x
6	Ocuera	*Pollesta discolor*		x	
7	Pichirina	*Vismia brasilensis*	Clusiaceae	x	
8	Capirona	*Capirona decorticans*	Rubiaceae	x	
9	Huacapu	*Lindackeria paludosa*	Flacourtiaceae	x	
10	Cashapona	*Iriartea exorrhiza*	Palmae		x
11	Huacrapona	*Socratea deltoidea*	Palmae		x
12	Topa	*Ochroma lagopus*	Bombacaceae		x
13	Soldado caspi	*Chimarrhis glabriflora*	Rubiaceae	x	

both local materials and sawn lumber. The roundwood species and other building materials extracted from purmas (table 10.3) differ from those extracted from monte alto (table 10.4).

Species of roundwood and other construction materials generally are not planted in purmas. However, people in the community tend to protect them. For instance, when people clean their fields they usually leave and protect the seedlings of useful tree species. In contrast, useful species in monte alto are not cultivated to any degree. As a result, some of the monte alto species are overexploited. A high market value in Iquitos for a forest species generally leads to its overexploitation. Two such roundwood species are extremely rare at present: huacapu (*Lindackeria paludos*) and tortuga caspi (*Duguetia lucida*). Similarly, chuchuhuasha (*Heisteria pallida*), a medicinal species now widely favoured as an alcohol extract, is quite scarce. These are all slow-growing species, and regeneration in the forest appears to be absent.

Fruit species are also collected from both monte alto and purmas. The number of fruit species collected from monte alto (table 10.5) is greater than that collected from purmas (table 10.6). However, owing to the greater density of fruit-bearing tree species in the more accessible purmas, extraction of fruits from there is more intensive than from monte alto. Nonetheless, two fruit species from monte alto with high value in Iquitos and in the community appear to be overexploited: ungurahui (*Jessenia batua*) and meto huayo (*Loretoa* spp.). Fortunately, these two species can be regenerated in both monte

Table 10.4 **Species of roundwood and other construction materials collected from monte alto in San Rafael, Iquitos, July 1989**

No.	Common name	Scientific name	Family	R	Com
1	Huacrapona	*Socratea deltoides*	Palmae		x
2	Quinilla blanca	*Franchetella gongrijpee*	Sapotaceae	x	
3	Carahuasca negra	*Guatteria decurren*	Annonacae	x	
4	Yarina	*Phytelephas macrocarpa*	Palmae		x
5	Quinilla colorada	*Pouteria laciocarpa*	Sapotaceae	x	
6	Carahuasca blanca	*Guatteria elata*	Annonaceae	x	
7	Puca shimbillo	*Inga* sp.	Mimosaceae	x	
8	Espintana negra	*Xylopia* sp.	Annonaceae	x	
9	Remocaspi	*Aspidosperma excelsum*	Apocynaceae	x	
10	Vara blanca	*Unonopsis stipitata*	Annonaceae	x	
11	Espintana blanca	*Xylopia conjugens*	Annonaceae	x	
12	Yutubanco	*Heisteria* sp.	Olacaceae	x	
13	Tortuga caspi	*Duguetia lucida*	Annonaceae	x	
14	Cashapona	*Iriathea exorriza*	Palmae		x
15	Vino huayo	*Cocoloba* sp.	Polygonaceae	x	
16	Shapaja	*Sheelea cephalotes*	Palmae		x
17	Yanavara	*Trema* sp.	Ulmaceae	x	
18	Pinsha callo	*Xylopia aromatica*	Annonaceae	x	
19	Rifari	*Miconia aurea*	Melasstomataceae	x	
20	Huacapu	*Lindackeria paludosa*	Flacourtaceae	x	
21	Quillosica	*Cassia* sp.	Caesalpinaceae	x	
22	Tahuari blanco	*Tabebuia capitata*	Bignoniaceae	x	
23	Chontaquiro	*Unonopsis peruviana*	Annonaceae	x	
24	Estoraque	*Psychotria* sp.	Rubiaceae	x	
25	Rifari blanco	*Miconia aulocalyx*	Melastomataceae	x	
26	Espintana colorada	*Xylopia cuspidata*	Annonaceae	x	
27	Acero caspi	*Cassia* sp.	Caesalpinaceae	x	
28	Aceite caspi		Annonaceae	x	
29	Lanza caspi	*Flusaea longifolia*	Annonaceae	x	
30	Quinilla amarilla	*Pouteria* sp.	Sapotaceae	x	
31	Vara negra	*Guatteria* sp.	Annonaceae	x	
32	Paliperro	*Tabebuia* sp.	Bignoniaceae	x	
33	Quinilla	*Pouteria rufonervia*	Sapotaceae	x	

alto and in purmas. In fact, many people from the community have already planted them in their fields and fallows.

6 Prospects for sustainable management

We suggest that, in San Rafael, management may be an inappropriate term for describing ribereño use of monte alto resources at pres-

Table 10.5   **Fruit species collected from monte alto in San Rafael, Iquitos, July 1989**

No.	Common name	Scientific name	Family
1	Huicungo	Astrocarium huicungo	Palmae
2	Shimbillo blanco	*Inga* sp.	Mimosaceae
3	Cacao	*Theobroma cacao*	Sterculiaceae
4	Zapotillo	*Quararibea wittii*	Bombacaceae
5	Ubos	*Spondias mombin*	Anacardiaceae
6	Misho chaqui	*Perebea* sp.	Moraceae
7	Conta		Palmae
8	Pairajo shimbillo	*Inga corymbifera*	Mimosaceae
9	Poroto shimbillo	*Inga canaminensis*	Mimosaceae
10	Metohuayo	*Loretoa* sp.	Rubiaceae
11	Cacahuillo	*Theobroma subincanum*	Sterculiaceae
12	Huiracaspi	*Carpotroche grandiflora*	Flacourtaceae
13	Ungurahui	*Jessenia bataua*	Palmae
14	Charichuelo	*Rheedia acuminata*	Clusiaceae
15	Pelejo shimbillo	*Peltogyne densiflora*	Caesalpinaceae
16	Camucamu de altura	*Calyptranthes simulata*	Myrtaceae
17	Chicle huayo	*Lacnellea aculeata*	Apocynaceae
18	Shapajilla	*Sheelea* sp.	Palmae
19	Charapilla	*Coumarouna charapilla*	Papilionaceae
20	Shapaja	*Sheelea cephalotes*	Palmae
21	Vino huayo	*Cocoloba* sp.	Polygonaceae

ent. In contrast, successional forests of purmas appear to support a higher degree of human manipulation. Purmas, however, are by no means stable islands of forest. They are part of a cycle of swidden agriculture. The agricultural phases of that cycle provide the principal source of income from the land of ribereños in San Rafael. Elsewhere, forest and fallow products may be as important (Padoch, 1987).

When considering community use of forest resources in monte alto and purmas, people's attitudes toward the forest must be taken into account. Local people continue to believe that monte alto resources are inexhaustible, despite their awareness of the decline in availability of a few valuable forest products. Padoch (1987) has identified a similar pattern of behaviour in the Ucayali region.

The principal goal of the San Rafael communal reserve is to protect the forest from commercial timber extraction by companies from Iquitos. Secondarily, communal rules serve to regulate the extraction of high value species within the reserve by people from the community and neighbouring communities (Pinedo-Vasquez, 1988). Sustainable use of the resources of monte alto within the context of

Table 10.6 **Fruit species collected from purmas in San Rafael, Iquitos, July 1989**

No.	Common name	Scientific name	Family	IN/55
1	Pijuayo	*Bactris gasipaes*	Palmae	33
2	Guineo	*Musa paradisiaca*	Musaceae	32
3	Macambo	*Theobroma bicolor*	Sterculiaceae	11
4	Piña	*Ananas comosus*	Bromeliaceae	17
5	Guava	*Inga edulis*	Mimosaceae	23
6	Naranja	*Citrus reticulata*	Rutaceae	3
7	Cidra	*Citrus* sp.	Rutaceae	11
8	Caimito	*Pouteria caimito*	Sapotaceae	26
9	Toronja	*Citrus* sp.	Rutaceae	1
10	Zapote	*Matisia cordata*	Bombacaceae	1
11	Aguaje	*Mauritia flexuosa*	Palmae	1
12	Casho	*Anacardium occidentale*	Anacardiaceae	1
13	Pan del arbol	*Artocarpus altilis*	Bombacaceae	3
14	Sacha mangua	*Griia peruviana*	Lecythidaceae	1
15	Vacaba	*Oenocarpus mapora*	Palmae	1
16	Caña de azucar	*Saccharum officinarum*	Poaceae	3
17	Umarí	*Poraqueiba sericea*	Icacinaceae	5
18	Shimbillo	*Inga* spp.	Mimosaceae	2
19	Limón	*Citrus aurantifolia*	Rutaceae	1
20	Dale dale	*Calathea allouia*	Marantaceae	1
21	Cacao	*Theobroma cacao*	Sterculiaceae	1

a communal reserve will require not only local knowledge, but also some technical input from outside the community. A forest management plan blending the two can promote not only the sustainable use of the forest resources but also the participation of local people in management decisions.

Acknowledgements

We thank the community of San Rafael and the Federación Departamental de Campesinos y Nativos de Loreto. J. Chota-Inuma and M. Rios-Quiroz provided invaluable assistance in the field. Recent fieldwork has been supported by the Inter-American Foundation, the Tropical Forestry Program of the World Wildlife Fund/Conservation Foundation, the Homeland Foundation, and the Tropical Resources Institute of Yale University.

References

Benedict, R. 1959. *Patterns of culture*. Mentor, New York.

Chaumeil, J.P. 1984. "Between zoo and slavery: The Yagua of eastern Peru in their present situation." *IWGIA* 49. Copenhagen.

Chibnik, M. 1986. "New sources of credit in Peruvian Amazonian communities." Paper presented at the meeting of the American Anthropological Association, Philadelphia, 7 December.

DeBoer, W. 1981. "Buffer zones in the cultural ecology of Amazonia." *American Antiquity* 48: 364–77.

Hiraoka, M. 1985. "Floodplain farming in the Peruvian Amazon." *Geographical Review of Japan* 58: 1–23.

———. 1986. "Zonation of mestizo riverine farming systems in northeast Peru." *National Geographic Research* 2: 354–71.

———. 1988. "Agricultural systems on the floodplain of the Peruvian Amazon." Paper presented at the symposium "Fragile Lands in Latin America: The Search for Sustainable Uses," held in conjunction with the 14th Congress of the Latin American Studies Association, New Orleans, 17–19 March.

Maroni, P. 1988. "Noticias auténticas del famoso rio Marañon." *Monumenta Amazonica* B 4. CETA-IIAP (Centro de Estudios Teológicos de la Amazonía–Instituto de Investigaciones de la Amazonía Peruana), Iquitos.

Ministerio de Educación. 1986. *Memorias anuales*. Dirección Departamental de Educación de Loreto, Iquitos.

Padoch, C. 1987. "The economic importance and marketing of forest and fallow products in the Iquitos region." *Advances in Economic Botany* 5: 74–89.

Padoch, C., J. Chota Inuma, W. de Jong, and J. Unruh. 1985. "Amazonian agroforestry: A market-oriented system in Peru." *Agroforestry Systems* 3: 47–58.

Pinedo-Vasquez, M. 1988. "The river people of Maynas." In J. Denslow and C. Padoch (eds.), *People of the tropical rainforest* (University of California Press, Berkeley), 141–3.

Pinedo-Vasquez, M., D. Zarin, P. Jipp, and J. Chota-Inuma. 1990. "Use-values of tree species in a communal forest reserve in northeast Peru." *Conservation Biology* 4: 405–16.

Posey, D.A. and W. Balée (eds.). 1989. *Resource management in Amazonia: Indigenous and folk strategies*. Advances in Economic Botany 7. New York Botanical Garden, New York.

Redfield, R. 1953. *The primitive world and its transformations*. Cornell University Press, Ithaca.

Roosevelt, A.C. 1989. "Resource management in Amazonia before the conquest: Beyond ethnographic projection." In Posey and Balée, 1989: 30–62..

San Román, J. 1975. *Perfiles históricos de la Amazonia Peruana*. Ediciones Paulinas, Lima.

Part IV
The semi-arid North-East

11

White sand soils in North-East Brazil

Eiji Matsumoto

1 Introduction

White sand soils are amongst the most infertile of the generally infertile tropical soils. They are composed mainly of quartz sand, and support a distinctive vegetation. This, varying from open savanna to closed forest, is characterized by pronounced sclerophylly, low diversity, and high endemism. Forests on white sand soils are reported from several humid tropical regions of the world and are variously designated: Amazon *caatinga* or *campinarana* in Amazonia (Anderson, 1981); *wallaba* forest or *muri*-bush in Guyana, and heath forest, *kerangas* or *padang*, in Borneo.

As shown in figure 11.1, extensive areas of white sand soils and related vegetation (white sand formations) are present in Amazonia, occurring in the Rio Negro basin, in Serra do Cachimbo on the Pará–Mato Grosso boundary, on the Chapada dos Parecis in Rondônia, and along the Atlantic coast near the mouth of the Amazon, as well as in Maranhão. Small patches are present in many other parts of Amazonia.

Amazonian white sand soils occur under diverse geological and geomorphological conditions. They are found on the low uplands (called *terra firme*), mainly composed of arenaceous sediments; on natural

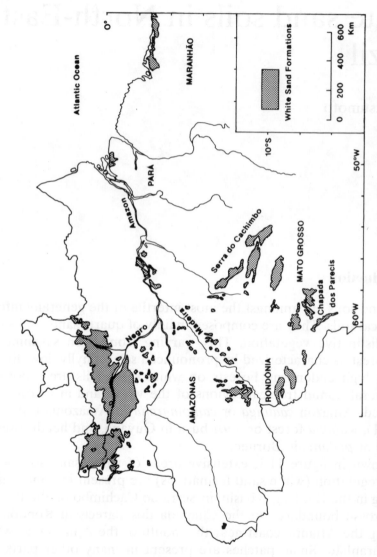

Figure 11.1 **Distribution of the vegetation on the white sand (white sand formation) in Brazilian Amazonia. (After Whitmore and Prance, 1987.)**

levees in a floodplain (*várzea*); on sand ridges or dunes in a coastal lowland (*restinga*); and on plateaux (*chapadas*) of Cretaceous sandstone, or on hill areas of granitic rocks (Whitmore and Prance, 1987).

White sand soils also cover a considerable area of North-East Brazil, or the Nordeste. The objective of this paper is: (1) to clarify the distribution of white sand soils in North-east Brazil; (2) to examine their characteristics and genetic processes; and (3) to consider the influence of deforestation on their formation.

2 Site characteristics

Broadly speaking, the North-East consists of three distinctive geo-ecological regions: the *zona da mata*, the *agreste*, and the *sertão* (Andrade, 1980). They are arranged zonally in this order from the Atlantic coast to the inland (fig. 11.2).

The *zona da mata do Nordeste* is part of the extensive forest zone that stretches along the Atlantic coast from the north-east to the south-east of Brazil. It enjoys a sub-humid climate with marked seasonality. That is, the annual rainfall amounts 1,000 to 2,000 mm, but there is a weak dry season for two or three months when the monthly rainfall is less than 50 mm. Its original plant cover was generally a

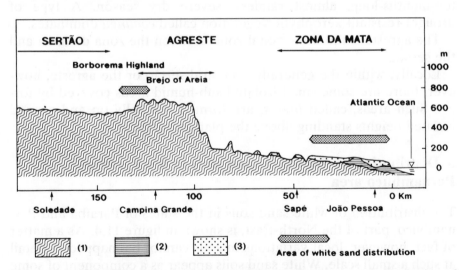

Figure 11.2 **Schematic cross-profile of landform and geology, and distribution of white sand soils in the state of Paraíba, along the latitude of about 7°S. (After Machida et al., 1976.) (1) crystalline basement (Precambrian gneiss, granite, schist, etc.); (2) Cretaceous sedimentary rocks (sandstone, limestone, etc.); (3) Pliocene and Pleistocene sediment (Barreiras Group).**

tropical evergreen seasonal forest, although because of long continued developments in the region, little original vegetation remains.

The geomorphology of the zona da mata is characterized by low uplands called *tabuleiros*, although in some parts, such as southern Pernambuco, there are low, rounded hills ("half oranges" or *colinas*) of deeply weathered crystalline rocks. The tabuleiros are low uplands 30 to 200 metres above sealevel. They have been dissected to a greater or lesser degree by numerous valleys; consequently, some appear as extensive flat uplands; others are only residual fragments (fig. 11.3). They are composed of sandy, permeable, and unconsolidated sediments of Pliocene to Pleistocene age (Barreiras Group). The tabuleiros are largely grouped into three geomorphic surfaces: the higher and older erosional surface; the lower and later depositional surface; and the lowest fluvial terrace surfaces (Matsumoto, 1983). Geologically and geomorphologically, the tabuleiros in the North-East are correlated with the terra firme uplands that predominate in the Amazonian lowland.

The sertão is a semi-arid inland area, and a part of Brazilian plateau (Borborema highland), on which low-relief erosional plains (pediplains) have developed on the crystalline rocks. The annual rainfall in the sertão ranges 500 to 800 mm, and there is a six- to ten-months-long, almost rainless, severe dry season. A type of drought-resistant xerophytic vegetation called *caatinga* dominates.

The agreste is the transitional zone between the zona da mata and the sertão.

Locally, within the generally semi-arid sertão or the agreste, however, there are some small isolated sub-humid areas covered by forest. Such areas, called *brejos*, are formed generally on and around isolated heights standing above the plateau surface.

3 Distribution of the white sand soils in the Paraíba– Pernambuco area

The distribution of white sand soils in the states of Paraíba and Pernambuco, part of the North-East, is shown in figure 11.4. As a matter of fact, however, local variations in soils cannot be mapped in detail at such a small scale. White sand soils appear as a component of some soil association units which form a mosaic of various soils, such as red-yellow podzolic soils, red-yellow lateritic soils, and so on. Consequently, figure 11.4 shows only the distribution of the soil association units including white sand soils. The areas shown in darker shade are

Figure 11.3 **Distribution of tabuleiros in the coastal region of the states of Paraíba and Pernambuco. (After Matsumoto, 1983.) (1) higher tabuleiro (Tab-H) Surface; (2) lower tabuleiro (Tab-L) Surface; (3) fluvial terrace surfaces; (4) principal roads.**

the areas where the white sand soils appear as the most dominant component of the soil association unit; the medium-shaded areas are those where they constitute the second most dominant component; and the lightest shaded areas those where the white sand soils are less dominant.

257

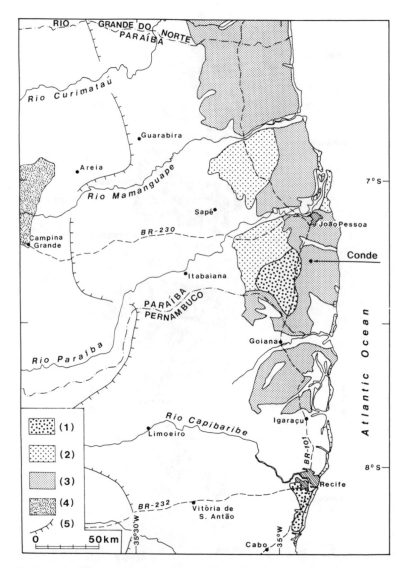

Figure 11.4 **Distribution of white sand soils in the eastern Paraíba–Pernambuco area. (After the soil maps by MA and SUDENE, 1972, 1973.) (1)–(3): white sand developed densely (1), moderately (2), and sparsely (3); (4): dystrophic regosol around *brejos*; (5): escarpment between the coastal plain and the Borborema highland.**

According to this figure and figure 11.2, white sand soils are principally found in the sub-humid areas. They are distributed mainly in the zona da mata along the coast. In addition, they are found also in the area around the brejos, such as Areia in Paraíba and Garanhuns in Pernambuco. Although the white sand soils in both areas are similar in appearance, they are of a different pedological nature. The white sand around the brejos, developed on the granitic rocks, contains a lot of unweathered minerals (mainly quartz and feldspars) derived from parent rocks. This immature soil is classified as "dystrophic regosol" on the soil maps and explanations by MA and SUDENE (1972, 1973).

On the other hand, the white sand soil in the zona da mata develops on the unconsolidated sandy sediments of tabuleiros, as well as on sand ridges or dunes on the coastal lowland, and is composed of almost exclusively of quartz sand. This type of white sand soil, henceforth simply "white sand," is classified in pedology as "hydromorphic podzol," for the formation of which, in tropical environments, acidic parent material, and shallow groundwater table are considered necessary conditions.

The white sand in the zona da mata is, in turn, classified into two types according to the geomorphological and geological conditions under which it develops. One type, found in strips along the coast, for example, around the cities of Recife and João Pessoa, is the hydromorphic podzol developed on the dune or sand ridge deposits in the coastal lowlands, where the groundwater table is constantly very shallow. This type of white sand has been known widely on the Brazilian Atlantic coast from Amazonia to Rio de Janeiro (Anderson, 1981). Another white sand, here called upland white sand, develops on the surface of tabuleiros. This paper discusses the character and formation of this type of upland white sand. The discussion is based on a detailed field survey on the Conde upland near the city of João Pessoa, the capital of Paraíba state.

4 White sand on the Conde upland, Paraíba

The Conde upland, part of the higher tabuleiro surface, with an altitude of about 110 metres, is located about 15 km south of João Pessoa (fig. 11.4). Most of it has been deforested and converted to farming or left as a low thicket.

The results of field survey on this upland were reported by Matsumoto and Watanabe (1986). This report and subsequent results undergird much of what follows. The distribution of white sand on the Conde upland (fig. 11.5) shows a distinctive pattern: (1) the white sand alternates horizontally with brown-coloured sandy soil (red-

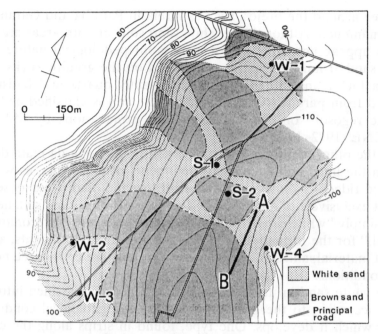

Figure 11.5 **White sand and brown sand on the Conde upland. Contour interval: 2 metres. S-1 and S-2: Sampling locations of the white and brown sands respectively (cf. figs. 11.6 and 11.7). W-1 ~ W-4: Spring water sampling location (cf. table 11.1). A–B: Measuring line for penetration test in fig. 11.8.**

yellow podzolic soil), here called simply "brown sand;" (2) the two kinds of sand reveal a clear-cut boundary; (3) the white sand occupies a slightly depressed portion of the upland; (4) a dissecting valley follows the downslope of the white sand zone; (5) springs are found near the head of the dissecting valleys.

Richards (1952) suggested that tropical rain-forest rivers flowing out from the white sand area, such as the Rio Negro in Amazonia, always carry "black water." The spring water of the Conde upland

Table 11.1 **Chemical properties of spring water of the Conde upland, at W–1 ~ W–4 in figure 11.5**

Location no.	Water temperature (°C)	pH	Electrical conductivity (μS/cm)
W–1	28.3	4.67	29.5
W–2	25.9	4.78	32.3
W–3	27.0	4.48	33.7
W–4	26.0	4.20	38.4

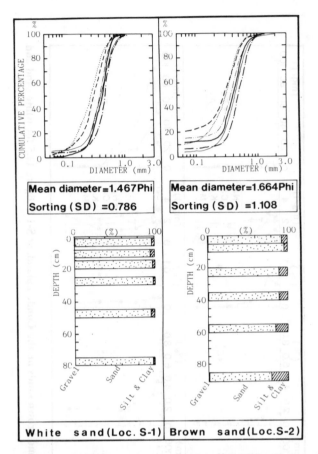

Figure 11.6 **Grain size distribution of white sand (at S-1 in fig. 11.5) and brown sand (at S-2) on the Conde upland.**

is also transparent, but somewhat smoky in colour, quite similar to the "black water" of the Amazonian rivers. It shows a low electric conductivity (*c.* 30 to 40μS/cm) and rather low hydrogen concentration (pH = 4.2 to 4.8), as shown in table 11.1.

Compared to the grain size of brown sand, the white sand is slightly coarser in mean diameter and better in sorting measure, i.e. the mean diameter in phi units for the white and brown sands is 1.467 (0.36 mm) and 1.664 (0.32 mm), respectively; the sorting measure (standard deviation in phi units) is 0.786 and 1.108, respectively (fig. 11.6). These characteristics are explained by the paucity of silt and clay fractions in the white sand.

Concerning chemical properties (fig. 11.7), the hydrogen ion con-

261

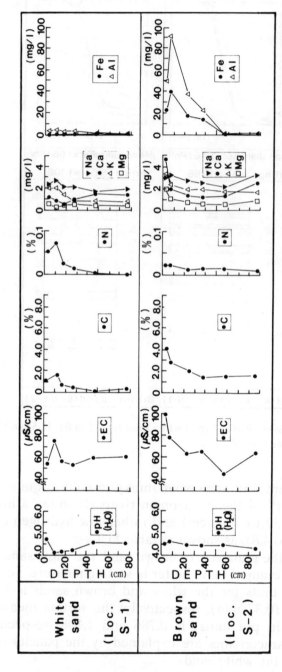

Figure 11.7 Chemical properties of white and brown sands on the Conde upland, at S-1 in figure 11.5 for white sand and S-2 for brown sand.

262

centration of soil solution is low (pH = 4.0 to 5.0) in both soils, and the concentration of elements such as sodium (Na), calcium (Ca), potassium (K), and magnesium (Mg) in soil solution is generally poor. Iron (Fe) and aluminum (Al) concentrations in soil solution appear as mere traces in the case of white sand, being high in the upper portion of the brown sand. The content of carbon (C) is low in white sand and moderate in brown sand; that of nitrogen (N) is low in both sands.

5 Origin of upland white sand

The white sand is the result of removal by the action of subsurface water (soil water and groundwater) of clay and various minerals other than quartz from the brown sand. The abundance of subsurface water on the seemingly water-deficient tabuleiros, originally composed of thick and permeable sandy sediments, is explained by the existence of "hardpan" (a lateritic duricrust) formed near the surface. This hardpan acts as an impermeable layer to maintain a shallow groundwater table beneath the tabuleiro surface.

Results of penetration resistance (hardness) tests for the soil layers on the Conde upland (fig. 11.8) may indicate this process. The tests were carried out at several points along a line across the boundary of white and brown sands (A–B in fig. 11.5). In the soil profile of the white sand, a well-developed hard layer (hardpan) is found relatively close to the surface (2–3 m in depth), on which shallow groundwater remains. On the other hand, generally no hardpan or groundwater body is evident at a shallow depth in the brown sand profiles. In the soil profile at the narrow transitional zone between the white and brown sands, a thin hard layer develops nearly at the same depth as the duricrust in white sand, indicating the embryonic stage in the formation of the hard layer at a shallow level.

The existence of a shallow hard layer and groundwater under white sand is observed also in many outcrops of upland podzol in the Paraíba–Pernambuco area, where groundwater issues as springs at the boundary between the layers of loose white sand and the underlying consolidated, yellow-coloured sand (hardpan).

The formation of the hard layer is related to the precipitation of iron and/or aluminum oxides at the level of the groundwater table or where soil water evaporates. Once such an impermeable hard layer is formed at a shallow level, the groundwater developed on it

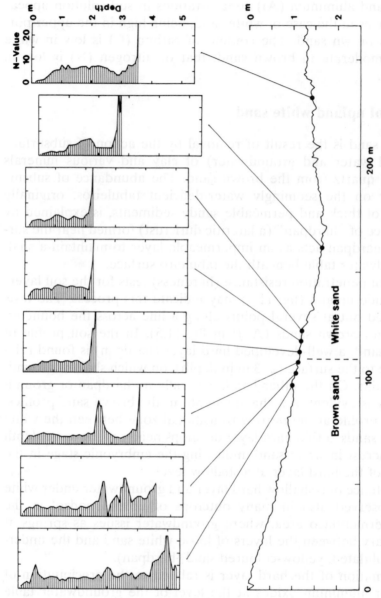

Figure 11.8 Penetration resistance value (N-value) of soil layers near the boundary of white and brown sands on the Conde upland, along the line A–B in figure 11.5. N-value means the number of impacts required to penetrate each 10 cm depth of soil, when one end of a rod, equipped with a cone (23 mm in base diameter and 60° of apex) at the other end, is struck by dropping a weight of 5 kg from a height of 50 cm.

accelerates the eluviation of elements and clay in the surface soil layer, leading to the formation of white sand.

6 The effect of deforestation

The formation of white sand may be mainly the outcome of natural processes under existing site conditions, such as geological, climatic, and vegetational ones. However, humans are also believed to accelerate this process through deforestation.

It may be clear from the preceding description that the abundance of subsurface water, maintaining shallow groundwater, should favour the formation of white sand. On sandy soils like the ones on tabuleiros, deforestation may decrease evapotranspiration and increase soil water. Such an outcome leads to the elevation of the groundwater table, which, in turn, results in the formation of the impermeable hard layer near the surface. In this manner, white sands may expand spatially.

The increase in soil water in the deforested terrain was ascertained through the comparison of water content in the soil profiles under the thicket and under the barren land on the Conde upland (fig. 11.9). The soil under the cleared land, both of white and brown sands,

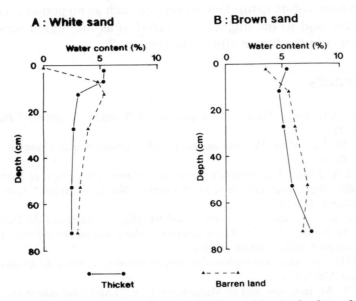

Figure 11.9 **Soil water content profile under thicket and barren lands on the Conde upland.**

dried out only superficially, while, at depth, it contains more soil water than the soil under vegetation. Owing to poor capillary action in the coarse sandy soil, little soil water may evaporate from the soil surface, and the absorption and transpiration through the roots and leaves of plants is the dominant process for the output of water into the air.

This situation was reported also by Kashiwagi (1986) from the sandy soil area near Campina Grande, Paraíba, where the soil of a nearly bare cropped field contained more than double the moisture present in the soil under the caatinga.

The zona da mata of North-East Brazil has a history of deforestation of some five hundred years, beginning with the extraction of Brazil-wood (pau brasil; *Caesalpinia echinata*) in the sixteenth century, followed by clearing for sugar cane plantations and the cutting of firewood for sugar production. Recently, after the establishment of the Pró-Álcool Project, which aims to produce fuel alcohol for automobiles from sugar cane, the sugar cane fields have been extended even onto the surface of tabuleiros. Through such a long continued and repeated deforestation, the soil on the tabuleiros must have been severely modified, especially in the form of the expansion of the white sand areas.

The *zona da mata do Nordeste*, having many similarities with Amazonia in terms of its natural environment, such as on geology, climate, vegetation, and so on, might be referred to as the region suggesting "Amazonia in the future after development."

References

Anderson, A.B. 1981. "White-sand vegetation of Brazilian Amazonia." *Biotropica* 13: 199–210.

Andrade, M.C. de. 1980. *The land and people of Northeast Brazil*. University of New Mexico Press.

Kashiwagi, Y. 1986. "A preliminary report on soil moisture content of bare ground and inside plant community in semi-arid region, Northeast Brazil." *Latin American Studies* 8: 155–60.

MA [Ministerio da Agricultura] and SUDENE [Superintendência do Desenvolvimento do Nordeste]. 1972. *Levantamento exploratório-reconhecimento de solos do Estado da Paraíba*. Rio de Janeiro.

———. 1973. *Levantamento exploratório-reconhecimento de solos do Estado de Pernambuco*. Vol.1. Recife.

Machida, T., M. Inokuchi, and E. Matsumoto. 1976. "Land condition in the Eastern Nordeste Region." *Tokyo Geography Papers* 20: 9–22.

Matsumoto, E. 1983. "A note on the tabuleiros in the coastal region of the Brazilian

Northeast – A geomorphological approach." *Latin American Studies* 6: 1–13.

Matsumoto, E., and T. Watanabe. 1986. "Site conditions and formation of white sand in Northeast Brazil." *Latin American Studies* 8: 31–48.

Richards, P.W. 1952. *The tropical rain forest: An ecological study*. Cambridge University Press, Cambridge.

Whitmore, T.C., and G.T. Prance (eds.). 1987. *Biogeography and Quaternary history in tropical America*. Clarendon Press, Oxford.

12

Changing aspects of drought-deciduous vegetation in the semi-arid region of North-East Brazil

Ichiroku Hayashi

1 Introduction

The semi-arid regions of North-East Brazil, the *Nordeste*, are covered by drought-resistant xerophytic vegetation (*caatinga*), which have been utilized for ranching and charcoal production. After clearing the vegetation, these areas have also been used for the cultivation of beans, cassava, and maize. Such human activities have degraded lands that now support only a poor harvest of crops and livestock. In order to learn how to conserve the vegetation under present land-use, I have carried out the following investigations:
1. The floristic composition of the caatinga;
2. The successional trend of the caatinga under pressure from human activities;
3. Quantitative feature of caatinga trees and phytomass production of the study sites;
4. The nitrogen and carbon content in soils of the study sites.
The results, we hope, should be useful in drawing up plans for rational land management of the area.

2 Study sites and methods

The study sites are situated between 7° and 8°S and between 32° and 38°E in the Brazilian North-East (fig. 12.1). Mean annual temperature

Figure 12.1 **The study area in North-East Brazil. 1. João Pessoa; 2. Campina Grande; 3. Patos.**

and total annual precipitation are 20°C and 800–1,000mm, with a severe dry season from October to the following February (Nishizawa, 1976; Rizzini and Pinto, 1964). The soils are classified as solodized solonetz and regosols (Ministério da Agricultura e Ministério do Interior, 1971).

The vegetation varies from place to place, according to land use, which includes ranching, cultivation, firewood collection, and charcoal production.

269

The intensive study sites were located in the vicinity of Campina Grande and Patos, where the vegetation is typical for the region. Nine 10m × 10m quadrats were set out at sites dominated by *Mimosa tenuiflora* (synonym of *Mimosa hostilis*) and *Caesalpinia pyramidalis*. In each quadrat, I measured the diameter of tree stems at 130 cm high (DBH) for each species, and counted the number of shrubs less than 150 cm tall for each species.

For selected specimens of *Caesalpinia pyramidalis*, *Mimosa tenuiflora* and *Aspidosperma pyrifolium*, the weight of stems (Ws:kg), branches (Wb:kg), and leaves (Wl:kg) was taken after first measuring tree height (H:m) and stem diameter (D:cm) at 130 cm high.

The nitrogen and carbon contents of stems and leaves and of the surface soil were determined in the laboratory.

3 Results

The floristic composition of the caatinga in Campina Grande is shown in table 12.1. *Mimosa tenuiflora* and *Caesalpinia pyramidalis* predominate, with *Pithecellobium foliorosum* and *Aspidosperma pyrifolium* also present. In the shrub layer, *Croton sonderiana*, *Sida cordifolia*, and *Croton campestris* were the dominant species. Observation indicated that the bare sites produced by disturbance were covered first by *Sida cordifolia* and *Croton campestris*. These were then replaced by *Mimosa tenuiflora* and *Caesalpinia pyramidalis*. The final stage of succession of this area appears to be *Aspidosperma pyrifolium*, be-

Table 12.1 **Floristic composition of the caatinga at the vicinity of Campina Grande (quadrat area 10 m × 10 m; 1st and 2nd layers above and less than 1 m in height)**

Species	1st layer		2nd layer
	Mean DBH (cm)	No. of trunks	No. of individuals
Caesalpinia pyramidalis	4.4	12	7
Pithecellobium foliorosum	4.2	4	0
Mimosa hostilis	4.0	28	3
Croton sonderiana	3.3	4	13
Aspidosperma pyrifolium	2.7	4	3
Encholrium spectabile	—	—	8
Spondias tuberosum	—	—	1
Croton species	—	—	1
Pilosocereus peutedrophorus	—	—	1
Unidentified species 1	—	—	2
Unidentified species 2	—	—	2

Table 12.2 **Quantitative characteristics of caatinga stand at the experimental station, Campina Grade**

Number of species per 100 m^2	
Tree layer	7
Herb layer	13
Number of trees per 100 m^2	39
Mean DBH (cm)	4
Above-ground biomass (kg per 100 m^2)	
Trunks and branches	246
Leaves	29
Total	275
Herbs	19
Gross total	294

cause the trees are of big stature, with erect stems, emerging above the other tree species.

The *Caesalpinia pyramidalis* stand included 11 species and 52 individuals per 100 m^2. The height of the tree layer was about 5 m. The density and mean DBH of the trees were 39–52 individuals per 100 m^2 and 3.7–4 cm. The aboveground phytomass of the stand was 294 kg per 100 m^2, including 246 kg of trunks and branches, 29 kg of leaves and 19 kg of herbs and grasses (table 12.2).

The relationship between mean DBH and number of trees per 100 m^2 (tree density) is shown in figure 12.2, which was obtained by the survey of 9 stands of caatinga. The relationship shown in this figure is described as follows:

$$N = 217 \exp\left(-0.42\,D\right) \tag{1}$$

where N and D are tree density and mean DBH. This equation suggests that the number of trees per unit area decreased exponentially with increment of mean DBH.

The relationship between DBH (cm) and weight mass of trees (W:kg), trunks and branches (Wt:kg) and leaves (Wl:kg) is shown in figure 12.3. These relationships are as follows:

$$W = 0.226\,D^{2.274} \tag{2}$$

$$Wt = 0.206D^{2.273} \tag{3}$$

$$Wl = 0.018D^{2.369} \tag{4}$$

After measuring the diameter of stem, we are able to estimate the tree weight from equation (2). The tree weights of *Caesalpinia pyra-*

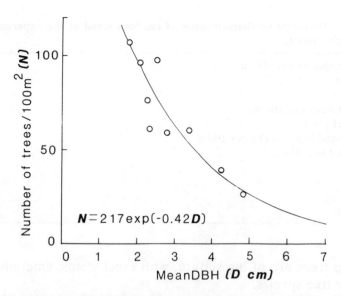

Figure 12.2 **Relationship between mean diameter at breast height of tree stem (DBH) and number of trees per unit area (N) of caatinga stand.**

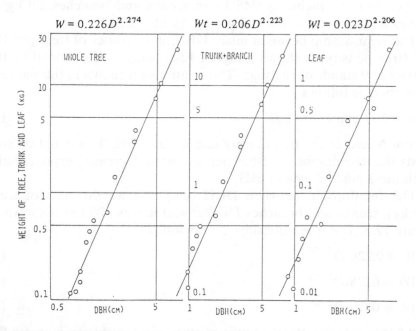

Figure 12.3 **Relationship between DBH and weight of leaves, trunk, and branches and whole tree of caatinga species.**

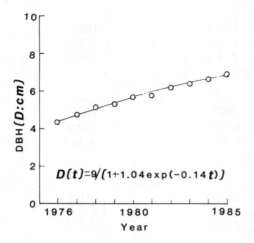

Figure 12.4 **DBH growth of *Pithecellobium foliorosum* (Jurema-branca) from 1976 to 1985. Open circles are measured value.**

midalis and *Aspidosperma pyrifolium* were 13.3 kg and 22.8 kg in estimated, and 14.5 kg and 23.0 kg in measured values, respectively (Hayashi, 1986).

The area of the annual ring formed in the stem of *Pithecellobium foliorosum* was computed for each year from 1975 to 1985. Based on the area of annual ring (s:cm^2), I obtained the stem diameter (d:cm) using the following equation:

$$d = 2 \, (s/\pi)^{1/2} \tag{5}$$

The DBH was obtained by adding bark thickness to the stem diameter (d). The growth of DBH obtained above is shown in figure 12.4. for *Pithecellobium foliorosum*.

The growth curve of DBH of *P. foliorosum* was described as

$$D \, (t) = 9/\{1 + 1.04 \exp [-0.14 \, t]\} \tag{6}$$

where $D \, (t)$ is DBH at year t, t is year from 1976 (1976 is 0 year). As shown by this figure, the logistic curve obtained by the least-squares method describes the growth of this tree. According to the equation, the maximum DBH and relative growth rate are 9 cm and 0.14 per year.

In a previous paper (Hayashi, 1986), I reported the same relationship for *Caesalpinia pyramidalis* and *Aspidosperma pyrifolium*, which are the dominant species of the caatinga. These equations were as follows:

273

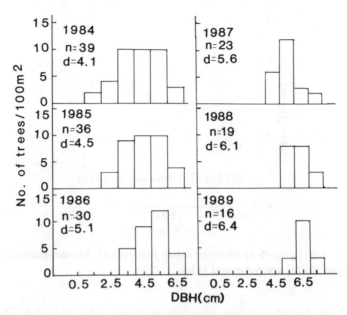

Figure 12.5 **Predicted changes in DBH histogram of caatinga stand from 1984 to 1989. *n* and *d* are number of trees and mean DBH of the stand.**

$$D~(t) = 7.7/\{1 + 1.16 \exp~(-0.098~t)\} \qquad (7)$$

(*Caesalpinia pyramidalis*: from 1963 to 1984)

$$D~(t) = 12.3/\{1 + 2.33 \exp~(-0.067~t)\} \qquad (8)$$

(*Aspidosperma pyrifolium*: from 1963 to 1984)

Assuming that the trees in the caatinga grow in accordance with equations (6), (7), and (8), based on a computer simulation, I predicted a change of DBH histogram of a caatinga stand from 1984 to 1989. The DBHs of trees measured in 1984 in Campina Grande were used in the simulation. The changes in the DBH histogram produced by computer simulation are given in figure 12.5. According to these results, the mean DBH changed from 4.1 cm in 1984 (measured value) to 6.4 cm in 1989.

The number of trees per unit area (predicted value) is expected to decrease according to equation (1) from 39 individuals per 100m² in 1984 to 16 individuals in 1989. During this period, the tree mortality in the stand from self-thinning is expected to be 3 from 1984 to 1985, 6 from 1985 to 1986, 7 from 1986 to 1987, 4 from 1987 to 1988 and 3

Table 12.3 **Carbon and nitrogen content of the plants of the dominant species in caatinga**

Species	Carbon (%)	Nitrogen (%)	C:N
Mimosa hostilis			
Wood	46.0	1.0	49.7
Bark	52.1	1.7	31.2
Leaf	43.1	2.4	18.0
Caesalpinia pyramidalis			
Wood	47.1	1.0	49.5
Bark	45.5	1.2	37.6
Leaf	46.1	2.5	19.0
Aspidosperma pyrifolium			
Wood	47.4	1.1	43.1
Leaf	42.2	2.7	15.7
Panicum trichoides			
Whole plant	44.2	2.8	15.7
Encholrium spectabile			
Whole plant	46.1	1.7	26.5
Herbaceous plants	41.5	2.5	16.6

from 1988 to 1989. A total of 23 trees from the stand are expected to die during the five years.

The mass of leaves, trunks, and branches from dead trees was estimated, using equations (2), (3), and (4). Based on the DBH shown in figure 12.5 and using the above equation, it is possible to estimate the total mass of litter for each year. Substituting the DBH of dead trees (which are assumed to be the smaller trees within the stand), with equation (3), the mass of trunks and branches from the dead trees were estimated for each year. The mass of fallen leaves at the end of rainy season was also estimated using equation (4). Thus, the total mass of litter supplied to the stand is expected to be 280 kg (164 kg of leaves and 116 kg of trunks and branches) per 100m^2 during the five years from 1985 to 1989 (Hayashi, 1986, 1988).

The carbon and nitrogen content of the plants are given in table 12.3. Nitrogen content was 2.4–2.8 per cent in the leaves, 1.0–1.1 per cent in the wood and 1.2–1.7 per cent in the bark. The C:N ratios were 43.1–49.7 for the wood and 15.7–19.0 for the leaves, respectively. Uhl et al. (1982) reported that the leaves of tree shoots from the Amazonian caatinga contained 0.78 per cent nitrogen, which is one third of the nitrogen content in the leaves of caatinga trees in North-East Brazil. The plant carbon contents were: wood 46–47 per

Table 12.4 Amount of plant litters and of carbon and nitrogen in the litters produced by the caatinga stand for 5 years (kg/100m²)

	Litter	Carbon	Nitrogen	Carbon dioxide
Leaf	164	71.8	4.10	264
Trunk and branch	116	55.0	1.16	202
Total	280	126.8	5.26	466

Table 12.5 Soil texture of the caatinga stands under different human impacts in the vicinity of Campina Grande

Soil depth (cm)	Content in percentage				
	Clay	Silt	Fine sand	Coarse sand	
Site 1					
0–5	14.0	10.2	71.3	4.5	SL
6–10	19.4	11.4	62.0	6.9	SCL
11–15	23.7	12.8	57.3	6.2	SCL
16–20	25.1	11.0	58.5	4.9	SC
21–25	23.5	12.1	58.0	6.4	SCL
Site 2					
0–5	19.4	9.1	54.1	17.4	SCL
Site 3					
0–5	5.0	9.3	71.0	14.7	SL

Site 1: developed stand of caatinga; site 2: disturbed stand of caatinga 11 km south from C. Grande; site 3: heavily disturbed stand in the vicinity of C. Grande.

cent, leaves 42–46 per cent and bark 45–52 per cent. Multiplying 2.4 per cent and 1.05 per cent by total mass of leaf and trunk litter, 5.26 kg/100m² of nitrogen is expected to be supplied to the stand in the form of plant litter during a five-year period. The carbon supplied to ground surface by the litter is expected to be 126.8 kg during the same period, which is equivalent to 466 kg of carbon dioxide (table 12.4). This suggests that the vegetation absorbs the 466 kg per 100m² of carbon dioxide from the atmosphere during the five-year period.

The texture of caatinga soils is given in table 12.5. The fine sand decreases with depth, although the coarse sand content remains constant. By contrast, the clay content increased with soil depth. Surface soils of disturbed and severely disturbed sites contained a larger proportion of coarse sand than that of developed stands.

Soil nitrogen and carbon concentrations are given in table 12.6. The top 20 cm of caatinga soil contained 0.01–0.14 per cent of nitro-

Table 12.6 **Carbon (C) and nitrogen (N) content (%) of the soils of caatingas under different human impacts at the vicinity of Campina Grande**

Soil depth (cm)	Site 1		Site 2		Site 3	
	C	N	C	N	C	N
0–5	1.14	0.02	1.65	0.14	0.67	0.05
6–10	0.56	0.02	0.75	0.07	–	
11–15	0.43	0.01	0.46	0.05	–	
16–20	0.39	0.01	0.43	0.04	–	

Site 1: developed stand of caatinga; Site 2: disturbed stand of caatinga 11 km south from C. Grande; Site 3: heavily disturbed stand of caatinga at the vicinity of C. Grande.

gen and 0.39–1.65 per cent of carbon. The soil nitrogen is very low comparable to B horizon for soils of well-developed temperate forest. Grove et al. (1986) reported that the surface soil of a *Eucalyptus marginata* forest in south-western Australia, which is similar to caatinga in physiognomy, contained 0.14 per cent of nitrogen. After burning, the soil nitrogen increased to 0.17 per cent. The nitrogen content before the fire was similar to the caatinga soil.

4 Discussion and conclusion

The flora of the semi-arid region of North-East Brazil was described by Luetzelburg (1922–23). According to him, the dominant species in the caatinga were *Caesalpinia ferrea, Caesalpinia pyramidalis, Caesalpinia echinata, Aspidosperma pyrifolium, Spondias tuberosa, Magonia pubescens, Hymenaea martiana, Mimosa verrucosa, Mimosa tenuiflora, Cereus squamosus, Cereus jamacaru,* and *Pilocereus gounellei.* Recently, Gomez (1981) studied the vegetation of Cariris Velhos, Paraíba state, and reported that the dominant species in that region were *Caesalpinia pyramidalis, Mimosa tenuiflora, Croton sonderianus, Combretum leprosum, Aspidosperma pyrifolium, Jatropha pholiana, Spondias tuberosa, Pithecellobium foliorosum,* and *Pilocereus gounellei.* These floristic compositions are similar to my results in Campina Grande and Patos.

According to Whittaker (1970), the average biomass of shrubland formation is in the range of 2 to 20 kg per m², which includes the value of 2.94 kg m², thus bracketing our value of 2.94 kg m² obtained from stands used for firewood and ranching. The phytomass of the stands varies from site to site according to the intensity of human activities.

Figure 12.6   **A fence for goat raising in the vicinity of Campina Grande.**

The area has been degraded by varying human impacts such as insufficient fallowing period within the shifting cultivation; charcoal production; felling wood for fuel used in brick production; demand for fuel wood by the bakeries in Campina Grande and Patos; and fence construction to enclose goats (fig. 12.6).

According to Saito et al. (1988), productivity of cultivated crops for 1986 in the *município* of Patos was 1,050 kg per 9,683 ha, for perennial and annual cotton; 44 kg per 2,299 ha, for maccather bean; 600 kg per 1,962 ha, for maize; and 1,200 kg per 60 ha, for rice. Livestock figures in Patos in 1980 were 14,274 head of cattle, 1,762 head of sheep, and 293 head of horses for the total area of 59,499 ha. Nishizawa and Pinto (1988) reported that during 1981, 16,253 tons of charcoal and 1,569,612m³ of firewood were consumed in the region, including Seridó Paraibano, Piemonte da Borborema, Depressão do Alto Piranhas, Cariris Velhos, and Agreste da Borborema. In 1981, 1,890m³ of timber was produced for house and fence construction. Saito et al. (1988) noted that a single family consumes 100 kg of firewood in a week (five tons per year). Increasing demand for firewood by the bakeries in Patos was also reported by Nishizawa and Pinto (1988).

These human activities have resulted in a lot of bare ground within North-East Brazil, thus promoting land degradation. Once the vegetation has been removed, tropical rains create a sandy surface soil and vegetation recovery, including seed germination and seedling establishment, is limited by the severe condition of the soil surface (Hayashi 1981, 1988). We should, with proper use of the land, conserve plant cover to protect the soil against erosion. It is necessary, therefore, that the production of livestock, crops, and fuels be managed within the capabilities of the natural biological potential for the area.

References

Gomez, M.A.F. 1981. *Padrões de caatinga nos Cariris Velhos, Paraíba*. Ceará, Fortaleza.

Grove, T.S., A.M. O'Connell, and G.M. Dimmonk. 1986. "Nutrient changes in surface soil after an intense fire in jarrah (*Eucalyptus marginata* Donn ex Sm.) forest." *Australian Journal of Ecology* 11: 303–17.

Hayashi, I. 1981. "Plant communities and their environments in the caatinga of Northeast Brazil." *Latin American Studies* 2: 66–79.

———. 1986. "Vegetation and soils of humid and semi-arid regions in Northeast Brazil." *Latin American Studies* 8: 49–62.

———. 1988. "Changing aspect of caatinga vegetation in semi-arid region, Northeast Brazil." *Latin American Studies* 10: 61–76.

Luetzelburg, P. von. 1922–23. *Estudo botânico do Nordeste*, vols. 2, 3. Rio de Janeiro.

Ministério da Agricultura e Ministério do Interior. 1971. *Mapa exploratorio-reconhecimento de solos: Estado da Paraíba* (1:500,000). FIBGE, Rio de Janeiro

Nishizawa, T. 1976. "Some characteristics of rainfall in the Northeast of Brazil." *Tokyo Geography Papers* XX: 53–61.

Nishizawa, T., and M.M.V. Pinto. 1988. "Recent changes in firewood and charcoal production and their affects on deforestation." *Latin American Studies* 10: 122–31.

Rizzini, C.T., and M.M. Pinto. 1964. "Áreas climático-vegetacionais do Brasil, segundo os métodos de Thornthwaite e Mather." *Revista Brasileira de Geografia* 26 (4): 523–47.

Saito, I., H. Maruyama, and K.D. Muller. 1988. "A comparative study of land use between the Campo Alegre in the sertão and Sitio Açude de Pedra in the agreste, Paraíba, Northeast Brazil." *Latin American Studies* 10: 78–99.

Uhl, C., C. Jordan, K. Clark, H. Clark, and R. Herrera. 1982. "Ecosystem recovery in Amazon caatinga forest after cutting, cutting and burning, and bulldozer clearing treatments." *OIKOS* 38: 313–20.

Whittaker, R.H. 1970. *Communities and ecosystems*. Collier–Macmillan, London.

13

Characteristics and utilization of tree species in the semi-arid woodland of North-East Brazil

Toshie Nishizawa, Akio Tsuchiya, and Maria Magdalena Vieira Pinto

1 Introduction

A large expanse of deciduous thorny woodland, *caatinga*, covers the semi-arid interior of North-East Brazil. The annual rainfall, which occurs mostly between December and April, varies from 400 to 800 mm. Owing to the dryness of the climate, aridisols, alfisols, and entisols are dominant. The capacity of these soils to hold water is limited by their shallowness and low organic matter content.

The Tupi word *caatinga*, literally "white forest," is descriptive of the open vegetation, the bleached appearance of the light-coloured trees and soils found during the dry season. With the arrival of the rainy seasons the caatinga changes completely: a paradise of lush vegetation bursts forth, birds sing, and butterflies flutter around.

Subsistence agriculture and open-range cattle grazing were introduced to the semi-arid area in the seventeenth century. Although crop farming provides greater economic benefits, it is limited mostly to the floodplains of intermittent rivers, and the moist bottoms of reservoirs (*açudes*), uncovered as the level of impounded water drops.

Agriculture gradually changed during the past two hundred years with the introduction of cash crops such as cotton and agave. However, subsistence farming of the moist areas still continues, especially the practice of interplanting crops such as maize, two or three kinds of beans, and squash. Normally, the following sequence occurs annually in the semi-arid interior, the *sertão*. During the dry season livestock graze in the fields. At the end of the rainless season fields are prepared for planting, and if the rains arrive on time and in adequate amounts the crops grow sufficiently to produce a harvest. This pattern of agricultural land use is repeated annually. In the past, after several years the cultivated fields were left to fallow and a second growth, or *capoeira*. However, recent population increases and economic pressures have modified this pattern of land use. Fallow periods are shortened or eliminated. The result of this overuse is accelerated erosion and depletion of soils, as well as the invasion of less desirable plant species and a general degradation of the ecosystem.

Livestock consists of cattle, sheep, and goats. Which of these animals are chosen is determined, not only by the variable forage production due to the interannual fluctuation of rainfall, but also by the mix of the preferred forage species. Moreover, the choice of livestock types is influenced strongly by the investment which individual farmers are willing – or financially able – to risk: cattle and sheep require greater capital than goats.

In addition to forage, the caatinga provides farmers with construction materials, fuelwood, charcoal, honey, fruits, fibres, and medicinal plants. Furthermore, trees are removed from the caatinga for commercial fuel in bakeries and in both nearby and distant brick and tile factories. Thus the caatinga provides an environment for multiple land use under traditional forest management.

This paper will discuss: (1) the strategies for adaptation of caatinga trees to the severe natural conditions of the semi-arid interior; and (2) possible improved utilization of the caatinga stand.

2 Bioclimatic divisions of North-East Brazil and the floristic composition of the caatinga stand

Two major subdivisions are commonly recognized in the Brazilian North-East, or *Nordeste*. There is the western Nordeste (roughly the states of Maranhão and Piaui), often called the *Meio Norte* ("Half North") because its climate and vegetation are transitional in respect to those of Amazonia (the *Norte*). Then there is the eastern Nordeste, which will be the focus of this paper. This region is, in turn, divided longitudinally, starting from the humid coastal strip (*zona da mata*), through a transitional belt (*agreste*), to the semi-arid backlands

Table 13.1 **Climatic indices for bioclimatic division (after Golfairi and Caser, 1977)**

Region	Mean annual air temp. (°C)	Annual rain-fall (mm)	Annual water deficit (mm)	Humidity index	Relative humidity (%)
1	20 ~ 27	1,500 ~ 1,350	0 ~ 100	+20 ~ +100	78 ~ 90
2	20 ~ 27	1,000 ~ 1,700	50 ~ 300	0 ~ +20	70 ~ 80
3	20 ~ 27	700 ~ 1,300	200 ~ 600	0 ~ −33	65 ~ 76
4	21 ~ 28	500 ~ 1,000	500 ~ 1,000	−33 ~ −66	60 ~ 70
5	23 ~ 28	250 ~ 550	800 ~ 1,300	−66 ~ −100	45 ~ 65

(*sertão*). Golfairi and Caser (1977) divide the Nordeste into five bio-climatic regions, (table 13.1 and fig. 13.1. The pocket-shaped area which includes Region 4 and Region 5, except for small but ecologi-cally and culturally significant enclaves, was originally covered by caatinga vegetation. These regions lie in areas of less than 1,000 mm of annual precipitation and annual water deficits greater than 500 mm. However, the amount of 300 mm/m as a soil's water-holding ca-pacity, used by Golfairi and Caser for the calculation of water deficit, is much too great for the shallow soils in the caatinga.

From the correlation between seasonal discharge and water surplus in three drainage basins of the semi-arid backland, Tsuchiya (1990) calculated the value of 50 mm/m as the soil water-holding capacity of the caatinga region from 1968 to 1987. Table 13.2 shows annual water storage and deficit, using a water-holding capacity of 50 mm/m at three stations.

Although Campina Grande and Patos, both in Paraíba State, are located in the same Region 4 defined by Golfairi and Caser, annual water deficits differ by about 600 mm. While Patos and Petrolina, Pernambuco State, are located in different regions, their annual water deficits are almost the same, as are their figures for the seasonal marches of the water balance.

The dominant species and the floristic composition of the caatinga are affected initially by natural conditions such as water balance and soil properties, but also by human activity. The magnitude of human impact on the caatinga has increased rapidly in recent years, owing to population and economic pressure, which results in greater scarcity of mature stands.

Trees of the caatinga stand with heights greater than 1 m are de-scribed by their floristic composition for five sites, but trees with heights smaller than 1 m are included at Campo Alegre I (table

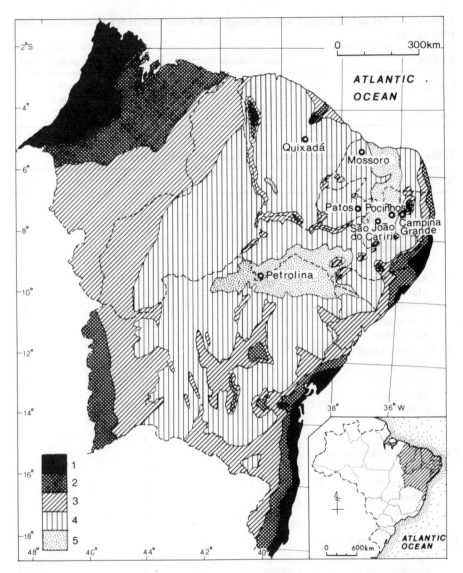

Figure 13.1 **Bioclimatic regions of North-East Brazil. (After Golfairi and Caser, 1977.)**

13.3). Campo Alegre, located 15 km north of Patos, is in Region 4; Pocinhos is in Region 5, as are Nogueira and Varginha, both 40 km east of Petrolina.

The floristic composition of Campo Alegre I is characterized by a two-year regrowth of caatinga. At Campo Alegre II, cattle grazing

283

Table 13.2   **Means of annual water storage and water deficit for twenty years from 1968 to 1987**

Station	Water storage (mm)	Water deficit (mm)
Campina Grande	181	443
Patos	118	1,093
Petrolina	62	1,047

Table 13.3   **Floristic composition of the caatinga stand at five sites**

Sites	No. of stems	(%)
(1) Campo Alegre I (10m × 10m)		
Malva	506	92
Pinhão	25	5
Marmeleiro	10	2
Jurema-preta	3	1
(2) Campo Alegre II (10m × 10m)		
Marmeleiro	79	72
Jurema-preta	23	21
Catingueira	6	6
Mofumbo	1	1
(3) Pocinhos (10m × 10m)		
Jurema-preta	23	52
Catingueira	10	23
Marmeleiro	7	16
Pinhão	2	5
Cipo	1	2
Mestracio	1	2
(4) Varginha (20m × 20m)		
Catingueira	34	57
Jurema-preta	20	33
Faveleira	3	5
Pinhão	2	3
Umbuzeiro	1	2
(5) Nogueira (10m × 10m)		
Catingueira	18	58
Pinhão	7	23
Jurema-preta	3	10
Burra-leiteira	2	6
Faveleira	1	3

occurs with selective cutting of trees for charcoal production. Nogueira has low-density cattle grazing, whereas in Varginha only goats and sheep browse. Malva is by far the dominant species in Campo Alegre I, while marmeleiro and jurema-preta prevail in Campo Alegre II. For Pocinhos, the jurema-preta species dominates, followed by catingueira and marmeleiro. Generally, jurema-preta is one of the dominant species at disturbed sites (Hardesty et al., 1988). Catingueira is the dominant species in both Nogueira and Varginha. Three sites have five species over one metre high, with jurema-preta and/or catingueira dominant. However, young jurema-preta never appear with mature catingueira, while young catingueira trees occur with mature jurema-preta and with other trees. Thus, it can be concluded that, following clear-cutting species such as malva and/or marmeleiro, jurema-preta, and catingueira dominate at different phases of caatinga regrowth. (For local and scientific names of caatinga trees, see Appendix, p. 298.)

3 Response and stress tolerance of caatinga trees to various water conditions

A better knowledge of response rates, which are expressed by α and β in equations (2) and (3), and stress tolerance of trees to water conditions in the tropical semi-arid region is important to an understanding of the adaptation of the caatinga trees to their natural environment. For this purpose, the relationship between annual growth rate of trees and water storage and water deficit were studied. Two hundred and fifty samples from sixteen tree species were collected at five sites, Pocinhos, Patos, Mossoro, Quixada, and Petrolina (see fig. 13.1).

Annual tree growth is expressed by the relative ring width, which is called relative growth ratio in order to eliminate the influence of the micro-environment, such as topography and, soils, and in order to allow comparison of samples with each other, is defined to be:

$$G_r = \Delta_r/R \tag{1}$$

where Δ_r = annual tree ring width, R = radius of tree sample in direction of measurement.

Tsuchiya (1990) expresses the relationship between tree age and tree radius as a linear equation throughout the entire growth period for the two samples of the dominant tree species: jurema-preta and catingueira, 20 and 13 years old, respectively. The Thornthwaite and Mather method is employed to calculate the water balance, assuming the water-holding capacity of the soil as 50 mm/m, (Tsuchiya, 1990).

Water storage and water deficit must be considered for the period of tree growth rather than the calendar year or the water year. Tree growth is found once per year in the rainy season, usually from Octo-

285

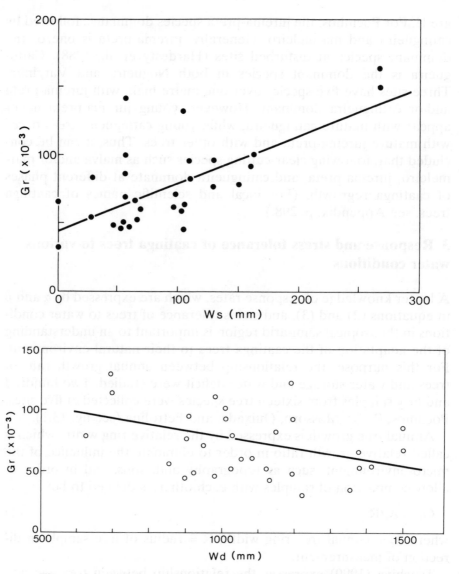

Figure 13.2–1 **Relationships between G_r and W_s and W_d (faveleira).**

ber to April or May. Thus, the tree growth year is defined by the period from the appearance of water storage to just before the next appearance. However, if water storage is absent throughout a given year, the next year begins only when the water deficit records the minimum value in the year.

Figures 13.2–1 and 13.2–2 exemplify the relationships between the relative growth ratio (G_r) and annual water storage (W_s), and that

286

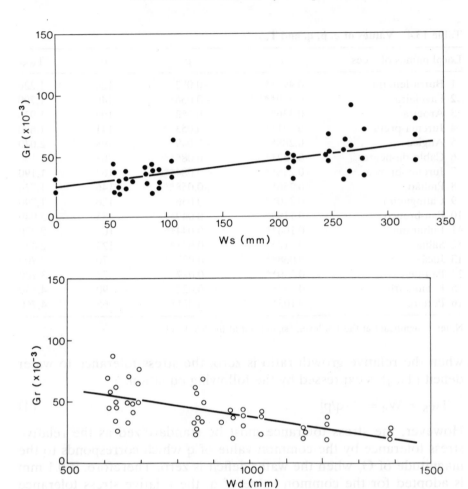

Figure 13.2–2 **Relationships between G_r and W_s and W_d (pau-branco).**

between relative growth ratio and annual water deficit (W_d) for faveleira and pau-branco, respectively. These relationships are expressed by the following equations:

$$G_r = a \, W_s + \beta \qquad (2)$$

$$G_r = p \, W_d + q \qquad (3)$$

$> a, \beta, p, q$: parameters $<$

In these equations, the parameters a and β represent the response rate of trees to the annual water storage and annual water deficit, respectively.

Assuming the magnitude of stress tolerance equals water deficit

287

Table 13.4 **Values of a, p, q, and T_{ws*}**

Local names of trees	a	p	q	T_{ws*}
1 Burra-leiteira	0.494**	−0.082	124	1,220
2 Faveleira	0.389**	−0.056*	140	1,790
3 Aroeira	0.336**	−0.052*	103	1,920
4 Jurema-preta	0.321**	−0.053**	141	1,890
5 Angico	0.288**	−0.049*	98	2,040
6 Cablo-de-negro	0.332**	−0.086**	203	1,160
7 Jurema-branca	0.258**	−0.084**	162	1,190
8 Pinhão	0.256**	−0.058**	146	1,720
9 Catingueira	0.230**	−0.056**	126	1,790
10 Pau-branco	0.119**	−0.049**	85	2,040
11 Imburana	0.104**	−0.044**	105	2,270
12 Sabiã	0.112*	−0.041*	123	2,440
13 Jucã	0.068**	−0.027**	70	3,700
14 Pau-de-casca	0.250**	−0.027	73	3,700
15 Espinheiro	0.133*	−0.022	90	4,550
16 Pereiro	0.105*	−0.021*	65	4,760

Note: **significant at the 1% level; *significant at the 5% level.

when the relative growth ratio is zero, the stress tolerance to water deficit (T_{ws}) is expressed by the following equation:

$$T_{ws} = W_d = |-q/p| \tag{4}$$

However, the stress tolerance must be standardized as the relative stress tolerance by the common value of q which corresponds to the magnitude of G_r when the water deficit is zero. Therefore, if 0.1 mm is adopted for the common value of q, the relative stress tolerance (T_{ws*}) is expressed by the following equation:

$$T_{ws*} = |-q_{0.1}/p| \tag{5}$$

Values of T_{ws*} for sixteen species are also shown in table 13.4. Next, the relationship between two independent parameters and T_{ws*} is found (fig. 13.3).

Sixteen tree species are classified into three groups. Group A includes tree species which have low stress tolerance although the response rate is large; group B varies little from group A in forms of the stress tolerance, but the response rate is larger; and group C includes trees whose response is similar to group B, but whose tolerance is the highest of all.

When comparing these results with the floristic composition of caatinga stands at the five sites, it can be estimated that the dominant

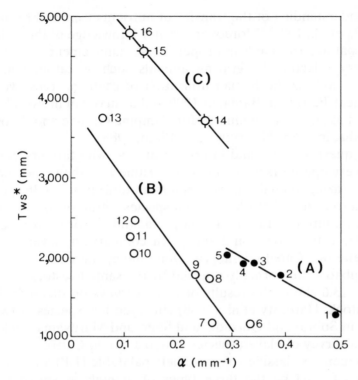

Figure 13.3   **Relationship between a and T_{WS*}.**

species transit successively from group A to group B, and from group B to group C. Trees of group A are dominant species in the primary stage of plant succession, which includes pioneer species. Trees of group C are dominant in the mature stage and trees of group B belong to the transition stage between group A and group C.

4 Utilization of the caatinga trees

Trees of the caatinga are utilized for a variety of purposes: browsing by livestock, production of firewood and charcoal, fencing, and medicine. There is abundant evidence that thoughtless removal of trees results in land degradation. Therefore, if the caatinga is to continue as a viable ecosystem, practices based on a knowledge of the ecological characteristics of trees are essential. Response rate and stress tolerance of trees as a function of soil water conditions are important factors in assuring the continuity of the caatinga. Partition rates of chemical elements among trees, soil, and bedrock are also important to an understanding of the transfer of nutrients from soil to the trees (Masuda et al., 1989). Moreover, greater knowledge of the utilization of the caatinga trees aids in proper forest management.

Dietary selection by grazing animals such as cattle, goats, and sheep, as well as the human utilization of caatinga trees, were surveyed near Petrolina, Bahia, in 1990 and a survey of firewood utilization for bakeries was conducted for Campina Grande and Patos, both in Paraíba, in 1986 (Nishizawa and Pinto, 1988).

Both questionnaires and interview surveys with farmers, ranchers, and bakery operators were employed. Table 13.5 shows dietary selection by grazing animals, as well as human utilization, of 36 species of caatinga trees near Petrolina. Seven species – arapiraca, calumbi, juazeiro, jucá, jurema-branca, jurema-preta, and mororo – are most preferred by cattle, goats, and sheep. In comparison, seven species – burra-leiteira, Cabelo-de-negro, João-mole, pereiro, quipa, and rompe-jibão – are normally rejected by the same livestock.

Table 13.6 shows the results of three surveys on dietary selection by livestock. Hardesty et al. (1988) surveyed five species at two sites located in Sobral and Quixada, and Saito and Maruyama (1988) conducted a survey of eleven species at São Joao do Cariri.

Catingueira is classified as extremely palatable (EP) and somewhat preferred $(++)$ by the three types of animals as stated both by Hardesty et al. (1988) and our survey in 1990, mentioned above. However, Saito and Maruyama identified catingueira as a non-edible tree for goats and sheep. In spite of this finding we observed goats eating very young foliage of catingueira at Fazenda Varginha, and cattle at Fazenda Nogueira. Catingueira is one of the first trees to produce new leaf growth with the arrival of seasonal rains, and the foliage is eagerly sought by livestock. As the rains begin, within a few days the foliage releases a strong pungent smell which livestock find offensive, and consequently they ignore the leaves until they dry and fall at the start of the dry season. This characteristic ensures that the catingueira foliage is available for animal consumption during the dry season (Hardesty et al., 1988). Pfeister and Malechek (1986) state that catingueira is relatively unpalatable as green foliage and that the dry, nutritious tree leaves provide the bulk of the late dry season foliage. Thus, animal preference for catingueira depends on the season. Jurema-preta, one of the most common trees in the early succession of the caatinga stand, is identified by Hardesty et al. and Nishizawa et al., respectively, as extremely palatable (EP) and somewhat preferred by livestock. However, Saito and Maruyama (1988) identified jur-

Table 13.5 Utilization of caatinga trees

Local name of tree	Dietary selection by livestock			Human utilization					
	Cattle	Goats	Sheep	Lumber	Firewood		Brickyards	Fencing
					Charcoal	Bakeries		
Angico	Man-	++	+	++	+	++	+	–
Arapiraca	da-	+++	+++	+++	++	+++	++	–
Aroeira	caru	+	++	+	++	+	++	–
Bolusu	Malva	+	++	++	++	+	++	–
Brauna	Mar-	+	++	++	++	+	++	–
Burra-leiteira	me-	–		–		–		–
Cabelo-de-negro	leir-	–		–		–		–
Calumbi	o-br-	+++		+++		+++		–
Carqueijo	anco	++		++		++		–
Canafístula	Maria-	++		++		++		–
Catingueira	dura	++		++		++		–
Espinheiro	Mo-	+++		++		++		–
Faveleira	fum-	++		++		++		++
Imburana (Umburana)	bo	++		++		++		+
João-mole		–		–				+
Juazeiro		+++		+++		+++		–
Jucá		+++		+++		+++		–
Jurema-branca		+++		+++		+++		–
Jurema-preta		++		++		++		–

291

Table 13.5 (continued)

| Local name of tree | Dietary selection by livestock | | | Human utilization | | | | |
| | Cattle | Goats | Sheep | Lumber | Firewood | | | Fencing |
					Charcoal	Bakeries	Brickyards	
Mororó	+++	+++	+++	–	–	–	–	++
Pau-branco	+	+	+	–	++	+	++	++
Pau-de-casca	+	+	+	–	+	+	++	++
Pereiro	–	–	–	–	+	+	++	++
Pinhão	–	–	–	–	–	–	–	–
Quebra-facão	++	+++	+++	–	++	+	–	+
Quipá	–	–	–	–	–	–	+	–
Rompe-jibão	–	–	–	–	–	–	–	–
São-joão	+	+	–	–	++	++	++	+
Sobiá	++	+++	+++	–	?	+	+	?
Uricuri	+++	++	++	–	–	–	–	–
Xiquexique	+	+	+	–	–	–	–	–

Key: *Dietary selection*: + + +: highly preferred; + +: somewhat preferred; +: slightly preferred; –: never preferred. Utilization: + +: most utilized; +: utilized; –: not utilized.

Table 13.6 **Comparison of three surveys on dietary selection by livestock**

Local Name	Name of researcher	Dietary selection		
		Cattle	Goats	Sheep
Angico	Hardesty et al. (H)			
	Nishizawa et al. (N)	+ +	+ +	+ +
	Saito et al. (S)	NE	NE	NE
Braúna	Hardesty et al. (H)			
	Nishizawa et al. (N)	+	+	+
	Saito et al. (S)	E	E	NE
Catingueira	Hardesty et al. (H)	EP	EP	EP
	Nishizawa et al. (N)	+ +	+ +	+ +
	Saito et al. (S)	E	NE	NE
Jurema-branca	Hardesty et al. (H)			
	Nishizawa et al. (N)	+ + +	+ + +	+ + +
	Saito et al. (S)	NE	E	E
Jurema-preta	Hardesty et al. (H)	EP	EP	EP
	Nishizawa et al. (N)	+ + +	+ + +	+ + +
	Saito et al. (S)	NE	E	E
Malva	Hardesty et al. (H)			
	Nishizawa et al. (N)	+ + +	+ +	+ +
	Saito et al. (S)	NE	E	E
Mandacaru	Hardesty et al. (H)			
	Nishizawa et al. (N)	+	+	+
	Saito et al. (S)	E	NE	NE
Marmeleiro	Hardesty et al. (H)			
	Nishizawa et al. (N)	+ +	+ +	+ +
	Saito et al. (S)	E	E	E
Pau-branco	Hardesty et al. (H)	P	NP	NP
	Nishizawa et al. (N)	+	+	+
	Saito et al. (S)			
Pinhão	Hardesty et al. (H)			
	Nishizawa et al. (N)	–	–	–
	Saito et al. (S)	NE	NE	NE
Sobiá	Hardesty et al. (H)		EP	EP
	Nishizawa et al. (N)	+ +	+ + +	+ + +
	Saito et al. (S)	E	E	E
Xiquexique	Hardesty et al. (H)			
	Nishizawa et al. (N)	+	+	+
	Saito et al. (S)	E	E	E

Key: (Hardesty et al.):   (Nishizawa et al.):   (Saito et al.):
    EP: extremaly palatable   + + +: highly preferred   E: edible
    P: palatable   + +: somewhat preferred   NE: non-edible
    NP: non-palatable   +: slightly preferred
                  –: never preferred

ema-preta as a non-edible tree for cattle. Marmeleiro is a principal species preferred by livestock, according to the survey by Nishizawa et al., but Pfeister et al. (1988) state that livestock mainly browse on it during relatively less severe dry seasons.

In the semi-arid interior of North-East Brazil, both temporal and spatial variations in rainfall cause pronounced fluctuations in the quality, quantity, and distribution of available foliage as well as changes in the floristic composition with successive plant stages. Therefore, the dietary selection by livestock is different from place to place and from season to season.

Near Petrolina, seventeen species are identified as being used for charcoal production, twenty-one for firewood at bakeries, twenty for firewood at brick and tile manufacturers, and seventeen for fencing. Fifteen species of caatinga trees are commonly used for all of the these purposes (table 13.5).

Almost all the bakeries in Campina Grande and Patos, except three that also employ supplementary electric ovens, use firewood to bake bread. Total consumption of firewood only for bakeries is approximately 600 tons per month in Campina Grande (population 300,000) and 50 tons per month in Patos (population 70,000).

Trees for firewood use by bakeries mainly consist of two species, jurema-preta and catingueira. There is a little difference in the composition for firewood of these two species used by bakeries in Campina Grande and Patos (table 13.7). In Campina Grande, catingeira is prevalent, followed by jurema-preta. On the other hand, in Patos, jurema-preta predominates, followed by catingueiro.

Almost all the bakeries in Campina Grande purchase firewood through brokers from the Cariri, where human population is sparse and thus human impact on the caatinga has been comparatively

Table 13.7 **Tree species for firewood used by bakeries in Campina Grande and Patos**

	Campina Grande		Patos	
Tree species	Frequency	%	Frequency	%
Jurema-preta	51	34	12	33
Catingueira	69	46	10	28
Pereiro	19	13	3	8
Aroeira	4	3	4	11
Juazeiro	3	2	3	8
Other species	3	2	4	11

small. However, the bakeries in Patos obtain their firewood directly from the environs of the town, and thus human impact is relatively greater.

While catingueira and jurema-preta are also used by the bakeries in Petrolina, other species, such as angico and calumbi, are generally used. However, there are some differences between species preferred by bakeries in the region around Petrolina, on the São Francisco River in Pernambuco, and the interior of Paraíba State.

Dominant trees for firewood used by bakeries also vary from place to place, as in the case of dietary selection by livestock. Although fencing materials of wood are now being replaced by concrete, several types of traditional fences are still constructed from caatinga trees (Barros, 1985; Ribaski, 1986).

Although many of the trees from the semi-arid interior of North-East Brazil are used as stated above, not all are useful species, nor are they always available in any given region, because floristic composition of the caatinga stand varies with stages of plant succession and the magnitude of human impact.

5 Deforestation associated with increased firewood consumption and charcoal production

Utilization of caatinga trees is a matter of increasing concern, mainly because of the increasing population and changing lifestyles. For example, recently new types of bread are being introduced in North-East Brazil, which indicates a change in the traditional dietary patterns. This change has caused an increase in the number of bakeries and deforestation of the caatinga for firewood in baking.

Along with changes in dietary patterns, the construction materials used in housing have also been gradually upgraded. Even in the rural areas, houses with mud walls and thatched roofs are changing to brick walls and tiled roofs. Therefore, consumption of firewood at brick yards and tile factories has also increased.

More accurate estimates of deforestation due to firewood and charcoal consumption are necessary in order to understand better the associated problems, as well as to suggest appropriate methods of sustainable development and sound management of the caatinga.

The rate of deforestation per month can be expressed as follows:

$$Adf = Mdf/r_t r_s P_f \tag{6}$$

where Mdf = consumption of firewood (kg/month); P_f = mass of trunks and branches (kg/100 km^2); r_t = utilization rate of trunks and branches; r_s = rate of mass of useful species for firewood to total mass of the stand.

Further, P_f is expressed as follows:

$$P_f = N(D)W_t(D) \tag{7}$$

where $N(D)$ is the tree density in a unit of the stand, which is usually expressed by the number of trees with breast height having diameter D in 100 m^2, and $W_t(D)$ is the weight of the trunks and branches of trees with breast height diameter D.

Hayashi (1981, 1988) has proposed the following empirical equations of $N(D)$ and $W_t(D)$:

$$N(D) = 217 \exp\cdot(-0.42D) \tag{8}$$

$$W_t(D) = 0.206D^{2.233} \tag{9}$$

Accordingly, total mass of trunks and branches with the magnitude of D from D_1 to D_2 per 100m^2 is calculated with the following equation:

$$\int_{D1}^{D2} N(D)W_t(D)dD = 44.7 \int_{D1}^{D2} D^{2.223} \exp(-0.42D)dD \tag{10}$$

Although the diameter of a firewood log is seldom larger than 10 cm, it ranges roughly from 5 cm to 8 cm. Assuming that D_1 and D_2 are 5 cm and 8 cm, respectively, the total mass is calculated at approximately 690 kg per 100m^2 by equation (10).

The magnitudes of r_t and r_s in equation (6) vary with the floristic composition, which differs by the stage of plant succession and the magnitude of human impact.

Consequently, assuming further that two pairs of r_t and r_s are as follows:

$$r_t = 0.6, \ r_s = 0.6$$

in the first pair of parameters,

$$r_t = 0.4. \ r_s = 0.4$$

in the second pair of parameters.

Adf in equation (6) is expressed as follows: in the first case

$$Adf = (1/248) \ Mdf \tag{11}$$

and in the second case

$$Adf = (1/110) \, Mdf \tag{12}$$

Inserting the firewood consumption of 6.0×10^5 kg per month by bakeries in Campina Grande into equations (11) and (12) yields the values of 2.4×10^5 m^2 per month and 5.5×10^5 m^2 per month respectively, as Adf.

The deforestation area per year is approximately 2.9 km^2 and 6.6 km^2 in the first and second pair of parameters, respectively.

If the consumption of bread per person for all of North-East Brazil, with a population of about forty million, is assumed to be at the same rate as in Campo Grande, and the firewood for bakeries is also assumed to be from the caatinga stand, then the total deforestation area for firewood from bakeries alone would be 312 km^2 for the first parameter and 715 km^2 for the second.

The deforestation of caatinga trees caused by charcoal production is also a great concern of ours. Deforestation area can be estimated for charcoal production by employing equation (6), employed above with firewood for bakeries.

Generally, one unit mass of charcoal is produced from about two unit mass of freshly cut green caatinga wood (Hayashi, 1988). Equation (6) for charcoal production is then converted to the following:

$$\begin{aligned} Adf &= Mdf/r_t r_s P_f \\ &= 2Mdc/r_t r_s P_f \end{aligned} \tag{13}$$

where Mdc is charcoal production (kg/year).

Charcoal production in North-East Brazil is roughly 500,000 tons per year (IBGE, 1991). Therefore, about 1,000,000 tons of green wood is consumed in charcoal production.

Employing equations (11) and (12), the deforestation area per year is approximately 4,000 km^2 and 9,000 km^2 in the first and second pair of parameters, respectively.

Although no scientific data is available for firewood use at brick and tile factories, rough estimates from factory managers suggest that the total area deforested for brick and tile production is about 1,000 to 1,500 km^2 per year.

Combining all the above uses, the total deforestation area of caatinga trees associated with firewood and charcoal production in the semi-arid interior of North-East Brazil is estimated in the range of 5,300 km^2 to 11,200 km^2 per year.

6 Conclusions and a proposal

Response rate and stress tolerance, which indicate the adaptabilities of caatinga trees to the semi-arid interior, are ascertained by measuring tree growth of 16 plant species. Moreover, the characteristics of their adaptabilities are classified into three tree groups, A, B, and C, associated with plant succession after clear-cutting.

Trees for animal grazing and human utilization are found not only in the mature stage (Group C) of plant succession but also in the primary stage (Group A) and the transitional stage (Group B). Trees belonging to Group A, such as aroeira and jurema-preta, require about fifteen years to reach maturity. These two, and other tree species, reach sufficient size for firewood and charcoal production in less than ten years. Trees in Group B normally have sufficient growth for firewood and charcoal production within fifteen years.

The area covered by the potential caatinga stand is about 930,000 km². It is assumed today that only about one-fourth of the potential caatinga stand still remains. Therefore, an area of about 230,000 km² is still available for firewood and charcoal production.

As stated above, the most useful caatinga trees provide sufficient firewood and charcoal production for a continuous recycling period of fifteen years. Thus, sustained use of the caatinga stand allows for regrowth of trees, if careful forest rehabilitation programmes are implemented. Moreover, it would be theoretically possible to supply about 400,000 more tons of charcoal from the caatinga area than is presently consumed.

Acknowledgements

The writers wish to express their sincere gratitude to SUDENE, IBGE, and CNPq. We would like to also thank Prof. Em. Hilgard O'Reilly Sternberg, University of California, Berkeley, and Dr Keith Muller, Kent State University, for their academic discussions and fruitful suggestions.

Appendix

Local and scientific names of caatinga trees

1	Angico	*Anadenanthera macrocarpa* Brenth.
2	Arapiraca	*Pithecollobirum foliorosum* Benth.
3	Aroeira	*Astronium urundeuva* Engl.
4	Bolusu	(unknown)

5	Braúna	*Schinopsis brasiliensis* Engl.
6	Burra-leiteira	*Sapium cicatricosum* Pax et K. Hoffm.
7	Cabelo-de-negro	(unknown)
8	Calumbi	*Mimosa malacocentra* Mart.
9	Carqueijo	*Calliandra depauperata* Benth.
10	Canafistula	*Cassia excelsa* Schrad.
11	Catingueira	*Caesalpinia pyramidalis* Tul.
12	Espinheiro	*Piptadenia viridiflora* Benth.
13	Faveleira	*Cnidoscolum phyllacanthus* Muell. Arg. Pax et Hoff.
14	Imburana (Umburana)	*Bursera leptophloeos* Mart.
15	João-mole	(unknown)
16	Juazeiro	*Ziziphus joazeiro* Mart.
17	Jucá	*Caesalpinia ferrlea* Mart. ex Tul.
18	Jurema-branca	*Piptadenia stipulacea* Ducke
19	Jurema-preta	*Mimosa hostilis* Benth.
20	Mandacaru	*Cereus jamacaru* DC.
21	Malva	*Gaya aurea* St. Hill.
22	Marmeleiro-branco	*Croton argirophylloides* Muell. Arg.
23	Maria-dura	(unknown)
24	Mofumbo	*Combretum leprosum* Mart. et Eichi.
25	Mororó	*Bauhinia cheilantha* Steud.
26	Pau-branco	*Fraunhofera multiflora* Mart.
27	Pau-de-casca	*Tabebuia spongiosa* Rizzini
28	Pereiro	*Aspidosperma pyrifolium* Mart.
29	Pinhão	*Jatropha mutabilis* Baill.
30	Quebra-fação	*Phisocalymma scaberrimum* Pohl
31	Quipá	*Opuntia palmadora* Br. et Rose
32	Rompe-jibáo	*Erythroxylum* sp.
33	São-joão	*Cassia excelsa* Schrad.
34	Sobiá	*Mimosa caesalpiniifolia* benth.
35	Uricuri	*Cocos coronata* mart.
36	Xiquexique	*Pilosocereus gounellei* Byl. et Rowl.

References

Barros, S. 1985. *Cercas sertanejas – traços ecológicos do sertão pernambucano.* Secretaria de Educação, Departamento de Cultura, Fundação Joaquim Nabuco, Recife.

Golfairi, L., and R.L. Caser. 1977. *Zoneamento ecológico da região nordeste para experimentação florestal.* Centro de Pesquisa Florestal de Região do Cerrado, Série Técnica, 10.

Hardesty, L.H., T.W. Box, and J.C. Malechek. 1988. "Season of cutting affects biomass production by coppicing browse species of the Brazilian caatinga." *Journal of Range Management*, 41 (6): 447–80.

Hayashi, I. 1981. "Plant communities and their environments in the caatinga of Northeast Brazil." *Latin American Studies* 2: 65–79.

———. 1988. "Changing aspect of caatinga vegetation in semi-arid region, Northeast Brazil." *Latin American Studies* 10: 61–71.

IBGE [Fundação Instituto Brasileiro de Geografia e Estatística]. 1991. *Anuário Estatístico do Brasil, 1991*, 528–9.

Masuda, F., T. Nishizawa, and Y. Sakamoto. 1989. "Element partition among tree, soil, and basement rock in thorny shrub in Northeast Brazil: A preliminary note." *Ann. Rep. Inst. Geosci.* (University of Tsukuba) 15: 88–91.

Nishizawa, T., and M.M.V. Pinto. 1988. "Recent changes in firewood and charcoal production and their effects on deforestation." *Latin American Studies* 10: 121–31.

Pfeister, J.A., and J.C. Malechek. 1986. "Dietary selection by goats and sheep in a deciduous woodland of Northeastern Brazil." *Journal of Range Management* 39 (1): 24–8.

Pfeister, J.A., J.C. Malechek, and D.F. Balph. 1988. "Foraging behavior of goats and sheep in the caatinga of Brazil." *Journal of Applied Ecology* 25, 379–88.

Ribaski, J. 1986. "Avaliaçao do uso dos recursos florestais em imoveis rurais na região de Ouricuri, PE." *Boletin de Pesquisa* 31, EMBRAPA.

Saito, I., and H. Maruyama. 1988. "Some types of livestock ranching in São João do Cariri on the upper Paraiba Valley, Northeast Brazil." *Latin American Studies* 10: 103–20.

Tsuchiya, A. 1990. "Hypertrophic growth of trees of the caatinga plant community and water balance." *Latin American Studies* 11: 51–70.

14

Drought, irrigation, and changes in the sertão of North-East Brazil

Isao Saito and Noritaka Yagasaki

1 Introduction

In Brazil's North-East, the semi-arid interior known as *sertão* (back-country) is in marked contrast ecologically with the coastal zone (*zona da mata*) and the transitional zone (*agreste*). While the coastal zone is humid, receiving more than 1,600 mm of rain per annum, precipitation decreases toward the interior, less than 800 mm falling in the sertão. The humid coast was originally covered with dense forest, though little of this remains today. In the sertão, on the other hand, the *caatinga*, the drought-resistant thorn scrub and xerophytic vegetation, predominates.

Such ecological regions have been the basis for different types of human land use, settlement, and economy. On the coast, sugar cane cultivation and sugar production have been important from the early stage of colonization and settlement up to the present. In the transitional zone, intensive farming of livestock and food crops has supported a dense population of peasants. The sertão, on the other hand, has been characterized by extensive cattle grazing and large-scale properties held by absentee owners. Thus, the three regions of zona da mata, agreste, and sertão differ in terms of environment, type of economy, and process of development (Andrade, 1968; Saito and Yagasaki, 1987).

301

While the fragility of the humid tropical environment of Amazonia is attracting worldwide attention, the sertão, whose ecological conditions and history of human use and occupancy differs substantially from those of Amazonia, is also considered susceptible to the process of desertification. The sertão suffers from chronic scarcity of water and recurrent drought. Severe droughts have often caused hunger, poverty, mass migration, and even the deaths of many people as well as of animals.

While the first drought since the Portuguese colonization and settlement was officially recorded in the late sixteenth century in Pernambuco, six droughts occurred in the seventeenth century, fourteen in the eighteenth century, twelve in the nineteenth century, and twelve so far in this century, according to the Superintendency for Development of the North-East (Superintendência do Desenvolvimento do Nordeste) (SUDENE, 1981). Such droughts have become nationally recognized, especially since the late nineteenth century. An influx of people into the interior accelerated with the development of commercial cultivation of arboreal cotton, and the increased population, consequently, further exacerbated the region's susceptibility to drought. Despite attempts by various public organizations and projects to relieve drought problems, the region remains today one of the most underdeveloped sections of Brazil.

For the people in the semi-arid sertão, maximum use of limited water resources has been their major concern. Traditionally, people took advantage of the *brejos*, or the humid mountain environment with orographic rainfalls. Farming was practised during the low-water season in the riverbeds, as the flow ceased, in the moist soil known as *vazante*. More recently, small reservoirs (*açudes*) were constructed for storing and supplying water. Such reservoirs now constitute an important landscape element of the sertão (Saito et al., 1986). These efforts were traditional adaptations of the people to the semi-arid environment.

In recent years, the sertão is changing, as federal and state governments endeavour to promote regional development by establishing irrigation projects, which attempt to utilize scarce water resources by constructing dams, reservoirs, and irrigation canals and by introducing electric pumps and other irrigation facilities. The land covered with caatinga is being transformed into farmland. Irrigation farming, regardless of the scale and type, gradually – and sometimes drastically – changes agriculture, land use, and rural communities of the sertão.

Although the contemporary sertão in transition can hardly be understood without considering irrigation farming, there is still limited knowledge concerning the process of irrigation development, land-use systems, and agricultural management on the farm and local scales. We also do not know if contemporary development policy will be able to remedy the sertão's chronic problems. In order to assess the government's irrigation approach for development, the socio-economic and ecological consequences of contemporary irrigation farming need to be scrutinized. Such examinations have to be made on a local scale, based on careful field investigation. Geographers concerned with people, land use, and environment have much to contribute here. An accumulation of case-studies will offer the basis for considering ecologically sound land-use systems and the social well-being of residents, and for reconsidering the regional development policies.

In this paper we intend to examine, on a small scale, the contemporary changes due to irrigation. Presented are two examples of small-scale, spontaneous irrigation farming around reservoirs in Boqueirão and Teixeira municípios in the state of Paraíba, and a large-scale irrigation development in the middle São Francisco Valley, around the twin cities of Petrolina and Juàzeiro (fig. 14.1). These areas emerged as important centres of irrigation farming during the past decade or so. We pay special attention to the development process of irrigation, farming types, and land use rotation systems. Details of each case are elaborated in our previous reports (Saito and Yagasaki, 1989, 1991; Saito et al., 1991; Yagasaki et al., 1989).

2 Reservoir irrigation in Paraíba

Reservoirs in Paraíba

Reservoirs in Paraíba, including those constructed by federal, state, and local governments, may be classified into three categories by size and type of use (table 14.1). A large reservoir has water storage capacity of over 200 million m^3, a medium-size reservoir ranges from 10 to 50 million m^3, and a small-scale reservoir holds less than 1 million m^3. Large reservoirs are constructed by damming up major rivers, while those of small to medium size are found around urban settlements. In addition, numerous small reservoirs of less than 1 million m^3 of water are found in cattle fazendas.

The National Department of Works Against the Drought (Departamento Nacional de Obras Contra as Secas, DNOCS) is a federal

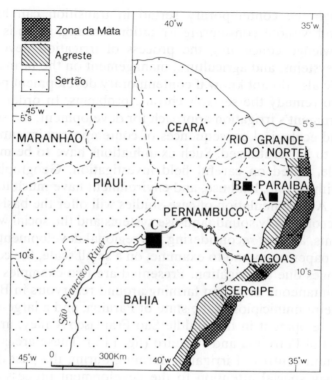

Figure 14.1 **Study area in North-East Brazil. A: Boqueirão area; B. Teixeira area; C: Petrolina–Juàzeiro area.**

organization for regional development of the North-East, which was established as early as the first decade of this century. DNOCS has constructed reservoirs intended as a development strategy against aridity and rural poverty. The intention is to augment agricultural production and to promote commercial agriculture in order to alleviate rural poverty and to stabilize the population in the semi-arid regions, which are characterized traditionally by extensive livestock grazing and subsistence farming (Hall, 1978).

Up to the end of 1981, DNOCS had built 261 public dams and reservoirs in the North-East, with a total water storage capacity of 12.3 billion m³. Among them, 38 are found in the state of Paraíba, with a capacity of 2.5 billion m³. In addition, 596 dams were constructed by DNOCS in the North-East for private water storage; their reservoir capacity amounted to 1.3 billion m³. Paraíba has 59 such reservoirs (Araújo, 1982). However, it has often been pointed out that these reservoirs are not necessarily utilized efficiently for local farming activities, despite the vast amount of water stored in them.

Boqueirão reservoir and its vicinity

Boqueirão município is situated on the eastern edge of the Paraiban sertão in the middle Paraíba valley. Here the caatinga vegetation predominates with jurema-preta (*Mimosa hostilis* Benth.), catingueira (*Caesalpinia pyramidalis* Tul.), and pereiro (*Aspidosperma pyrifolium* Mart.), as well as such xerophytic plants as facheiro (*Cereus squamosus* Guerke) and mandacaru (*Cereus jamacaru* DC). Although annual precipitation fluctuates substantially, the region receives 400 to 600 mm in an average year. The rainy season is from March through August.

The Paraíba River was dammed up by DNOCS in 1956. Boqueirão reservoir, with a water capacity of over 500 million m³, belongs to the large-scale category. It is variously utilized for urban consumption, electric power generation, irrigation, fishery, recreation, and flood control.

Boqueirão's economy has depended traditionally on livestock grazing and rainfed cultivation of maize, beans, cotton, and palma, a cactaceous plant used for cattle feed. Cattle are the most important animals, grazed in the caatinga as well as in the stubble of crops. Beans, maize, and cotton are cropped together for three to four years after the scrub is cleared. Palma and xerophytic plants become increasingly important as fodder for cattle during the dry season. Absentee landlords are not numerous. The landholding pattern of Boqueirão shows the transitional characteristics from the agreste to the sertão.

Although irrigation farming was primarily undertaken on the floodplain to grow elephant grass, a type of sorghum used for cattle feed, it gradually expanded to the interfluvial areas using water pumped from the reservoir and the Paraíba River. Irrigated acreage increased substantially in the late 1970s, when tomatoes, bell peppers, and bananas became particularly important. In 1980, the area under irrigation amounted to around 400 hectares. Boqueirão reservoir, blessed with an ample quantity of water, is able to provide water for farming all the year round, and the area under irrigation is expanding.

During our field study in this area in October 1988, we identified 31 irrigation fields operated by 26 farmers (fig. 14.2). These fields are situated within two kilometres' distance from either the reservoir or the Paraíba River. The total area under irrigation, crop production, and the type of irrigation were investigated. We also interviewed fourteen farm households regarding land tenure, family structure, residence, previous occupation, and crop marketing methods. Land-use surveys were also conducted. Figure 14.3 shows an example of

305

Table 14.1   **Classification of reservoirs in Paraíba, North-East Brazil**

Size	Name of reservoir	Construction		Storage capacity ('000 m³)
		Year	Agency	
Large	Coremas	1942	DNOCS	720,000
	Mãe D'Agua	1956	DNOCS	638,000
	Boqueirão	1956	DNOCS	536,000
	Engenheiro Avidos	1936	DNOCS	255,000
Medium	São Gonçalo	1936	DNOCS	44,600
	Sume	1962	DNOCS	36,800
	Eng. Arco Verde	1936	DNOCS	35,000
	Soledade	1933	DNOCS	27,058
	Jatoba I	1954	DNOCS	17,520
	Santa Luzia	1933	DNOCS	11,960
	Taperoa	198?	Canaã[a]	?
Small	Lagoa de Meio	1955	DNOCS	6,648
	Riacho de S. Antonio	1956	DNOCS	6,834
	Serra Branca	1966	DNOCS	2,117
	Poços	1923/53	DNOCS	2,000
	Bodocongo	1915	DNOCS	1,020
	São Francisco	1984	Canaã[a]	9,000
	Communal açudes	1930 ~	Community	
	Açudes in Fazendas	1950 ~	Individual	
	Roadside açudes	1970 ~	Community	

Source: Based on Araújo (1982): *Dams in the northeast of Brazil*, DNOCS, and field observation.
a. Governmental project of Paraíba.

an irrigation farm on the left bank of the Paraíba River. In this farm, operated by a tenant farmer, tomatoes were first cultivated after clearing of the caatinga. Watermelons followed tomatoes. Then the field appears to have been rotated to either cotton or maize and beans (*feijão*), and eventually returned to caatinga. The details of the study are elaborated elsewhere (Saito and Yagasaki, 1989).

While the produce is sold locally at the periodic market known as the *feira*, most crops are shipped to the public wholesale produce markets (CEASA) of large cities in Paraíba and Pernambuco. Boqueirão's tomatoes and bell peppers are particularly important at the wholesale market of Recife, where they represented 12.3 per cent and 13.2 per cent respectively of the total receipt in 1987.

	Irrigation							
Hydro-electric	Gravity	Pump	Urban	Individual	Animal	Fishing	Recreation	Flood Control
○	○		○		○	○	○	○
○		○	○		○			○
○	○	○	○		○	○	○	○
					○			
○	○		○		○	○	○	
			○		○	○		
	○				○			
					○	○		
	○		○		○	○		○
			○		○			
		○	○		○	○		○
			○					
			○		○	○		
			○		○	○		
		○	○		○			
			○					
		○			○			
			○	○	○			
				○	○			
			○	○	○	○		

Irrigation farms are mobile and transient, easily shifting from one location to another. The repeated use of land causes plant diseases and declining productivity. Simple irrigation equipment and the acquisition of land by tenancy facilitate such mobility. In the fields, crops are typically rotated. After the land is rented, the caatinga cover is cleared and burned, the field is prepared, the irrigation ditch is dug, and water is secured by installing electric pumps and water pipes.

Tomatoes are generally grown for the first one to two years. The field is then planted in bell peppers, and afterwards rotated to cotton. Cotton fields eventually turn to banana fields before being abandoned and returning to caatinga. The crop rotation systems are summarized in table 14.2.

Although the production and marketing of irrigated crops have so

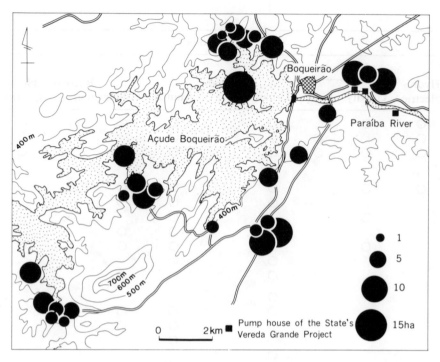

Figure 14.2 **Irrigation farms around Boqueirão Reservoir, Paraíba. (Based on interviews.)**

far been successful, it is rather doubtful whether spontaneous irrigation farming has expanded employment opportunities in Boqueirão.

Teixeira plateau

The Teixeira plateau is located in the heart of the Paraiban sertão, some 270 km inland from João Pessoa and overlooking the Patos basin. Due to its high elevation, ranging from 750 to 900 m above sea level, the region has relatively mild climatic conditions with rather stable precipitation. February through April is the main rainy season, when 80 per cent of the annual precipitation is received. The environment, resembling that of the brejos typically found in eastern Paraíba, is rather favourable for farming activities.

Teixeira município is dominated by small landholdings. Cattle and goats are the main animals, but the role of livestock in the economy of Teixeira is limited (Saito and Maruyama, 1988). Maize and beans are important food crops, while sisal and cashew nuts constitute the major cash crops.

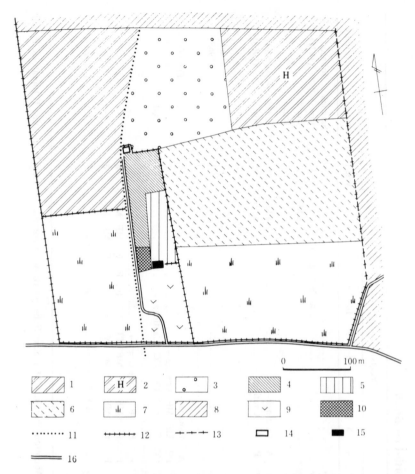

Figure 14.3 **Land use of an irrigation farm on the Paraíba River. 1: tomatoes; 2: tomatoes harvested; 3; watermelons; 4: bell peppers; 5: cotton; 6: maize and beans; 7: wasteland; 8: caatinga; 9: uncultivated land; 10: corral; 11: irrigation pipes; 12: fences; 13: *avelós* hedgerow; 14: simple hut; 15: residence; 16: road. (Based on field observation.)**

Although the local residents attempted to construct a small reservoir in the late nineteenth century by damming up a small stream of the Poços River, the present Poços Reservoir was completed by DNOCS (then called IFOCS) in 1923. Reconstructed thirty years later, the reservoir now holds 2 million m^3 of water. However, the reservoir alone did not promote the development of irrigation farming. The real growth took place after 1984, when the São Francisco reservoir was built on the Poços River upstream of the Poços reser-

Table 14.2 Land use cycles in the sertão, North-East Brazil

Irrigation method	Location	1	2	3	4	5	6	7	8	9	10	11	12	13	14	15	Land use cycle (yrs)	Use of caatinga	Reference
								Years											
No irrigation (rain)	Caatinga/sertão	▲	Caatinga →														30	Charcoal/firewood/fence	Johnson (1971)
	Caatinga/Boa Ventura	▲	Caatinga →								▲	Caatinga →					10		
		MF	Caatinga →													▲MF	15		
	Field/sertão	MF	MFA	A	A	Caatinga →										▲MF	15	Fence/charcoal	Andrade (1968)
	Field/Boqueirão	MF	MFP	P	P	P	Caatinga →									▲MF	15		
River — Flood	Várzea (floodplain)	MF →															1	–	Andrade (1968)
		B →															1	–	
		R →															1	–	
Açude and river — Pump	Boqueirão	TT	TT	A	A	Banana →											?	–	Field Observation
	Boqueirão	PP	PP	PP	MF	MF	MF	Orange →									?	–	
	Teixeira	TT	TT	CC	CC	CC	CC	CC	Caatinga →								?	Ash	
	Petrolina	F	F	Grapes →													?	–	
Açude and river — Canal	Petrolina	TT	TT	TT	F	F	F	F	Tree crops →								?	–	
	Petrolina	TT	TT	F	F	F	MF	MF	MF	TT	TT	F	F	F	MF	MF	8	–	
	Petrolina	N	N	F	F	F	MF	MF	N	N	F	F	F	MF	MF		8	–	
Ground water (pumpwell)	Mossoró (Rio Grande do Norte)	N	Capoeira →				▲N Capoeira →							▲N Capoeira →			5	Ash	Interview

▲: clearing of caatinga; Capoeira: second growth; A: cotton; P: palma; M: maize; F: beans; B: sweet potatoes; R: rice; N: melons; T: tomatoes; P: bell peppers; C: carrots; → ......: continuous land use.

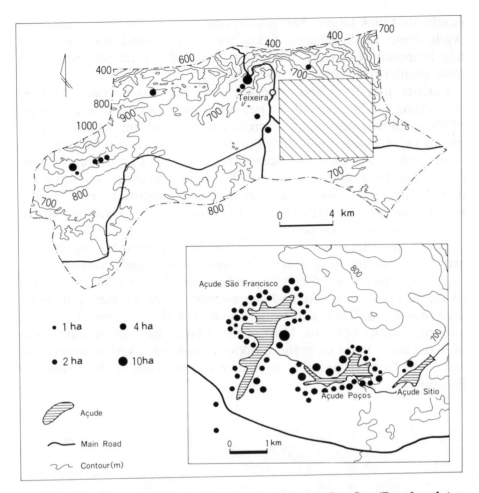

Figure 14.4 **Distribution of irrigation farms in Teixeira, Paraíba. (Based on interviews and data from the Bank of Brazil.)**

voir as part of the state-sponsored Cana project. This reservoir, with a capacity of 9 million m^3, effectively promoted irrigated farming. In 1987, a third reservoir, named Sítio, was constructed downstream on the same river. Although these three reservoirs belong to the small-scale group in our overall classification of Paraíba's reservoirs, they have played important roles in intensifying Teixeira's farming.

In our field research, 88 farms utilizing irrigation were identified in the Texeira município, based on our interviews and the data supplied at the branch office of Bank of Brazil (for details see Yagasaki et al., 1989). The total irrigated area amounted to 261 ha. This figure is

311

nearly six times larger than that enumerated in the 1980 Census of Agriculture. Most irrigated fields are found around the Poços and São Francisco reservoirs, while others are dispersed, utilizing water from smaller reservoirs or rivers (fig. 14.4).

Carrots, tomatoes, and table beets are the major irrigated crops, accounting for 74 per cent, 16 per cent, and 5 per cent, respectively, of the total irrigated areas. Carrots are the most important, and are grown twice a year on wide mounds called *canteiros* with plenty of water and care. Figure 14.5 shows the land use of an irrigation farm on the São Francisco reservoir, with carrots and tomatoes being the major crops. The owner plans to continue planting carrots for the next fifteen years. After tomato is harvested, the field will be planted with bell pepper and onions.

There are three types of irrigation farms, operated by owner-growers (*proprietários*), renters (*arrendatários*), and share-croppers (*meieros*). Since it is difficult to purchase farmland within easy access to the reservoirs, renters and share-croppers are becoming increasingly dominant. They constitute one-half both in terms of acreage and the number of farms. Most of these farms have taken advantage of agricultural loans from the Bank of Brazil. Such agricultural credit can cover from 70 per cent to nearly 100 per cent of the necessary investments.

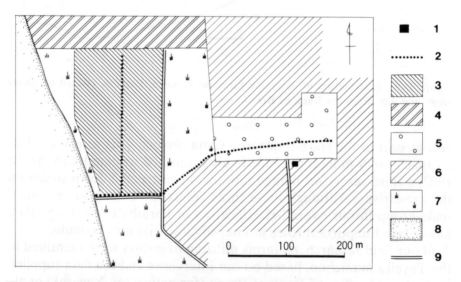

Figure 14.5 **Land use of an irrigation farm in Teixeira, Paraíba. 1: farm shed; 2: irrigation pipes; 3: carrots; 4: caatinga; 5: tomatoes; 6: other land use; 7: wasteland; 8: São Francisco reservoir; 9: road. (Based on field observation.)**

Carrots and tomatoes are marketed to the CEASAs in the major cities of the North-East. Carrots are particularly important in Fortaleza, Recife, and Salvador. In 1987, Fortaleza received some 2,000 tons of carrots from Teixeira, amounting to 34 per cent of the total receipt. In Recife, Teixeira's carrots accounted for 11 per cent. Teixeira is considered one of the major carrot-producing areas in the North-East. This development took place in a relatively short period of time.

3 Middle São Francisco Valley

Sobradinho dam, CODEVASF, and irrigation projects

The São Francisco River, originating in the state of Minas Gerais, is the largest permanent river of North-East Brazil. Enjoying semi-arid tropical conditions and an abundant supply of water all year round, the river's environs have great potential for agricultural development.

The middle São Francisco Valley, particularly the area around the twin cities of Petrolina and Juàzeiro, attracted national attention during the 1980s, when the region began to change rapidly from traditional sertão covered with caatinga into a productive farming area. The nature of the transformation process, as well as the type of irrigation farming, differs substantially from the spontaneous development exemplified by Boqueirão and Teixeira.

The construction of the Sobradinho dam in 1978, some 30 km upstream from the urban settlements of Petrolina and Juàzeiro, was one of the most important factors in transforming the region's economy, society, and landscape (fig. 14.6). There is a hydroelectric power plant with a capacity of 1 million kW. The Sobradinho lake has over 4,000km² of surface areas and a water storage capacity of 34 billion m³. The water area is comparable to the Japanese inland sea of Setonaikai. The dam has contributed not only to stabilizing the volume of water flowing downstream but also to providing water for large irrigation projects.

The construction of the Sobradinho dam and the subsequent development of irrigation agriculture brought about a substantial influx of people. In 1940, the municípios of Petrolina and Juàzeiro had a combined population of some 30,000. This increased to 124,000 in 1970 and to 222,000 in 1980, reaching 332,000 in 1989. The din and bustle of the urbanized sections of Petrolina and Juàzeiro remind us of the boom towns of the frontier.

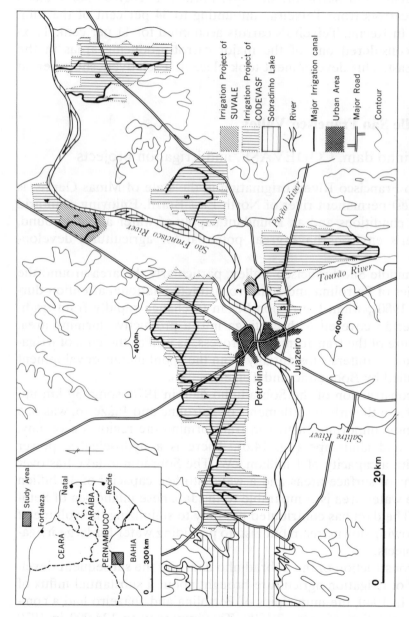

Figure 14.6 Irrigation projects in the middle São Francisco Valley. 1 to 7 correspond to projects in Table 3. (Based on the project plans of CODEVASF, aerial photographs, and field observation.)

The São Francisco Valley is presently administered by the Development Company of the São Francisco Valley (Companhia de Desenvolvimento do Vale do São Francisco, CODEVASF), while the rest of the North-East falls under the jurisdiction of the aforementioned DNOCS. CODEVASF, a public corporation established in 1974 on the basis of SUVALE (Superintendency of the São Francisco Valley), has five districts with headquarters in Brasilia. The Petrolina–Juàzeiro area belongs to the third district, whose regional office is situated in Petrolina (CODEVASF, 1989).

CODEVASF has promoted regional development by organizing large irrigation projects (table 14.3). In the late 1960s and early 1970s, SUDENE and SUVALE launched the pilot project of Bebedouro in the Petrolina município, and another pilot project, Mandacaru, in the Juàzeiro município, for the settlement of small farmers. When CODEVASF took over the implementation of such colonization projects, it established the Tourão project in 1976, the Bebedouro II and Maniçoba projects in 1981, the Curaçá project in 1982, and the Senador Nilo Coelho project in 1984. These projects offer small *parcelas* (plots) for small farmers, as well as medium to large parcelas to corporate farms. The emphasis is increasingly on corporate farming, as can be seen particularly in the Tourão project. While Bebedouro and Mandacaru have limited areas under irrigation, CODEVASF's new developments have vast amounts of land under irrigation, including 10,000 ha in Tourão and over 4,000 ha each in Maniçoba and Curaçá. In the Senador Nilo Coelho project, the largest development in the area, 20,000 ha would be irrigated upon its completion.

Small farms and corporate farms

Provided that a sufficient amount of water is supplied, the semi-arid tropical environment with ample sunshine promotes rapid plant growth. Agricultural production increased substantially in the 1980s, when tomatoes, melons, cotton, grapes, mangoes, and sugar cane became major crops. In the Juàzeiro município, the area planted with tomato increased sharply from less than 900 ha in 1984 and 3,800 ha a year later to 4,700 ha in 1988, according to the Brazilian Institute of Geography and Statistics (Instituto Brasileiro de Geografia e Estatística, IBGE). Melons were important throughout the decade, occupying 770 ha in 1988. The area under grapes also increased substantially in the mid-1980s, reaching over 200 ha in 1988. Mangoes, the most

Table 14.3 **Irrigation projects of CODEVASF in the middle São Francisco Valley**

Project	Establishment	Total area (ha)	Irrigable area (ha)	Pumping capacity (m³/s)	Colono area			Corporate area		
					Lot	Area (ha)	Average	Lot	Area (ha)	Major firm
1 Bebedouro I	1968	7,797	2,418	3.7	104	1,090	10.5	6	1,328	
2 Mandacaru	1973	823	382	0.72	331	331	6.5	1	51	EMBRAPA
3 Tourão	1976	10,713	10,454	11.06	32	182	5.7	M:17 / L:2	2,034 / 8,238	Agrovale/Frutivale
4 Bebedouro II	1981	2,064	667	–	–	–	–	1	2,064	EMBRAPA
5 Maniçoba	1981	12,236	4,317	5.43	232	1,890	8.1	S/M:50 / L:1	1,321 / 500	Maniçoba Agrícola
6 Curaçá	1982	15,059	4,436	5.66	267	1,964	7.3	16	2,280	CAC/Frutinor/
7 Senador Nilo Coelho	1984	56,286	20,018	23.2	1,432	8,592	6.0	S/M:105 / L:8	12~59/lot / 60~320/lot	

S: Small; M: Medium; L: Large.

Sources: CODEVASF (1989): *Informação gerais dos perímetros irrigados da 3ª directoria regional da CODEVASF.* CODEVASF (1982): *Inventário dos projetos de irrigação.*

recent addition to the list of commercial crops, increased from 20 ha in 1986 to 240 ha in 1987. Although the area under sugar cane was only 1 ha in 1980, over 6,000 ha were recorded in 1988. As these statistics show, development of agriculture in this region took place only during the last decade. Small farms, medium- to large-scale corporate farms, and agro-industries have played their respective roles in this rapid development.

Small farmers in irrigation projects are called *colonos*. They own five to ten hectares of farmland, and cultivate such cash crops as melons, tomatoes, onions, bell peppers, and cotton. Colono farming is typically observed in the Bebedouro and Mandacaru projects, where agricultural cooperatives are effectively organized for cooperative purchase and marketing. The Agricultural Cooperative of Bebedouro (CAMPIB) has 130 members, and that of Mandacaru (CAMPIM) has 50 members.

Japanese farmers, widely known in Brazil as skilled producers of vegetables and fruits, are actively engaged in farming in this area. Although a small number of Japanese farmers started to produce melons in the 1970s, the real development took place in the mid-1980s, when the Agricultural Cooperative of Cotia (Cooperativa Agrícola de Cotia), the largest agricultural cooperative in Brazil, founded by Japanese immigrants in the 1920s, started a colonization project. Obtaining some 1,000 ha from CODEVASF in the Curaçá project, thirty plots for settlers were prepared. Twenty-nine Japanese families with ample experience and capital from the states of São Paulo and Paraná took advantage of this opportunity. After clearing caatinga and preparing fields in 1983, they initially planted tomatoes and melons for immediate returns. As grape vines grew, the colony developed as a centre of grape cultivation. Grapes are shipped to the domestic market as well as to Europe. Beside Cotia's colonization project, many Japanese are independently engaged in farming.

Japanese farmers function as agricultural innovators who experiment with new crops, technology, and marketing. They have contributed a great deal to producing and marketing melons for São Paulo. Double harvesting of grapes and year-round shipment of mangoes became successful due to their experiments. A winery with extensive vineyards is operated by a Japanese resettled from São Paulo. In support of their endeavours, the Agricultural Cooperative of Cotia, as well as the Agricultural Cooperative of South Brazil (Cooperativa Agrícola Sul Brasil), another Japanese-founded cooperative, opened branch offices in Juàzeiro. This region is thus becoming an outpost of Japanese colonization outside of the cultural and agricultural centres in São Paulo and northern Paraná.

Corporate farms, diverse in size, management, and origin, also play important roles in this region. The Bompreço company, operating a large supermarket chain in the North-East with headquarters in Recife, operates a 5,000 ha farm of Frutivale in Juàzeiro in and around the Tour o project. The DAN (Desenvolvimento Agrícola do Nordeste S.A.) company, financed by the American Express Company and Brazilian investors, is operated by an Israeli firm with advanced technology for arid-land agriculture. An attempt by non-farming investors to make profits in agriculture is well exemplified by the Frutinor company. With headquarters in Salvador, it owns 8,000 ha in three locations. Figure 14.7 shows the land use of a Frutinor farm in the Curaçá project. With four centre-pivot irrigation systems, 500 ha are under irrigation, and the fields are rotated for continuous harvest (for details, see Saito et al., 1991).

In addition, local cattle fazendas attempt to intensify parts of their land use by introducing irrigation farming. These corporate farms typically have gigantic centre-pivot irrigation facilities and expensive drip irrigation equipment.

Agro-industries

The Petrolina–Juàzeiro area has also attracted agricultural processing industries, which, in turn, promote farming activities. There are processing plants for tomatoes, cotton, and bell peppers. Wine, sugar, and alcohol are also produced. Some of these agro-industries have headquarters in south-eastern Brazil, while others are multinational corporations.

The first enterprise to start agricultural processing was the São Francisco Valley Winery (Vinicola do Vale do São Francisco, Fazenda Milano), which initiated wine production in 1974. A decade later the second winery, operated by a Japanese Brazilian, appeared. Both wineries are managed by people resettled from the state of São Paulo.

Probably most important was the establishment of tomato processing plants. The Cicanorte company, established in 1978 in Juàzeiro, was the first to start processing tomatoes. It is a subsidiary of Cica headquartered in Jundiaí, São Paulo. Two other major tomato processors, Etti and Costa Pinto, established their factories in Petrolina's

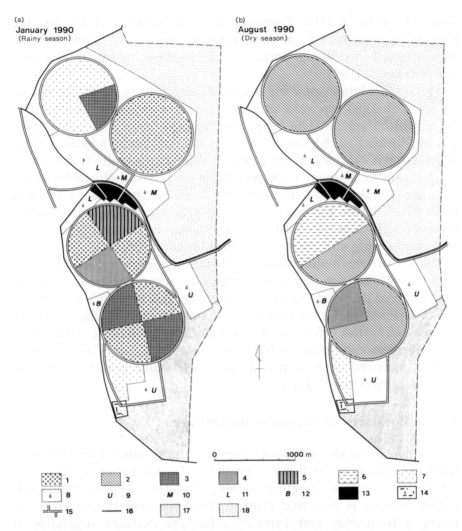

Figure 14.7 **Land use of the Frutinor company's industrial farm. 1: watermelons; 2: tomatoes; 3: maize; 4: beans; 5: crotaralia; 6: under preparation; 7: harvested; 8: fruits; 9: grapes; 10: mangoes; 11: lemons; 12: bananas; 13: administrative facilities; 14: agrovila; 15: road; 16: irrigation canals; 17: capoeira; 18: caatinga. (Based on field observation and aerial photographs.)**

industrial district in 1984 and 1988 respectively. The Paulo Coelho group, headed by a local economic and political leader in Petrolina, also started the Frutos do Vale company in 1986. These four tomato processors collect tomatoes by contracting with small farmers as well as large corporate growers. The area under contract amounted to some 15,000 ha in 1989. Tomato cultivation starts in March and the processing continues from June through November. Contracts are well planned in order to secure a stable supply of tomatoes (Saito and Yagasaki, 1991).

The establishment of a sugar and alcohol factory by the Agrovale company in 1980 was very striking. The company owns some 16,000 ha, of which over 7,000 ha are planted to sugar cane. The Usina Mandacaru, located in the centre of the vast cane fields, functions from May through November. Its calendar differs substantially from that of the traditional sugar cane regions of the coastal North-East. Sugar-cane yields amount to some 120 tons per hectare, more than twice than that on the coast, and even higher than that in the cane-growing regions of São Paulo. The operation is financed mainly by a civil engineering and construction firm based in Maceio.

There are two multinational corporations operating in this area. One is the Algodeira São Miguel company, started in 1984, a subsidiary of one of the world's largest cotton manufacturers, Coats Viyella, headquartered in Great Britain. Not only does it manage directly 1,200 ha of cotton fields, but it also has 2,500 ha under contract with small farmers. The other is Nisshin Seifun do Brasil. This Japanese firm extracts red dyes from bell peppers to make poultry feed. The product is exported to Japan.

4 Consequences of irrigation agriculture

During the 1980s the sertão experienced a substantial transformation where irrigation water became available. In this paper we have observed two types of irrigation farming. Small-scale spontaneous irrigation farming is practised around reservoirs constructed on small rivers in Boqueirão and Teixeira. After the caatinga vegetation is cleared and burned, the field is irrigated by pumping up water. Although such fields are limited in area and tend to shift after several years of cultivation, this type of intensive farming plays a significant role in the metropolitan markets of the North-East.

On the other hand, large-scale transformations are taking place in the middle São Francisco Valley. With the influx of capital, manpower and technology, and with governmental planning and support, the Petrolina–Juàzeiro area has emerged as a productive farming region known as "New California." It produces fruits such as melons, grapes, and mangoes, as well as tomato pulp, cotton, wine, sugar, and alcohol for the national and international markets. The region is a contemporary frontier of Brazil.

If sufficient and regular supply of water is secured, the dry tropical environment has great merits for farming free from plant diseases. Besides, abundant sunshine throughout the year promotes uninterrupted plant growth. The unexploited soils are fertile enough. The construction of better roads and the development of trucking have improved the sertão's access to the coastal North-East as well as to the south-eastern metropolises.

Although intensive farming in our study areas has only a short history of development, taking place during the last decade, various consequences are already observed. More time is needed to evaluate critically the total consequences of irrigation farming in the sertão, but it is worth while mentioning some effects that we observed in the field.

Irrigation farming has introduced a new land-use system. The long-term, extensive use of land was replaced by the repeated cultivation system. Plant diseases have started to appear and soil productivity has begun to decline. Thus, the yield per unit area is decreasing. Consequently some fields have already been abandoned. In order to cultivate continuously, pesticides and fertilizers are increasingly applied. In addition, effective crop rotation systems need to be introduced. In the spontaneous irrigation areas around the reservoirs in Boqueirão and Teixeira, the system of crop rotation depends on the farmers' empirical knowledge, taking into consideration the ecological responses of crops to the soil conditions. For example, tomatoes are a typical short-term crop, and carrots and bananas long-term crops.

In the industrial farms of the middle São Francisco Valley, on the other hand, careful study of the soil and of market conditions decides the rotation system. It can be practised only with substantial aid of pesticides and fertilizers. Beans and crotalaria are also used in the crop rotation as cleaning crops. Tree crops are introduced and are becoming increasingly important.

Repeated application of irrigation water and excess use of pesticides and fertilizers often cause salinization of the soil. In the spontaneous farming regions of Boqueirão and Teixeira, farms are mobile and fields are abandoned after several years of cultivation. In the Petrolina–Juàzeiro area, the fields are permanent and more intensively utilized. This is because the producers own the land and invest substantial capital in it. Crops are more carefully rotated and drainage ditches are often observed in the fields to remove accumulated salt.

Social and economic consequences are also substantial in the middle São Francisco Valley. Irrigation farming and agro-industries have created a sharp increase in job opportunities in both field and factory. This has caused a rapid increase in the population of Petrolina and

Juàzeiro, and their urban centres have grown rapidly. There are numerous seasonal workers who find work in the fields during the busy harvesting season. Manufacturers of irrigation equipment have also been attracted to the region. Brazil's two major manufacturers have branch offices here, and one company has built a factory to supply irrigation equipment for the entire North-East, as well as for large-scale developments in the cerrado region. The twin cities of Petrolina and Juàzeiro, with the landscape and atmosphere of the frontier's boom towns, are the most important inland centres of the North-East.

Concentration of land has also taken place in the process of agricultural development in the middle São Francisco Valley. Early public irrigation projects, such as Bebedouro and Mandacaru, aimed to settle small farmers by giving them titles to the land. However, CODEVASF's recent development policy appears to promote large-scale industrial farms (see table 14.3). In addition, turnover of land ownership appears to be frequent. Developed parcelas in irrigation projects are sold and purchased, while large farms and undeveloped land covered with caatinga are also on the market. Thus, land ownership is easily concentrated in the Petrolina–Juàzeiro area. The largest industrial farm owns 15,000 ha.

In the small-scale spontaneous developments of Boqueirão and Teixeira, on the other hand, the traditional system of land tenure persists and increased concentration is less apparent. In Boqueirão, where irrigation farming is undertaken by renting land and ample uncleared caatinga still exists, purchasing land decreases mobility and productivity. In Teixeira, where half of the irrigation farms are tenant-operated, the area accessible to the reservoir water is already extensively used and landowners are not willing to sell their properties. Under these conditions, it is difficult to accumulate farmland. Besides, large-scale industrial farms appear to have little interest in these areas.

Our observations clearly suggest that irrigation farming has largely modified the traditional landscape and land use of the sertão. Has it, then, transformed fundamentally its traditional social and economic structure? Is irrigation agriculture a successful strategy for the economic development of the North-East? Is the new farming system ecologically and economically viable in the long run? Do these farming regions become development centres for the diffusion of the intensive cultivation system? We do not yet have complete answers to these questions. Continued observation of the changes currently taking place in the sertão is required to this end.

Acknowledgement

The field studies for this paper were financed by overseas research grants from the Ministry of Education, Science and Culture of Japan.

References

Andrade, M. C. de. 1968. *A terra e o homen no Nordeste*. Livraria Editoria Ciéncias Humanas, São Paulo. (English translation: *The land and people of Northeast Brazil*. University of New Mexico Press, Albuquerque).

Araújo, J. A. da A. 1982. *Dams in the Northeast of Brazil*. DNOCS, Fortaleza.

CODEVASF. 1989. *Informação gerais dos perimetros da 3° diretoria regional da CO-DEVASF*. CODEVASF, Petrolina.

Hall, A.L. 1978. *Drought and irrigation in North-East of Brazil*. Cambridge University Press, Cambridge.

Saito, I., and H. Maruyama. 1988. "Some types of livestock ranching in São João do Cariri on the upper Paraíba valley, Northeast Brazil." *Latin American Studies* 10: 101–20.

Saito, I., and N. Yagasaki. 1987. "Zonal pattern of agricultural land use in the state of Paraíba, Northeast Brazil." *Geographical Review of Japan* B60: 66–82.

———. 1989. "Irrigation farming in Boqueirão in the middle Paraíba valley, Northeast Brazil." *Tsukuba Studies in Human Geography* 13: 23–52.

———. 1991. "Agro-industries in the middle São Francisco Valley, Northeast Brazil." *Annals of the Japan Association of Economic Geographers* 37: 225–44.

Saito, I., N. Yagasaki, and H. Maruyama. 1991. "Irrigation projects and corporate agriculture in the middle São Francisco valley, Northeast Brazil." *Tsukuba Studies in Human Geography* 15: 269–300.

Saito, I., N. Yagasaki, E. Pazera, and K. Muller. 1986. "Agriculture and land tenure in Salgado de São Félix along the middle reaches of the Paraíba river in Northeast Brazil." *Latin American Studies* 8: 91–124.

SUDENE. 1981. *As secas do nordeste*. SUDENE, Recife.

Yagasaki, N., I. Saito, and K. Muller. 1989. "Irrigation farming in Teixeira, Northeast Brazil." *Journal of the Yokohama National University* (Sec. 1) 35: 71–98.

Contributors

GILBERTO C. GALLOPÍN Leader, Land Management, Centro Internacional de Agricultura Tropical, Calí, Colombia.

ICHIROKU HAYASHI Professor and Director, Sugadaira Montane Research Center, University of Tsukuba, Nagano, Japan.

MARIO HIRAOKA Professor, Department of Geography, Millersville University of Pennsylvania, USA.

PETER JIPP Graduate student, School of the Environment, Duke University, USA.

WIL DE JONG Research Associate, Institute of Economic Botany, New York Botanical Garden, New York, USA.

EIJI MATSUMOTO Associate Professor, Institute of Geoscience, University of Tsukuba, Ibaraki, Japan.

BETTY J. MEGGERS Research Associate, National Museum of Natural History, Smithsonian Institution, Washington, DC, USA.

EMILIO F. MORAN Professor and Director, Anthropological Center for Training and Research on Global Environmental Change (ACT), Indiana University, USA.

ROBERTO MOTTA Professor of Anthropology, Universidade Federal de Pernambuco, Recife, Brazil.

TOSHIE NISHIZAWA Professor, Tokyo Seitoku University, Chiba, Japan.

CHRISTINE PADOCH Scientist, Institute of Economic Botany, New York Botanical Garden, New York, USA.

MIGUEL PINEDO-VASQUEZ Research Associate, Yale School of Forestry and Environmental Studies, USA.

ISAO SAITO Professor, Institute of Geoscience, University of Tsukuba, Ibaraki, Japan.

HILGARD O'REILLY STERNBERG Emeritus Professor of Geography, University of California, Berkeley, USA.

MINORU TANAKA Research Associate, Meteorological Research Institute, Ibaraki, Japan.

AKIO TSUCHIYA Assistant Professor, Faculty of Integrated Arts and Sciences, Department of Natural Environmental Studies, Hiroshima University, Hiroshima, Japan.

JUHA I. UITTO Academic Officer, The United Nations University, Tokyo, Japan.

MARIA MAGDALENA VIEIRA PINTO Fundação Instituto Brasileiro de Geografia e Estatística (retired), Rio de Janeiro, Brazil.

MANUEL WINOGRAD Director, Grupo de Análisis de Sistemas Ecológicos (GASE), Buenos Aires, Argentina.

NORITAKA YAGASAKI Associate Professor, Department of Geography, Yokohama National University, Kanagawa, Japan.

DANIEL ZARIN Postdoctoral Research Associate, Department of Geology, University of Pennsylvania, USA.